D1488520

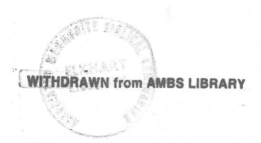

WITHDRAWN from AMBS LIBRARY

German-American
History and Life

ETHNIC STUDIES INFORMATION GUIDE SERIES

Series Editor: Curtis W. Stucki, Head, Catalog Division, University of Washington Libraries, Seattle

Also in this series:

WITHDRAWN from AMES LIBRARY

BASQUES IN AMERICA—*Edited by William A. Douglass and Richard Etulain**

BIBLIOGRAFIA CHICANA—*Edited by Arnulfo D. Trejo*

DUTCH AMERICANS—*Edited by Linda Pegman Doezema*

ITALIAN AMERICANS—*Edited by Francesco Cordasco*

JEWISH AMERICANA—*Edited by Michael Keresztesi and Bette Roth**

ROMANIANS IN THE UNITED STATES—*Edited by Vladimir Wertsman*

UKRAINIAN AMERICANS—*Edited by Aleksander Sokolyszyn and Vladimir Wertsman**

*in preparation

The above series is part of the
GALE INFORMATION GUIDE LIBRARY

The Library consists of a number of separate series of guides covering major areas in the social sciences, humanities, and current affairs.

General Editor: Paul Wasserman, Professor and former Dean, School of Library and Information Services, University of Maryland

Managing Editor: Denise Allard Adzigian, Gale Research Company

German-American History and Life

A GUIDE TO INFORMATION SOURCES

Volume 4 in the Ethnic Studies Information Guide Series

Michael Keresztesi

*Associate Professor
Division of Library Science
Wayne State University
Detroit*

Gary R. Cocozzoli

*Librarian
Lawrence Institute of Technology
Southfield, Michigan*

WITHDRAWN from AMBS LIBRARY

Gale Research Company
Book Tower, Detroit, Michigan 48226

WITHDRAWN from AMBS LIBRARY

Library of Congress Cataloging in Publication Data

Keresztesi, Michael.
   German-American history and life.

   (Ethnic studies information guide series ; v. 4)
(Gale information guide library)
    1. German Americans—History—Bibliography.
2. German Americans—History—Sources—Bibliography.
I. Cocozzoli, Gary, joint author. II. Title.
Z1361.G37K47 [E184.G3]   016.973'04'31   79-24065
ISBN 0-8103-1459-2

Copyright © 1980 by
Michael Keresztesi and Gary R. Cocozzoli

No part of this book may be reproduced in any form without permission in
writing from the publisher, except by a reviewer who wishes to quote brief
passages or entries in connection with a review written for inclusion in a
magazine or newspaper. Manufactured in the United States of America.

VITAE

Michael Keresztesi has been teaching courses in library science in the division of library science at Wayne State University, Detroit, Michigan, since 1973. Previously he worked in various positions in academic and public libraries over a period of twenty years. He holds a Ph.D. in library science from the University of Michigan, a Master's degree in library science from the same institution, and a Master's degree in history from Eastern Michigan University. He has been active in professional organizations and made several contributions to the literature of library science. The present project grew out of a course in American ethnic heritage bibliography offered in the Wayne State University library science program.

Gary R. Cocozzoli received his M.S. in library science from Wayne State University in 1974. Since 1975, he has been on the staff of the library at the Lawrence Institute of Technology as serials, interlibrary loan, and reference librarian. He has been active in state and local professional organizations.

CONTENTS

Contents

Contents

Contents

Contents

ACKNOWLEDGMENTS

A work of this type is by necessity the result of a collective effort, because it requires the cooperation of many people acting privately or as representatives of institutions. It is, therefore, appropriate that we first express our appreciation to individuals who assisted us in our labors in a variety of ways. We thank Clarence A. Phillips, director of the library, Lawrence Institute of Technology, Southfield, Michigan, for his interest in our project and for bringing many new items to our attention. Our need for copies of works not available in the Detroit area libraries placed a heavy burden on the staff of the interlibrary loan department of the Wayne State University Library. We thank Judith Pullan, Elizabeth Kruz, and Brenda Smith for their cheerful cooperation and prompt assistance in getting books for us from libraries all over the country. We are grateful for the inquiries and encouragements received from Dr. Sidney Heitman, professor of history and German Russian Research Project coordinator at Colorado State University, and from Professor J. Anthony Burzle of the Max Kade Document and Research Center, University of Kansas. The material for the directory of archival and literary repositories could not have been assembled without the collaboration of the archivists and librarians who responded to our questionnaire. We sincerely thank them for their cooperation. We are indebted to the staff of Wayne State University, the Detroit Public Library, the Michigan State Library, and the University of Michigan Harlan Hatcher Graduate Library for letting us use their collections on the premises, and for granting us borrowing privileges. We also thank Dr. H. Curt Vogt, director of Information Center, of BASF Wyandotte Corporation, Wyandotte, Michigan, for loaning some recent publications held in the company's library. We want to single out the staff of the Burton Historical Collection, Detroit Public Library, who shared their splendid resources for this project with us. Our special thanks go to Peter de Klerk, theology librarian, Calvin College, Grand Rapids, Michigan, who graciously assisted in the assembling of information on the history of the German Reformed Church in America.

Finally, we wish to acknowledge the contribution of Thomas E. Cocozzoli of the Michigan State University libraries in assisting us by obtaining materials and for some typing, as well as Phyllis Bostwick who helped with the preparation of the manuscript.

INTRODUCTION

The subject literature of German-American history and life and the attendant written records have been accumulating for the past three hundred years, forming an extremely rich body of individual works that can be counted in the tens of thousands. They are both in English and German. The contemporary bibliographer of German Americana confronts not the task of inventorying this literature, but of facilitating access to it. With H.A. Pochmann and A.R. Schultze's BIBLIOGRAPHY OF GERMAN CULTURE IN AMERICA TO 1940 (1953) and D.H. Tolzmann's GERMAN-AMERICANA: A BIBLIOGRAPHY (1975), together with K.J.R. Arndt and M.E. Olsen's 2-volume THE GERMAN LANGUAGE PRESS OF THE AMERICAS: HISTORY AND BIBLIOGRAPHY 1732-1968 (1973-75), the basic inventorial work had been essentially accomplished. Having reached this stage, the bibliographic elaboration of the field can now concentrate on the task of opening up this enormously varied and fascinating literary terrain for the aspiring researcher, the interested public, and not the least, for young Americans of German descent who wish to explore the nature of their ancestral heritage.

This book was conceived to serve such a purpose. It brings together a selection of "penetrator" works, basic treatises, landmark writings, and documents which constitute the best available sources of information in their respective topical areas, on several levels. Wherever the existing material allowed it, a conspectus of writings was assembled to furnish a multiplicity of factual accounts and approaches. Only materials in the English language were considered. With a few exceptions, the authors examined, described, and assessed every item in the main body of the work in terms of their research value and information yielding capability. The listing includes a few works which could not be obtained for examination despite repeated attempts, consequently, they were left unannotated. Although cognizant of its great significance, the authors gave less attention to the periodical literature, mainly for reasons of space, and because it was felt that the standard abstracting and indexing tools provide adequate access and content disclosure to German-American scholarly and popular writings in journals, magazines, and newspapers.

Reflecting the variety and uniqueness of the German experience and contribution to America, the titles of works, the subject matter covered, and the annotations themselves may appear too specialized and too esoteric to the uninitiated.

Introduction

In order to facilitate acquaintance with the subject literature here presented, a glossary has been prepared and placed in front of the bibliography. The glossary attempts to define almost every unfamiliar term, event, concept, and organization mentioned in the book titles and in the annotations. Taken together, the entries of the glossary provide a topical outline for the entire scope of German-American history and life.

An added feature of the work is a complete analytical listing of the writings included in the three major historically significant series: (1) Publications of the Pennsylvania German Society, (2) Pennsylvania German Folklore Society Yearbooks, and (3) the Americana Germanica Series. It is hoped this feature will save the user considerable inconvenience in finding and identifying individual items in these series. At the same time, this feature gives an idea of the range of intellectual concerns and research involvements of scholars and students of German Americana, over many decades, who found a forum in these publications.

Perhaps the most problematic task of this project was the establishment of a reliable list of scholarly journals, past and present. No attempt was made to compile a comprehensive inventory here. Our intent was merely to identify the major specialized periodicals which together have carried on their pages the bulk of the literary and scholarly products. The American-German language daily and weekly press was deliberately omitted from our purview to avoid unnecessary duplication. There are several standard reference tools where information on these types of publications can be readily found.

Several previous bibliographic compilations have enumerated repositories of German-American materials without specifying and describing the actual resources they held. Since the major objective of this work is to stimulate interest and facilitate research in German Americana, it was considered imperative that we include a census of archival and library collections in the United States dealing with the German experience in America, with a realistic account of their resources and activities. Because the English-language subject literature has become an intrinsic part of our nation's broader literary spectrum, books on the German participation in the building of America are included in the collections of most American libraries as standard procedure. For our purposes, what was needed was a directory of archival and literary repositories which specialize in German Americana, or have concentrations on some aspects of it. The directory includes seventy such institutions which supplied information on their holdings and activities on a questionnaire furnished for this purpose. It is estimated that outside the Library of Congress and the large research and metropolitan public libraries, the institutions described in the directory section taken together, may account for the bulk of the highly specialized available research resources.

The structure of this guide grew out of the internal logic of the materials brought together and analyzed. The strength of the coverage usually depended on the quantity of the monographic literature available on a particular subject. While the abundance of writings dealing with religious sects and denominations, for example, made the selection of the most appropriate information sources for this work a difficult task, the scarcity of materials in some other fields forced us to list whatever we found on the subject in order to provide a modicum of coverage.

Admittedly, the broad categories into which the works are fitted may not always do justice to the complexity of their content, they can, however, be penetrated through the detailed subject index. This feature suggested that instead of mechanically following an alphabetical listing of main entries within each of the subject categories, the arrangement should have its own logic, either chronological, if appropriate, or hierarchical according to the breadth of the scope or level of treatment. Thus, the reader may assume that the first item appearing in a constellation of works would be a work in which research on a germane topic might most fruitfully begin. The subject index itself points to many topical relationships implicit not only in the titles of the books listed but also in the annotations and glossary entries as well.

Last, there remains a few words to be said about some lexicographic problems. Many German surnames appear in the literature in several versions. For example, the name of the famous early German-American printer is spelled alternately Sauer, Saur, or Sower. We adopted the policy of rendering German names as they are given in the original text. To provide the "Umlaut," an extra "e" has been added to the transliteration. Since many of the books in their original editions have long been out-of-print, but have recently been reprinted, we were obliged to write the annotation from the reprint copy. In general, no effort was spared in assembling and verifying bibliographic details, but when dealing with reprinted works issued prior to 1929, imprint data for the original copy were kept to the minimum.

I. GLOSSARY

1   Adelsverein: A corporate enterprise for colonization and development in Texas under the full name "Verein zum Schutze Deutscher Einwanderer in Texas," organized by a group of wealthy noblemen in Germany, some of whom were reigning princes. It was referred to briefly as "Adelsverein," or association of noblemen. The corporation sent Prince von Solms-Braunfels to Texas to administer the first settlement which received more than seven thousand Germans between 1844 and 1846. In 1845 the community of New Braunfels was founded, followed by Fredericksburg and several other widely scattered settlements. The Verein brought emigrants from Hannover, Braunschweig, Hesse-Darmstadt, Thueringia, and Wuerttemberg. The ultimate intent of the company was to establish a German sovereign territory and eventually a German state in Texas. The Verein fell into bankruptcy in 1847, but the influx of German settlers to Texas continued in subsequent years.

2   Amana: The name designates seven small settlements in Iowa, near Iowa City. They were founded in 1855 by a group of German pietists who left their homes in Wuerttemberg in 1842 and came to America. The seven villages, Amana, East Amana, West Amana, Middle Amana, High Amana, South Amana, and Homestead functioned until the end of World War I as a communal religious society under the corporate name "The Community of True Inspiration." In the inter-war period modern industrial methods were introduced and after World War II the communal life based on agriculture practically disappeared as the group adopted modern industrial and business methods. The Amana appliances, furniture, and textile industries have gained good reputation for their quality.

3   Amerika-Deutscher Volksbund: See German-American Bund.

4   Amish: The Amish separated from the Mennonite church and followed Jakob Amman when the Swiss Mennonite bishop, in 1693, criticized his fellow Mennonites for their laxity of doctrine and practice. He advocated orthodoxy and the strict enforcement of "shunning," the social and religious ban against violators of church rule. The Amish are ultraconservative in observance of their creed: they do not bear arms, do

1

Glossary

not take oaths, nor seek public office, and are reluctant to introduce convenient technology into their lives. They tend to isolate their well-integrated communities from the surrounding world. They use hooks and eyes instead of buttons. The Amish migrated to America in three streams. The first, in the eighteenth century, brought the Amish to Eastern Pennsylvania from Switzerland and the Palatinate. The second wave occurred in the nineteenth century when Alsatian, Bavarian, and Hessian Amish crossed the Atlantic to settle primarily in western Pennsylvania, Ohio, and Ontario. The third strain of migration, in 1847, included the Volhynian Amish who went to Kansas and South Dakota.

5   Anabaptists: A Protestant secessionist group originating in Switzerland in 1524. Imbued with an idealistic vision of uncompromising Christian love, the group advocated adult baptism, strict separation of church and state, pacifism, and refusal to pay taxes for purposes of war. Perceived as a threat to the established churches, both Catholic and Protestant, as well as to the local political authorities, the Anabaptists were persecuted all over Europe, bringing upon themselves sufferings resulting occasionally from their own fanaticism. The movement later split into several branches. Among them, the German Hutterites, the Mennonites, and the Amish began to seek refuge in America, beginning in the seventeenth century.

6   Aurora, Oregon: A religiously inspired communitarian colony in the Willamette Valley organized by Wilhelm Keil in 1855 on the same principles as Bethel, Missouri (see 9). In 1900 Aurora had a population of 122.

7   Barns: The barns of German and Swiss settlers were a conspicuous feature of colonial architecture and of the landscape where they lived. In the continental European tradition, the farmer's first enterprise after clearing his fields was to build an immense and elaborately designed barn to shelter his animals from the excesses of the climate. These barns and the care of animals partially explain why German and Swiss farmers were often more productive than their English and Scottish neighbors who did not bring with them from England the tradition of constructing sturdy barns.

8   Beachy Amish (or Burkholder Amish): A branch of the Amish groups in the United States named for their leader Moses M. Beachy. The group seceded from the more conservative Amish in 1927 mainly over the issues of the use of the automobile and the strict discipline. They are concentrated mainly in Somerset County, Pennsylvania, and they number between three thousand and five thousand.

9   Bethel, Missouri: A communitarian settlement of some five hundred German farmers, founded in 1844 by Wilhelm Keil of Prussia, in Shelley County, Missouri. Keil was a mystic who converted to Methodism and permitted no church ritual beside the confessional. All land, produce, and goods were held in common in the group. Eye witnesses reported that despite a rigorous regime of work and religion, life in the community was not without relief and band concerts were frequently held. The

commune was dissolved in 1879 and the settlement was incorporated as a town in 1883.

10   Brethren: Several German-American religious groups who came to America to avoid persecution in Europe, adopted the term "Brethren" in their names to designate their fellowship and signify their unity. They include: Church of the Moravian Brethren (Unitas Fratrum), the Swiss Brethren which refers to the Hutterites and Mennonites, the Church of Brethren (Dunkers), the River Brethren which were branches of German Baptists, and the Evangelical United Brethren Church which was formed in Pennsylvania in 1767 from some Mennonite and Reformed churches.

11   Brethren in Christ: See River Brethren.

12   Bruderhof: The term designates German-Hutterian religious communities organized as collective farms where everything is communally owned. Such communities were formed in the United States and Canada by Hutterian Brethren in the second half of the nineteenth century and the early part of the twentieth century.

13   Buffington-Barba Transliteration System: Traditionally, writers in the Pennsylvania Dutch vernacular have used various systems of spelling. While some writers based spelling on English sound values, others followed the German tradition. Albert F. Buffington of Arizona State University and Preston A. Barba of Muhlenberg College have systematized the treatment of the dialect in writing by offering a transliteration system more closely aligned with the German tradition which they considered more suitable for rendering Pennsylvania Dutch pronunciation than the one based on English.

14   Bund: See German-American Bund.

15   Burkholder Amish: See Beachy Amish.

16   Bush-Meeting Dutch: The term is used by some writers in reference to the revivalistic churches which were gaining ground among German inhabitants of eastern Pennsylvania beginning in the early nineteenth century. The "Bush-Meeting Dutch" constituted the third religious grouping in popular nomenclature, the first being the "Church People," and the second the "Plain People."

17   Captains' Lists: Rosters of passengers of ships which carried emigrants from European ports to America. The names were taken down at the time of embarkation. The personal data given on these lists varied. Some registered only adult males by name, stating merely when wife and children were accompanying the head of the household. The number of children in the family, their ages and sex were indicated. Other lists were made

more carefully, registering every person by name, sex, age, and even place of origin. Such lists can be valuable sources of genealogical information. One difficulty associated with some captains' lists is that the names of German passengers appearing on them were deliberately or unwittingly distorted, taken down by the official in charge of registration presumably not as they were spelled, but as they sounded. Thus, in many instances, the names of Germans were rendered in an Anglicized form which made identification a difficult, or an entirely impossible task. In such a case, the true identity of a passenger can be traced by comparing a name on the captain's list with a name appearing on the roster of the same shipload of emigrants listed when they took the oaths of abjuration and allegiance. (q.v.)

18   Carl Schurz Memorial Foundation: Organized in Philadelphia in 1930 with support of wealthy German-American businessmen and industrialists to promote cultural exchange programs and to acquaint Americans with German cultural achievements through an attractive magazine, the AMERICAN-GERMAN REVIEW, launched in 1934. In 1962 the name of the organization was changed to the National Carl Schurz Association.

19   Church of the Brethren: Members of this religious group were historically known also as German Baptists, Dunkers, Dunkards, Tunkers, Taufer, and Dompelaars. The founder of the Brethren movement was Alexander Mack, Sr., (1679-1735). Dissatisfied with the formal religion of the state churches, and being persecuted for their faith, pietists under Mack's leadership organized themselves into church groups. The first group came to America in 1719 and settled in Germantown, Pennsylvania. In 1729 Mack arrived and began to organize intensive missionary work. The church spread rapidly all over America. The German Baptists were known for their educational interests. In Germantown, Christopher Sower and his son were printers who published the first religious magazine on the continent. The church controls several educational institutions, among them Juniata College in Pennsylvania, Manchester College in Indiana, and Blue Ridge College in Maryland. The headquarters of the church is the Brethren Publishing House, Elgin, Illinois. The GOSPEL MESSENGER is its main organ.

20   Church of the Moravian Brethren: The origin of this group is traced to a remnant of followers of John Huss (Czech religious reformer, ca. 1369-1415) who, under the patronage of Count Nicholas Zinzendorf, came to America and settled in Bethlehem, Pennsylvania in 1741. Moravian colonies were soon established in Philadelphia, Nazareth, Lititz, Pennsylvania, and Salem, North Carolina.

The Moravian Church is governed by provincial synods. The United States contains two provinces, a northern and southern, whose headquarters are in Bethlehem, Pennsylvania, and Winston-Salem, North Carolina, respectively. Historically, the Moravian Church has been associated with extensive missionary activities among the American Indians and Negro slaves. Hymn singing and church music have had a prominent place in Moravian church services.

21 Church People: A popular term designating German people in Pennsylvania who belong to congregations of the Lutheran, Reformed, United Brethren, and the Evangelical or Schwenkfelder denominations. They were distinguished from the "Plain People" who belonged to the Amish, Mennonite, and German Baptist (Dunkers) congregations, and the "Bush-Meeting Dutch" who were adherents of various revivalistic denominations.

22 Communitarian Experiments: Religious and secular experiments in communal living have existed in America since colonial times. Many German groups came to America specifically for the purpose of establishing communities where everything was collectively owned, produced, and shared. Some of these communities have prospered, but most of them lasted only until the departure of the founders. The German religious communitarian settlements included Woman in the Wilderness, founded in 1683 near Germantown, Pennsylvania; Ephrata, Pennsylvania (1732); Harmony Society, Butler County, Pennsylvania (1805); Zoar in Ohio (1817); Amana in Iowa (1842); Bethel, Missouri (1844); and the agricultural communities of the Hutterite Brethren in South Dakota (1847); St. Nazianz in Wisconsin (1854); and Aurora, Oregon (1855). Among these, only the Hutterite collectives have survived. They now count about twenty thousand members in scattered settlements in South Dakota, Montana, Minnesota, Washington, and the Western provinces of Canada.

23 Community of True Inspiration: See Amana.

24 The Concord: The "Mayflower" of German Americans; the ship that brought the first group of German immigrants to America. Under the command of Captain Jeffreys, the Concord left Gravesend, England, 24 July 1683, and arrived in Philadelphia 6 October 1683. The first immigrants were Mennonites from Krefeld German Rhineland who settled near Philadelphia and founded Germantown.

25 Conestoga Wagon: The Conestoga wagon, which played an important role in the winning of the West, was a direct descendant of Rhine River mercantile wagons. The first Palatine immigrants in 1683 brought with them the craft of coachmaking and fashioned their American vehicles from the old country models.

26 Conservative Amish Mennonite: A group which separated from the Old Order Amish and formed the Conservative Mennonite Conference. They held their first conference at Pigeon, Michigan in 1910. These Amish introduced meeting houses, Sunday schools, and the use of English in worship. They allow the use of modern conveniences and cooperate with the larger Mennonite groups.

27 Creole: The term originally applied in Latin America to the nativeborn descendants of European conquerors. It was also adopted early in Louisiana to designate the descendants of the original French settlers and to

distinguish them from the "Cajuns." Descendants of German settlers in Louisiana were also called creoles.

28   Deutsch-Amerikanische Buergerbund: German-American Citizen's League, organized in Chicago in January of 1921 to replace the discredited National German-American Alliance. The league was avowedly ethnocentric and political in orientation. They supported Warren G. Harding in his bid for the presidency attempting to deliver him the German-American block vote. The organization could not claim national leadership because its influence was limited to Chicago and the Midwest.

29   Deutsch-Amerikanische Reform Bund: A German-American liberal political organization which supported Robert LaFollette for the presidency in 1924.

29a   Deutsche Evangelisch-Lutherische Synode von Missouri, Ohio und andern Staaten: This was the original name of the Lutheran Church--Missouri Synod, the nucleus of which can be traced to the Lutheran congregation founded in 1838 in Perry County, Missouri by Martin Stephan, a powerful preacher and vigorous organizer. The synod under this name was established in Chicago in April 1847. In 1947, the German name was changed to Lutheran Church--Missouri Synod.

30   Deutscher Evangelische Kirchenverein Des Westens: A religious organization which had considerable impact on the shaping of religious development of German communities and the molding of German culture on the American frontier. The Kirchenverein emerged in Missouri in 1840, and its activities were soon extended to Illinois, Indiana, Iowa, and other states. In 1866, it assumed the name German Evangelical Synod of the West, and in 1877 was renamed German Evangelical Synod of North America, by which name it was known until 1925, when the word "German" was dropped. In 1934 the Evangelical Synod and the Reformed Church of the United States merged into the Evangelical and Reformed Church.

31   Deutsches Ausland Institut (DAI); German Foreign Institute: Originally founded in 1917 and headquartered in Stuttgart. Initially its purpose was to counteract Allied propaganda abroad and to strengthen ties with people of German ancestry living in various parts of the world. During the Weimar regime the institute functioned as a research and information center on Germandom abroad. After Hitler's takeover, DAI's activities expanded. The government and the Nazi Party found it a convenient instrument for disseminating and orchestrating Nazi propaganda among the "Auslandsdeutsche" (Germans residing outside of Germany) in order to win their allegiance and support. In the United States, such propaganda efforts were directed toward German-American groups and organizations particularly in Pennsylvania and Texas. Resuming its cultural mission, the institute was reconstructed after World War II under the name Institut fuer Auslandsbeziehungen (Institute for Relations with Abroad) in Stuttgart.

32   Dickstein Committee: During the seventy-third Congress, Representative Samuel Dickstein of New York was the chairman of the House Committee on Immigration and Naturalization. In October 1933 Dickstein initiated a congressional inquiry into Nazi activities in the United States which was formally approved in March, 1934 by the resolution of the House of Representatives. Congressman John W. McCormack of Massachusetts was the chairman, and Dickstein, vice-chairman of the committee. The committee was officially called the "Special Committee on Investigation of Nazi and Other Foreign Activities in the United States." The committee held more than thirty hearings, meeting often in executive sessions which were not open to the public.

33   Dies Committee: A Congressional committee created in 1938 and chaired by Martin Dies to look into aspects of subversive activities in the United States. One of the targets of the committee's inquiry was the German-American Bund (Nazi Party) and its leader Fritz Kuhn.

34   Dompelaars: A variant popular name for German Baptists, also called "Dunkers." See Church Of The Brethren.

35   Dreissiger: A group which came to America following the 1830 disturbances in German. Many of the immigrants were leaders of student groups (Burschenschaften) who challenged the established authorities in various German cities.

36   Dunkards: See Church of the Brethren.

37   Dunkers: See Church of the Brethren.

38   "Dutchified" German: The term used by German-American folklorists mainly in the context of revivalist religious services in the Pennsylvania Dutch country in the nineteenth century. In the course of these religious services, original German-language hymns were sung, but the words already reflected their adaptation to the peculiar local dialect which had been in formation in the past two hundred years through interaction with the American environment.

39   Ephrata: A religious retreat and communitarian settlement initiated in 1728 by a few German Seventh Day Baptists (Dunkards), under the leadership of Conrad Beissel. By 1735 it developed into a full-fledged community. The community operated a variety of industries, including a paper mill, printing press, and bookbindery. This was the first printing press in America to produce printed music. Music played an important role in the life of Ephrata due mainly to Beissel's devotion. He was also a composer. The communal buildings were called cloisters, and two monastic orders, Sisters and Brothers, were part of the community. In its heyday, Ephrata had about three hundred members. The monastic features disappeared after 1800, and the congregation was dissolved in

1891 when Ephrata became an incorporated borough of the Commonwealth of Pennsylvania. Today, Ephrata is preserved as a historical monument and park.

40 Evangelical and Reformed Church: A religious body with strong German-American affiliations which came into existence in 1934 through the merger of the Evangelical Synod of North America and Reformed Church of the United States.

41 Evangelische Gemeinschaft: This was the name by which the Evangelical Church was known in the United States in the early nineteenth century. The church was founded by Jacob Albright in 1803.

42 Forty-Eighters: The Forty-Eighters were refugees of the Revolution of 1848 in Germany. There were many republicans, liberal and radical reformers, and some utopists among them. They were influential in invigorating German culture, as well as social and political life in America, alienating in the process some segments of society.

43 Fraktur: The generic term used to describe illuminated manuscripts based on the sixteenth-century Gothic typeface of the same name.

44 Franz Sigel Society: An organization particularly active in the 1920s to honor the memory of the Civil War general of German ancestry, Franz Sigel, and all liberal German immigrants of 1848. In cultivating their memory, the society sought to achieve a fuller recognition of the contribution they made to their adopted country.

45 Freie Gemeinde: An umbrella term encompassing, in the middle of the nineteenth century, a variety of "freethinking" societies, anticlerical groups, and nationalistic and humanistic congregations brought into existence in many American cities by German intellectuals of the post 1848 immigration wave. They were led by "speakers" (Sprecher). Eduard Schroeter and Friedrich Schuenemann-Pott were among the prominent figures of the movement. The Freie Gemeinde had considerable influence on various German-American cultural societies and the Turnverein.

46 Friends of Germany: A short-lived pro-Hitler organization in the United States, which emerged around March 1933. The address of the organization was the office of the German consul in New York City. It was under the leadership of Colonel Edwin Emerson, "a soldier of fortune, author, and war correspondent, as well as a secret agent for Germany" (J.L. Spivak, SECRET ARMIES [New York: Modern Age Books, 1939, pp. 73-74]). In May 1934 the "Friends of Germany" withdrew from the scene, suggesting that its members join the newly formed "Friends of the New Germany" (q.v.).

47   Friends of the Hitler Movement: An early attempt by the German National Socialist Party (N.S.D.A.P.) to organize a branch in the United States. After coming to power in 1932, Rudolf Hess, who was in charge of the foreign activities of the Nazi Party, took action under pressure by the American government to dissolve the organization in the United States. Almost immediately a new organization, called "The Friends of the New Germany," or Bund, sprang up under the leadership of Heinz Spanknoebel, an immigrant (Reichsdeutsche). His strong-arm tactics against the established German-American newspapers and societies alienated their leaders. Facing deportation, Spanknoebel disappeared from the United States and later reappeared as a general in the SS, Hitler's elite corps. After Spanknoebel's disappearance from America, the German Nazi Party instructed the Bund to turn its leadership over to American-born citizens of German descent.

48   Friends of the New Germany, Or "New Germany": The official name of the Bund, a Nazi organization in the United States. See also Friends of the Hitler Movement and German-American Bund.

49   German-American Alliance: See National German-American Alliance.

50   German-American Bund: This organization was the successor to the Friends of New Germany which in 1936 continued its existence under the name "Amerika-Deutscher Volksbund" (American-German Peoples Society) or German-American Bund, briefly referred to as Bund. Fritz Julius Kuhn, the former head of the Detroit local of the Friends and a chemist at the Ford Motor Company, was named the Bund leader. Kuhn resided in the United States since 1924 and became an American citizen. The Bund adopted and publicly flaunted all Nazi paraphernalia: Nazi uniforms, swastika flags, storm troops, training camps, and an organizational structure modeled after Hitler's Nazi Party. The Bund staged its most spectacular rally in New York's Madison Square Garden on 20 February 1939. It was attended by twenty-two thousand Nazi sympathizers. The speakers denounced President Roosevelt and members of his cabinet. There were various estimates of the Bund's strength ranging from three hundred fifty thousand in 1937, according to the Dickstein committee, to six thousand members in close organization. The latter figure was confidentially conveyed by the German ambassador to the German foreign ministry. The Madison Square Garden demonstrations led to numerous investigations. Kuhn was arrested, but freed on bail and ultimately left the country. In all, the Bund had little success among the German-American population. Most of its members were recent immigrants, and according to Kuhn's testimony, 40 percent of the Bund's membership was drawn from right wing elements in the population at large.

51   German-American Historical Society: The society was founded in 1901 through the efforts of Marion D. Learned, the head of the German department of the University of Pennsylvania. Under the auspices of the society, the department launched the journal, GERMAN AMERICAN AN-

NALS, and issued many scholarly monographs in the AMERICANA GER-
MANICA series.

52   German Baptist Brethren: This was the legal name until 1908 of the
Church of the Brethren whose members were also known popularly as
Dunkers, Dunkards, or Tunkers. See Church of the Brethren.

53   German Coast of Louisiana: A strip of German settlements founded in
1723 along the Mississippi River about thirty miles above New Orleans.
Today it comprises the St. Charles and St. John parishes.

54   German Creoles: See Creoles.

55   German Evangelical Synod of North America: See Deutscher Evangelische
Kirchenverein Des Westens.

56   German Flats: The term refers to an area in Herkimer County, New
York, in the vicinity of Utica, settled in 1723 by German Protestants
from the Palatinate. They were part of the group of three thousand
Germans brought to America in 1710 by the English Board of Trade to
make tar, pitch, and so forth, for the English naval stores industry.

57   Germanna, Virginia: An early German settlement established in 1714
in Orange County, Virginia. Many of the settlers worked in Governor
Spotswood's mines.

57a   German Reformed Church in America: See Reformed Church in the United
States.

58   German Settlement Society of Philadelphia: The society was founded in
1836 for the purpose of promoting land acquisition for its members in the
newly opened Missouri territory.

59   Germantown, Pennsylvania: The founding of Germantown is associated
with the name of Francis Daniel Pastorius, a German religious leader who
brought from Europe a group of Mennonites and Quakers in 1683 and settled them on twenty-five thousand acres, six miles from Philadelphia.
Pastorius purchased the land from William Penn as the agent of the Frankfurt Land Company. This event marked the beginning of large-scale German immigration to America. For the next hundred years Germantown
served as a distribution point of newly arrived immigrants toward the in-
terior. In 1854 Germantown was annexed to metropolitan Philadelphia.

60   Germantown, Virginia: A settlement founded in 1721 by German colonists
along the Licking Run, about ten miles from the Little Fork of the Rappa-
hannock River. The colonists had originally gone to Germanna but de-

parted at the expiration of their period of service because of a dispute with Governor Spotswood over some land.

61   Harmony Society: The Society was organized by Georg Rapp, a separatist preacher from Iptingen, Wuerttemberg, who migrated to America in 1804 with several hundred followers. They organized themselves into a Christian communitarian society at Harmony, Butler County, Pennsylvania. Following the War of 1812, Rapp and his followers moved to a site near the mouth of the Wabash River in the Territory of Indiana. Here they established a new settlement which was also called Harmony. This property was sold in 1824 to the Scottish reformer, Robert Owen, who renamed it New Harmony. The Rappists returned to Pennsylvania, where in Beaver County, about twenty miles from Pittsburgh, they constructed the town of Economy which was intended to become a manufacturing center.

Georg Rapp died in 1847. Technological advances and the Society's strict adherence to celibacy contributed to the community's decline, and in 1905 Harmony Society was dissolved.

62   Herrenhuter: An early name for the Church of the Moravian Brethren (q.v.).

63   Hessians: German soldiers brought to the colonies by the British to fight for their cause in the American Revolution. The men were recruited mainly in the principalities of Hesse-Kassell, Hesse-Hanau, and Braunschweig by their rulers in return for monies. It is estimated that about thirty thousand Hessian soldiers were fighting in the war and presumably six thousand of them settled in the United States after the close of the Revolutionary War. They were scattered among established German settlements from New York to North Carolina.

64   Hex Signs: Decorative barn signs using a wide variety of symbols that appeared in Pennsylvania Dutch country. It is generally assumed that these barn adornments were brought to America from the old country by early settlers. While there is no agreement as to what the symbols represent, it is suggested that originally they were charms used to ward off witches and to keep them from harming cattle and crops.

65   Hexerei: German word for witchcraft.

66   Hutterites: The present day Hutterites are descendants of the pacifist and collectivistic Anabaptist sect founded by Jakob Hutter (a Tyrolean religious reformer, condemned to death and burned at the stake at Innsbruck, 1536). Suffering from continuous persecutions through centuries, surviving German Hutterites fled to Russia in the eighteenth century. To avoid conscription, the remaining colonies migrated from Russia to the United States between 1874-77 and settled in South Dakota. From here their colonies spread to Montana and to Canada's prairie provinces where the majority of the Hutterite communities can now be found.

Glossary

67   Indentured Servants: The term refers to a system of labor in colonial times by which a white adult person was bound to labor for a period of years. There were three distinct categories of indentured servants: (1) redemptioners, (q.v.) who bound themselves to labor for a definite time mainly because they had no other means to pay for their passage to America, (2) the people who were kidnapped or forced to leave their home country because of poverty, political, or religious reasons, and (3) convicts. Seven years was a common term for such service. A great many German, English, and Scottish Irish came to America as indentured servants. The Germans were mainly redemptioners (q.v.).

68   Inspirationists: See Amana.

69   Kameradschaft U.S.A.: An organization of returnees to Hitler's Germany from the United States. At the initiative of Fritz Gissibl, formerly a leading Nazi organizer in the United States who held an important position in the Stuttgart based Deutsches Ausland Institut, the organization provided assistance and social outlet for repatriated members of the American Nazi Party. At the outbreak of World War II, the Kameradschaft U.S.A. counted an enrollment of about 450. In August 1939 Gissibl launched the periodical, DER AMERIKADEUTSCHE, to disseminate news from America.

70   Kentucky Rifle: Also known as the Pennsylvania rifle. It had a long, grooved barrel and was assumedly created by German craftsmen in Pennsylvania, who brought with them from the old country the skills and technique of making hunting weapons.

71   Kirchenverein: See Deutscher Evangelische Kirchenverein Des Westens.

72   Labadists: A Calvinist sect from the Rhineland which followed the French religious reformer Jean de Labadie. A colony of Labadists came to Maryland in 1683 under the leadership of Augustine Herrmann, and a second group settled in New York shortly thereafter.

73   Latin Farmers: A nickname given to highly educated German refugees and immigrants to the United States who left Germany after the defeat of the 1848 democratic revolution and took up farming in the new land.

74   Liebhaberbuehnen: Amateur and minor stages in New York City where German-language plays were produced in the 1850s.

75   Loyalty Oath: A formal procedure in colonial times administered to new immigrants upon arrival to America. After disembarking the passengers, the shipmaster took them to the local authorities in one group. Here, the immigrants took an oath pledging allegiance to the king of England and were officially registered. The official register taken on this occa-

sion recorded names and personal data more accurately than the list prepared by the ship's captain at embarkation, making the official register a valuable resource for genealogical research. (See annotation for 171-74).

75a Lutheran Church--Missouri Synod: See Deutsche Evangelisch-Lutheranische Synode von Missouri, Ohio und andern Staaten.

76 Lutherans: German Lutherans began to come to America in 1626 and scattered throughout the colonies, founding congregations, and erecting churches wherever they settled. An important event in the history of the German-American Lutheran churches was the arrival in 1741 of pastor Heinrich Melchior Muhlenberg who organized in 1748 the first Lutheran Synod in America, the Ministerium of Pennsylvania. With the heavy influx of Lutheran immigrants from Germany in the subsequent two hundred years, synods were established in many parts of the country, yielding great influence in the German-American community. The first union of Lutheran synods occurred in 1820, called the "General Synod." Political and doctrinal issues later created divisions in the church.

77 Mennonites: The followers of Menno Simons, an Anabaptist reformer, who profess adult baptism, pacifism, and a high degree of community discipline through the moderate use of "shunning" -- an instrument of discipline invoked by the community against a member who violates church rules. Persecuted in Europe, Mennonites began to arrive in America in 1683 seeking religious freedom. They settled mostly in Pennsylvania, but later spread to other parts of the country as well, breaking up into several groups. A second wave of Mennonites came in 1870 from Russia. The major Mennonite denominations and the approximate number of their adherents in the 1970s were as follows: General Conference of the Mennonite Church, 36,000; Old Order Amish, 15,000; General Conference of Mennonite Brethren Churches, 13,000; Old Order (Wisler) Mennonite Church, 8,000; Church of God in Christ, 6,000; Beachy Amish Mennonite Churches, 4,000; Evangelical Mennonite Brethren, 3,700; Hutterian Brethren, 3,400; Reformed Mennonite Church, 500 members. Due to their refusal to bear arms, the Mennonites had to endure various degrees of hostility from the American population in times of war.

77a Mercersburg Theology: The term designates a protestant theological movement in the German Reformed Church in the United States between 1836 and 1866. The movement originated in Marshall College and in the Theological Seminary of the German Reformed Church located at that time in Mercersburg, Pennsylvania. The leaders of the Mercersburg school of thought were Frederick A. Rauch, John W. Nevin, and Philip Schaff. The movement generated a body of vigorous polemical literature in which the writers addressed themselves to the main theological doctrines of Calvinistic Reformation, arguing their theses from a "Christocentric" position. The Mercersburg Theology had considerable impact on American Protestantism in later decades.

Glossary

78   Moravians: See Church of the Moravian Brethren.

79   National Association of Teutonia: The first identifiably Nazi organization in the United States founded in Detroit by Friedrich Gissibl and dissolved in 1932. It never had a large following, but was significant for providing cadres for future Nazi groups. The organization had small local chapters in New York, Rochester, Chicago, Philadelphia, Detroit, and Milwaukee. It published the irregular newspaper, VORPOSTEN, in Chicago, dedicated to "News of the German Freedom Movement in the United States."

80   National Carl Schurz Association: See Carl Schurz Memorial Foundation.

81   National German-American Alliance: Chartered in 1899 by the Congress of the United States, the alliance was brought into existence to function as an umbrella organization espousing noble cultural objectives. In 1914 it claimed two million members. During its existence, the alliance became absorbed in the battle against prohibition and blue laws, neglecting its other obligations. During World War I the organization was openly sympathetic to the Allied cause. In the wake of the pervasive anti-German sentiment following the war, the National German-American Alliance was voluntarily dissolved after a prolonged Congressional investigation.

82   Nativism: In the context of American history, the term refers to organized expressions of policy giving preference to native inhabitants of the country over immigrants. In the nineteenth century nativism flared up especially at times of heavy influx of immigrants from Catholic countries in Europe. Nativism was the platform of the "Know-Nothing" movement. Street fights between natives and immigrants were common. In the big cities, German workers, Catholics, and Turnverein headquarters were frequent targets of nativist hostility.

83   New Germany: See Friends of the New Germany.

84   Nordamerikanischer Turnerbund: See Turnerbund.

85   Oath of Abjuration: New immigrants in colonial times were required by local authorities upon arrival in ports of entry to renounce in a formal procedure their allegiance to former rulers. (See also Loyalty Oath).

86   Old Order Amish: The most conservative body of the Mennonite groups who avoid the use of electricity and the automobile. They are characterized by their distinctive dress. They are concentrated mainly in Lancaster County, Pennsylvania, Holmes County, Ohio, and Lagrange and Elkhart counties, Indiana. The church body was established in 1865, and its membership hovers around twenty thousand.

87   Old Order Brethren: In 1881 a small group of conservatives left the church of the German Baptist Brethren and called themselves the Old Order Brethren. They do not believe in missions, Sunday schools, or higher education. Their membership amounts to a few thousand. See also Church of the Brethren.

88   Palatinate: "Pfalz" in German, the name designates a region in Germany along the Rhine River, whose boundaries have varied throughout history. The core area of Pfalz has been the territory bounded by Alsace-Lorraine in the south, and Hesse in the north. Inhabitants of the area had suffered a great deal from ravages of wars and recurring invasions, especially in 1674 and 1689. Tens of thousands of Palatinates came to America during colonial times on various schemes and settled in New York, Pennsylvania, and other parts of the colonies.

89   Passenger Lists: See Captains' Lists.

90   Peace Churches: In the context of German-American history, this term has been associated with the Mennonite Church and its derivatives, the members of which were conscientious objectors, an alternative to serving in the military.

91   Pennsylvania Dutch: A name erroneously assigned to the inhabitants of Pennsylvania of German ancestry; it was derived from the corruption of the word "Deutsch." Entering the province under William Penn's charter, Germans were among the first European settlers. The massive immigration from the Palatinate in the eighteenth century rapidly increased the German element creating compact settlements in the southeastern part of the colony. At the time of the revolution, German Americans comprised one-third of Pennsylvania's population. Historically, the German population has predominated in Lancaster, Lebanon, Lehigh, Berks, Northhampton, and York counties, often referred to as "Pennsylvania Dutch Country."

92   Pfaelzer: German immigrants from the Palatinate, "Pfalz" in German. They were among the early settlers of Pennsylvania.

93   Pietists: Many of the German religious immigrant groups seeking freedom of conscience in colonial America had been inspired by pietism, a movement which arose in Germany in the seventeenth century against the growing formalism of the established Protestant churches. Pietism advocated Christianity as a life rather than a creed, and laid stress on missionary activities. Among the German religious bodies in America, the Lutherans in their early stages, and especially the Moravians, were pietistic in orientation.

94   Plain People: A term given to German people belonging to the Amish, Mennonite, and Dunkard congregations in early Pennsylvania.

95   Pow-Wow: A secret art, practiced in the past in Pennsylvania Dutch country backwoods, to heal by laying of the hand, by magic words, or by charmed objects.

96   Putz: Putz comes from the word "putzen" which in German means to adorn, to decorate, or to dress up. Among Pennsylvania Germans it has come to mean the Christmas creche scene.

97   Rappites: See Harmony Society.

98   Redemptioners: A system established in early colonial times by which an emigrant from Europe could secure transportation to America without having the means to pay for the passage. These emigrants sold their services upon arrival for from three to seven years. The majority of redemptioners from 1730 until the early nineteenth century were Germans and Scottish-Irish. Because of the scarcity of slaves in Pennsylvania, there was a great demand for this form of servitude labor. The abuses in the traffic of redemptioners were curtailed through successive measures by the Pennsylvania legislature. The sale of redemptioners was finally abolished in 1820. (See also Indentured Servants.)

98a   Reformed Church in the United States: The history of this denomination goes back to the first half of the eighteenth century when large masses of Germans of the Reformed faith emigrated to America via Holland from the Rhineland of Germany and Switzerland. Their plight aroused the interest and sympathy of the Reformed Church of Holland and for the first seventy-five years the German Calvinistic congregations in the colonies developed under the patronage of the Reformed Church of Holland. The first German Reformed Church was founded in Philadelphia in 1727 and by 1751 there were forty-six congregations in Pennsylvania alone. The separation from the Holland Church took place in 1792 when the name German Reformed Church was adopted. In subsequent decades the church expanded its influence to Ohio and North Carolina and a number of colleges and theological schools were also founded. In 1869, the word "German" was dropped from the name. In 1934, the Reformed Church and the German Evangelical Synod of North America (Deutscher Evangelische Kirchenverein des Westens, q.v.) merged to form a new ecclesiastical body under the name Evangelical and Reformed Church. At the time of the merger the Reformed Church reported 345,000 members. In 1959 the Evangelical and Reformed Church, then having 810,000 communicants in 2,740 churches, decided to merge with the Congregational Christian Churches to form a new denominational body under the name United Church of Christ. A historical note: at the time of the first merger in 1934, the Eureka classis in the Dakotas insisted on continuing its existence as the Reformed Church in the United States and is known today under this name. It has 22 churches and over 4,000 members.

99   River Brethren: A German-Protestant religious sect clustered along the Susquehanna River in Pennsylvania who followed a way of life similar to

that of the Mennonites or Dunkers. They had originally belonged to the United Brethren, which was an amalgam of religious communities in Lancaster County consisting of Swiss Mennonites, German Baptist Brethren, some German Lutherans, and reformed groups. The River Brethren ultimately broke away from the United Brethren because of differences over rituals. Their religious life was informal, but when their members were drafted into the Union army during the Civil War they were forced to establish formal organizations to protect conscientious objectors. The sect took the name Brethren in Christ in 1863. Today they maintain about 150 congregations with a membership of around 8,000.

100 Russian Germans: The first German settlements in Russia were initiated along the Volga River by Catherine II. In 1804, Alexander I opened up new areas for German settlement in the Black Sea region inviting colonists of various religious denominations from the Palatinate, Wuerttemberg, Baden, Alsace, and Switzerland. They included Lutherans, Mennonites, Hutterites, and Roman Catholics. Enjoying various privileges, the German colonies prospered, their numbers reaching several million and gradually spreading to the Crimea, Caucasus, and Bessarabia. After Alexander III abrogated their privileges in 1874, they began to leave Russia in large masses and came to America establishing settlements in the Dakotas, Nebraska, and California's San Joaquin valley.

101 Salzburgers: Early settlers in Georgia whose history goes back to 1731 during the time when all people who were not adherents of Catholicism were expelled from the Austrian bishopric of Salzburg. About 30,000 Lutherans were affected. Encouraged by the British government, many of the Salzburg Lutherans came to America, settling in the marshlands of Georgia. In 1736 they founded the city of Ebenezer along the Savannah River. The Salzburgers later spread out into other territories of Georgia.

102 Schwenkfelders: Members of the Schwenkfelder Church are followers of Kasper von Schwenkfeld (1490-1561), the German mystic and religious leader whose differences with orthodox Protestantism led to his condemnation. He was able to attract many followers who underwent severe persecution. A group of 212 Schwenkfelders migrated to Pennsylvania in 1734 settling in Philadelphia, as well as Montgomery, Berks, and Lehigh Counties. The church has five congregations, a library in Pennsburg, Pennsylvania, and a school. The documents, records, and writings of the leaders of the church have been published in cooperation with the Hartford Theological Seminary in a twenty-nine volume set (1907-61) under the title CORPUS SCHWENKFELDIANORUM.

103 Separatist Society of Zoar: See Zoar.

103a Silver Shirts: A fascist organization founded by William D. Pelley in Ashville, North Carolina, on the day Hitler took power in Germany.

Glossary

104 Stephanites: A German-Lutheran group; followers of Martin Stephan, a self-appointed bishop who came to America in 1838 settling in Perry County, Missouri. Stephan was soon deposed on charges of improper behavior.

105 Steuben Society: Founded in May 1913 in New York with local chapters in various communities, the society came into being in reaction to the decline of German-American culture in the aftermath of World War I. Named after Baron Friedrich Wilhelm von Steuben (1730-94), German general, a volunteer in the Continental Army and Washington's adviser, the society aimed at enlightening the American public about the contribution that Americans of German origin have made to the nation, to cultivate pride among members in their ancestry, and protect people of German ancestry from misrepresentation and discrimination.

106 St. Nazianz: A Catholic communitarian society in Wisconsin, composed of 113 colonists from Baden, Germany, established in 1854 by Father Oschwald. Because of friction with the Catholic hierarchy, Father Oschwald led his followers to the forest where he bought three thousand acres and founded in the Spiritual-Magnetic Association of the Holy St. Gregor of Nazianz. The founder died in 1873, but the community continued to exist. In 1902 there were still one hundred members of the commune living in the cloisters.

106a Swiss American Historical Society: The society was founded in 1927 in Chicago on the occasion of a Swiss Singing Festival by a group of midwestern Swiss Americans. The initiative came from Ernst A. Kubler of Ithaca, New York; Bruno Buchmann of Chicago; and August Ruedy of Cleveland, all three of whom had long been active in Swiss American social and cultural affairs. The society set itself the task of conducting and encouraging historical research and of recording the achievements and influences of Swiss Americans in all spheres of life of the United States. In addition to holding regular meetings and discussions with speakers presenting scholarly papers on Swiss American themes, the society has been active in promoting and disseminating publications of author-members. Headquartered in Washington, D.C., the society has throughout its whole existence kept close contact with the Swiss Embassy.

107 Swiss Germans: Since the arrival of secessionist Protestant groups from Calvinist Switzerland in colonial times, a steady flow of German-speaking Swiss arrived in America. They organized settlements in almost every part of the country with heavier concentrations in New York, New Jersey, Wisconsin, and regions of the Midwest. As their cultural background was German, they intermingled with German groups throughout the nineteenth and early twentieth centuries. It was only after World War I that they began to divorce themselves from the Germans to establish their own organizations. The Swiss-American Historical Society was founded in 1927 to promote research on the contribution of Swiss Germans to America.

108 Swiss Mennonites: This group began to arrive in America in 1711. Their departure from Switzerland was encouraged and facilitated by the authorities of Berne who offered them free transportation to Holland if they pledged never to return to Switzerland. They settled in Lancaster County.

109 Taufer: See Church of the Brethren.

110 Teutonia: See National Association of Teutonia.

111 Tunkers: See Church of the Brethren.

112 Turnerbund, North American. Nordamerikanischer Turnerbund. See Turnerbund.

113 Turnerbund: This body was the national organization of the local German gymnasts' clubs (Turnvereine) which flourished in the nineteenth century. In 1855 the Turnerbund represented sixty societies, and in 1909 its membership was 40,000. The organization rapidly declined after 1932. In its heyday, the Turnerbund espoused liberal causes. Sixty percent of its members volunteered to fight with the Union armies in the Civil War. Advocating the physical and mental progress of the individual, the Turnerbund was instrumental in introducing physical education in public schools. The organization itself maintained a German teacher training institution in Milwaukee and issued DIE TURNERZEITUNG, a national newspaper of the "Turner" movement.

114 Turnverein: The word means "gymnasts' association," a movement which originated in Germany in the first part of the nineteenth century and was transplanted to America mainly by the refugees of the 1848 revolution. The movement's aspirations was expressed in the Latin motto: "Mensa sana in corpore sano" literally, a sound mind in a sound body, or in philosophical terms, "a chainless body and a fetterless mind." The first Turnverein was organized in Cincinnati in 1848, and local clubs sprang up there after in almost every community with a sizable German population. In the initial period, the Turner's political orientation was reformist and anticlerical and aroused the suspicion and hostility of conservative and nativistic elements of society. For many decades, the local Turnverein served as the center of the cultural life of the German community with singing and dramatic sections, maintaining a reading room and library, offering lectures, play productions, concerts, and organizing athletic and song festivals (Turnfeste, Saengerfeste).

115 Unitas Fratrum: See Church of the Moravian Brethren.

116 United Brethren: The movement which resulted in the formation of the United Brethren Church began with the evangelistic efforts of Philip William Otterbein (1726-1813) and Martin Boehm (1725-1813). The two religious leaders were working among the German settlers in Pennsylvania,

disseminating a theology similar to that of Methodism. The Methodist bishops were not willing to accept German-speaking congregations, and this refusal left them no choice but to found a new denomination.

117 Utopian Communities: See Communitarian Experiments.

118 Verein Zum Schutze Deutscher Einwanderer in Texas (Association for the Protection of German Immigrants in Texas): See Adelsverein.

119 Volga Germans: Descendants of farmers and artisans who were brought to Russia and settled along the Volga River by Empress Catherine II in 1763. After Tsar Alexander abrogated their privileges in 1871, which included exemption from military service, the Volga Germans began to leave Russia in large masses and come to America. First they settled in Kansas, Nebraska, and Colorado, then moved into Idaho and Montana, following the expansion of the sugar beet industry.

120 Wachovia Tract: A 98,985 acre tract covering about two-thirds of Forsyth County, purchased by the Moravian Church for the North Carolina settlement in the Piedmont section of the state. Bethabara, Bethania, Friedberg, Friedland, and Hope were villages with Moravian congregations.

121 Woman in the Wilderness: The term is associated with a group of German mystics led by Johann Kelpius who believed that the world was coming to an end in 1694. They decided to await the Judgment Day in the wilderness of America. They came to America in 1693 and settled near Germantown, Pennsylvania. "The Woman in the Wilderness," is a reference to Revelations, 12:14.

122 Zoar: A German religious communitarian settlement founded in 1817 in Tuscarawas County, Ohio, and disbanded in 1898. Members of the sect believed that Christ would return in 1836. They refused to do military service, and to send their children to public school. They also distinguished themselves by wearing quaint clothes.

II. REFERENCE WORKS

GENERAL BIBLIOGRAPHIC WORKS

123 Pochmann, Henry August, comp., and Schultz, Arthur R., ed. BIB-
LIOGRAPHY OF GERMAN CULTURE IN AMERICA TO 1940. Madison:
University of Wisconsin Press, 1953. 483 p.

Pochmann's bibliography represents the first attempt to compile
a comprehensive inventory of German Americana. In it, thirty
thousand items were scrutinized from which twelve thousand
were selected for inclusion. The listing encompasses a wide
spectrum of materials, from standard works, archival records,
and dissertations, to popular writings. The author made a special effort to choose judiciously from among a mass of club
records, local histories, memorabilia, propaganda materials,
documents, hymnals, prayer books, and a variety of other items.
The arrangement of entries is alphabetical by author or title
word. The work is equipped with a superb subject, name, and
geographic index which provides not only a multitude of access
points, but defines the subject scope of the field as well. In
discussing his sources in the introduction, the author conveys a
great deal of useful information on library collections, archives,
and documentary repositories of organizations and associations.
This work is indispensible for research in German Americana.

124 Tolzmann, Don Heinrich, comp. GERMAN-AMERICANA: A BIBLIOG-
RAPHY. Metuchen, N.J.: Scarecrow Press, 1975. 384 p.

Pochmann and Schultz's pioneering efforts in inventorying
German-American materials were continued by Tolzmann, whose
bibliography covers the 1941-73 period. This work adds 5,300
items to the census established by Pochmann, thus contributing
to a contiguous bibliographic apparatus of the literary manifes-
tations and historical records of the German-American experience in the United States. The listing encompasses books,
pamphlets, government publications, newspapers, periodical
articles, dissertations, records, photo albums, and materials in
other formats.

In contrast with Pochmann's conception, Tolzmann gave his bibliography a classified structure with a detailed author index. The material is organized under ten subject categories: (1) German-American history, (2) language and literature, (3) the press and the book trade, (4) religious life, (5) education, (6) cultural life, (7) business and industry, (8) German-American radicalism, (9) biography, and (10) genealogical works. The first chapter takes up almost one third of the work. It is devoted to a survey of depositories of materials, such as libraries, archives, research centers, organizations, historical societies, and other sources. This section is followed by a listing of bibliographical guides and an enumeration of general and state histories extending over seventy pages. Works dealing with the social and political aspects of the German-American experience are also incorporated in this section.

In addition to providing a bibliographic census, Tolzmann also made an effort to indicate library location in selected cases. The work is complemented by a ten-page listing of journals indexed. The bulk of the material brought together in this bibliography is in the English language and should be generally available in larger public and academic libraries.

The works of Pochmann and Tolzmann are of pivotal importance for researching German Americana. The lack of annotations in both, however, diminish their value as guides to the subject literature.

125 Miller, Wayne Charles, ed. A COMPREHENSIVE BIBLIOGRAPHY FOR THE STUDY OF AMERICAN MINORITIES. 2 vols. New York: New York University Press, 1976. Index.

The work encompasses about 29,000 entries, representing the essential English-language literature dealing with every major ethnic group in the United States. Forty pages, containing over a thousand entries, are devoted to German Americans. The material is presented in classified arrangement. Some of the entries carry brief notes.

126 Baginsky, Paul Ben, ed. GERMAN WORKS RELATING TO AMERICA: 1493-1800. A LIST COMPILED FROM THE COLLECTIONS OF THE NEW YORK PUBLIC LIBRARY. Reprinted with revisions and corrections from the BULLETIN OF THE NEW YORK PUBLIC LIBRARY, vols. 42, 43, 44 (1938, 1939, 1940). New York: New York Public Library, 1942. 217 p.

In the preface of his work, Baginsky stated that in his attempt to write a study on the conception of how Germans viewed America from the time of its discovery to 1800, he was stymied by the lack of bibliographic access to the subject. To remedy the situation, he set out to compile and survey pertinent German-language materials dealing with the discovery, exploration, and development of America, as seen through German eyes. He

concentrated on the relevant holdings of the New York Public
Library, which forms the basis of this bibliography. To make
the work more inclusive, titles from Joseph Sabin, DICTION-
ARY OF BOOKS RELATING TO AMERICA (New York: Sabin,
1868, 1936), and Christian G. Kayser, VOLLSTAENDIGES
BUECHER-LEXICON, 1750-1910 (1834-1911), were added in
in the supplement. Periodical articles which project the image
of America, even in such esoteric fields as forestry, medicine,
and science, were also brought under purview.

All this material is presented in chronological arrangement by
date of publishing. References can be found to book reviews
on works dealing with America. Popular interest in the New
World was stimulated by letters, reports, and diaries from over-
seas, which often received wide circulation in hometown periodicals in Germany. References to such materials are also included in this bibliography. Detailed subject, author, and
title indexes make this work easy to use. No index, however,
was prepared for the supplementary material.

127 Bowers, David Frederick, ed. FOREIGN INFLUENCES IN AMERICAN
LIFE: ESSAY AND CRITICAL BIBLIOGRAPHIES. Princeton Studies in
American Civilization. Princeton, N.J.: Princeton University Press,
1944. Reprint. New York: Peter Smith, 1952. 254 p. Bibliog.

This collection of essays seeks to define the scope of foreign
influence in American life, including the influences exerted by
Americans of German origin. The first eight essays analyze
foreign influences in the social and cultural realms, and specifically in the economic and political life, as well as in art,
literature, and philosophy. Of particular interest are the bibliographic essays, complementing these writings, which discuss
the nature of the literature and sources of information relating
to the themes covered. Although the material included is somewhat dated, it may contain items overlooked elsewhere.

128 Cashman, Marc, and Klein, Barry, eds. BIBLIOGRAPHY OF AMERICAN
ETHNOLOGY. Bicentennial first ed. Rye, N.Y.: Todd Publications,
1976. 304 p.

Devoted to the general subject of ethnicity in America, this
bibliography highlights fifty-nine selected publications relating
to German Americans out of a total listing of 4,500 works.
The subject areas covered are: history, immigration, literature,
and politics. The significance of this listing is that it included
only items currently in print. The work is based essentially on
the 1976 edition of SUBJECT GUIDE TO BOOKS IN PRINT.

THE GERMAN-AMERICAN PRESS

129 Seidensticker, Oswald. THE FIRST CENTURY OF GERMAN PRINTING

IN AMERICA, 1728-1830. 1893. Reprint. New York: Krause, 1966. 253 p.

A composite bibliography of works such as books, pamphlets, almanacs, handbooks, catechisms, calendars, and newspapers printed by German presses primarily in Pennsylvania, New York, Massachusetts, Ohio, Virginia, and Nova Scotia. The listing is arranged first by the year of printing, then by city, and then by author. Most of the items listed are in the German language, and they carry annotations in English. Locations are indicated for older and rarer works. A directory of printers and publishers is provided. One of the listings offers an enumeration of places of German printing arranged by date of first issue. As a special feature, the work includes a bibliography of the writings of Francis Daniel Pastorius. The work is supplemented by Gerhard Friedrich, "A New Supplement to Siedensticker's American-German Bibliography" (PENNSYLVANIA HISTORY 7 (October 1940): 213-24).

130   Hocker, Edward W. THE SOWER PRINTING HOUSE OF COLONIAL TIMES. Pennsylvania German Society Proceedings and Addresses, vol. 53. Norristown: Pennsylvania German Society, 1948. 125 p. Bibliog.

A basic history of the Sower dynasty which played an important part in the early history of press in America. The founder, Christopher Sower, came to the United States in 1724, established a printing shop in 1738 in Germantown, Pennsylvania, and in the following year launched the GERMANTOWN ZEITUNG, the first German-language newspaper in America. After Sower's death in 1758, his son continued the family business, and in 1772 established the first foundry. Successive generations have kept the business alive. This work provides checklists of the publications of the Sower press. The bibliography of sources gives many leads for further research. Six facsimiles of book title pages issued by the Sower press give an inkling of the typographical quality of the early products.

131   Reichmann, Felix, comp. CHRISTOPHER SOWER, SR., 1694-1758, PRINTER IN GERMANTOWN; AN ANNOTATED BIBLIOGRAPHY. Bibliographies on German-American History. Philadelphia: Carl Schurz Memorial Foundation, 1943. 79 p. Bibliog., index.

This is a descriptive bibliography with biographical detail and printing history of the 193 items issued during the lifetime of Christopher Sower, the founder. The listing is chronological by date of publishing. A source bibliography of sixty-three works is included.

132   Hildeburn, Charles Swift Riche. A CENTURY OF PRINTING: THE ISSUES OF THE PRESS IN PENNSYLVANIA, 1685-1784. 1885. Reprint. 2 vols. American Classics in History and Social Science, no. 41. New York: Burt Franklin, 1968. 392 p.; 516 p. Index.

A two-volume bibliography of all types of printed literary products which were put forth by the presses in Pennsylvania during
these hundred years. In all, the two volumes enumerate,
describe, and briefly annotate 4,700 items, many of which are
in German. The work is a result of six years of careful research. The listing is by year of printing, and then alphabetical by title. There is an index to authors, or titles if the work
is anonymous. For many items, library location is given. There
is a list of printers in chronological arrangement according to
their appearance on the scene.

133 Heckman, Marlin L. "Abraham Harley Cassel, Nineteenth Century Pennsylvania German American Book Collector." PENNSYLVANIA GERMAN
SOCIETY PUBLICATIONS 7 (1973): 105-224. Breinigsville: Pennsylvania German Society, 1973. Bibliog., notes.

Originally a thesis at the University of Chicago, this work is
a detailed treatment of Cassel as a book collector, librarian,
and writer. According to the author, Cassel's effort to establish a research collection related to the Pennsylvania Germans
was a pioneering undertaking. Following a biography of Cassel, who died in 1908, the author discusses the nature and dis-
persal of the collection. The major beneficiaries were Mount
Morris College in Illinois, Juniata College in Pennsylvania,
and the Historical Society of Pennsylvania, from where the material was transferred to the Library Company of Philadelphia.
A 250-item bibliography, used to reconstruct the story, complements the work.

134 Bausman, Lottie M. A BIBLIOGRAPHY OF LANCASTER COUNTY,
PENNSYLVANIA, 1747-1912. Publications of the Pennsylvania Federation of Historical Societies. Philadelphia: Patterson and White, 1916.
460 p. Index.

All told, six thousand items including books, almanacs, magazines, journals, and other works are listed chronologically in
this bibliography. German-American materials are adequately
represented. Two supplements bring in many added items which
could not be included in the main listing on account of insuf-
ficient bibliographic evidence. Has an author-title index.

135 Shoemaker, Alfred L[ewis]. A CHECK LIST OF IMPRINTS OF THE GER-
MAN PRESS OF NORTHAMPTON COUNTY, PENNSYLVANIA, 1766-
1905, WITH BIOGRAPHIES OF THE PRINTERS. Northampton County His-
torical and Genealogical Society Publications, vol. 4. Easton, Pa.:
Northampton County Historical and Genealogical Society, 1943. 162 p.
Bibliog., index.

Preceded by a historical sketch, the work enumerates by imprint
year all types of materials produced in the county during the
period indicated. A list of German newspapers is provided giv-

ing title, frequency, size, and a short history. Library holdings of books are given. A rundown of German presses with a
biographical directory of their owners complements the work.

136 _____. A CHECKLIST OF IMPRINTS OF THE GERMAN PRESS OF LE-
HIGH COUNTY, PENNSYLVANIA, 1807-1900, WITH BIOGRAPHIES OF
THE PRINTERS. Lehigh County Historical Society Proceedings, vol. 16.
Allentown, Pa.: Lehigh County Historical Society, 1947. 240 p. Bib-
liog., index.

A chronological listing of publications with many added features.
In addition to bibliographic description and library locations,
the work includes a list of publishers, a list of German-language
newspapers in the county, and the biographical directory of publishers based on obituaries. The bibliography is introduced by
an essay discussing the history of printing in Lehigh County with
pertinent sources.

137 Cazden, Robert Edgar. GERMAN EXILE LITERATURE IN AMERICA,
1933-1950; A HISTORY OF THE FREE GERMAN PRESS AND BOOK
TRADE. Chicago: American Library Association, 1970. 250 p. Bibliog., index.

An exhaustive treatment of the literary activities in the United
States of exiles from Germany, Austria, and Czechoslovakia who
used the German language as a vehicle of communication. A
substantial part of the work consists of a detailed historical
overview covering roughly two decades up to 1954. The focus
here is on the various types of periodical publications reflecting the complicated political, national, and religious alignments
of the group. Aspects of book publishing, the import trade,
and the plight of emigre authors are also explored.

The discourse is complemented by a rich bibliographical section
presenting relevant information in a variety of ways. The first
is a list of retail distributors of free German publications in the
United States from 1933-50, with company, dates active, spe-
cialities, and city location. The second is a checklist of free
German and free Austrian newspapers and periodicals in the
United States from 1933-50. The third is a checklist of free
German books and pamphlets published in the United States from
1933-54. Here the arrangement is by publisher, and then by
author. The entries carry informative annotations. The enu-
merative section is followed by a numerical analysis of the publications in tabular form. A 360-item source bibliography listing unpublished manuscripts, newspapers, monographs, journal
articles, bookdealers' and publishers' catalogs complete the work.

NEWSPAPERS AND PERIODICALS

138 Wittke, Carl Frederick. THE GERMAN-LANGUAGE PRESS IN AMERICA.

Louisville: University of Kentucky Press, 1957. Reprint. New York: Haskell House, 1973. 311 p. Bibliog. notes, index.

A narrative survey of important German-language newspapers and periodicals throughout the ages, beginning with 1732 to the end of World War I. Their role in the social process of their respective communities is emphasized. As such, the work can provide many pointers for social historians and genealogists. A very detailed index helps pinpoint specific information in the text.

139 Arndt, Karl John Richard. GERMAN-AMERICAN NEWSPAPERS AND PERIODICALS, 1732-1955: HISTORY AND BIBLIOGRAPHY. 2d rev. ed. New York: Johnson Reprint, 1965. 810 p. Bibliog., index.

For annotation, see below.

140 Arndt, Karl John Richard, and Olson, May E. THE GERMAN LANGUAGE PRESS OF THE AMERICAS: HISTORY AND BIBLIOGRAPHY 1732-1968. 2 vols. Vol. 1: United States of America. 3d rev. ed. Vol. 2: Argentina, Bolivia, Brazil, Canada, Chile, Columbia, Costa Rica, Cuba, Dominican Republic, Ecuador, Guatemala, Guyana, Mexico, Paraguay, Peru, U.S.A. (addenda), Uruguay, Venezuala. Munchen: Verlag Dokumentation, Pullach, 1973-75. Bibliog., index.

This work is the definitive bibliographical directory of its kind which took decades to compile. It inventories about five thousand German-American newspapers and periodicals in the United States. The arrangement is by state, then by city, with an introductory statement concerning the German element in each. The bibliographic information includes the title of the periodical, the date of launching, and the date when it ceased publication, if applicable. This is followed by a brief publishing history, title changes, library locations with holdings, and the authors' sources of information. More than two hundred works were consulted. Their titles are given in the accompanying bibliography. A few facsimiles illustrate the work, among which the most interesting are Abraham Lincoln's contract as a reporter with the ILLINOIS STAATS-ANZEIGER, and of the original copy of the German-language version of the Declaration of Independence.

As seen from the above entries, these works have a long publishing history. In 1973 volume two was published covering Canada and South America. This edition also carried a 145-page supplementary listing to the material presented in the 1965 U.S. volume. In 1975 a new edition of the U.S. volume was issued with a forty-eight page addendum. At this writing a third volume is projected: GERMAN AMERICAN PRESS RESEARCH FROM THE TIME OF THE REVOLUTION TO THE BICENTENNIAL.

Reference Works

141   Dolmetsch, Christopher L. "Locations of German Language Newspaper
and Periodical Printing in the United States: 1732-1976." MONAT-
SHEFTE 68 (Summer 1976): 188-95.

> "The studies of German settlement in the United States have
> been furthered by the research into German newspaper and
> periodical publication by Karl J.R. Arndt and May E. Olson.
> Their reference works to date, however, have not included
> any maps. The presentation of two maps showing: (Map 1)
> locations of German language newspaper and periodical publi-
> cation between 1732 and 1976, and (Map 2) locations of Ger-
> man language newspaper and periodical publication prior to
> 1830 is intended primarily as an addition to their work. These
> maps have an important advantage over other visual depictions
> by taking into account almost all areas of German settlement
> in the U.S. irrespective of the date of immigration--not the
> case, for example, with earlier U.S. Census Bureau maps.
> Because of their content and character, prisoner of war
> (P.O.W.) publications have been excluded. All other news-
> papers and periodicals, regardless of duration, have been
> included." (Author's abstract)

142   Miller, Daniel. EARLY GERMAN AMERICAN NEWSPAPERS. Pennsylvania German Society Proceedings, vol. 19 (1908). Lancaster: Pennsylvania German Society, 1910. 107 p.

> The chronological scope of this work extends from the eigh-
> teenth century to the middle of the nineteenth century and
> covers Pennsylvania, Maryland, New York, the South, and
> the West, with particular emphasis on eastern Pennsylvania.
> The German-language press of the period is discussed in the
> context of each city and county where such press existed.
> The paper's title, founder's name, dates of publication, and
> information on editorial policy are given. There are many
> facsimiles of mastheads and pages.

143   Park, Robert Ezra. THE IMMIGRANT PRESS AND ITS CONTROL.
Americanization Studies. 1922. Reprint. New York: Greenwood
Press, 1970. 487 p. Bibliog. notes, index.

> German-American newspapers receive substantial treatment in
> this general study of the immigrant press. Their history, pur-
> pose, and impact are explored in some depth. A great deal
> of useful information can also be extracted from diagrams and
> comparative statistical tables.

144   Arndt, Karl John Richard. THE ERNST STEIGER COLLECTIONS OF GER-
MAN-AMERICAN NEWSPAPERS AND PERIODICALS IN HEIDELBERG AND
VIENNA DILIGENTLY COMPARED AND CATALOGUED FOR CO-OPE-
RATING LIBRARIES AS A GUIDE TO MICROFILM COPIES OF THE HEI-
DELBERG COLLECTION. Worcester, Mass.: Clark University, 1964.
51 leaves.

The Vienna Collection described here originated as an American exhibit at the Vienna International Exhibition of 1873. Steiger, a New York publisher, sent samples of contemporary German-language periodicals, as well as of books, as his firm's contribution to the exhibit. This material ultimately found its way to the Austrian National Library, and it is now available on microfilm. This bibliography describes the items in the collection bearing testimony to the vitality of German-language periodical publishing in the United States in the second half of the nineteenth century. If Steiger's sampling was complete, there were at that time 363 active German-language periodicals distributed among the states as follows: California, 9; Colorado, 1; Connecticut, 1; Dakota, 1; Delaware, 1; Georgia, 1; Illinois, 20; Indiana, 14; Iowa, 14; Kansas, 3; Kentucky, 8; Louisiana, 4; Maryland, 5; Massachusetts, 2; Michigan, 10; Minnesota, 7; Missouri, 25; Nebraska, 4; New Jersey, 13; New York, 74; Ohio, 40; Oregon, 1; Pennsylvania, 60; South Carolina, 1; Tennessee, 2; Texas, 4; Virginia, 1; Wisconsin, 37. The bibliographic data for each periodical listed includes title, size, frequency, publisher, place of publication, and the identity of the issue in the collection.

145   Hunter, Edward. IN MANY VOICES; OUR FABULOUS FOREIGN-LANGUAGE PRESS. Norman Park, Ga.: Norman College, 1960. 190 p.

Intended to supplement Park's treatise on the same subject (see 143), this work surveys key foreign-language newspapers in major U.S. cities, highlighting interest groups which were behind the publications. The German-language press is given the largest space among them.

ARCHIVES AND ARCHIVAL MATERIALS

146   Hamer, Philip M., ed. A GUIDE TO ARCHIVES AND MANUSCRIPTS IN THE UNITED STATES. Compiled for the National Historical Commission. New Haven, Conn.: Yale University Press, 1961. 775 p. Index.

Lists and describes by state and by city major repositories of archival materials, reflecting their status as of 1960. The holdings of libraries, archives, and historical societies are enumerated in terms of subject matter, chronological range, and quantity. The papers of 7,600 prominent persons were included in the inventory, together with the records of many organizations, corporations, and institutions. A considerable amount of material of German-American interest can be identified through the index, as for example: German-American Cultural Alliance, German Baptist Church, German Christian Agricultural and Benevolent Society of Ora et Labora, German Evangelical Church, Fraktur, German Methodist Church, German Reformed Church, German Seventh Day Baptist Conference, German Society of Pennsylvania, Germantown Pennsylvania, Germantown Historical Society, Mennonite Church, Mennonite Publishing, Moravian Church, and many others. The index also enables the researcher to locate material on a particular individual by the individual's name. Since individuals are indexed solely by name and not by affiliation, the papers of persons with German-American affiliation can be located only if the researcher knows this to be a fact.

147 NATIONAL UNION CATALOG OF MANUSCRIPTS COLLECTIONS. 1959/61-- . Hamden, Conn.: Shoe String Press, 1962-- . Annual.

Essentially, this catalog continues Hamer's work (see 146). It is based on reports from American repositories of manuscripts. The collections inventoried consist of private and corporate records in a variety of format. The shortcomings that characterize Hamer's index are also present in this compilation.

148 U.S. Library of Congress. UNITED STATES LOCAL HISTORIES IN THE LIBRARY OF CONGRESS: A BIBLIOGRAPHY. 4 vols. Edited by Marion J. Kaminkow. Baltimore: Magna Carta Book Co., 1975.

An indispensable reference work of several thousand pages listing materials of all types. The geographical distribution is as follows: volume 1, Atlantic states (Maine to New York); volume 2, South Atlantic states (New Jersey to Florida); volume 3, Middle West, Alaska, Hawaii; volume 4, The West. The listing includes books, serials, city directories, and bibliographies, with the cutoff date of 1972. The arrangement is according to the Library of Congress classification scheme. Genealogies have been omitted.

149 Griffin, Appleton Prentiss Clark. BIBLIOGRAPHY OF AMERICAN HISTORICAL SOCIETIES (THE UNITED STATES AND THE DOMINION OF CANADA). 2d ed., rev. and enl. Annual Report of the American Historical Association, vol. 2 (1905). 1907. Reprint. Detroit: Gale Research Co., 1966. 1,374 p. Index.

Writings dealing with aspects of German Americana are well represented in this listing. Content notes are given for most items. A copious subject-author index as well as biographical and society indexes help locate materials. Further listings are included in the annual issues of WRITINGS ON AMERICAN HISTORY (Washington, D.C.: Government Printing Office, 1902--).

150 DIRECTORY OF HISTORICAL SOCIETIES AND AGENCIES IN THE UNITED STATES AND CANADA. Madison, Wis.: American Association for State and Local History, 1956-- . Biennial.

The most comprehensive listing in this field, with addresses, libraries, and museums, and additional information on hours, publications, and other useful data.

151 Learned, Marion Dexter. GUIDE TO MANUSCRIPT MATERIALS RELATING TO AMERICAN HISTORY IN THE GERMAN STATE ARCHIVES. Carnegie Institution. Publication no. 150. 1912. Reprint. New York: Kraus Reprint, 1965. 352 p. Index.

Sponsored by the Carnegie Institution, the author made a systematic study of archives in Germany for the purpose of inventorying materials of interest to American history. The result of this study is a listing of a variety of records, papers, passenger lists, personal diaries, letters, and others, originating mostly from the eighteenth and nineteenth centuries. The material is organized in descending order from state to municipal archives, and in each section the items found are enumerated in alphabetical sequence. The bulk of the records are in German, English, and French. An explanation of the German archival system in the introduction and a very detailed index facilitate the use of the work.

152 Faust, Albert Bernhardt. GUIDE TO THE MATERIALS OF AMERICAN HISTORY IN SWISS AND AUSTRIAN ARCHIVES. Carnegie Institution. Publication no. 220. 1916. Reprint. New York: Kraus Reprint, 1966. 299 p. Index.

Faust surveyed forty archives and six libraries in Switzerland and Austria and a few in German-inhabited sections of France and Italy, where he found a considerable amount of material related to emigration of Germans to America and elsewhere. The collections of state, cantonal, and municipal institutions were consulted and the material is presented in this arrangement. Most of the entries are in German with a capsule statement regarding their content given in English. The work has a fine index.

153 Allison, William Henry. INVENTORY OF UNPUBLISHED MATERIAL FOR AMERICAN RELIGIOUS HISTORY IN PROTESTANT CHURCH ARCHIVES AND OTHER REPOSITORIES. Carnegie Institution. Publication no. 137. 1910. Reprint. New York: Kraus Reprint, 1965. 254 p. Index.

A great deal of the material inventoried here consists of the official papers of the governing bodies of the various Protestant denominations, their missionary societies, and of their various subsidiaries. In addition, a tally of the papers and correspondences of prominent figures are also enclosed. The listing is by state, then by city. The student of German-American religious history may find some relevant materials here.

154 Spalek, John M. GUIDE TO THE ARCHIVAL MATERIALS OF THE GER-
MAN-SPEAKING EMIGRATION TO THE UNITED STATES AFTER 1933.
In collaboration with Adrienne Ash and Sandra H. Hawrlchak. Charlottes-
ville: Published for the Bibliographical Society of the University of
Virginia by the University Press of Virginia, 1978. Index.

Item not available for examination.

155 Historical Records Survey. Pennsylvania. GUIDE TO THE MANUSCRIPT
COLLECTIONS IN THE HISTORICAL SOCIETY OF PENNSYLVANIA.
Prepared by the Historical Records Survey, Division of the Professional
and Service Projects, Works Project Administration. Compiled by Paul
Bleyden. Edited by Bernard S. Levin. 2d ed. Philadelphia: The So-
ciety, 1949. 350 p.

Because of its local nature, the collection has many implications for German-American research. This edition describes
over sixteen hundred various collections with a total holdings
of more than four million items. References to published collections of documents are indicated.

156 PENNSYLVANIA GERMAN FOLKLORE SOCIETY YEARBOOK, vol. 7
(1942). Allentown: Pennsylvania German Folklore Society, 1943. 102 p.

The whole issue is devoted to Pennsylvania German historical
societies and museums. Each of the six articles focuses on
one particular institution giving historical background and a
detailed description of their holdings. Numerous photographs
of buildings and objects accompany the text. The yearbook
consists of the following contributions: (1) Horace M. Mann,
"The Bucks County Historical Society"; (2) Elmer E.S. Johnson, "The Schwenkfelder Historical Library"; (3) Mabel E.
Bitner, "The Pennsylvania State Museum"; (4) Gurney W.
Clemens, "The Berks County Historical Society"; (5) Richard
Light, "The Hershey Museum"; and (6) Felix Reichmann, "The
Landis Valley Museum."

156a Hobbie, Margaret. MUSEUMS, SITES, AND EXHIBITS OF GERMANIC
CULTURE IN NORTH AMERICA: AN ANNOTATED DIRECTORY OF
GERMAN IMMIGRANT MATERIAL CULTURE IN THE UNITED STATES
AND CANADA. Westport, Conn.: Greenwood Press, in press.

A description of over 250 museum collections and historic
sites of German-Americana. A name index of institutions and
a subject index based on Robert G. Chenhall's NOMENCLA-
TURE FOR MUSEUM CATALOGING: A SYSTEM FOR CLAS-
SIFYING MAN-MADE OBJECTS (Nashville: American Association for State and Local History, 1978) are provided. In
an appendix, the author lists a number of European sources
and the cultural attaches of German, Swiss and Austrian em-
bassies in the United States and Canada.

157 Historical Records Survey. Pennsylvania. INVENTORY OF THE COUNTY ARCHIVES OF PENNSYLVANIA. Prepared by the Historical Records Survey, Division of Professional and Service Projects, Works Project Administration. No. 6, Berks County; no. 36, Lancaster County. Philadelphia: The Historical Records Survey, 1940-- . Var. pag.

> Contains a detailed enumeration of municipal, county, and agency records covering the period 1750 to 1940. The material inventoried includes not only documents generated by the respective governmental units, but also any items having relevancy to local history. Among the graphic materials one would find maps of townships and boroughs, charts of governmental organizations, floor plans of buildings, and others. A subject index and a chronological index to the records facilitate the use of this inventory. A list of Berks County officials is appended covering the years 1752 to 1940.

GENEALOGICAL RESOURCES

Encyclopedic Guides

158 Smith, Clifford Neal, and Smith, Anna Piszczan-Czaja. ENCYCLOPEDIA OF GERMAN-AMERICAN GENEALOGICAL RESEARCH. New York: Bowker, 1977. 273 p. Index.

> For annotation, see below.

159 _____. AMERICAN GENEALOGICAL RESOURCES IN GERMAN ARCHIVES (AGRIGA): A HANDBOOK. New York: Bowker, 1977. 336 p. Index.

> A comprehensive treatment of topics that anyone attempting to do genealogical research in Germany must know. The first chapter deals with genealogical resources in the United States, listing the cities where German-language periodicals were published. Further chapters are devoted to: sources on the illegal emigrations from Germany in the seventeenth and eighteenth centuries; German ethnic religious bodies and locations of German-speaking congregations in the United States; language and dialect clues, especially for surnames; political and administrative organization of the various units that made up Germany beginning with the Holy Roman Empire; genealogical sources in Germany, including church records, local land, and civil records; an explanation of the German court system; a directory of archival repositories and information on what kind of assistance is available for research; Jews in southwestern Germany; and heraldry. The last chapter concentrates on German-American genealogical materials in governmental agencies. It discusses the nature of military records, immigration records, and others.

Item 158 is supplemented by AGRIGA which is a directory of 290 archival collections in Germany of interest to American genealogical researchers. In addition to directory information, the subject matter, the nature of the collections, and their chronological span, size, and location code within the institution are supplied. The work is equipped with three separate indexes: name, geographic, and subject.

160 Rubincam, Milton. RESEARCHING EUROPEAN ORIGINS OF PENNSYL-VANIA FAMILIES. Philadelphia, 1968. Offprint from PENNSYLVANIA GENEALOGICAL MAGAZINE 25 (1968): 227-45.

Intended for the uninitiated who wish to trace their ancestry in Europe. The article is full of hints as to how to go about finding the original home of ancestors in Germany. The nature of the various types of relevant records are also discussed. This essay can serve as an introduction prior to consulting the more sophisticated tools.

Genealogical Atlas

161 Hall, Charles M. THE ATLANTIC BRIDGE TO GERMANY. 5 vols. Logan, Utah: Everton, 1974-- .

A five-volume set of thematic atlases showing areas from which large-scale emigration to America had taken place. At the writing of this review, only the following three volumes were published: I. Baden-Wuerttemberg, II. Rheinland-Pfalz (Palatinate), and IV. Saarland, Alsace-Lorraine, Switzerland. A gazeteer in each volume identifies the place, its map location, and the records available. The presentation of the material varies from volume to volume. When applicable, the availability of the records on microfilm at the Library of the Genealogical Society of the Church of Jesus Christ of Latter-Day Saints at Salt Lake City, or at some other institution located in the United States, is indicated. Each volume has an introductory section with a short list of suggested sources.

Bibliographies and Indexes

162 U.S. Library of Congress. GENEALOGIES IN THE LIBRARY OF CON-GRESS, A BIBLIOGRAPHY. 2 vols. Edited by Marion Kaminkow. Baltimore: Magna Carta Book Co., 1972.

This massive compilation of family histories in the Library of Congress can be extremely useful for German-American genealogical research, provided one has a specific family in mind. The listing is alphabetical by family name, and the subsequent arrangement is chronological. The material inventories ranges from books to typescripts and handwritten materials. Variant spellings of family names are cross-referenced. The work is intended to be used with the supplement, 1972-76, published in 1977.

163 THE AMERICAN GENEALOGICAL-BIOGRAPHICAL INDEX TO AMERICAN GENEALOGICAL, BIOGRAPHICAL, AND LOCAL HISTORY MATERIALS. Edited by Fremont Rider. Middletown, Conn.: Godfrey Memorial Library, 1952-- .

This monumental compilation can be considered as a master index to genealogical and biographical material in the United States. It is based on the 48-volume AMERICAN GENEA-LOGICAL INDEX, edited by Fremont Rider and published between 1942 and 1952 by Wesleyan University Station, Middletown, Connecticut. At this writing, the present edition, issued in five-volume units per year, has already surpassed one hundred volumes, having reached the middle ranges of the alphabet.

The concept of this work involves name indexing of a multitude of works such as family histories, genealogies, biographical sketches, vital records of towns, and counties, local histories, the first U.S. Census of 1790, rolls of the armies of the Revolution, and others. Arrangement is alphabetical by surname, and a typical index entry gives first name and initial, maiden name if applicable, date of birth, state of residence, and references to works where information on the person can be found. This work is all inclusive in its approach, but for German-American genealogical research it is best used when the name of an ancestor is known.

164 INDEX TO AMERICAN GENEALOGIES, AND TO GENEALOGICAL MATERIALS CONTAINED IN ALL WORKS SUCH AS TOWN HISTORIES, COUNTY HISTORIES, LOCAL HISTORIES, HISTORICAL SOCIETY PUBLI-CATIONS, BIOGRAPHIES, HISTORICAL PERIODICALS, AND KINDRED WORKS, ALPHABETICALLY ARRANGED. 5th ed., rev., improved, and enl. 1900. Reprint. With Supplement 1900 to 1908. Detroit: Gale Research Co., 1966. 352, 107 p.

165 THE AMERICAN GENEALOGIST, BEING A CATALOGUE OF FAMILY HISTORIES. A BIBLIOGRAPHY OF AMERICAN GENEALOGY, OR A LIST OF THE TITLE PAGES OF BOOKS AND PAMPHLETS ON FAMILY HISTORY, PUBLISHED IN AMERICA, FROM 1771 TO DATE. 5th ed. Albany, N.Y.: J. Munsell's Sons, 1900. 406 p.

General in scope, the first work (see 164) covers Germanic family names as well, thus can be very useful for German-American genealogical research. The surnames are given in bold-faced type, followed by titles of works containing information on each surname with title and page references to works in which information on families can be found. The biblio-

graphical description is skeletal, which necessitates consulting
THE AMERICAN GENEALOGIST for complete bibliographic
information.

166 Stewart, Robert Armistead. INDEX TO PRINTED VIRGINIA GENEA-
LOGIES, INCLUDING KEY AND BIBLIOGRAPHY. Richmond, Va.:
Old Dominion Press, 1930. Reprint. Baltimore: Genealogical Publish-
ing, 1970. 265 p. Bibliog.

More than nine hundred works, including family histories,
biographies, and Virginia county histories are brought together
in this index. The entries of published works are given full
bibliographic treatment and are arranged alphabetically by the
name of the author or by the family name if the work is anonymous. The bulk of the book is the index which consists of
name entries with source references to items in the bibliographic section where related information can be found. The
bibliographic source listing contains some items lacking imprint
and location data.

Resource Materials

167 Lancour, Harold, comp. A BIBLIOGRAPHY OF SHIP PASSENGER LISTS
1538-1825; BEING A GUIDE TO PUBLISHED LISTS OF EARLY IMMI-
GRANTS TO NORTH AMERICA. 4th ed., corrected. With a List of
Passenger Arrival Records in the National Archives by Frank E. Bridgers.
New York: New York Public Library, 1978. 137 p. Index.

An inventory of an assortment of publications carrying information on passenger lists. The chronological scope covers the
period 1538 to 1900, but the inclusion beyond 1825 is less
comprehensive. The arrangement of the material is by name
of the state of respective ports of entry, under which the items
containing passenger lists are enumerated in chronological order. Notes accompanying the items reveal the contents of
each entry.

168 Knittle, Walter Allen. EARLY EIGHTEENTH CENTURY PALATINATE
EMIGRATION; A BRITISH GOVERNMENT REDEMPTIONER PROJECT TO
MANUFACTURE NAVAL STORES. Ithaca, N.Y.: Cayuga Press, 1937.
Reprint. Baltimore: Genealogical Publishing, 1970. 320 p.

Contains twelve thousand names of emigrants from 1683 to 1717
(see 289).

169 Faust, Albert Bernhardt, and Brumbaugh, Gaius Marcus, comps. and eds.
LISTS OF SWISS IMMIGRANTS IN THE EIGHTEENTH CENTURY TO THE
AMERICAN COLONIES. 2 vols. in one. Vol. 1, Zurich, 1734-44,
1920. Vol. 2, Berne, 1706-95; Basel, 1734-94. 1925. Reprint. Baltimore: Genealogical Publishing, 1968.

The 1968 reprint edition consists of one physical volume divided into three parts. Part 1 is a listing of German emigrants from Zurich and its environs to Pennsylvania and the Carolinas between 1734-44. The list was discovered by the authors while doing research in the state archives of Zurich. Parts 2 and 3 were their own compilations, made from minutebooks of governing councils of the cities involved, from lists of citizenships withdrawn, records of withdrawal of property, account books, church and parish records, and other official papers.

In the first part, the names are grouped under the name of the parish and subdivided by dates of departure. In part 2, two hundred Bern immigrants are listed by family name, with departure dates. Part 3 is primarily a listing of the emigrants from Basel, arranged chronologically by year of departure. There is a name index for each volume of the book. The illustrative material includes facsimiles of lists and documents. The work is intended to complement Rupp's lists (see 171). The listings are accompanied by some documented historical notes.

170 Hinke, William John, and Stoudt, John Baer, eds. "A List of German Immigrants to the American Colonies from Zweibruecken in the Palatinate, 1728-1749." PENNSYLVANIA GERMAN FOLKLORE SOCIETY YEAR-BOOK 1 (1936): 101-24. Allentown: Pennsylvania German Folklore Society, 1936.

An incomplete list of emigrants who left the former Duchy of Zweibruecken between 1728-49, based on a document preserved in the German state archives. Altogether 404 names appear here, enumerated according to the original place of residence in chronological sequence. Notes give variants of names as recorded in various Pennsylvania lists together with the place of settlement in Pennsylvania. A map of the Palatinate and Middle Rhine region delineates the area covered.

171 Rupp, Israel Daniel. A COLLECTION OF UPWARD OF THIRTY THOUSAND NAMES OF GERMAN, SWISS, DUTCH, FRENCH, AND OTHER IMMIGRANTS IN PENNSYLVANIA FROM 1727 TO 1776, WITH A STATEMENT OF THE NAMES OF SHIPS, WHENCE THEY SAILED, AND THE DATE OF THEIR ARRIVAL IN PHILADELPHIA, CHRONOLOGICALLY ARRANGED TOGETHER WITH THE HISTORY AND OTHER NOTES . . . CONTAINING LISTS OF MORE THAN 1,000 GERMAN AND FRENCH NAMES IN NEW YORK PRIOR TO 1712. 2d ed., rev. and enl. 1880. Reprint. Baltimore: Genealogical Publishing, 1965. 583 p.

For annotation, see 174.

172 Koger, Marvine Vastine, comp. INDEX TO THE NAMES OF 30,000 IMMIGRANTS--GERMAN, SWISS, DUTCH AND FRENCH--INTO PENNSYLVANIA, 1727-1776, SUPPLEMENTING THE I. DANIEL RUPP SHIP LOAD VOLUME. Pennington Gap, Va.: the author, 1935. 232 p.

For annotation, see 174.

173 Egle, William Henry. NAMES OF FOREIGNERS WHO TOOK THE OATH OF ALLEGIANCE TO THE PROVINCE AND STATE OF PENNSYLVANIA 1727-1775, WITH THE FOREIGN ARRIVALS, 1786-1808. PENNSYLVANIA ARCHIVES, 2d series, vol. 17, 1890. 1892. Reprint. Baltimore: Genealogical Publishing, 1967. 788 p.

For annotation, see 174.

174 Strassburger, Ralph Beaver. PENNSYLVANIA GERMAN PIONEERS: A PUBLICATION OF THE ORIGINAL LISTS OF ARRIVALS IN THE PORT OF PHILADELPHIA FROM 1727 TO 1808. Edited by William John Hinke. Pennsylvania German Society Proceedings, v. 42-44. Norristown: Pennsylvania German Society, 1934. Reprint. 2 vols. Baltimore: Genealogical Publishing, 1966. Index.

The various types of immigrant name lists constitute important sources for genealogical research. Three varieties occur most frequently in archival records. The so-called "captains' lists" were drawn up upon embarkation and usually contained the names of adult males over sixteen years of age. One peculiarity of many "captains' lists", which gave a roster of passengers from Germany, is that in them the German names were often transliterated into English, resulting in the anglicization of both Christian and surnames. The other two lists were the "allegiance list," and the "abjuration lists." Many of these have been preserved among the official records of the commonwealth of Pennsylvania.

The following excerpts from the foreword of R.B. Strassburger, and W.J. Hinke, PENNSYLVANIA GERMAN PIONEERS (pp. viii-ix) shed some light on the origin of the allegiance lists, and the abjuration lists:

When the pioneers arrived, the government of Pennsylvania was in the hands of British subjects. Penn's agents were Englishmen; the English language was used; English common law was in force. It early became a matter of concern to these Englishmen that so large a body of continentals, speaking another language and accustomed to another form of government, should be admitted to the land, even though they came at the invitation of Penn himself. Therefore, in 1727, the Provincial Council, at the recommendation of Governor Patrick Gordon, passed a law, suggested ten years before by Governor William Keith, requiring all continentals who arrived at Philadelphia to take oaths of allegiance to the British crown. Two years later the continental immigrants were required also to take oaths of abjuration and fidelity to the proprietor and the laws of the province. The oaths were

administered and subscribed to before public officials. . . . In violation of the Provincial Council's
instructions, the captains' lists were prepared care-
lessly and without regard to uniformity. Few gave
complete lists of names, and the occupations of the
passengers and the places of their origin were ig-
nored. The lists were handled indifferently and
many were lost. The oath of allegiance lists were
incomplete, in that they contained only the signa-
tures of the adult males who did not happen to be
ill on the day they had to sign their names. But
the lists of the signers of the oath of abjuration
were preserved in bound books.

The first official version of allegiance lists for the period
1727-36 was published in the PENNSYLVANIA COLONIAL
RECORDS in 1852. I.D[aniel]. Rupp made an attempt to compile a roster of immigrants to Pennsylvania from 1727-76 using
captains' lists, allegiance lists, and other sources. An expanded version of his first compilation (1856) was published
in 1880 (see 171). Rupp compared the names on the various
lists and made an effort to eliminate duplication by referring
to the original German form of a name, entering the name
of a particular immigrant only once. His contribution is
evaluated by Strassburger and Hinke (p. ix) in these words:

> Rupp strove to arrange the names of the ships in
> chronological form, but the names of the passen-
> gers were not printed in the order in which they
> appeared on the official lists. The names were
> generally written in the German script, and many
> required translation. It should be stated, in justice
> to Rupp, that he worked in the face of great dif-
> ficulties in publishing his book, together with other
> editions, including the names of children and adults,
> covering a period of twenty years.

The original editions of Rupp's work had no indexes. In 1935
M.V. Koger prepared an index to names giving references to
year of arrival and location in the body of the work. Although this index appeared in typewritten form, presumably
it received considerable circulation. (In Michigan, a copy
can be found in Detroit Public Library's Burton Historical Collection.)

A further extension of coverage of name lists was W.H. Egle's
work (see 173). This listing encompassed allegiance lists from
1727-75 and captains' lists from 1786 to 1808.

Strassburger and Hinke were dissatisfied with the status of passenger lists as presented by Rupp. They re-did the lists from
the original German, more accurately, with names spelled
correctly and without omissions or errors of deciphering, as
they claim were found in Rupp. They expanded the time

period of Rupp, 1727-75, by adding 1785 to 1808. There
was little immigration during the American Revolutionary war.
Arrangement is similar to Rupp, by chronological arrival of
ship. For each arrival, each of the three types of lists are
included when they are available. At the end of volume two,
a battery of indexes appear: of captains, of ships, of officials
and merchants, of the pioneers themselves, with reference to
date and page of appearance. Another list demonstrates the
various forms of German-Christian names and their first appearance in the list.

175 Krebs, Friedrich. EMIGRANTS FROM THE PALATINATE TO THE AMERI-
CAN COLONIES IN THE 18TH CENTURY. Edited with introduction by
Milton Rubincam. Pennsylvania German Society. Special study, no. 1.
Norristown: Pennsylvania German Society, 1953. 32 p.

This contribution consists of a pamphlet intended as an addendum to Strassburger's and Hinke's lists (see 174) prepared by
the author who held the position of state archivist in Speyer,
Germany. Krebs identified more than 160 families who emigrated from the Palatinate to America in the eighteenth century. The name entries provide brief biographical and historical information on the families mentioned. The bibliography
includes many valuable references for genealogical research.

176 Philadelphia. Mayor. RECORD OF INDENTURES OF INDIVIDUALS
BOUND OUT AS APPRENTICES, SERVANTS, ETC., AND OF GERMAN
AND OTHER REDEMPTIONERS IN THE OFFICE OF THE MAYOR OF THE
CITY OF PHILADELPHIA, OCTOBER 3, 1771 TO OCTOBER 5, 1773.
Pennsylvania German Society Proceedings and Addresses, vol. 16. 1907.
Reprint. Baltimore: Genealogical Publishing, 1973. 364 p. New in-
dex.

Lists the name of passenger, date, port of embarkation, occupation, the name to whom indentured, residence of indenturer,
terms of servitude, and dollar amount of indenture. Arrangement is chronological by date of entry into the port of Philadelphia. The 1973 reprint edition has a name index, lacking
in previous editions.

177 Langguth, Otto. "Pennsylvania German Pioneers from the County of Wertheim." Edited and translated by Don Yoder. PENNSYLVANIA GER-
MAN FOLKLORE SOCIETY YEARBOOK 12 (1947): 147-289. Allentown: Pennsylvania German Folklore Society, 1948. Bibliog. notes.

Otto Langguth's, AUSWANDERER AUS DER GRAFSCHAFT WER-
THEIM, served as the basis of this work. Yoder excerpted
only those parts which dealt with emigrants from the county
of Wertheim to Pennsylvania in the eighteenth century. In
addition to names, a great amount of personal biographical
material is brought together here, along with a historical survey of the movement itself. The biographical data shed light

on the place and date of emigration, reasons for leaving, family members, and other information. The appendices include a number of pertinent contemporary documents.

178 Yoder, Donald Herbert, ed. "Emigrants from Wuerttemberg: The Adolf Gerber Lists." PENNSYLVANIA GERMAN FOLKLORE SOCIETY YEARBOOK 10 (1945): 103-237. Allentown: Pennsylvania German Folklore Society, 1945. Bibliog. notes.

A valuable contribution to the genealogical literature of early immigration of Germans from Wuerttemberg and the general area of Swabia to the United States. In all, about six hundred families are dealt with. The work is based on Adolf Gerber's lists which were prepared from local tax lists and land warranties, abstracts of wills, parish registers, and others. Yoder organized Gerber's disparate listings into a cogent whole providing information on individuals named in alphabetic sequence. Standard items of information include village of former residence, occupation, economic status, conduct of passage, reasons for emigration, and other data.

179 Braun, Fritz, and Weiser, Frederick S. "Marriages Performed at the Evangelical Lutheran Church of the Holy Trinity in Lancaster, Pennsylvania, 1748-1767." PENNSYLVANIA GERMAN SOCIETY PUBLICATIONS 7 (1973): 225-99. Bibliog., index.

Potentially useful for tracing German settlers who may have moved from Pennsylvania to other areas. Arranged sequentially by year, month, and day, the information includes the name of the newlyweds, previous marital status, former residence in Germany, occupation if specified, and occasionally some brief observation by the recorder. To facilitate identification, an approach by place of origin is provided separately. Case histories can be further researched by means of the index which under the name entry indicates whether the person's name appears on ship lists and other compilations (i.e., Strassburger and Hinke [see 174]).

180 Easton, Pennsylvania. First Reformed Church. SOME OF THE FIRST SETTLERS OF "THE FORKS OF THE DELAWARE" AND THEIR DESCENDANTS; BEING A TRANSLATION FROM THE GERMAN OF THE RECORD BOOKS OF THE FIRST REFORMED CHURCH OF EASTON, PENNA., FROM 1760 TO 1852. Translated and published by Henry Martyn Kieffer, with a historical introduction. 1902. Reprint. Baltimore: Genealogical Publishing, 1973. 404 p.

This is a history of Easton, Pennsylvania, based on the records of the First Reformed Church of the city, combining the historical narrative with the records themselves. The latter constitute section two of the work. The documentation ranges from baptismal to burial records, but the details vary from period to period. The coverage includes branches of the church at Greenwich, Dryland, and Plainfield, as well. As this area was heavily populated by Germans, this item can be useful for German-American historical and genealogical research.

181   Egle, William Henry. PENNSYLVANIA: GENEALOGIES CHIEFLY SCOTCH-IRISH AND GERMAN. 2d ed. 1896. Reprint. Baltimore: Genealogical Publishing, 1969. 798 p. Index.

A considerable part of this work consists of references to German-American families in Pennsylvania in the eighteenth and nineteenth centuries. The line of descendants is given in the main entry. There is an index to surnames.

182   Smith, Clifford Neal, ed. SHIP LISTS OF GERMAN AND CENTRAL EUROPEAN EMIGRANTS TO AUSTRALIA, BRAZIL, CANADA, CHILE, AND THE UNITED STATES SHOWING THEIR EUROPEAN PLACES OF ORIGIN; TWO PARTS, INCLUDING THE "DIREKT" LISTS FOR 1850, SURNAMES A-H; SURNAMES P-Z. Hamburg Emigration Series. McNeal, Ariz.: Westland Publications, 1978.

COLLECTED WORKS

183   MAKERS OF AMERICA. 10 vols. Edited by Wayne Moquin. Chicago: Encyclopedia Britannica Educational Corporation, 1971. Index.

A compilation of contemporary literary and pictorial materials documenting the contribution of ethnic groups to the building of America. Each volume encompasses a distinct historical period giving a panorama of the lives and aspirations of the immigrant masses rather than chronicling the achievements of prominent individuals. The coverage of the entire set spans the period 1536-1970. MAKERS OF AMERICA includes over one hundred documentary pieces and a multitude of illustrations presenting almost every facet of the German-American experience. The emphasis is on social history. The work is especially suitable for school and public libraries and can serve as a valuable resource for courses in American social history and ethnic studies.

PICTORIAL WORKS—MAPS AND ATLASES

184   Piltz, Thomas, ed. ZWEIHUNDERT JAHRE DEUTSCH-AMERIKANISCHE BEZIEHUNGEN, 1776-1976: EINE DOKUMENTATION [Two hundred years of German American relations, 1776-1976: a documentary with 391 illustrations and plates]. Muenchen: Heinz Moos Verlag, 1975. 188 p.

This book was published on the occasion of the bicentennial

year to celebrate two hundred years of German-American relations. The main thrust of the work is the tracing of historical connections between the two countries and the examination
of reciprocal cultural influences over the past four hundred
years. The book was written in German and English, with
the two texts appearing side-by-side on the same page. The
entire range of the German-American experience is covered,
with particular emphasis on the cultural and scientific contributions.

The work is copiously illustrated with many black and white,
as well as color, photographs and reproductions of people,
events, places, things, documents, excerpts, and letters.
Added features include a listing of addresses of organizations
which promote German-American culture in the United States,
and organizations in Germany promoting cultural understanding
between the two countries. In addition, the book contains
a chronology of events from 1456 through 1976, and a list of
prominent emigres from Germany to the United States, in the
period from 1933-41. This is a well-designed pictorial work
which could have become a valuable reference tool if it had
a detailed index and more meticulous documentation.

185   Wust, Klaus German, and Muehlen, Norbert. SPAN 200: A COM-
PANION PIECE TO THE SPAN 200 EXHIBIT, THE STORY OF GERMAN-
AMERICAN INVOLVEMENT IN THE FOUNDING AND DEVELOPMENT
OF AMERICA. Philadelphia: Published in behalf of Institut fuer Aus-
landbeziehungen, Stuttgart, by the National Carl Schurz Association,
1976. 95 p. Bibliog.

A brief overview in popular style of German-American involvement in the founding and development of America, attractively
illustrated with black and white photographs and reproductions.
The contribution of people of German origin to American culture and industry is emphasized.

186   Kloss, Heinz. ATLAS DER IM 19. UND FRUEHEN 20. JH. ENTSTAN-
DENEN DEUTSCHEN SIEDLINGEN IN USA [Atlas of 19th and early 20th
century German-American settlements]. Marburg, Germany: N.G. El-
wert, 1974. 17 p., 108 leaves.

This compendium of maps of German settlements in the United
States is the first cartographic treatment of the subject ever
to see print. The first such attempt was made by Earl Meynen before World War II, but the project never materialized.
The chronological scope of the maps ranges from 1800 to 1930
and excludes Mennonite, Hutterite, and Amish settlements.
The maps are arranged in twelve topical sections, subdivided
into regional and state units. In each of these units, large
black and white foldout maps show the distribution of German
settlements and various cultural and demographic features.

The subjects highlighted include, among other things: the ratio of the German stock in the white population of the United States as of 1910 in cities and rural areas, existence of secular clubs, Roman Catholic congregations, Evangelical and Reformed churches, and German participation in other denominations. Several maps are devoted to Germans originating outside Germany, especially Russian Germans. The reader will not find full chronological coverage for each subject surveyed here, as most of the maps illustrate a situation as it existed in a particular year. The choice of the year depended upon the availability of pertinent data.

The introduction describes and discusses the sources used. In addition to the United States census data, heavy reliance was made on information supplied by German-American organizations themselves. References to sources provide excellent starting points for further research. Unfortunately, the absence of an index or gazetteer makes the use of this atlas somewhat awkward. The work is based on meticulous research and is cartographically well presented.

187 Handlin, Oscar. A PICTORIAL HISTORY OF IMMIGRATION. New York: Crown Publishers, 1972. 344 p. Bibliog., index.

Among the more than one thousand illustrations of various kinds, many of the photographs, engravings, etchings, paintings, and other reproductions have German themes. They show Germans in typical occupations, farm life, and cultural pursuits such as the Turnverein and singing societies.

DIRECTORY

188 Wasserman, Paul, and Morgan, Jean, eds. ETHNIC INFORMATION SOURCES OF THE UNITED STATES: A GUIDE TO ORGANIZATIONS, AGENCIES, FOUNDATIONS, INSTITUTIONS, MEDIA, COMMERCIAL AND TRADE BODIES, GOVERNMENT PROGRAMS, RESEARCH INSTITUTES, LIBRARIES AND MUSEUMS, RELIGIOUS ORGANIZATIONS, BANKING FIRMS, FESTIVALS AND FAIRS, TRAVEL AND TOURIST OFFICES, AIRLINE AND SHIP LINES, BOOKDEALERS AND PUBLISHER'S REPRESENTATIVES, AND BOOKS, PAMPHLETS, AND AUDIOVISUALS ON SPECIFIC ETHNIC GROUPS. Detroit: Gale Research, 1976. 751 p. Bibliog., index.

Contains a thirty-three page section on Germans. The listing includes: organizations, museums, newspapers and magazines, radio programs, festivals, bookdealers specializing in German materials, and a brief reading list, along with a few audio-visual items on Germany.

CHRONOLOGY

189   Furer, Howard B., comp. and ed.   THE GERMANS IN AMERICA, 1607–1970; A CHRONOLOGY AND FACT BOOK.   Dobbs Ferry, N.Y.: Oceana Publications, 1973.   156 p.   Bibliog., index.

> This is a year-by-year listing of events based on a few standard treatises on German Americans.   The coverage is reasonably good up to the middle of the twentieth century.   Mostly biographical features are highlighted.   Appended to the chronology section is a collection of twenty-five documents ranging from government and commission reports to letters and excerpts from contemporary periodicals.   This is followed by a lay-level reading list of about 150 items with one-sentence annotations, suffering from some bibliographic inaccuracies.

III. IMMIGRATION

GENERAL WORKS

190 Jones, Maldwyn Allen. AMERICAN IMMIGRATION. Chicago History
of American Civilization Series. Chicago: University of Chicago Press,
1960. 359 p. Bibliog., index.

> The coverage is from 1607-1959. The Germans are one of
> the most strongly represented groups in this work. The econom-
> ic, social, and political aspects of immigration are empha-
> sized. There are critical bibliographic essays at the end of
> each chapter.

191 Hansen, Marcus Lee. THE IMMIGRANT IN AMERICAN HISTORY. Edited, with a foreword by Arthur M. Schlesinger. Cambridge, Mass.:
Harvard University Press, 1940. Reprint. New York: Harper and Row,
1964. 230 p.

> For annotation, see below.

192 _____. ATLANTIC MIGRATION 1607-1860: A HISTORY OF THE
CONTINUING SETTLEMENT OF THE UNITED STATES. Edited, with a
foreword by Arthur M. Schlesinger. Cambridge, Mass.: Harvard University Press, 1940. Reprint. Gloucester, Mass.; P. Smith, 1972.
386 p. Bibliog. notes, index.

> A broad overview from a universal perspective. Useful for
> general background reading on the topic.

193 Bennett, Marion Tinsley. AMERICAN IMMIGRATION POLICIES: A
HISTORY. Washington, D.C.: Public Affairs Press, 1963. 362 p.
Bibliog., index.

> A useful reference work on official policies and measures re-
> garding immigration, with a bibliography of two hundred items.

194 Stephenson, George Malcolm. A HISTORY OF IMMIGRATION 1820-

1924. 1926. Reprint. New York: Russell and Russell, 1964. 316 p. Bibliog., index.

> Explores how immigration affected the political and social process in the context of the U.S. official immigration policies. It has many references to Germans.

195 Taylor, Philip. THE DISTANT MAGNET: EUROPEAN EMIGRATION TO THE U.S.A. London: Spottiswoode, 1971. 326 p. Bibliog., index.

> A general treatise on the subject from a British vantage point. The coverage of Germans is adequate.

196 THE IMMIGRANT EXPERIENCE IN AMERICA. Edited by Frank J. Coppa, and Thomas J. Curran. Immigrant Heritage of America Series. Boston: Twayne Publishers, 1976. 232 p. Bibliog.

> A collection of popular essays which grew out of a television series on CBS in 1973. Eight groups are represented, including the Germans. In each case, the conditions leading to mass emigration, their reception in America by established populations, and their social, economic, and cultural impact are explored. Among the German-American personalities, Gustav Koerner and Carl Schurz are highlighted. In addition, the McCarran-Walter Act (1952) is analyzed in terms of its impact on U.S. immigration policies.

DOCUMENTARY MATERIALS

197 Abbott, Edith, ed. IMMIGRATION: SELECT DOCUMENTS AND CASE RECORDS. 1924. Reprint. American Immigration Collection. New York: Arno Press, 1969. 809 p. Bibliog. notes, index.

> For annotation, see below.

198 _____. HISTORICAL ASPECTS OF THE IMMIGRATION PROBLEM: SELECT DOCUMENTS. 1926. Reprint. American Immigration Collection. New York: Arno Press, 1969. 881 p. Bibliog. notes, index.

> A massive compilation of public and private documents, case studies, and articles on every facet of immigration.

199 A CENTURY OF POPULATION GROWTH FROM THE FIRST CENSUS OF THE UNITED STATES TO THE TWELFTH, 1790-1900. 1909. Reprint. Baltimore: Genealogical Publishing, 1967. 303 p. Index.

> Contains a great deal of useful statistics on German Americans.

200 U.S. Immigration Commission, 1907-10. EMIGRATION CONDITIONS IN EUROPE. Reports of the Immigration Commission, vol. 4. 61st Congress,

3d session, Senate document 748. Washington, D.C.: Government Printing Office, 1911. 424 p. Index.

The reports contain a considerable amount of data on immigrants from Germany, as well as on ethnic Germans who came to the United States from other countries.

201 _____. STATISTICAL REVIEW OF IMMIGRATION, 1820-1910. DISTRIBUTION OF IMMIGRANTS, 1850-1900. Reports of the Immigration Commission, vol. 3. 61st Congress, 3d session, Senate document 756. Washington, D.C.: Government Printing Office, 1911.

A compendium of immigration statistics from 1820 through 1919 by country. Extremely useful for the study of immigration of Germans.

202 Carpenter, Niles. IMMIGRANTS AND THEIR CHILDREN. U.S. Bureau of the Census Monographs, no. 7. 1920. Reprint. American Immigration Collection. New York: Arno Press, 1969. 431 p. Bibliog. notes, index.

203 Hutchinson, Edward Prince. IMMIGRANTS AND THEIR CHILDREN, 1850-1950. Census Monograph Series. New York: Wiley, 1956. Reprint. New York: Russell and Russell, 1976. 391 p. Bibliog. notes, index.

The chronological scope of item 202 is 1850 to 1920. It contains 146 statistical tables with interpretive texts in the body of the work, plus 46 detailed displays of data in the appendix. Data regarding Germans can be located within the index. This item is a sequel, covering the period to 1950.

SPECIALIZED WORKS

204 Bennion, Lowell Colton. "Flight from the Reich: A Geographic Exposition of Southwest German Emigration, 1683-1815." Ph.D. dissertation, Syracuse University, New York, 1971. 385 p.

The focus is southeast Germany and all destinations of immigrants: Russia, Austrian Empire, and colonial America are dealt with.

205 Walker, Mack. GERMANY AND THE EMIGRATION, 1816-1885. Harvard Historical Monographs, vol. 56. Cambridge, Mass.: Harvard University Press, 1964. 284 p. Bibliog., index.

Emigration from Germany in the nineteenth century from the Napoleonic Wars (1815) to the rise of the German colonial empire in the 1880s was world-wide in scope and not limited just to the United States. The intent of this work is to examine the causes in Germany which both stimulated and discouraged emigration from its borders. The most useful sections for studying the background of emigration from Germany to America is the time period from 1830–54, when it was at its highest. The emigrants were first the "Auswanderers," the lower-class farmers seeking a better lot, and later the political refugees of the 1848 revolution. Much of the work of this scholarly inquiry was done from primary resources in German and American archives. The book includes a sizeable bibliography of both primary and secondary sources in German and to a lesser extent in English.

206   Meyer, Luciana Ranshofen-Wertheimer. "German-American Migration and the Bancroft Naturalization Treaties, 1868–1910." Ph.D. dissertation, City University of New York, 1970. 299 p.

An important work on the subject exploring the background, administration, and the legal implications of the treaties.

207   Bogen, Frederick W. THE GERMAN IN AMERICA, OR ADVICE AND INSTRUCTION FOR GERMAN IMMIGRANTS IN THE UNITED STATES OF AMERICA. 1856. Reprint. St. Clair Shores, Mich.: Scholarly Press, 1976. 195 p.

This is a bilingual pocketbook intended for German newcomers to America, designed partly to ease their "culture shock" and partly to introduce them to the traditions and culture of their new country. Following a "Welcome to America" essay, the book includes German on one side while on the opposite page there is the text of the Constitution, biographies of George Washington and Benjamin Franklin, travel tips, and a glossary of difficult American expressions. The author was a Boston clergyman. His effort to indoctrinate German immigrants in the values of the Protestant ethics and appreciation for their host country pervades the work, which is interesting for the study of social history.

208   AUFBAU ALMANAC. THE IMMIGRANT'S HANDBOOK. New York: German Jewish Club, 1941.

A bilingual source book consisting of informative articles on subjects of interest to Jewish refugees from Germany making their home in America. The articles deal with the National Refugee Service, routes to citizenship, types and names of meatcuts and butcher's terms, and other useful matters. The work also includes a bibliography of best books about America and a directory of organizations whose services immigrants could use.

IV. GENERAL WORKS DEALING WITH THE
GERMAN-AMERICAN EXPERIENCE

GENERAL WORKS

Guides

209　Wittke, Carl Frederick.　GERMANS IN AMERICA; A STUDENT'S GUIDE
TO LOCALIZED HISTORY.　New York: Teacher's College Press, 1967.
26 p.　Bibliog.

> Intended for students, this pamphlet introduces the reader to
> the main topics of the German-American experience.　It pro-
> vides basic information on the Pennsylvania Dutch, the Amish,
> Mennonites, the "Forty-Eighters," the Turnverein, German
> music, and the press.

Historical Treatises—Scholarly Works

210　Faust, Albert Bernhardt.　THE GERMAN ELEMENT IN THE UNITED
STATES WITH SPECIAL REFERENCE TO ITS POLITICAL, MORAL, SO-
CIAL, AND EDUCATIONAL INFLUENCE.　1927.　Reprint.　American
Immigration Collection Series.　New York: Arno Press, 1969.　1,277 p.
Bibliog., index.

> Faust's work is the first comprehensive, scholarly treatment of
> the history of Germans in America, which grew out of a con-
> test at the University of Chicago in 1907.　Section one deals
> with the story of settlements from region to region, providing
> a detailed account of the peopling of the colonies and the
> states by immigrants brought over from various parts of Ger-
> many under a variety of schemes.　The narrative is organized
> into the following chapters: earliest Germans; Germantown;
> increase of German immigration in the eighteenth century;
> Palatinates in New York; Germans in Pennsylvania; Germans
> in New Jersey and Maryland; Germans in Virginia; Germans
> in the Carolinas; six settlements before the Revolution in
> Georgia and New England; German settlers, 1775; the Revolu-
> tion and the War of 1812; Germans in Kentucky and Tennessee;

the Ohio Valley; Mississippi and Missouri Rivers; the Northwest, Southwest and the Far West; Germans and wars of the
United States in the nineteenth century; summary. Section
two concentrates on cultural aspects: German American population estimates; agriculture and manufacturing; technology
and craftsmanship; political influence; education; music and
fine arts; theater, literature and journalism; social and moral
influence, and traits.

The work is well documented, drawing extensively from English, German, and American sources. Illustrations, maps,
portraits, statistical tables on German population, and a
massive bibliography of 1600 items make Faust's treatise a
basic work in every respect. The indexes to each section
allow in-depth subject penetration to the book's rich information content. The two volumes in one cover the period to
1909, while a supplementary section updates the basic work
to 1927.

211   Billigmeier, Robert Henry. AMERICANS FROM GERMANY: A STUDY
IN CULTURAL DIVERSITY. Minorities in American Life Series. Belmont,
Calif.: Wadsworth Publishing, 1974. 189 p. Bibliog. notes, index.

A sensitively written, compact treatment of German-American
history and life, presented in an objective, balanced manner.
The author offers a multitude of historical, social, and cultural facts about the German contribution to America during
the three hundred years of mutual interaction. Set against
the background of the process of nation formation, Billigmeier
brings into sharp relief the events and forces which shaped
German destiny on the North American continent. The first
chapter surveys the coming of German groups to America before the Revolution. Chapter 2 discusses the role of German
Americans in the building of the nation. Chapter 3 is devoted entirely to the Pennsylvania Germans. Chapter 4 covers
the twentieth century. This is the most extensive and the best
part of the work. It deals with German-American literature
and politics, the First World War and the subsequent transfor-
mation of German-American life, the intellectual refugees
from Nazi Germany, the Nazi propaganda in the United States,
and social change and German-American churches.

212   Rippley, La Vern. THE GERMAN-AMERICANS. Boston: Twayne Publishers, 1976. 271 p. Bibliog., index.

Rippley's survey provides a highly readable overview of German-American history and life encompassing the entire historical period extending beyond World War II. The treatment of
the subject matter is somewhat uneven. The sections dealing
with social and cultural topics are considered superior than the
others. The uninitiated will find in Rippley's book a lot of
valuable information on such relatively unexplored topics as

Germans from Russia, Germans in the westward movement, and German Americans after World War II. The work is well documented and the selected bibliography of about one hundred items lists the essential standard literature on the subject.

213 Wittke, Carl. WE WHO BUILT AMERICA: THE SAGA OF THE IMMIGRANT. Rev. ed. Cleveland: Press of Western Reserve University, 1964. 550 p. Bibliog. notes, index.

The presence of Germans looms large in this book of broad appeal; more than one-third of the space is devoted to the discussion of the successive waves of German immigration, and the impact of Germans on American society, culture, and politics. Although the problem of assimilation is dealt with, the political aspects predominate. There are copious references to good sources; and the detailed index facilitates retrieval of general, as well as specific, information.

Popular Works

214 Dubois, Rachel Davis, and Schweppe, Emma, eds. THE GERMANS IN AMERICAN LIFE. Building American Culture Series. New York: Thomas Nelson and Sons, 1936. Reprint. Freeport, N.Y.: Books for Libraries Press, 1972. 180 p. Bibliog.

The purpose of this overview of German achievements in the United States was to arouse people's interest in their heritage and to dispel the shame the younger generation is often made to feel toward their ethnic ancestry. In a popular style, the book follows German-American history from the earliest days of discovery through the nineteenth century, with explorations into achievements of German Americans in education, journalism, economic life, literature, drama, music, and folkways. The author copiously quotes from pertinent key works. In its day, this work appealed to young readers despite the lack of illustrations.

215 Huebener, Theodore. THE GERMANS IN AMERICA. Philadelphia: Chilton, 1962. 168 p. Bibliog., index.

Intended for background reading on a popular level, this work condenses the findings of Faust, Skal, Hirschler, Zucker, and other writers on the subject. The entire sweep of American history is covered. German achievements are presented mainly through individual contributions, thus the approach is heavily biographical. The illustrations, portraits, and tables make the book attractive especially for high school and public library audiences.

216 O'Connor, Richard. THE GERMAN-AMERICANS, AN INFORMAL HISTORY. Boston: Little, Brown and Co., 1968. 484 p. Bibliog., index.

O'Connor's insightful book is a journalistic treatment of German-American history from the colonial period to the outbreak of World War II. All major highlights are dealt with, but German contribution to American military affairs is seemingly more emphasized. O'Connor drew heavily from secondary and biographical sources.

217   Tolzmann, Don Heinrich. AMERICA'S GERMAN HERITAGE: BICENTENNIAL MINUTES. Cleveland: German-American National Congress, 1976. 126 p. Bibliog., index.

This assemblage of sixty short articles was prepared for a Cleveland radio program series under the title "Bicentennial Minutes" for the occasion of the two hundredth anniversary of the birth of the United States. The series was produced under the aegis of the German-American National Congress. Each article is about three hundred words long. They highlight German participation in an important event in the life of the nation, or tell the story of the various ethnic and cultural subgroups within the German-American community. The majority of the articles, however, consists of biographical sketches of prominent Americans of German origin, some of whom are little known to the general public. The book also includes a brief chronology from 1607 to 1976, and a few poems.

218   Rippley, La Vern. OF GERMAN WAYS. Minneapolis: Dillon Press, 1970. 301 p.

219   Von Hagan, Victor Wolfgang. THE GERMANIC PEOPLE IN AMERICA. Norman: University of Oklahoma Press, 1976. 404 p. Bibliog., index.

This work on the impact of German exploration and settlement in North and South America is the English version of the author's DER RUF DER NEUEN WELT: DEUTSCHE BAUEN AMERIKA (1970). While the book was intended for a home-based audience, North American readers will find the chapters dealing with the following topics of particular interest: the Pennsylvania Germans, the Hessians, the explorers of the continent from Germany, the immigration waves of 1830 and 1848, the settling of Texas, California, and other parts of the West, and participation of German Americans in the Civil War.

The work is richly illustrated with an assortment of photographs, reproductions, facsimiles, and maps. Writing in a popular vein, the author omits footnote references, and the bibliography at the end inventories mainly German and Spanish-language sources.

Juvenile Works

220   Kunz, Virginia Brainard. THE GERMANS IN AMERICA. Minneapolis: Lerner Publishers, 1966. 86 p.

An attractive juvenile book with wide coverage. It provides an excellent introduction into the topic mainly through a biographical approach on a fourth- to sixth-grade level.

221 Holland, Ruth R. THE GERMAN IMMIGRANTS IN AMERICA. New York: Grosset and Dunlap, 1969. 61 p.

Designed for junior high school level and older readers.

222 Gay, Kathlyn. THE GERMANS HELPED BUILD AMERICA. New York: Messner, 1971. 96 p. Index.

A fine introductory work for young readers which highlights important events in the life of German Americans, presented in an appealing style and format. While the emphasis is on the cultural aspects, political and religious matters are also brought under purview. It includes a list of distinguished Americans of German extraction, indicating profession and dates.

Specialized Histories

223 Sachse, Julius Friedrich. THE FATHERLAND: (1450-1700) SHOWING THE DISCOVERY, EXPLORATION, AND DEVELOPMENT OF THE WESTERN CONTINENT, WITH SPECIAL REFERENCE TO THE COMMONWEALTH OF PENNSYLVANIA. Pennsylvania German Society Proceedings and Addresses, vol. 7. Philadelphia: Pennsylvania German Society, 1897. 234 p. Bibliog. notes.

This work yields a great deal of information on the first German contacts in North America by German merchants and early settlers. It also vividly describes the social and political conditions in Germany prior to 1700 which prompted many Germans to seek a better life in the American colonies. The discussion encompasses William Penn's efforts in Pennsylvania, as well as the promotional literature sent to Europe to encourage German immigration. The appendix includes fifty-six facsimile title pages of these materials. They are organized in chronological order from 1675 through 1708. The copious footnote references are extremely valuable for further research, as they are based on primary resources, including manuscripts, documents, and various archival records. The work is profusely illustrated with contemporary sketches, renderings of buildings, coats-of-arms, maps, and other objects. The lack of an index greatly impedes the exploitation of the informative material contained in the book.

224 Bittinger, Lucy Forney. THE GERMANS IN COLONIAL TIMES. 1901. Reprint. New York: Russell and Russell, 1968. 314 p. Bibliog., index.

This work was written with a popular audience in mind. Based mainly on secondary sources, the book describes the conditions in Germany that led to large-scale emigration, and subsequent settlements of many different groups of Germans in the American colonies. The story of the settlements is told vividly in individual chapters, extending from fifteen to twenty pages. Avoiding the details, the author concentrated only on main events and on prominent personalities. The book is particularly suited for high school readers. Added features include a map of German settlements, a chronological table, and a fairly detailed index.

225   THE OLD LAND AND THE NEW: JOURNALS OF TWO SWISS FAMI-LIES IN AMERICA IN THE 1820S. Edited and translated by Robert H. Billigmeier, and Fred Altschuler Picard. Minneapolis: University of Minnesota Press, 1965. 281 p. Bibliog. notes, index.

The journals referred to are: Johannes Schweizer, "Account of a Journey to North America and through the Most Significant Parts Thereof," and J. Jakob Ruetlinger, "Day Book on a Journey to North America in the Year 1823."

The authors of these journals were keen observers who brought under their purview all aspects of American life as they saw it in the 1820s. They comment on the American character as well as the material and cultural life of the country. In addition to the translation, Billigmeier and Picard corrected and footnoted the texts. A list of further readings on the topics covered is also provided. Sketches by Hans Erni.

226   Hawgood, John Arkas. THE TRAGEDY OF GERMAN-AMERICA: THE GERMANS IN THE UNITED STATES OF AMERICA DURING THE NINE-TEENTH CENTURY--AND AFTER. New York: G.P. Putnam's Sons, 1940. Reprint. New York: Arno Press, 1970. 334 p. Bibliog. notes, index.

Hawgood's analytical history concentrates on the social aspects of "New Germanies" on American soil, focusing on the nineteenth century. Part 1 surveys the characteristics of the Germans in the United States, tracing their provenance and destination. In part 2, the author devotes three chapters to the attempts aimed at founding a "New Germany" in Missouri, Texas, and Wisconsin, pointing out that the German communities in America lacked the political, social, and economic features needed for creating politics comparable to "New Spain," "New England," or "New France." The third part of the book is devoted to an inquiry into the painful assimilation process and integration of Germans in American society. The work is well documented. The copious bibliographic references provide excellent starting points for further research.

227 Higham, John, ed. ETHNIC LEADERSHIP IN AMERICA. The Johns Hopkins Symposia in Comparative History, no. 9. Baltimore: Johns Hopkins University Press, 1978. 214 p. Bibliog., index.

Contains nine papers presented at the symposium held at Johns Hopkins University, 5–6 February 1976. A 30 page paper, prepared by Frederick Luebke, professor of history at the University of Nebraska, critically surveys the role of the German-American social, cultural, and religious organizations in the interwar period. Particular attention is given to the Deutsch-Amerikanische Buergerbund, the Steuben Society, the National Carl Schurz Foundation, and the National Congress of Americans of German Descent.

228 THE GERMAN CONTRIBUTION TO THE BUILDING OF THE AMERICAS: STUDIES IN HONOR OF KARL J.R. ARNDT. Edited by Gerhard K. Friesen, and Walter Schatzberg. Worcester, Mass.: Clark University Press; Hanover, N.H.: distributed by the University Press of New England, 1977. 410 p. Bibliog. notes.

This Festschrift contains seventeen essays, some of them written in German. The contributions include: (1) A. Waldenrath, "The Pennsylvania-Germans: Development of Their Printing and Their Newspapers in the War for American Independence"; (2) H. Jantz, "German Men of Letters in the Early United States"; (3) R.E. Cazden, "Johann Georg Wesselhoeft and the German Book Trade in America"; (4) E.A. Albrecht, "Edward Dorsch and the Civil War"; (5) A.E. Schroeder, "The Survival of German Traditions in Missouri"; and (6) R.E. Ward, "The Case for German-American Literature." An important feature of the work is a bibliography of Arndt's writings covering the period from 1932–76, as well as a list of publications in process.

229 Feiler, Arthur. AMERICA SEEN THROUGH GERMAN EYES. Translated by Margaret Leland Goldsmith. 1928. Reprint. New York: Arno Press, 1974. 284 p.

The book is essentially a visitor's impressions of America. Of particular interest is the chapter, "German-Americans, Anglo-Americans and Americans," which summarizes the author's astute observations and thoughts on the German-American experience.

230 Meyer, Georg[e]. THE GERMAN-AMERICAN; DEDICATED TO THE CELEBRATION OF THE GERMAN-AMERICAN DAY HELD IN MILWAUKEE, OCTOBER 6TH, 1890. Milwaukee: Hake and Stern, 1890. 41 p.

A brief survey of the German-American experience, deploring the fading away of German culture in America.

GERMANS IN THE AMERICAN REVOLUTION

231 Rosengarten, Joseph G. THE GERMAN SOLDIER IN THE WARS OF THE
UNITED STATES. 1886. Reprint. San Francisco: R and E Research Associates, 1972. 175 p. Index.

> A broad treatment of German participation in America's wars
> from the 1700s, but with main emphasis on the Revolutionary
> War. The narrative centers around the individual soldiers
> whose exploits are recounted. It includes a list of German-
> American officers in the revolutionary army. A name index
> for the entire text identifies soldiers who took part in other
> wars. Excerpts from the 1860 census provide data on the
> number of German-American soldiers and their proportion to
> the population of individual states on the one hand, and the
> German population within the state on the other.

232 Greene, George Washington. THE GERMAN ELEMENT IN THE WAR OF
AMERICAN INDEPENDENCE. New York: Hurd and Houghton, 1875;
Cambridge, Mass.: Riverside Press, 1875. 211 p.

> Consists of three chapters: (1) Baron Von Steuben, (2) Gen-
> eral John Kalb, and (3) German mercenaries. The work
> draws heavily from Friedrich Kapp's German-language mono-
> graphs on the same subjects. Useful for introductory reading.

233 THE ETHNIC CONTRIBUTION TO THE AMERICAN REVOLUTION. Edited
by Frederick Harling, and Martin Kaufman. Westfield, Mass.: Westfield
Bicentennial Committee, 1976. 119 p. Bibliog.

> A balanced discussion on the participation of eighteen ethnic
> groups, mostly of European origin, in the American Revolution.
> Each group is treated in an essay. The section dealing with
> the Germans was written by James Naglack.

234 Schrader, Frederick Franklin. PRUSSIA AND THE UNITED STATES,
FREDERICK THE GREAT'S INFLUENCE ON THE AMERICAN REVOLUTION;
HISTORICAL SKETCH. Concord Society Historical Bulletin, no. 2. New
York: Concord Society, 1923. 16 p. Bibliog. notes.

> An interesting essay on Frederick the Great's opposition to the
> engagement of German soldiers against the nascent United
> States.

235 Lowell, Edward Jackson. THE HESSIANS AND THE OTHER GERMAN AUXIL-
IARIES OF GREAT BRITIAN IN THE REVOLUTIONARY WAR. 1884. Reprint. Williamstown, Mass.: Corner House, 1975. 328 p. Bibliog.,
index.

> A basic work for establishing essential facts on the Hessian
> contingent in the Revolutionary War, studded with biographical

and anecdotal digressions. Subjects highlighted include the German princes, the treaties for service, the soldiers from Germany in America, and an enumeration of battles and events the material for which was culled from original German sources. The appendices yield a great amount of systematized information, for example: names of Hessian regiments, number of troops sent from each German state and returned, and data on the wounded, killed, and missing. There are several maps and plans on the deployment of Hessians.

236 Eelking, Max von. THE GERMAN ALLIED TROOPS IN THE NORTH AMERICAN WAR OF INDEPENDENCE, 1776-1783. Translated and abridged from the German by J.G. Rosengarten. 1893. Reprint. Baltimore: Genealogical Publishing, 1969. 360 p. Bibliog., index.

In its day this was the first comprehensive account of Hessians as soldiers and prisoners of war written from a German viewpoint. The circumstances surrounding the engagement of the Hessians are discussed in detail. Includes a list of officers of the Hessian corps serving under British Commanders Howe, Clinton, and Carleton. The index is divided: one gives names for personal identification, the other gives places where events occurred.

237 Baurmeister, Carl Leopold. REVOLUTION IN AMERICA; CONFIDENTIAL LETTERS AND JOURNALS, 1776-1784, OF ADJUTANT GENERAL MAJOR BAURMEISTER OF THE HESSIAN FORCES. Translated and annotated by Bernhard A. Uhlendorf. New Brunswick, N.J.: Rutgers University Press, 1957. Reprint. Westport, Conn.: Greenwood Press, 1973. 640 p. Bibliog. notes, index.

In addition to organizing and referencing the material which constitutes about one-third of the Von Jungkenn Papers at the University of Michigan Clements Library, the translator furnished a survey history of the Hessian participation in the British campaign against the American Revolution.

238 Riedesel, Friederika Charlotte Luise (von Massow) Friefrau von. LETTERS AND JOURNALS RELATING TO THE WAR OF THE AMERICAN REVOLUTION, AND THE CAPTURE OF GERMAN TROOPS AT SARATOGA. 1867. Reprint. New York: New York Times, 1968. 235 p. Index.

The wife of one of the Hessian generals, Baroness Riedesel, followed her husband to America. Her diaries reveal a unique view of the Revolutionary War, especially in the New York and Pennsylvania theater.

239 Radloff, Herman, and Coyle, Alexander, comps. HESSIANS IN THE REVOLUTION, 1776-1783. St. Louis: St. Louis Genealogical Society, 1975. 27 p.

For annotation, see 241.

240 _____ . HESSIANS AND THEIR AMERICAN DESCENDANTS. St. Louis: St. Louis Genealogical Society, 1972. 7 p.

For annotation, see 241.

241 St. Louis Genealogical Society. INDEX OF NAMES OF THE BRAUNS-CHWEIG CORPS WHO REMAINED IN AMERICA 1776-1783. St. Louis: 1976. 11 p.

The first of the three pamphlets (item 239) is a bibliographic guide to reference sources, documents, and lists dealing with Hessians. It includes also the Hessian and Waldeck prisoner of war list held in the library of the Historical Society of Pennsylvania. The second item consists of a listing of Hessian officers with their rank. The third item is an alphabetical enumeration of 2,910 names of the muster rolls of the Braunschweig Corps personnel who remained in America after the Revolutionary War.

242 Coester, G.C. HESSIAN SOLDIERS IN THE AMERICAN REVOLUTION: RECORDS OF THEIR MARRIAGES AND BAPTISMS OF THEIR CHILDREN, IN AMERICA, PERFORMED BY THE REV. G.C. COESTER, 1776-1783, CHAPLAIN OF TWO HESSIAN REGIMENTS. Translated and abstracted from German by Marie Dickore. Cincinnati, 1959. 25 p. Index.

G.C. Coester was chaplain to the Hessian troops in the American Revolution, whose records were translated and abstracted here by Marie Dickore. The records range from marriage, baptisms, and confirmations in the Reformed Church to confessions of faith and obituaries.

243 Smith, Clifford Neal. BRUNSWICK DESERTER-IMMIGRANTS OF THE AMERICAN REVOLUTION. German-American Genealogical Research Monographs, no. 1. Thomson, Ill.: Heritage House, 1973. 55 p.

244 _____ . MERCENARIES FROM ANSBACH AND BAYREUTH, GERMANY, WHO REMAINED IN AMERICA AFTER THE REVOLUTION. German-American Genealogical Research Monographs, no. 2. Thomson, Ill.: Heritage House, 1974. 52 p.

245 _____ . MUSTER ROLLS AND PRISONER-OF-WAR LISTS IN AMERICAN ARCHIVAL COLLECTIONS PERTAINING TO THE GERMAN MERCENARY TROOPS WHO SERVED WITH THE BRITISH FORCES DURING THE AMERICAN REVOLUTION. German-American Genealogical Research Monographs, no. 3. DeKalb, Ill.: Westland Publishers, 1976. 177 p.

246 _____ . EMIGRANTS FROM SAXONY (GRANDDUCHY OF SACHSEN-WEINER-EISENACH) TO AMERICA, 1854, 1859. German-American Genealogical Research Monographs, no. 4. DeKalb, Ill.: Westland Publishers, 1974. 32 p.

247 _____. MERCENARIES FROM HESSEN-HANAU: WHO REMAINED IN CANADA AND THE UNITED STATES AFTER THE AMERICAN REVOLUTION. German-American Genealogical Research Mongraphs, no. 5. DeKalb, Ill.: Westland Publishers, 1976. 105 p.

> With the exception of number four, the works in this series (items 243, 244, 245, 246) provide information on German mercenaries of various provenance who fought in the American Revolutionary War. The lists are based on official documents, and their locations, whether in European or American archives, are given. The lists are arranged chronologically by the date of compilation. Under the name of units, the officers and men are enumerated with their ranks. Additional information is given in other parts. For example, there is a list of engagements in which German mercenaries fought with an index showing which units were involved. Also, statistical tables give quantitative data on the mercenaries. A name index provides access to data on each individual soldier mentioned.

248 Schoepf, Johannes David. TRAVELS IN THE CONFEDERATION [1783-84]. 2 vols. From the German of Johannes David Schoepf, translated and edited by Alfred J. Morrison. 1911. Reprint. Burt Franklin Research and Source Series, 206. New York: Burt Franklin, 1968. Bibliog., index.

> Personal impressions of Pennsylvania, New Jersey, and the South with many references to people and places, describing the situation after the Revolutionary War.

IMPACT OF THE 1848 GERMAN REVOLUTION

249 Bruncken, Ernest. GERMAN POLITICAL REFUGEES IN THE UNITED STATES DURING THE PERIOD FROM 1815-1860. Special print from the DEUTSCH-AMERIKANISCHE GESCHICHTSBLAETTER, 1904. San Francisco: R and E Research, 1970. 59 p. Bibliog. notes.

> A good overview of the political conditions in Germany that caused the departure of politically active elements for the United States. The impact of these well-educated groups on German settlements, and their achievements in the United States are also explored. Much of the material was drawn from contemporary periodicals.

250 Wittke, Carl Frederick. REFUGEES OF REVOLUTION: THE GERMAN FORTY-EIGHTERS IN AMERICA. Philadelphia: University of Pennsylvania Press, 1952. Reprint. Westport, Conn.: Greenwood Press, 1970. 384 p. Bibliog. notes, index.

> The fullest treatment of the 1848 German refugees so far. Topics highlighted: the German element before 1848; the revolution and migrations "Latin farmers"; Freethinkers; political radicalism; nativism; slavery; the German vote; the Civil

War; postwar politics; journalism; German social patterns;
learning and letters; labor; and Bismarck and the German uni-
fication in Europe. The author contends that the German
"Forty-Eighters" had an invigorating effect that extended be-
yong the German-American community. Among óther things,
they provided the intellectual leadership needed to combat
nativism. A highly informative work, meticulously documented.
The bibliographic references include a mass of primary and
secondary sources both in English and German.

251 Zucker, Adolf Eduard, ed. THE FORTY EIGHTERS; POLITICAL REFU-
GEES OF THE GERMAN REVOLUTION OF 1848. New York: Columbia
University Press, 1950. Reprint. New York: Russell and Russell, 1967.
379 p. Bibliog., index.

Prepared for the commemoration of the one-hundredth anniversary of the 1848 German revolution, this anthology surveys
the contribution of the "Forty-Eighters" to the United States.
The essays, written by prominent specialists, deal with the
European background, the American scene in 1848, adjustment
of the refugees to the United States, the Turnverein, the
"Forty-Eighters" in politics, radicals, the "Forty-Eighters" in
the Civil War, and Carl Schurz. A substantial part of the
work consists of a biographical dictionary of the "Forty-Eighters"
providing a considerable amount of personal and career information, with references to sources.

252 Goldmark, Josephine Clara. PILGRIMS OF '48; ONE MAN'S PART IN
THE AUSTRIAN REVOLUTION OF 1848: AND A FAMILY'S MIGRATION
TO AMERICA. New Haven, Conn.: Yale University Press, 1930. Reprint.
Modern Jewish Experience [Series]. New York: Arno Press, 1975. 311
p. Bibliog., index.

An articulate account of the "Forty-Eighter" experience in
Europe and America from the personal perspective of the
author's family and circle of friends. Part one deals with
events leading to the 1848 revolution. Part two describes
the journey to America and the group's responses to the challenges of the new environment. In depicting this process,
the author gives a sweeping panorama of practically every
facet of contemporary America from a German-Jewish vantage
point. The story is reconstructed from family papers, memoirs,
public documents, and the best published sources.

THE CIVIL WAR

253 Dorpalen, Andreas. "The German Element and the Issues of the Civil
War." MISSISSIPPI VALLEY HISTORICAL REVIEW 29 (June 1942): 55-
76. Bibliog. notes.

A scholarly essay discussing German-American attitudes and opinions, especially those in the Midwest and Texas, with Abraham Lincoln's campaign for the presidency as its focus.

254 Rombauer, Robert Julius. THE UNION CAUSE IN ST. LOUIS IN 1861; A HISTORICAL SKETCH. St. Louis: Press of Nixon-Jones Printing, 1909. 475 p.

Because of heavy concentrations of German Americans in the city, the historical analysis of the pro-union movement can be considered, by extension, as being indicative of German-American attitudes. The attached documentary material seems to bear out this contention, as the union infantry and reserve roll, containing about ten thousand names, consists largely of identifiably Germanic surnames. The work is based on original documents, many of which are reprinted in the appendix.

WORLD WAR I

255 Child, Clifton James. THE GERMAN-AMERICANS IN POLITICS, 1914-1917. Madison: University of Wisconsin Press, 1939. Reprint. American Immigration Collection, Series II. New York: Arno Press, 1970. 193 p. Bibliog., index.

Deals with issues, events, organizations, and personalities revolving around America's participation in the war against Germany and its impact on German Americans. The activities of Richard Bartholdt, a congressman of German-American ancestry, and his National German-American Alliance are highlighted. The documentation was drawn from official and private sources, as well as from interviews. A good classified bibliography complements the text.

256 Luebke, Frederic C. BONDS OF LOYALTY; GERMAN-AMERICANS AND WORLD WAR I. Minorities in American History. DeKalb: Northern Illinois University Press, 1974. 366 p. Bibliog., index.

Inquires into the official and popular attitudes toward German Americans in three different time periods from 1870 to 1920, as reflected in contemporary newspapers, magazines, tracts, congressional hearings, and other records. The aim of the work is to show how social integration of the Germans which had been proceeding smoothly in the second part of the nineteenth century was disrupted by World War I, and how the benevolent public acceptance of them had turned into hostility. This is quite evident in political cartoons. Told with a wealth of detail, the author draws heavily from THE NEW YORK TIMES, THE WASHINGTON POST, THE ST. LOUIS DISPATCH, THE CHICAGO TRIBUNE, autobiographies, correspondences, and personal interviews. A bibliographic essay

critically discusses the literature on the subject. A detailed
index provides access to a great deal of specific information
in the text.

257 Wittke, Carl Frederick. GERMAN-AMERICANS AND THE WORLD WAR
(WITH SPECIAL EMPHASIS ON OHIO'S GERMAN-LANGUAGE PRESS).
Ohio Historical Collections, vol. 5. Columbus: Ohio State Archae-
logical and Historical Society, 1936. Reprint. The United States in
World War [Series]. New York: J.S. Ozer, 1974. 223 p. Bibliog.
notes, index.

This study analyzes the most important German-language newspapers published in Ohio, primarily in Cincinnati in the war
years, to find out how German Americans responded to the
war and its consequences. The choice is explained by the
fact that these newspapers were quoted extensively by other
German-language newspapers in the country. The early struggle for America's neutrality and accusations of disloyalty are
the major themes.

258 Strother, French. FIGHTING GERMANY'S SPIES. Garden City, N.Y.:
Doubleday, Page and Co., 1918. 275 p.

Discusses German intelligence in America in World War I, its
working methods, and accomplishments. The documentation is
interesting.

259 Kahn, Otto Hermann. RIGHT ABOVE RACE. New York: Century,
1918. 182 p.

A polemical work proclaiming the correctness of America's position in World War I, and an appeal to German
Americans to side with their government.

260 Hagedorn, Hermann. WHERE DO YOU STAND? AN APPEAL TO
AMERICANS OF GERMAN ORIGIN. New York: Macmillan, 1918.
126 p.

An apologetic work by a prominent German American calling
for fairness in judging the loyalty of German Americans to
America. The author's poem, FATHERLAND (Winter 1915),
is reprinted.

261 Viereck, George Sylvester. SPREADING GERMS OF HATE. New York:
Horace Liveright, 1930. 278 p.

Deals with pro- and anti-German propaganda during and after
World War I in Britain, France, Germany, and the United
States as seen by an agent actively involved. Interspersed
photographs and posters provide the illustrative material.

262 Ohlinger, Gustavus. THEIR TRUE FAITH AND ALLEGIANCE. Our National Problems [Series]. New York: Macmillan, 1916. 123 p.

> An example of anti-German propaganda of World War I vintage. Significantly, the author does not doubt the allegiance of the long established German Americans, the "Forty-Eighters," and the followers of Carl Schurz, but only of those German Americans who retained "Prussian mentality."

263 Swift, Lucius Burrie. GERMANS IN AMERICA. 3d ed. Indianapolis: Kautz Stationery, 1916. 30 p.

> A specimen of a propaganda pamphlet attacking German Americans, claiming that they were supporters of the Kaiser.

264 United States. Committee on Public Information. AMERICAN LOYALTY, BY CITIZENS OF GERMAN DESCENT. War Information Series, no. 6. Washington, D.C.: Government Printing Office, 1917. 24 p.

> A government pamphlet designed to combat anti-German prejudices during World War I. It consists of seven short essays quoting excerpts, editorials, and other sources.

265 Jones, John Price, and Hollister, Paul Merrick. THE GERMAN SECRET SERVICE IN AMERICA, 1914-1918. Boston: Small, Maynard and Co., 1918. 340 p.

> This work had been originally published in New York and in London under two different titles: THE GERMAN SPY IN AMERICA; THE SECRET PLOTTING OF GERMAN SPIES IN THE UNITED STATES AND THE INSIDE STORY OF THE LUSITANIA (London: Hutchinson, 1917) and AMERICA ENTANGLED; THE SECRET PLOTTING OF GERMAN SPIES IN THE UNITED STATES AND THE INSIDE STORY OF THE SINKING OF THE LUSITANIA (New York: A.C. Laut, 1917). This edition is a somewhat modified version of the previous editions. Jones was a reporter for THE NEW YORK SUN, and much of the material he gathered was from private and unauthenticated sources. He claimed that there existed a network of agents which ranged from individual spies to the Pan-German Party, and to the German lobby in Congress, which aimed at subverting the U.S. government, and bringing the European war to America. It is a plain journalistic exploit, with no documentation, except for some photographs and facsimiles.

THE NAZI MOVEMENT

Histories and Studies

266 Diamond, Sander A. THE NAZI MOVEMENT IN THE UNITED STATES,

1924-1941. Ithaca, N.Y.: Cornell University Press, 1974. 380 p. Bibliog., index.

The story of Nazi penetration into the United States is told here. It surveys Germany's relationship with the United States from 1923 through Hitler's rise to power. The rest of the work is devoted to the rise and fall of the Amerika-Deutscher Volksbund under the leadership of Fritz Kuhn. The work is based on primary sources in the National Archives, the German-American Bund collection of the Anti-Defamation League of the B'nai B'rith, and the Institute of Contemporary History in London. The sources are discussed in a bibliographic essay. The appendices include: (1) numbers of German immigrants entering the United States in 1880-1933; (2) the seven Bund membership regions in the United States; (3) a "who's who" of selected German officials and Bund personnel; (4) selected newspapers published by the American Bund Movement with dates and city of publication; and (5) selected Bund leaders and subordinates who returned to Germany in 1938-40.

267 Smith, Arthur Lee. THE DEUTSCHTUM OF NAZI GERMANY AND THE UNITED STATES. International Scholars Forum, vol. 15. The Hague: Martinus Nijhoff, 1965. 172 p. Bibliog., index.

An investigation of how Nazi Germany has attempted to exploit German immigrants abroad to promote its objectives through organizations in host countries. The history and activities of the Deutsches Ausland Institut, the Friends of the New Germany, the German-American Bund, and the Kameradschaft U.S.A. are described. The work is well documented and much of the material was drawn from captured Nazi documents. The work contains a good bibliography.

268 Rogge, Oetje John. THE OFFICIAL GERMAN REPORT: NAZI PENETRATION, 1924-1942; PAN ARABISM, 1939-TODAY. New York: Thomas Yoseloff, 1962. 478 p. Index.

A detailed exposition of the Nazi movement in the United States based on official documents and the movement's own literature and records. It focuses on the Bund, its propaganda activities, lobbying, political schemes, the sympathetic business community and other collaborationists, intelligence, espionage and sabotage activities, and American isolationists. It also contains much biographical information and material on the various pro-German or pro-Nazi organizations.

269 Frye, Alton. NAZI GERMANY AND THE AMERICAN HEMISPHERE, 1933-1941. Yale Historical Publications. Miscellany, vol. 86. New Haven, Conn.: Yale University Press, 1967. 229 p. Bibliog., index.

The story of how Nazi Germany attempted to undermine the

integrity of the political stability in the Western Hemisphere countries by means of propaganda and contrived crises. A separate chapter is devoted to the Nazi campaign to defeat Roosevelt in 1940. The role of key figures and organizations who directed the effort is explored. The study was based on the captured files of the German foreign ministry, and materials in the National Archives. A classified bibliography complements the text.

270 Bell, Leland V. IN HITLER'S SHADOW: THE ANATOMY OF AMERI-CAN NAZISM. Kennikat Press National University Publications. Series in American Studies. Port Washington, N.Y.: Kennikat Press, 1973. 135 p. Bibliog.

An analytical history of the emergence and decline of the German-American Bund and Nazi-inspired hate groups in the United States between 1936 and 1960. It is based on the author's Ph.D. dissertation entitled, "Anatomy of a Hate Movement: The German-American Bund, 1936-1941."

271 Turrou, Leon G. NAZI SPIES IN AMERICA, AS TOLD TO DAVID G. WITTELS. New York: Random House, 1939. 299 p.

271a _____. NAZI SPY CONSPIRACY IN AMERICA, AS TOLD TO DAVID G. WITTELS. London: G.G. Harrap, 1939. Reprint. Freeport, N.Y.: Books for Libraries Press, 1972. 276 p.

A chronicle of the exposure of the Nazi spy ring in America in 1938. It is told in a thrilling style with gripping details by a special agent of the Federal Bureau of Investigation who directed the operation.

272 Rollins, Richard. I FIND TREASON; THE STORY OF AN AMERICAN ANTI-NAZI AGENT. New York: William Morrow, 1941. 291 p. Index.

The internal life of pro-Nazi and anti-Semitic hate groups is revealed on these pages as told by an agent who infiltrated their ranks for eight years. Sixty-four pages are devoted to documentation which disclose correspondences of Nazi party members, membership file records, propaganda materials, forgeries, and others.

273 Bischoff, Ralph Frederic. NAZI CONQUEST THROUGH GERMAN CUL-TURE. Cambridge, Mass.: Harvard University Press, 1942. 198 p. Bibliog. notes, index.

Two propositions are advanced in this work, first that German cultural organizations have always been vehicles of German nationalism, and second that the activities on American soil of organizations such as the German-American National Alliliance, the Pennsylvania German Society, the Turnverein, the Amerikadeutscher Volksbund, and by extension, the German-language churches and schools, are all dangerous to the interests of the United States. The author comes to this conclusion by surveying the history of these cultural organizations through the examination of their record and through personal observations made when he was an exchange student in Germany.

Documents

274 U.S. House of Representatives. HEARINGS, No. 73. 73d Cong., 2d sess., 9-12 July 1934; New York: 29 December 1934; Washington, D.C.: 16-17 October 1934; New York. Washington, D.C.: Government Printing Office, 1935.

Contains the transcripts of the hearings conducted by the "Special Committee on Investigation of Nazi and Other Foreign Activities in the United States," under the chairmanship of John W. McCormack of Massachusetts.

275 U.S. House of Representatives. HEARINGS, No. 76. 76th Cong., 1st sess. 16, 17, 18, 21, 22, 23, 24, 28, 29 August 1939; Washington, D.C. Washington, D.C.: Government Printing Office, 1939.

The hearings were conducted by a committee chaired by Congressman Martin Dies which inquired into the activities of the German-American Bund (Nazi Party) and its leader Fritz Kuhn.

276 American Historical Association. Committee for the Study of War Documents. GUIDES TO GERMAN RECORDS MICROFILMED AT ALEXANDRIA, VA. 67 vols. Washington, D.C.: National Archives and Records Service, 1958-- .

Altogether, this study consists of sixty-seven booklets, each providing access to the contents of microfilm reels containing captured World War II documents.

277 U.S. War Department. NAZI PARTY MEMBERSHIP RECORDS. SUBMITTED BY THE WAR DEPARTMENT TO THE SUBCOMMITTEE ON WAR MOBILIZATION OF THE COMMITTEE OF MILITARY AFFAIRS, UNITED STATES SENATE. Washington, D.C.: Government Printing Office, 1946. 1,060 p.

This compilation was made from the card files found in the U.S. sector of Germany after World War II. The tabulation is made in four parts: (1) United States and Argentina; (2) United States, supplement 1, and the Latin American countries; (3) United States, supplement 2, and Nazi membership in countries outside Germany; and (4) list of Nazis who returned to Germany from abroad, United States, and selected countries. The data given for each individual includes: name, membership number, date entered the Nazi Party, birth date, birthplace, last recorded address, and occupation.

278 THE GERMAN REICH AND AMERICANS OF GERMAN ORIGIN. Edited by Charles Burlingham et al. New York: Oxford University Press, 1938. 45 p.

The purpose of this booklet was to bring together a number of key documents of the German Nazis to reveal their true nature and political aspirations. Among the documents, nine relate to legislative measures concerning the courts, taxation, the Nazi Party, and foreign travel of educators. Further, there are official pronouncements formulated by Hitler, Goering, Lange, and Hess, regarding the relationship of the Nazi government and Germans abroad, especially those Germans who lived in the United States.

PACIFISM

279 Brock, Peter. PACIFISM IN THE UNITED STATES, FROM THE COLONIAL ERA TO THE FIRST WORLD WAR. Princeton, N.J.: Princeton University Press, 1968. 1,005 p. Bibliog., index.

The work covers the various religious groups and movements which have resisted military service and participation in war. Although the focus of the discussion is the Quakers, considerable space is devoted to German-American religious groups which are also discussed under the following chapter headings: "German Peace Sects in Colonial America" (Mennonites, Amish, Brethren, Schwenkfelders); "Peace Testimony of Early American Moravians;" "Mennonites in the Civil War;" "Religious Pacifism Outside the Major Peace Sects" (Harmonists, Inspirationists of Amana). The text is copiously documented with primary sources. The 700-item bibliography is an almost complete inventory of secondary materials on pacifism prior to 1914, published up to 1968. The index is an excellent finding tool for information in the text.

280 Herschberger, Guy Franklin. WAR, PEACE, AND NON-RESISTANCE. Scottdale, Pa.: Herald Press, 1944. 415 p. Bibliog., index.

The study focuses on two main groups: the Quakers and the Mennonites. Relevant chapters devoted specifically to the Mennonites are: (chapter 6) Mennonites in America: Revolutionary War, War of 1812, Civil War; (chapter 7) World War I; (chapter 8) Postwar migrations and relief; (chapter 9) World War II; (chapter 12) Pacifism today, including the U.S. Civilian Public Service; (chapter 13) Non-resistance and industrial conflict: the growth of organized labor. There are also numerous appendices: (1 and 2) scripture quotations on non-resistance; (3) some practical questions on non-resistance considered; (4) Dortrecht Confession of 1632, excerpt on non-resistance; (5) Mennonite General Conference Statement on Peace, War, and Military Service (1937); (6) Statement of the General Conference of Brethren in Christ Church and the Mennonite General Conference on Industrial Relations (1941); (7) Memorandum on Alternate Service (10 January 1940); (8) Mennonite colleges and wartime problems; (9) excerpt of Policy in Mennonite Central Committee Relief (1943); (10) Statement for Guidance of Mennonite Central Committee Workers (1942); (11) Mennonite Central Committee Message to Mennonite and Other Non-resistant Christians (1942); and (12) Mennonite Civilian Public Service (1943). Footnote references and bibliographic essays are given at the end of each chapter.

281 Horst, Samuel. MENNONITES IN THE CONFEDERACY: A STUDY IN CIVIL WAR PACIFISM. Scottdale, Pa.: Herald Press, 1967. 148 p. Bibliog.

The persecutions and sufferings that the Mennonites of the Shenandoah Valley were made to endure because of their belief in pacifism is the subject of this treatise.

282 Gingerich, Melvin. SERVICE FOR PEACE; A HISTORY OF MENNONITE CIVILIAN PUBLIC SERVICE. Akron, Pa.: Mennonite Central Committee, 1949. 508 p. Bibliog.

This is the first scholarly and comprehensive study of the Mennonites, America's largest group of conscientious objectors during World War II, and other groups.

283 Hartzler, Jonas Smucker. MENNONITES IN THE WORLD WAR, OR NONRESISTANCE UNDER TEST. 2d ed. Assisted by a committee appointed by Mennonite General Conference. 1922. Reprint. New York: J.S. Ozer, 1972. 246 p.

An apologetic work expounding the doctrinal position of the denomination and informing about Mennonite experiences during World War I. After a retrospective glance at Mennonite attitudes in previous wars, the author discusses the issues of World War I, the draft, the treatment of Mennonites in camps and barracks, and their role in relief work. There are no footnotes, but numerous letters from Mennonite nonresistants are reprinted in the narrative.

284 Yoder, Sanford Calvin. FOR CONSCIENCE SAKE: A STUDY OF MENNONITE MIGRATIONS RESULTING FROM THE WORLD WAR. Goshen, Ind.: Mennonite Historical Society, 1940. Reprint. Studies in Anabaptist and Mennonite History, vol. 4. Scottdale, Pa.: Herald Press, 1945. 300 p.

Although this work has a worldwide scope, some parts of it deal with Mennonites in the United States during World War I.

285 Parish, Arlyn John. KANSAS MENNONITES DURING WORLD WAR I. Fort Hays Studies. New Series. History Series, no. 4. Hays: Fort Hays Kansas State College, 1968. 62 p. Bibliog.

Provides insight into the ordeals of the Mennonite communities and their draftees during World War I. The tone is objective, and the work is extremely well documented.

286 Wright, Edward Needles. CONSCIENTIOUS OBJECTORS IN THE CIVIL WAR. Philadelphia: University of Pennsylvania Press, 1931. Reprint. New York: A.S. Barnes, 1961. 274 p. Bibliog., index.

The Quakers are the center of the author's attention, but other pacifist groups are also dealt with, namely, the Mennonites, Church of German Baptist Brethren (Dunkers), Community of True Inspiration (Amana), and the Schwenkfelders. The author deals with the struggle of these pacifist groups for political legitimacy of their positions, describes the attitudes of civil and military authorities toward conscientious objectors, and compares the treatment of conscientious objectors in the Civil War to that of World War I. A 150-item bibliography is given.

V. REGIONAL AND STATE HISTORIES

GERMANS IN THE EASTERN UNITED STATES

New England

287 Solomon, Barbara Miller. ANCESTORS AND IMMIGRANTS: A CHANG-ING NEW ENGLAND TRADITION. Cambridge, Mass.: Harvard University Press, 1956. 276 p. Bibliog., index.

> This work, based on a doctoral dissertation, deals with the changing attitudes of the New England elite toward immigrants at the turn of the century. Its relevancy to German-American history consists in the author's thesis that by this time this group's traditional distaste for German and Irish immigrants had almost disappeared and was now directed toward other immigrant groups.

New Jersey

288 Chambers, Theodore Frelinghuysen. THE EARLY GERMANS OF NEW JERSEY; THEIR HISTORY, CHURCHES, AND GENEALOGIES. 1895. Reprint. Baltimore: Genealogical Publishing, 1969. 667 p. Index.

> Concentrates on Hunterdon, Morris, Sussex, and Warren Counties, and on Roxbury Township from 1710 to 1890. Part 1 is a chronicle of the settlements and the story of their churches. Part 2 is a compendium of family histories and genealogies. Part 3 consists of several appendices including: (1) who's who of ministers; (2) Mt. Olive churches; (3) Churches of Flanders; (4) "Old Straw" Lutheran church; (5) German Reformed churches; (6) persons naturalized, settlers on "society lands," signers to Weygand's call, customers of German Valley storekeeper John Peter Nizer (1763); and (7) public institutions and improvements. The material was drawn from local records. There are 60 illustrations, mostly portraits. Only part 2 is indexed.

New York

HISTORY AND SETTLEMENT

289   Knittle, Walter Allen. EARLY EIGHTEENTH CENTURY PALATINE EMI-
GRATION; A BRITISH GOVERNMENT REDEMPTIONER PROJECT TO
MANUFACTURE NAVAL STORES. Ithaca, N.Y.: Cayuga Press, 1937.
Reprint. Baltimore: Genealogical Publishing, 1970.   320 p.   Bibliog.,
index.

> Originated as a thesis at the University of Pennsylvania in
> 1931, this well-documented study inquires into the background
> of the British government's effort to settle a large number of
> Palatine emigrants in New York and North Carolina in the
> early 1800s. Much of the material was drawn from official
> and unofficial sources. The list containing twelve thousand
> names of Palatine emigrants is particuarly important for genea-
> logical research. The arrangement is by ships. The textual
> material is accompanied by twenty-five maps, illustrations,
> and portraits. There is a detailed index to the text and il-
> lustrations.

290   Reid, William Maxwell. THE MOHAWK VALLEY, ITS LEGENDS AND
ITS HISTORY. New York and London: G.P. Putnam's Sons, 1901.
455 p.   Index.

> Chapter 5 of this work is of particular interest for German-
> American studies. It deals with the emigration and settlement
> of Palatine immigrants. Illustrations and photographs by J.
> Arthur Maney.

291   Benton, Nathaniel Soley. A HISTORY OF HERKIMER COUNTY, INCLUD-
ING THE UPPER MOHAWK VALLEY, FROM THE EARLIEST PERIOD TO
THE PRESENT TIME: WITH A BRIEF NOTICE OF THE IROQUOIS INDI-
ANS, THE EARLY GERMAN TRIBES, THE PALATINE IMMIGRATIONS IN-
TO THE COLONY OF NEW YORK, AND BIOGRAPHICAL SKETCHES OF
THE PALATINE FAMILIES, THE PATENTEES OF BURNETSFIELD IN THE
YEAR 1725 . . . ALSO BIOGRAPHICAL NOTICES OF THE MOST PROMI-
NENT PUBLIC MEN OF THE COUNTY: WITH IMPORTANT STATISTICAL
INFORMATION. Albany: J. Munsell, 1856.   497 p.   Index.

> A broadly gauged narrative with a wealth of detail covering
> about 150 years beginning with the early 1700s. It deals with
> people, institutions, public administration, land transactions,
> and others. A gold mine for genealogical research. There
> are illustrations, maps and an index.

292   Simmendinger, Ulrich. TRUE AND AUTHENTIC REGISTER OF PERSONS
STILL LIVING, BY GOD'S GRACE, IN THE YEAR 1709, UNDER THE
WONDERFUL PROVIDENCES OF THE LORD, JOURNEYED FROM GER-
MANY TO AMERICA, OR THE NEW WORLD, AND THERE SEEK THEIR

PIECE OF BREAD AT VARIOUS PLACES; REPORTED WITH JOY TO ALL ADMIRERS, ESPECIALLY TO THEIR FAMILIES AND CLOSE FRIENDS. Translated from the German by Herman F. Vesper. St. Johnsville, N.Y.: Enterprise and News, 1934. Reprint. New York: Genealogical Publishing, 1962. 20 p.

> A list of German immigrants from the Palatinate who settled in the Mohawk Valley in New York and in New Jersey between 1709-17. There is no indication in the work how the author collected the information, but the work was intended to let the folks at home know their friends and relatives arrived at their destination. The arrangement is alphabetical by name and the name entry includes the place of settlement. A brief introduction deals with the history of Palatine immigration.

293 Berczy, William. "William Berczy's Williamsburg Documents." Edited by A.J.H. Richardson, and Helen I. Cowan. ROCHESTER HISTORICAL SOCIETY PUBLICATIONS 20 (1942): 139-265. Bibliog. notes, index.

> This is the journal with some attached documents of a man who was commissioned in the early 1790s by land owner Colquhoun to recruit German settlers for his tract in Genessee County, New York. Berczy was paid a commission for each settler. The project was a failure. In this journal, Berczy tells his side of the story, defending himself for the failure and the disappointments of the settlers. The work contains two interesting items in the appendix: some correspondences between Berczy and the settlers detailing complaints, and the agreement of Colquhoun and Berczy with regard to procuring Germans for settlements.

SOCIAL ASPECTS

294 Bayor, Ronald H. NEIGHBORS IN CONFLICT: THE IRISH, GERMANS, JEWS, AND ITALIANS OF NEW YORK CITY, 1929-1941. Johns Hopkins University Studies in Historical and Political Science, 96th series, no. 2. Baltimore: Johns Hopkins University Press, 1978. 232 p. Bibliog. notes, index.

GERMANS IN PENNSYLVANIA

Bibliographies

295 Meynen, Emil, comp. and ed. BIBLIOGRAPHIES DES DEUTSCHTUMS DER KOLONIALZEITLICHEN EINWANDERUNG IN NORDAMERIKA: INSBESONDERE DER PENNSYLVANIEN-DEUTSCHEN UND IHRER NACHKOMMEN, 1683-1933 [Bibliography on German Settlements in Colonial North America, especially on the Pennsylvania Germans and Their Descendants].

Leipzig: O. Harrassowitz, 1937. Reprint. Detroit: Gale Research Co., 1966. 636 p. Index.

The intent of this work was to update and consolidate relevant bibliographic entries scattered among various publications compiled between 1900-29. Arranged by subject, the eight thousand items in English and German included here are listed alphabetically by author, with local histories by county constituting a separate section. The materials inventoried encompass books, essays, personal papers, periodical articles, addresses, pamphlets, diaries, personal narratives, church records, and histories. They were culled principally from the holdings of the Historical Society of Pennsylvania, Library of Congress, Pennsylvania State Library, the University of Pennsylvania Library, and various church libraries and archives. Writings in the local dialect, historical romances, and fictional works were omitted. The time span ranges from the colonial beginnings to the early 1900s, but the subject matter seldom goes beyond the Civil War. While the main focus is Pennsylvania, parts of the United States and Canada, where Pennsylvania Germans migrated in substantial numbers, are also covered. This bibliography boasts a number of fine extra features, for example, a list of libraries and archives with pertinent holdings, enumerations of important listings of emigrants, ship passengers and redemptioners, and land title holders. In addition, many family histories and biographical materials are noted for which there is a separate surname index. This work is of central significance for research on the Pennsylvania Germans.

296 Pennsylvania. Historical and Museum Commission. BIBLIOGRAPHY OF PENNSYLVANIA HISTORY. 2d ed. Compiled by Norman B. Wilkinson. Edited by S.K. Stevens, and Donald H. Kent. Harrisburg: Pennsylvania Historical and Museum Commission, 1957. 826 p. Index.

In addition to a special section devoted entirely to Pennsylvania Germans, materials on this subject are scattered throughout the work. More than nine thousand items have been inventoried here, cutting across the whole spectrum of genre and format published prior to 1952. For later materials, the reader should consult BIBLIOGRAPHY OF PENNSYLVANIA HISTORY: A SUPPLEMENT, edited by Carol Wall (Harrisburg: Pennsylvania Historical and Museum Commission, 1976).

297 Barton, Ruth A., and Graham, Robert L., Jr., comps. "The Pennsylvania Dutch Country; A Bibliography of Books and Other Materials." Lancaster, Pa.: Lancaster Free Public Library, 1963. Mimeographed. 31 leaves.

This is a useful list of over four hundred items of popular appeal, dealing with arts and crafts, cooking, music, folklore, customs, religion, fiction, and other subjects.

298   Washburn, David E. THE PEOPLES OF PENNSYLVANIA: AN ANNOTATED
       BIBLIOGRAPHY OF RESOURCE MATERIALS. Pittsburgh: University Center
       for International Studies, University of Pittsburgh, 1978.

       A compendium of materials dealing with the ethnic experience in
       Pennsylvania. The listing contains printed material, as well as a
       variety of audiovisual aids. About three thousand items are cited.

DIRECTORY

299   Washburn, David E. DIRECTORY OF ETHNIC STUDIES IN PENNSYLVANIA.
       Pittsburgh: University Center for International Studies, University of Pitts-
       burgh, 1978.

       Contains detailed descriptions of the ethnic studies offerings of the
       commonwealth's post-secondary schools, public school systems, and
       nonpublic schools.

Pictorial Works

300   Brand, Millen. FIELDS OF PEACE: A PENNSYLVANIA GERMAN ALBUM.
       Garden City, N.Y.: Doubleday, 1970. 159 p. Bibliog.

       This is a compendium of photographic essays in black and white
       portraying contemporary life, arts, crafts, and customs of the
       Pennsylvania Amish, Mennonites, and Schwenkfelders. The narra-
       tive text provides the historical background with subjective insights
       of the author. An appealing work for the general reader of any age.
       Photographs by George A. Tice.

301   Smith, Edward Costello, and Thompson, Virginia van Horn. TRADITIONALLY
       PENNSYLVANIA DUTCH. New York: Hastings House, 1947. 81 p. Index.

       This work illustrates, through charcoal sketches, highlights from
       the history and life of German people in Bucks, Berks, Lancaster,
       and York counties. They show, for example, barn raisings, barn
       signs, fraktur writing, quilting bees, cider pressings, utensils, fur-
       niture, food products, and many other things. The book grew out
       of an advertising project launched by the Old Reading Brewery,
       which was so successful that the authors decided to continue the
       initial graphic work for the advertisements to make up an entire
       book. The text and sketches are indexed.

Immigration

302   Diffenderffer, Frank Ried. THE GERMAN EXODUS TO ENGLAND IN 1709.
       Pennsylvania German Society Proceedings and Addresses, vol. 7. Lancaster:
       Pennsylvania German Society, 1897. 157 p. Index.

       For annotation, see 304.

303 Jacobs, Henry Eyster. THE GERMAN EMIGRATION TO AMERICA, 1709-1740. Pennsylvania German Society Proceedings and Addresses, vol. 8. Lancaster: Pennsylvania German Society, 1898. 120 p.

For annotation, see 304.

304 Richards, Matthias Henry. THE GERMAN EMIGRATION FROM NEW YORK PROVINCE INTO PENNSYLVANIA. Pennsylvania German Society Proceedings and Addresses, vol. 9. Lancaster: Pennsylvania German Society, 1899. 100 p.

Items 302-4 constitute a trilogy. In a contiguous narrative, they follow the journey of Palatinates and Swabians, led by Reverend J. Kocherthal to Holland, England, and ultimately to Pennsylvania. Diffenderffer's study deals with the events of 1708 and 1709 providing broad historical background for the causes and preliminaries of the journey. A body of municipal and other records are inserted in the appendix. Jacobs' study concentrates on the group's sojourn in New York, confronted with the alternatives of settling in South Carolina or Pennsylvania. The destiny of other immigrants that followed the Kocherthal group up to the year of 1740 is also discussed. Richards traces the gradual expansion of the Pennsylvania settlement and brings the narrative to the 1750s. The main subjects of his book include: relations with Indians, Conrad Weiser, churches and schools, the role of H.M. Muhlenberg, agriculture, industry, the establishment of W.W. Stiegel glass works, The French-Indian War, and the founding of towns and cities. Much documentation in the form of facsimiles is given in the text in all three works. In addition, they are also abundantly illustrated, but only Diffenderffer's work has an index.

305 Herrick, Cheesman Abiah. WHITE SERVITUDE IN PENNSYLVANIA: INDENTURED AND REDEMPTIVE LABOR IN COLONY AND COMMON-WEALTH. 1926. Reprint. Freeport, N.Y.: Books For Libraries Press, 1970. 326 p. Bibliog., index.

This work grew out of a University of Pennsylvania Ph.D. thesis originally prepared in 1899, but published in an expanded version twenty-six years later. Every example of colonial indentured servitude is examined in detail with particular reference to Pennsylvania and its German immigrants. The information was gathered from contemporary official documents such as the proceedings of the Pennsylvania legislature, and records of indentures, many of which are disclosed in the appendix. In addition, recourse was made to private papers and secondary works, listed in the 180-item bibliography. Facsimiles of types of documentary materials and a list of indentured servants with relevant data complement the work. Detailed index.

306   Diffenderffer, Frank Ried. THE GERMAN IMMIGRATION INTO PENN-
      SYLVANIA THROUGH THE PORT OF PHILADELPHIA FROM 1700-1775
      AND THE REDEMPTIONERS. 1900. Reprint. Baltimore: Genealogical
      Publishing, 1977. 328 p. Bibliog. notes, index.

      This work is considered a serious inquiry into the background
      and pattern of German immigration to Pennsylvania in the
      eighteenth century. The first part encompasses a wide range
      of topics from the causes of immigration to the process of
      adaption of the settlers to their new environment. The second
      part focuses on the "redemptioner" system of indentured servi-
      tude, used by some immigrants as a method of traveling to the
      New World. The research value of the work is enhanced by
      140 sketches and portraits, statistical tables, maps, and pas-
      senger lists. Footnoted quotations from original sources pro-
      vide many leads for further research. There is no bibliography
      appended, but the reasonably detailed index is helpful in lo-
      cating information in the text.

307   Hull, William Isaac. WILLIAM PENN AND THE DUTCH QUAKER MI-
      GRATION TO PENNSYLVANIA. Swarthmore College Monographs on
      Quaker History, no. 2. Swarthmore, Pa.: Swarthmore College, 1935.
      Reprint. Baltimore: Genealogical Publishing, 1970. 445 p. Bibliog.
      notes.

      In this study, Hull contends that "Dutchtown" would have
      been a more correct name for the Pennsylvania city of Ger-
      mantown because it was initially settled predominately by
      Dutch Quakers and not German Mennonites. He predicates
      this contention on the fact that when William Penn set out
      to recruit settlers for Pennsylvania, he first went to Holland
      and only subsequently made a trip to the neighboring German
      Rhineland. Implicit in this argument is the assumption that
      the Quakers recruited in Holland left first for the New World
      and settled in what later became known as Germantown, Penn-
      sylvania.

307a Kriebel, Martha B. RETRACING OUR ROOTS. Pennsylvania Dutch
      Studies, no. 8. Collegeville, Pa.: Institute of Pennsylvania Dutch
      Studies, and Pennsylvania Southeast Conference, United Church of Christ,
      1976. 61 p.

      Item not available for examination.

Cultural Aspects

308   Stoudt, John Joseph. SUNBONNETS AND SHOOFLY PIES; A PENN-
      SYLVANIA DUTCH CULTURAL HISTORY. South Brunswick, N.J.: A.S.
      Barnes, 1973. 272 p. Index.

      This is a handsome reference work on the many aspects of
      Pennsylvania German culture presented factually in topical

chapters by a recognized authority of Pennsylvania German art. An attempt was made to dispel romanticism and to avoid glamorization. The entire historical span is covered from 1650 onward. Stoudt allows the Pennsylvania German culture to speak for itself through abundant textual examples and quotations. Religion, mysticism, the local press, vernacular literature, foods, fashion, humor (cartoons and popular jokes), and the erosive impact of the surrounding wider American culture on local folkways are among the topics dealt with in particular detail. The work is profusely illustrated. References to documentary sources are integrated in the text. One of the chapters surveys the history of some of the major works about Pennsylvania Germans and their utilization in the writing of general histories of the American people. Their marginal use is noted.

Of special reference value are the illustrations which include color plates and facsimiles showing types of architecture, handicrafts, art objects, artifacts, utensils, fashion, specimens of printed matters, chorale books, and Fraktur. There is a detailed index to names and places, making the book easy to use for ready reference.

Poetry

309   Brand, Millen. LOCAL LIVES. New York: C.N. Potter, distributed by Crown Publishers, 1975. 526 p. Index.

This is a collection of 350 short poems written over a period of thirty years, reflecting Brand's feelings, observations, and thoughts inspired by his surroundings bounded by Reading, Bethlehem, and Philadelphia in Pennsylvania.

Study and Teaching

310   Washburn, David E. ETHNIC STUDIES IN PENNSYLVANIA. Pittsburgh: University Center for International Studies, University of Pittsburgh, 1978.

Reports on a survey conducted in educational institutions on all levels offering programs dealing with ethnic groups. The programs are described in terms of content and method.

Travel

311   Burgwyn, Diane. THE 1776 GUIDE FOR PENNSYLVANIA. New York: Harper and Row, 1975. 248 p.

This travel book describes fifteen trips of one or two days. Most of these excursions use Philadelphia as a starting point and cover many famous sites of German-American interest. The itinerary, sites suggested, car routes, recreational activities, and prices and times when applicable are included for each. The "historic insight" section encapsulates the background material essential to the understanding of a site's significance. The following places are highlighted: Germantown, Lancaster, Strasburg, Ephrata, Reading, Kutztown, Allentown, Bethlehem, and Old Economy. Maps are provided. Typical points of interest include museums, modern commercial attractions, churches, historic houses, parks, and nature areas.

312   Pennsylvania Dutch Tourist Bureau, Lancaster. PENNSYLVANIA DUTCH GUIDE-BOOK. Lancaster, Pa.: 1960. 100 p.

An illustrated guide to items of interest primarily to Lancaster county. Short essays describe the local lore and culture. Museums, landmarks, and monuments are highlighted. It contains much information on antiques, churches, local business, and farmers' markets.

General Works and Surveys

313   Klees, Frederic. THE PENNSYLVANIA DUTCH. New York: Macmillan, 1950. 451 p. Bibliog.

This is an eminently readable introduction to Pennsylvania Dutch history and culture. The author divides the Pennsylvania Dutch into three groups: the "Plain People" (Amish, Mennonites, Dunkards, or Brethren), the "Church People" (Lutherans, Reformed, United Brethren, Evangelical, or Schwenkfelder), and the Moravians. The geographic scope is the area in and around Berks County, and the time period covered is from the late 1600s to the Civil War. Subjects treated include religious groups, Ephrata, farming, industry, commerce, landscape, folkways, dialect, education, hexes, holidays, music, furniture, barns, and foods. The scope of the work precludes an in-depth treatment, but the resulting overview is a worthy contribution to the popular literature of the subject. Footnote references are omitted. A bibliographic essay on the sources used is appended to the end of the text. There is no index.

314   Parsons, William T. THE PENNSYLVANIA DUTCH: A PERSISTENT MINORITY. Boston: Twayne Publishers, 1976. 316 p. Bibliog., index.

Parsons offers a historical view of the conditions which made it possible for the Pennsylvania Dutch to flourish for such an extended period. Both the "Church Germans" and the "Plain Folk" sects who settled between 1684 and 1835 are described. Beyond the history of migration and the background of the fatherland, subjects treated include education and publishing, folk arts and crafts, formal art, local and national politics, home life, the westward movement and the Civil War, the uncomfortable minority during the two World Wars, and the ethnic traditions today. Footnotes are numerous and are based on many primary works and scholarly journals. A selected bibliography, over 320 items, classes works into primary and secondary, and by books and articles. There is also a chronology of main events from 1517 to 1974.

315 Jenkins, Howard Malcolm, ed. PENNSYLVANIA: COLONIAL AND FEDERAL, A HISTORY 1608-1903. 3 vols. Philadelphia: Historical Publishing Association, 1903. 600 p.; 585 p.; 608 p. Index.

This massive history of Pennsylvania treats the German contribution in an integrated fashion. The individual chapters were written by specialists, and each chapter is devoted to a particular chronological period. Embedded in the work are many informative items of interest to research in German Americana. For example, volume two has a civil list under each department of government listing officeholders with their dates of service. Dates of county organization with constituent localities are also given. The work is illustrated and each volume is separately indexed.

316 Eshelman, Henry Frank. HISTORIC BACKGROUND AND ANNALS OF THE SWISS AND GERMAN PIONEER SETTLERS OF SOUTHEASTERN PENNSYLVANIA AND THEIR REMOTE ANCESTORS FROM THE MIDDLE OF THE DARK AGES DOWN TO THE TIME OF THE REVOLUTIONARY WAR; AN AUTHENTIC HISTORY, FROM ORIGINAL SOURCES WITH PARTICULAR REFERENCE TO GERMAN-SWISS MENNONITES OR ANABAPTISTS, THE AMISH, AND OTHER NON-RESISTANT SECTS. 1917. Reprint. Baltimore: Genealogical Publishing, 1969. 386 p. Index.

This narrative is a year-by-year account of major political, social, and religious events in Europe from 1009 to 1782 which induced large scale immigration to southeast Pennsylvania. The text often mentions names of passengers of ships, based on official lists, indicating their points of destination. Limited access to the names of immigrants is provided in the name index. In addition, the work also includes a subject index. More detailed references to sources would have enhanced the value of this chronological reference tool for historical and genealogical research.

317 Kuhns, Levi Oscar. THE GERMAN AND SWISS SETTLEMENTS OF COLONIAL PENNSYLVANIA; A STUDY OF THE SO-CALLED PENNSYLVANIA DUTCH. 1901. Reprint. New York: AMS Press, 1971. 268 p.

Kuhns addresses himself to the task of providing an objective and factual history of German immigration to Pennsylvania as a unique historical and social phenomenon. Its uniqueness lies in the fact that in Pennsylvania the German element was preponderant, whereas in the other colonies German immigrants constituted only a minority of the population. The historic background of the immigration, the formation of German counties of Pennsylvania, the life, work, customs, and culture of the inhabitants are discussed in a lively prose, based on contemporary sources. The appendix "Pennsylvania German Family Names" is of special value for genealogical research showing patterns of derivations of present names from German and Swiss origin. Equally valuable is the bibliography of German and English materials, which does not include church and town records, and congressional papers which the author consulted in the preparation of the manuscript.

318 Beidelman, William. THE STORY OF THE PENNSYLVANIA GERMANS; EMBRACING AN ACCOUNTING OF THEIR ORIGIN, THEIR HISTORY, AND THEIR DIALECT. 1898. Reprint. Detroit: Gale Research, 1969. 254 p.

The focus of this study is the "Pfaelzer," inhabitants of the Palatinate, their history and movements from their home territory to Pennsylvania and elsewhere. More than half of the work is taken up by the cultural aspects of their lives, such as language, dialect, schools, churches, religious sects, social life, customs, and administration of justice. Appendices extending to forty-five pages deal with: (1) examples of Pfaelzisch, south German and Pennsylvania German dialects, (2) vocabulary, (3) brief personal sketches of English, German, and Palatinate rulers from 1682 to 1770, the period of the great exodus of German Palatinates to Pennsylvania, (4) chronological table of all the reigning princes of the Palatinate from the first elector in 1147 until 1801 and (5) a glossary.

319 Fisher, Sydney George. THE MAKING OF PENNSYLVANIA: AN ANALYSIS OF THE ELEMENTS OF THE POPULATION AND THE FORMATIVE INFLUENCES THAT CREATED ONE OF THE GREATEST OF THE AMERICAN STATES. Keystone State Historical Publications Series, no. 2. 1896. Reprint. Port Washington, N.Y.: I.J. Friedman, 1969. 364 p. Bibliog., index.

Chapters four and five of this treatise, comprising about one-fourth of the body of the work, are devoted to the various German groups and the Moravians. The chronological scope of the discussion ranges from 1682 through the middle of the nineteenth century. The end-of-the-chapter bibliographies indicate that secondary sources served as the basis for this history.

320 Rosenberger, Homer Tope. THE PENNSYLVANIA GERMANS 1891-1965, FREQUENTLY KNOWN AS THE "PENNSYLVANIA DUTCH": 75TH ANNIVERSARY VOLUME OF THE PENNSYLVANIA GERMAN SOCIETY. Pennsylvania German Society Publications, vol. 63. Lancaster: Pennsylvania German Society, 1966. 619 p. Bibliog., index.

For the seventy-five years covered, this is a key work. It is not a contiguous discourse of developments, but rather an inventory and synoptic discussion of events, trends, and achievements, primarily in the field of culture, as seen from the corporate vantage point of the Pennsylvania German Society. The revival of interest during this period in Pennsylvania German cultural heritage lends special significance to Rosenberger's sweeping review presented here.

The work begins with a retrospective glance to the settlement of Germans in Pennsylvania and traces the origin of the movement which led to the foundation of the Pennsylvania German Society in 1891. Subsequent sections chronicle major events and development in the life of the community highlighting successes in all spheres of life. Special chapters are devoted to Pennsylvania Germans who attained eminence, providing biographical sketches of Jane Addams, Pearl Buck, General John J. Pershing, Conrad Richter, and a multitude of other individuals. Among the chapters having special interest for librarians and researchers are those which are devoted to Pennsylvania German literary activity, publishing and archival collections. For example: chapter eleven deals with Pennsylvania German dictionaries and grammar; chapter twelve is a year-by-year analysis of the literature on Pennsylvania Germans produced between 1890 and 1965. Chapter fifteen discusses in almost sixty pages the outstanding collections of Pennsylvania German material. It should be mentioned that Rosenberger also updates Hostetler's ANNOTATED BIBLIOGRAPHY ON THE AMISH (1951) (see 414). The work closes with an evaluation of the prospects of survival of Pennsylvania German traditions. Illustrations and a detailed index further enhance the value of this work as an indispensable reference tool.

321 Brenner, Scott Francis. PENNSYLVANIA DUTCH, THE PLAIN AND THE FANCY. Harrisburg, Pa.: Stackpole, 1957. 244 p.

This book is an account of personal impressions presented in a popular style, relaying the spirit of Pennsylvania German life in the early 1950s. The subjects dealt with include customs and folkways, education, religious life, holidays, and folk art. Among the historical topics, the Ephrata Cloister and George Rapp's Harmony Society are discussed. The work is intended for easy background reading.

322 Jordan, Mildred. THE DISTELFINK COUNTRY OF THE PENNSYLVANIA DUTCH. New York: Crown Publishers, 1978. 258 p. Index.

Written in a popular vein, this attractive book reflects the author's subjective perceptions of the ways of life of the Pennsylvania Dutch country, stretching across the southeastern

part of the state where many of the old habits still prevail.
The author touches upon the history of the different sects,
dialect, traditions, customs, superstitions, folklore and tales,
architecture, farming and gardening, and the culinary art.
The last chapter contains some thoughts on the prospect of
survival of this culture. The book was illustrated by Howard
Berelson.

323   Rosenberger, Jesse Leonard. IN PENNSYLVANIA-GERMAN LAND,
1928-1929. Chicago: University of Chicago Press, 1929. 91 p. Index.

What started out as a quest for genealogical data on a rela-
tive in order to trace his own Pennsylvania Dutch roots, Rosenberger ended up writing a whole book. Rosenberger writes:
"I obtained all the information of interest and importance that
I conveniently could about what I have designated Pennsylvania Dutch land." This land includes Lancaster, York, Berks,
Bucks and Montgomery counties. He describes the land and
people, old buildings, churches, schools, farms, and traces
the genealogy of his ancestor, Matthias Helm of Freiburg.
There are many reproductions in this book of old photographs.

324   Gilbert, Russell Wieder. A PICTURE OF THE PENNSYLVANIA GERMANS.
3d ed., Rev. Pennsylvania History Studies, no. 1. Gettysburg: Pennsylvania Historical Association, 1971. 83 p. Bibliog.

This 83-page pamphlet, which describes itself as the "most
scholarly, all-inclusive, readable account of the Pennsylvania
Germans which has been produced in one small volume,"
serves as an easy-to-read introduction stimulating interest in
Pennsylvania German study. Subjects include: origin, problems of language, politics, education and prejudice, achievements, role in war, literature, music and art, decoration,
barn signs, Fraktur, pottery, furniture, and family names.
There are few illustrations and the booklet lacks an index,
but the detailed table of contents is helpful infinding one's
way in the text. The bibliography is grouped by subjects
and consists of books, pamphlets, and scholarly journals.
Basic recommended books are marked with an asterisk and
are briefly annotated.

325   Rosenberger, Jesse Leonard. THE PENNSYLVANIA GERMANS: A
SKETCH OF THEIR HISTORY AND LIFE, OF THE MENNONITES, AND
OF SIDE LIGHTS FROM THE ROSENBERGER FAMILY. Chicago: Uni-
versity of Chicago Press, 1923. 173 p. Index.

The intent of the author was to memorialize the traditions
and life-style of the Pennsylvania Dutch before "their quaintness is lost through encroachments of the modern world into
their territory. . . . " Subjects discussed begin with immigration, the process of leaving the hardships of the old world for

the hardships of the new, pioneer life, religion and education,
manners, customs and dress, proverbs, and superstitions. A
chapter focuses on the Mennonites as a distinct group within
the Pennsylvania Germans. The genealogy of the Rosenberger
family is also traced from old records. Twenty-eight contemporary photos of people and buildings accompany the work.
It lacks a bibliography and documentation, but has a detailed
index. In all, it is an interesting book for background reading and for the history of the Rosenberger family originating
in the Lancaster area.

Colonial Pennsylvania

326 Wertenbaker, Thomas Jefferson. THE FOUNDING OF THE AMERICAN
CIVILIZATION: THE MIDDLE COLONIES. New York: Charles Scribner's Sons, 1938. 367 p. Bibliog. notes, index.

A substantial part of the discussion is devoted to the history,
social, material, and cultural life of the Palatinate Germans
of Pennsylvania during the colonial period. A detailed index
and bibliographic notes make this work useful for introductory
study.

327 Lincoln, Charles Henry. THE REVOLUTIONARY MOVEMENT IN PENN-
SYLVANIA, 1770-1776. Publications of the University of Pennsylvania
Series in History, no. 1. Cas Cob, Conn.: J.E. Edwards, 1901. 300 p.
Bibliog., index.

This well-documented study concentrates on the political and
social process during the six years immediately preceeding the
Revolution, showing how local aspirations merged with the
national effort. While the focus of the inquiry is Pennsylvania
colonial society as a whole, attention is paid to the local
German population as well. The contemporary periodical
press, pamphlets, and various archival materials are used for
documentation. The index is detailed.

328 Rothermund, Dietmar. THE LAYMAN'S PROGRESS: RELIGION AND
POLITICAL EXPERIENCE IN COLONIAL PENNSYLVANIA, 1740-1770.
Philadelphia: University of Pennsylvania Press, 1961. 202 p. Bibliog.,
index.

An important interpretive historical work focusing on the social
and intellectual trends in the society of colonial Pennsylvania.
The research was based on primary resources consisting principally of private papers and church records. Thirty-six documentary items are included in the appendix. A classified
bibliography of relevant primary and secondary sources, as
well as a list of further reading material complement the work.

329   Richards, Henry Melchior Muhlenburg. THE PENNSYLVANIA-GERMAN
IN THE FRENCH AND INDIAN WAR: A HISTORICAL SKETCH. Penn-
sylvania German Society Proceedings and Addresses, vol. 15. Lancaster:
Pennsylvania German Society, 1906. 559 p.

      This narrative history, written from contemporary documents
      and records of personal testimonies, encompasses the entire
      subject of the role of the Pennsylvania Germans in the French-
      Indian wars, the major theaters of which were New York and
      Pennsylvania. The works contain numerous sketches, engrav-
      ings, maps of battlesites, and forts. The lack of an index
      severely limits the book's reference value.

330   Mittelberger, Gottlieb. JOURNEY TO PENNSYLVANIA. Edited and
translated by Oscar Handlin, and John Clive. 1898. Reprint. Cambridge, Mass.: Belknap Press of Harvard University Press, 1960. 102 p.

331   . GOTTLIEB MITTELBERGER'S JOURNEY TO PENNSYLVANIA
AND RETURN TO GERMANY IN THE YEAR 1754 CONTAINING NOT
ONLY A DESCRIPTION OF THE COUNTRY ACCORDING TO ITS PRE-
SENT CONDITION, BUT ALSO A DETAILED ACCOUNT OF THE SAD
AND UNFORTUNATE CIRCUMSTANCES OF MOST OF THE GERMANS
THAT HAVE EMIGRATED, OR ARE EMIGRATING TO THAT COUNTRY.
Translated from German by Carl T. Eben. Philadelphia: John Joseph
McVey, 1898. 129 p.

      This book (and item 330) is Mittleberger's account of his jour-
      ney to America in 1750 and his return to his homeland in 1754.
      The account includes a realistic description of Pennsylvania and
      the conditions of its German settlers. It was published in Ger-
      many in 1756 with the possible intent to discourage Germans
      from leaving for the New World. The translators supplied the
      introduction, footnotes, and some useful comments.

COLLECTED WORKS

332   Rose Hill Seminar, 3d, Waynesboro, Pennsylvania, 1965. INTIMATE
GLIMPSES OF THE PENNSYLVANIA GERMANS: PROCEEDINGS. Edited
by Homer Tope Rosenberger. Waynesboro, Pa.: Published with the assistance of the Pennsylvania German Society, 1966. 98 p. Bibliog.

      A compendium of excerpts from the following papers: "Volun-
      tarism and the Colonial Lutheran Clergy"; "Papers of David
      Rittenhouse"; "Pennsylvania-Germans in Partisan Politics 1754
      to 1965"; "Henry Snavely Herliman, Pennsylvania Bibliophile";
      "Pennsylvania-German Humor," with twelve examples in the
      dialect and English; and a "Treasury of Pennsylvania-German
      Literature," reviews and excerpts from key literature. Docu-
      mentation varies with individual articles, but is usually pri-
      mary when it is included.

333 Wood, Ralph Charles, ed. THE PENNSYLVANIA GERMANS. Prince-
     ton, N.J.: Princeton University Press, 1942. 299 p. Index.

   Ten essays by authors, prominent in Pennsylvania German research, explore early settlement, farmers, the "Plain People,"
   the "Church People," journalism, literature, military history,
   examples of Pennsylvania German dialect, and the history of
   Pennsylvania German study. The essays purport to interpret
   who the Pennsylvania Germans are, and what their place is
   in America. There is a map of concentrations of Pennsylvania Germans by county.

334 Gibbons, Phebe H. Earle. THE "PENNSYLVANIA DUTCH" AND OTHER
     ESSAYS. 3d ed , rev. 1882. Reprint. New York: AMS Press, 1971.
     427 p.

   This collection of essays has seen several editions, each edition expanded by further inclusions. The first included Gibbons's noted essay on the Pennsylvania Dutch, originally published in the ATLANTIC in October 1869. The second edition
   brought in additional material centering on the Amish and
   Dunker religious meetings, Ephrata, the Schwenkfelders, Bethlehem and Moravians, and Swiss exiles. Among the essays
   there was one devoted to the miners of Scranton. The third
   edition added some essays dealing with the English and Irish
   in Pennsylvania.

   Two essays from this collection were published separately in
   1963 under the titles: THE PENNSYLVANIA DUTCH. A RE-
   PRINT OF THE ESSAY FIRST PUBLISHED IN THE ATLANTIC
   MONTHLY IN OCTOBER 1869 (Lebanon, Pa.: Applied Arts,
   1963), and THE PLAIN PEOPLE (Witmer, Pa.: Applied Arts,
   1963), with illustrations taken from Henry Lee Fisher, OLDEN
   TIMES: PENNSYLVANIA RURAL LIFE SOME FIFTY YEARS
   AGO (York, Pa.: Fisher Brothers, 1888).

CITY HISTORIES

Allentown

335 Williams, David G. THE LOWER JORDAN VALLEY, PENNSYLVANIA
     GERMAN SETTLEMENT. Proceedings of the Lehigh County Historical
     Society, vol. 18. Allentown, Pa.: Lehigh County Historical Society,
     1950. 181 p. Bibliog., index.

   This work is the result of the author's prolonged involvement
   in land title searches and compilation of warrants in Allentown and in the region west of the Lehigh River. This interest
   led to a study of the early settlement patterns and architecture
   of the area. The first section of the book lists warrants and
   land patents in the Lehigh Valley, with survey data, maps,

dates, and owners' names. Subsequent sections provide a
listing of settlements and description of buildings. The narrative is substantiated by maps, foldout floor plans, and
architectural detail sheets. The sources of materials are
listed. The work is a gold mine of information for local
historians, genealogists, and architectural historians.

Bernville

335a Kline, Pearl B., and De Long, Janice C. BERNVILLE PENNSYLVANIA,
1851-1976. Bernville, Pa.: Bicentennial Committee, 1976. 148 p.

Item not available for examination.

Bethlehem

336 Levering, Joseph Mortimer. A HISTORY OF BETHLEHEM, PENNSYL-
VANIA WITH SOME ACCOUNT OF ITS FOUNDERS AND THEIR EARLY
ACTIVITY IN AMERICA. Memorial volume issued by the Sesquicentennial
committee of the Moravian Congregation of Bethlehem. 1903. Reprint.
New York: AMS Press, 1971. 809 p. Bibliog.

This history portrays Bethlehem, Pennsylvania, as a center of
Moravian settlement from earliest times to 1892. It narrates
in a scholarly style the factual story without stereotyping the
Moravians as "quaint, amusing, strangely eccentric" people.
Each chapter describes an epoch: settlement, relations with
Indians, growth, American Revolution, modernization, progress
of industry, and the Civil War. The work is based on primary
sources consisting of manuscripts, diaries, minutes, synod records, and various personal papers. The text is accompanied
by eighty illustrations. In addition to serving as a historical
background, this work can be used as a starting point for local
genealogical research.

337 BETHLEHEM OF PENNSYLVANIA: THE FIRST ONE HUNDRED YEARS,
1741-1841. Edited by Ross Yates, et al. Bethlehem, Pa.: Bethlehem
Book Committee, 1968. 226 p. Index.

338 BETHLEHEM OF PENNSYLVANIA: THE GOLDEN YEARS, 1841-1920.
Edited by Ross Yates, et al. Bethlehem, Pa.: Bethlehem Book Committee, 1976. 362 p. Index.

The first item (337) is a beautifully illustrated volume devoted
to the first hundred-year history of the city of Bethlehem,
Pennsylvania. The founding of the city, the Indian wars, the
American Revolution, the city's life-style and architecture are
shown through pictures and accompanying text. A special section concentrates on the culture of the city, presenting the
works of local artists. A chronology summarizes the main
events from 1457 to 1845. The second item (338) is a continuation of the first, bringing the history up to 1920.

Germantown

339 MacReynolds, George, comp. PLACE NAMES IN BUCKS COUNTY, PENNSYLVANIA, ALPHABETICALLY ARRANGED IN AN HISTORICAL NARRATIVE. 2d ed. Doylestown, Pa.: Bucks County Historical Society, 1955. 454 p. Index.

> This detailed gazetteer contains short articles on large, small, and even obscure places in Bucks County with a capsule history for each. The draft was initially distributed to members of Bucks County Historical Society, whose contributions and corrections were integrated in the text. The treatment of manors is sketchy. The index provides references to places, institutions, dates, and people connected with them.

340 Jenkins, Charles Francis. THE GUIDE BOOK TO HISTORIC GERMAN-TOWN. 4th ed. Germantown, Pa.: Site and Relic Society, 1926. 156 p. Bibliog., index.

> This edition of this guidebook to the eighteenth century sites and relics of Germantown, Pennsylvania, gives historic facts for each site in a narrative form. Its arrangement is suitable for walking tours. A chronology from 1683 to 1854 of Germantown, thirty-two sketches of buildings, a map of the town, biographical data on its founder Francis Daniel Pastorius, and a list of books and genealogies complement the work.

341 Hotchkin, Samuel Fitch. ANCIENT AND MODERN GERMANTOWN, MOUNT AIRY AND CHESTNUT HILL. Philadelphia: P.W. Ziegler, 1899. 548 p. Index.

> This book contains three sections, each dealing with the history of the respective areas which are now part of the city of Philadelphia. The material is essentially a collection of historical bits sketching the story of streets, buildings, organizations, and institutions such as clubs, library associations, companies, churches, hospitals, Y.M.C.A. and Y.W.C.A. of these three settlements. Collectively these sketches provide an insight into the evolution of these cities over a period of two hundred years beginning from 1680. The documentary material used as evidence is a goldmine of data and information on people in all facets of life. In all, this is an excellent source book of both documentary texts and contemporary illustrations with a fairly good index.

342 Hocker, Edward Wilhelm. GERMANTOWN 1683-1933: THE RECORD THAT A PENNSYLVANIA COMMUNITY HAS ACHIEVED IN THE COURSE OF 250 YEARS; BEING A HISTORY OF THE PEOPLE OF GERMANTOWN, MOUNT AIRY, AND CHESTNUT HILL. Germantown, Pa. and Philadelphia: the author, 1933. 331 p. Bibliog., index.

This history of Philadelphia's three former suburbs tells of their founding in colonial times, through 1854 when Germantown became part of the city, up to 1933. The narrative extends to municipal government, organizations, and institutions. The bibliographic references include many primary sources.

343 Pennypacker, Samuel Whitaker. THE SETTLEMENT OF GERMANTOWN, PENNSYLVANIA, AND THE BEGINNING OF GERMAN EMIGRATION TO NORTH AMERICA. Pennsylvania German Society Proceedings and Addresses, vol. 9. 1899. Reprint. New York: B. Blom, 1970. 310 p. Index.

A descendant of founders of Germantown, the author had been gathering facts for thirty years and conceived of writing the history of its early settlement as "a duty that could not be avoided." The history of the early settlement from the 1600s to the 1700s is brought to life through abundant quotations and excerpts from contemporary documents, diaries, memoirs, and biographies. The topical coverage extends to the immigrants from Krefeld and Kriegsheim, the Mennonites, Pietists, Frankfurt Land Company, communal life, and relations with the Indians. Among the personalities, Francis Daniel Pastorius and William Rittenhouse are discussed in considerable detail. The work is well documented. A particularly valuable feature of this work is the text of the charter and ordinances of Germantown, and a listing of municipal office holders from 1621 to 1707. The bulk of the index consists of name references.

344 Tinkcom, Harry Marlin; Tinkcom, Margaret M.; and Grant, Miles Simon. HISTORIC GERMANTOWN, FROM THE FOUNDING TO THE EARLY PART OF THE NINETEENTH CENTURY; A SURVEY OF THE GERMAN TOWNSHIP. Memoirs of the American Philosophical Society, vol. 39. Philadelphia: American Philosophical Society, 1955. 154 p. Bibliog., index.

Part one of this work is a history of the settlement of Germantown with maps and illustrations showing its growth and development. Part two comprises pictorial representations of houses, buildings, and structures with floorplans and dimensions for the purpose of assessing the requirements for their restoration. The work includes bibliographic notes, a checklist of maps, and a location map of historic buildings.

345 Sachse, Julius Friedrich, ed. QUAINT OLD GERMANTOWN IN PENNSYLVANIA, A SERIES OF SIXTY FORMER LANDMARKS OF GERMANTOWN AND VICINITY, DRAWN ON ZINC DURING THE YEARS 1863-1888 BY JOHN RICHARDS. Pennsylvania German Society Proceedings and Addresses, vol. 23. Lancaster: Pennsylvania German Society, 1913. 100 leaves.

This collection contains sixty 6 x 8 inch black and white plates of Germantown buildings and landmarks sketched between

1863-88. Each plate gives, when relevant, the building's owner, name, title, location, site number, builder, former uses, and contemporary (1913) uses.

346   Wolf, Stephanie Grauman. URBAN VILLAGE: POPULATION, COMMU-
NITY, AND FAMILY STRUCTURE IN GERMANTOWN, PENNSYLVANIA,
1683-1800. Princeton, N.J.: Princeton University Press, 1976. 361 p.
Bibliog., index.

A statistically oriented study of the social structure of Germantown's colonial society, presenting a picture of a dynamic,
autonomous, and individualistic community. The author contends that Germantown itself was a pluralistic polity where
no single ethnic or religious group could reach commanding
positions.

Lancaster

347   Worner, William Frederic. OLD LANCASTER TALES AND TRADITIONS.
Lancaster, Pa.: the author, 1927. 261 p.

This volume contains short pieces of prose on various aspects
of the history and life of Lancaster, Pennsylvania. Among
the topics are: Ephrata, the German Reformed Church, Johann
Conrad Beissel, and many others.

GERMANS IN THE MIDWEST

Bibliography

348   Hubach, Robert Rogers. EARLY MIDWESTERN TRAVEL NARRATIVES; AN
ANNOTATED BIBLIOGRAPHY, 1634-1850. Detroit: Wayne State University Press, 1961. 149 p. Bibliog., index.

Includes many references to Germans in the Midwest.

Illinois

349   Hofmeister, Rudolf. THE GERMANS OF CHICAGO. Champaign, Ill.:
Stipes Publishing, 1976. 285 p. Bibliog , index.

350   Townsend, Andrew Jacke. THE GERMANS OF CHICAGO. Chicago:
University of Chicago, 1927   160 p. Index.

Originally a doctoral dissertation at the University of Chicago
in 1927, this work examines the various roles Germans played
in the city's history from 1850 to 1920. The impact of the
"Forty-Eighters" is analyzed along with the rise of the various
radical movements. The social attitudes during World War I

are explored using contemporary documentation. Other aspects such as German churches, press, cultural, and civic organizations are also given serious attention. The study is supported by statistical and cartographic material.

Indiana

351 Fritsch, William August. GERMAN SETTLERS AND GERMAN SETTLE-MENTS IN INDIANA: A MEMORIAL FOR THE STATE CENTENNIAL. Evansville, Ind.: 1916. 61 p.

A basic study for the history of German Americans in Indiana surveyed from 1786 to the early 1900s. Chapters deal with early German settlers and their origin, New Harmony, Indiana Germans in the Civil War, the role of Germans in industry, the professions, and in public life. A separate chapter is devoted to the emergence of the German-American Alliance of Indiana.

Iowa

352 Ludwig, G.M. "The Influence of the Pennsylvania Dutch in the Middle West." In PENNSYLVANIA GERMAN FOLKLORE SOCIETY YEARBOOK vol. 10 (1945): 1-101. Allentown: Pennsylvania German Folklore Society, 1947.

An examination of the settling of the Midwest by the Pennsylvania Dutch and particularly their influence on the way of life on the population, with special emphasis on Iowa. One of the chapters discusses the effect of the Pennsylvania Dutch on the English language of the Midwest. A map shows German settlements.

Michigan

353 Russell, John Andrew. THE GERMANIC INFLUENCE IN THE MAKING OF MICHIGAN. Detroit: University of Detroit, 1927. 415 p. Bibliog., index.

A comprehensive treatise written in a popular style devoting half of its length to the history of German Americans in Michigan from the mid-1700s to the 1900s. A large amount of biographical and institutional information, as well as county and local history has been integrated into the narra-tive. Much of the material was drawn from the Michigan Pioneer Collection and the Burton Historical Collection of Detroit Public Library. The second half of the work consists of listings and tabulations such as Michigan place names of German origin, federal and state legislators of German extrac-tion, German-American officers from Michigan in the Civil

War, German-American military medal recipients and dead in World War I, and others. A 160-item bibliography provides an excellent path for further study and reading.

354 Florer, Warren Washburn. EARLY MICHIGAN SETTLEMENTS. Vol. 1 on Washtenaw, Westphalia, Frankenmuth, Detroit, 1848. Ann Arbor, Mich.: the author, 1941. 129 p.

Originally intended to be a five-part series, volume one concentrates on the history of Germans in Washtenaw County, Detroit, Westphalia, and Frankenmuth in 1848. All aspects of social and cultural life are dealt with. The appendix includes specimens of resource materials used for this study.

Missouri

355 Bek, William G. THE GERMAN SETTLEMENT SOCIETY OF PHILADEL-PHIA AND ITS COLONY, HERMANN, MISSOURI. American Germanica. New Series, Vol. 5. Philadelphia: Americana Germanica Press, 1907. 170 p. Bibliog. notes.

The German Settlement Society was founded in Philadelphia in 1836 for the purpose of facilitating land acquisition in the newly opened Missouri territory. The members bought shares in the company and they received land at the site which became the community of Hermann. This work relates the history of the society and the Hermann settlement, reconstructed from archival records, the minutes of the board of trustees of Hermann, and the society's official organ ALTE UND NEUE WELT. Facsimiles of documents, photographs, boundary maps, and a list of members containing 678 names are added to the text.

356 Forster, Walter Otto. ZION ON THE MISSISSIPPI; THE SETTLEMENT OF THE SAXON LUTHERANS IN MISSOURI, 1839-1841. St. Louis: Concordia Publishing House, 1953. 606 p. Bibliog., index.

This is the story of the Stephanite emigration from Saxony to St. Louis and Perry County in Missouri. The preparation, journey, establishment of the community, its breakdown and reconstruction are vividly described. The community was to be built on the CODES (the church's doctrinal formulations) as an autonomous religious and political colony. The text of the CODES is given here. The author worked from primary resources which included passenger lists integrated in the work. The lists enumerate Stephanite emigrant families by name, age, occupation, and former residence. There is a sizeable bibliography organized by form and a detailed topical index.

357 Gerlach, Russel L. IMMIGRANTS IN THE OZARKS; A STUDY IN ETH-NIC GEOGRAPHY. University of Missouri Studies, 64. Columbia: University of Missouri Press, 1967. 206 p. Bibliog., index.

Nearly half of this work is devoted to an in-depth study of German settlements in the Ozark Highland Region. The author describes the influx of Germans before and after the Civil War, giving special attention to the Amish and the Mennonites. The study centers around such aspects as settlement patterns, agriculture and land use, religion, language, attitudes on temperance, and hyphenism today. The study was based on primary resources and contains a substantial bibliography. The distribution of ethnic groups by county is shown in the appendix.

Ohio

358 Harlow, Alvin F. THE SERENE CINCINNATIANS. Society in America Series. New York: Dutton, 1950. 442 p. Bibliog.

Includes a section describing the German-American section of Cincinnati and its influence on the city at large.

Wisconsin

359 Dundore, M. Walter. "The Saga of the Pennsylvania Germans in Wisconsin." PENNSYLVANIA GERMAN FOLKLORE SOCIETY YEARBOOK 19 (1954): 33-166. Allentown: Pennsylvania German Folklore Society, 1955. Bibliog.

Prepared for the Wisconsin state centennial (1948), this history recounts how the Pennsylvania Germans who resettled in the state in the nineteenth century became a major force in its development. The range of subjects include: activities in farming, timber, fur trapping, leadmining and milling, politics, education, missionaries, pioneer women, folklore and customs, the professions, homes, statehood, place names and landmarks, the Pennsylvania German dialect, and a chapter on Edward S. Bragg. In addition to various photographs, there are two maps showing the westward trek of the Pennsylvania Germans to Wisconsin, and the German counties in the state, ranked according to the size of the German population. A listing of new settlers by year gives their county of origin in Pennsylvania and the county of settlement in Wisconsin. There are no footnote references.

360 Everest, Kate Asaphine. "How Wisconsin Came by its Large German Element." STATE HISTORICAL SOCIETY OF WISCONSIN. COLLECTIONS 12 (1892): 299-334.

361 _____. "Geographical Origins of German Immigration to Wisconsin." STATE HISTORICAL SOCIETY OF WISCONSIN. COLLECTIONS 14 (1898): 341-393.

The first of these two studies (item 360) is an overview of historical, political, and economic factors between 1830 and the 1880s which account for the attraction of the area for German settlers. The process of settlement is illustrated and interpreted by official documents, federal and state, and census and immigration reports. A color map shows concentration of Germans by county based on the 1880 census data. County population figures are also included. The sequel traces the economic and political reasons for the mass departure from the various areas of Germany. The settlement pattern in Wisconsin of Germans originating from the various parts of Germany is shown in a map.

362　Zeitlin, Richard H. GERMANS IN WISCONSIN. Madison: State Historical Society of Wisconsin, 1977. 30 p.

363　Holmes, Fred L. OLD WORLD WISCONSIN: AROUND EUROPE IN THE BADGER STATE. Eau Claire, Wisc.: E.M. Hale, 1944. Reprint. Madison: Wisconsin House, 1974. 368 p. Index.

This is a general treatment of the various ethnic groups in Wisconsin. Includes two chapters dealing with Germans and Luxemburgers who populated the Milwaukee, Manitowoc, and Sheboygan areas of the state. A map shows the distribution of ethnic groups in Wisconsin. Illus. with photos. and sketches by Max Fernekes. Additional materials on Germans are scattered throughout the book and are accessible through the subject index.

364　Lacher, John Henry A. THE GERMAN ELEMENT IN WISCONSIN. Milwaukee: Published for the Salomon Brothers Memorial Fund by Muhlenberg Unit, 36, Steuben Society of America, 1925. 60 p.

This short work intends to fill a gap in the historical literature of Wisconsin which heretofore had concentrated on the French and the English. The following topics are briefly surveyed: agriculture, religion, art, education, business, music, the professions, politics, press, sports, and role in war. There is also a section dealing with Germanic place-names. Sources used appear in bold print in the text and include historical chronicles, state government reports, newspapers, local histories, and some secondary works.

365　Frank, Louis Frederick, comp. GERMAN-AMERICAN PIONEERS IN WISCONSIN AND MICHIGAN; THE FRANK-KERLER LETTERS, 1840-1864. Translated from German by Margaret Wolff. Edited, with introduction and notes by Harry H. Anderson. Milwaukee: Milwaukee County Historical Society, 1971. 600 p. Bibliog. notes, index.

An impressive array of letters, papers, diaries, and other materials generated by the Frank, Kerler, Seyffard, and Buck families who emigrated from Germany and settled in Milwaukee, Wisconsin, and the Saginaw, Michigan area. They are arranged chronologically and reflect the settlers' perceptions of every facet of their situation in the new environment. The material brought together here transcends the scope of a family saga, as it is a documentary of the times. The supplementary material constitutes a valuable genealogical resource.

366 Still, Bayrd. MILWAUKEE, THE HISTORY OF A CITY. Madison: State Historical Society of Wisconsin, 1948. 638 p. Bibliog. notes, index.

Although a general history of the city, its German-American inhabitants are given considerable attention in it. The work traces the evolution of Milwaukee from a small village in 1795 to its rise as a metropolis in the twentieth century. The author assembled a mass of data from a great variety of sources. Information on German Americans is retrievable through the detailed index.

366a Conzen, Kathleen Neils. IMMIGRANT MILWAUKEE, 1836-1960: ACCOMMODATION AND COMMUNITY IN A FRONTIER CITY. Harvard Studies in Urban History. Cambridge, Mass.: Harvard University Press, 1976. 300 p. Bibliog.

The work explores the social life, customs and interrelationships of immigrant groups in Milwaukee with special emphasis on the Germans and the Irish.

GERMANS IN THE SOUTH

Georgia

367 Stroebel, Philip A. THE SALZBURGERS AND THEIR DESCENDANTS; BEING THE HISTORY OF A COLONY OF GERMAN (LUTHERAN) PROTESTANTS, WHO EMIGRATED TO GEORGIA IN 1734, AND SETTLED AT EBENEZER TWENTY-FIVE MILES ABOVE THE CITY OF SAVANNAH. 1885. Reprint. Foreword, appendix, and index by Edward D. Wells, Sr. Athens: University of Georgia Press, 1953. 318 p. Index.

A basic treatment of the founding of Ebenezer, Georgia, in 1733 and the settlement's development up to the middle of the nineteenth century. Religious and cultural aspects are highlighted. It includes some documentary material useful for genealogical research.

368 Urlsperger, Samuel, comp. DETAILED REPORTS ON THE SALZBURGER EMIGRANTS WHO SETTLED IN AMERICA. 3 vols. Edited by George Fenwick Jones. Translated by Hermann J. Lacher. Publications of the Wormsloe Foundation, no. 9. Athens: University of Georgia Press, 1968. 211 p.; 253 p.; 348 p. Bibliog. notes, index.

A compilation of the diaries, correspondence, and church
papers of Lutheran pastors who accompanied the Salzburger
immigrants to America, covering the years 1733-36. The
work is in three volumes. The first volume describes the
passage and settlement in Georgia in 1733; the subsequent
volumes deal with the experiences of the community in its
new setting centering around Ebenezer. The editor of the
present edition reorganized the material for easier access and
added his own notes and comments. Each volume is indexed
separately.

Louisiana

369   Deiler, John Hanno. THE SETTLEMENT OF THE GERMAN COAST OF
      LOUISIANA AND THE CREOLES OF GERMAN DESCENT. Americana
      Germanica, new series, no. 8. 1909. Reprint. With a new preface,
      chronology, and index by Jack Belsom. Baltimore: Genealogical Pub-
      lishing, 1969. 138 p.

      Gives interesting insights into the life of German villages on
      the north and south sides of the Mississippi in the vincinity
      of New Orleans from the 1700s to the 1770s. A special sec-
      tion is devoted to the Creoles with a listing by family names.
      One of the highlights of the work is the enumeration of two
      local censuses taken in 1724 and 1731. A supplemental enu-
      meration of Germans who were not included in these censuses
      is added as a special section. Some maps and documentation
      are integrated in the text.

370   Nau, John Frederick. THE GERMAN PEOPLE OF NEW ORLEANS, 1850-
      1900. Leiden: E.J. Brill, 1958. 154 p. Bibliog.

      Originally a dissertation at the University of South Carolina,
      1954, this work deals with the social and economic role of
      the Germans who emigrated to the South in general, and with
      those who settled in New Orleans and its surrounding area, in
      particular. The focus is the period between 1850 and 1900.
      The impact of slavery and the Civil War on the New Orleans
      Germans is examined. All aspects of life are touched upon.
      A section is devoted to prominent personalities. The documen-
      tation is drawn from local German-language newspapers, the
      records of churches and societies, census reports, some personal
      interviews, and personal accounts. A 250-item bibliography
      was assembled at the end of the work.

Maryland

371   Cunz, Dieter. THE MARYLAND GERMANS, A HISTORY. Princeton,
      N.J.: Princeton University Press, 1948. Reprint. Port Washington,
      N.Y.: Kennikat Press, 1972. 476 p. Bibliog., index.

A thorough investigation of the history of German settlers in Maryland from the colonial period until World War II. The various waves of immigrations and their impact on one another are discussed. Provides some biographical treatment of notable German Americans from Maryland. The work is carefully documented and includes a 350-item subject bibliography. Some portraits, maps, and a good index complement the work.

372 Nead, Daniel Wanderlich. THE PENNSYLVANIA-GERMAN IN THE SETTLEMENT OF MARYLAND. Pennsylvania German Society Proceedings and Addresses, vol. 22. 1914. Reprint. Baltimore: Genealogical Publishing, 1975. 304 p. Bibliog., index.

Devoted to the early history of Germans in Maryland, with particular emphasis on their participation in the French-Indian and Revolutionary Wars. Many illustrations, facsimiles, maps, and various lists are interspersed in the text.

North Carolina

373 Graeffenried, Baron Christoph von. CHRISTOPH VON GRAEFFENRIED'S ACCOUNT OF THE FOUNDING OF NEW BERN. Edited, with historical introduction and English translation by Vincent H. Todd in cooperation with Julius Goebel. Publications of the North Carolina Historical Commission. Reprint. Spartanburg, S.C.: Reprint Co., 1973. 434 p. Bibliog., index.

An authentic document on the city's origins and the life of the early settlers beginning with 1709, based on one of the settler's diaries, papers, and memoirs. The editor contributed the English translation and the historical introduction on the Palatinate immigration. The book includes a sketch of the plan of the city drawn by von Graeffenried himself.

Shenandoah Valley

374 Smith, Elmer Lewis; Stewart, John G.; and Kyger, M. Ellsworth. THE PENNSYLVANIA GERMANS OF THE SHENANDOAH VALLEY. Pennsylvania German Folklore Society Yearbook, vol. 26, 1962. Allentown: Pennsylvania German Folklore Society, 1964. 278 p.

This work is a compendium of writings on the spread of Pennsylvania Germans to Maryland, West Virginia, and Virginia, beginning with the eighteenth century. It is the contention of the authors that in this region the Pennsylvania German influence was so pervasive that it should be considered "Pennsylvania Dutch" country. The writings deal with Pennsylvania German pioneers, religion, the Ephrata and Shenandoah settlements, social life and customs, arts and crafts, printing, publishing, tombstones and cemeteries, and the local dialect. The documentation consists of primary resources, recorded interviews,

14240

unpublished materials, and pertinent monographic literature.
Numerous illustrations, facsimiles, and maps complement the
work.

South Carolina

375   Voight, Gilbert Paul. THE GERMAN AND GERMAN-SWISS ELEMENT
      IN SOUTH CAROLINA, 1732-1752. Bulletin of the University of South
      Carolina, no. 113. Columbia: University of South Carolina, 1922.
      60 p.

> This short history deals specifically with Saxe-Gotha township,
> Purrysburg, Orangeburg, and New Windsor in South Carolina
> at a time of the heaviest influx of German settlers to this
> area from 1732-52. It includes several lists of immigrants,
> but the information given is sketchy.

Tennessee

375a Slonina, Maria. GERMAN-SPEAKING PEOPLE IN TENNESSEE FROM
      COLONIAL TIMES TO WORLD WAR I: AN INTRODUCTION AND BIB-
      LIOGRAPHY. Edited by David Lee. Knoxville: University of Tennessee,
      Department of Germanic and Slavic Languages, 1976. 145 p.

> Item not available for examination.

375b Haecker, J.G. REPORT ABOUT AND FROM AMERICA, GIVEN FROM
      FIRST-HAND OBSERVATION IN THE YEARS 1848 AND 1849, AND PUB-
      LISHED FOR EMIGRANTS BY J.G. HAECKER. Translated with an intro-
      duction and notes by Richard B. O'Connell. 1849. Reprint. MVC
      Bulletin no. 3. Memphis: John Willard Brister Library, Memphis State
      University, 1970. 84 p.

> This volume is the translation of BERICHT AUS UND UEBER
> AMERIKA and includes writings of Haecker and others dealing
> primarily with the city of Wartburg and Morgan County, Ten-
> nessee.

Virginia

376   Wust, Klaus German. THE VIRGINIA GERMANS. Charlottesville: Uni-
      versity Press of Virginia, 1969. 310 p. Bibliog. notes, index.

> A major attempt to write a comprehensive history of Germans
> in Virginia from 1608 to World War I, inspired by Cunz's THE
> MARYLAND GERMANS, A HISTORY (see 371). Previous treat-
> ments of the subject were denominational or local in nature. The
> scope of the work consists of: early and colonial settlements,
> German population distribution, politics, bilingualism, German
> churches, the arts, folkways, slavery and nativism, and Ger-
> man Americanism. This is a well-documented work based on

archival materials, and illustrated by maps showing settlements
and distributions of congregations. The bibliographic notes
provide many leads for further research.

377 Schuricht, Herrmann. HISTORY OF THE GERMAN ELEMENT IN VIR-
GINIA. 2 vols. Issued as appendices to the Annual Reports of the Society for the History of the Germans in Maryland, Vol. 1 with the 11th-
12th Reports for 1897-98, and Vol. 2 with the 13th-14th Reports for
1899-1900. 1898. Reprint. Baltimore: Genealogical Publishing, 1977.
168 p.; 244 p. Bibliog., index, notes.

This work gives an extensive treatment to the history of Germans in Virginia during the colonial period, with particular
emphasis on the German contribution to the winning of the
area for the white man, which takes up the first volume.
The second volume concentrates on the post-Civil War period.
Special features include biographies of prominent Virginia
German citizens, a list of anglicized German names in Virginia, specimens of Virginia German poetry, lists of Virginia
delegates to the U.S. and Virginia legislatures in 1898,
school officials 1872-96, and a list of German-influenced
localities and post offices. The footnotes comprise a rich
selection of state and federal documents, papers, and directories.

378 Wayland, John Walter. THE GERMAN ELEMENT IN THE SHENANDOAH
VALLEY OF VIRGINIA. 1907. Reprint. Harrisonburg, Va.: Carrier,
1978. 312 p. Bibliog.

An important local history covering three hundred years up to
the early 1900s, with emphasis on the pre-1850 era. All
aspects of society are dealt with. The historian would probab-
ly find the information on the economic life particularly important, as it is authenticated with contemporary documents. A
wealth of archival materials are brought together in the appendix relating to Augusta, Frederick, Rockingham, and Shenandoah counties. The work offers excellent leads for genealogical research. The participation of local Germans in federal
and state politics is illustrated by lists of congressmen of German descent from the area. A substantial annotated bibliography complements the work.

378a Heavener, Ulysses S.A. GERMAN NEW RIVER SETTLEMENT: VIRGINIA.
Baltimore: Genealogical Publishing, 1976. 94 p. Index.

The area, which consists today of Giles, Montgomery, and
Pulaski counties, was settled in the mid-eighteenth century by
German emigrants from the Palatinate. The history of many
local families can be traced in this book. Several vital records, including baptismal records with full details are also
included.

379 Hinke, William John, and Kemper, Charles E., eds. "Moravian Diaries of Travels Through Virginia." VIRGINIA MAGAZINE OF HISTORY AND BIOGRAPHY 11 (1903); 12 (1904). Var. pag. Bibliog. notes.

These are selected excerpts from diaries kept by Moravian missionaries who traveled in Virginia and the middle colonies in the mid-1700s. The purpose of the journey was to convert German settlers to the Moravian faith. The diaries yield a wealth of information on local conditions. Names of German settlers visited by the missionaries are italicized in the text for easy identification. The editors added notes to clarify ambiguities in the text, and included a list of further reading material.

380 Wayland, John Walter. GERMANNA, OUTPOST OF ADVENTURE, 1714-1956. Staunton: Memorial Foundation of the Germanna Colonies in Virginia, 1956. 102 p. Bibliog., index.

A documented history of Germanna, Virginia, based on records left by former residents and chroniclers. An interesting feature is a description of reunions of German Americans who trace their origin to the city. It includes bibliographic sources, illustrations, maps, tables, and lists of personal names.

381 Memorial Foundation of the Germanna Colonies in Virginia. THE STORY OF GERMANNA DESCENDANTS IN REUNION AT SIEGEN FOREST, VIRGINIA. Harrisonburg, Va., 1957-- . Annual.

A series of annually issued pamphlets. The initial numbers were restricted to an account of the annual reunion with roster of attendants, membership, and some genealogical notes. Later issues assumed the characteristics of localized history featuring essays on Germanna's past, geography, folklore, family histories, relevant publications, and new additions to the Germanna Library.

382 Kemper, Willis Miller, and Wright, Harry Linn, eds. GENEALOGY OF THE KEMPER FAMILY IN THE UNITED STATES, DESCENDANTS OF JOHN KEMPER OF VIRGINIA, WITH A SHORT HISTORICAL SKETCH OF HIS FAMILY AND OF THE GERMAN REFORMED COLONY AT GERMANNA AND GERMANTOWN, VIRGINIA. Chicago: George K. Hazlitt, 1899. 268 p. Bibliog. notes, index.

In addition to its value for genealogical research, this work may be of interest to the historian as it contains authentic information on the German Reformed Church in America. The Kemper family was involved in the founding of Germanna, and this book identifies three thousand names connected with it.

GERMANS IN THE SOUTHWEST

Texas

383 Benjamin, Gilbert Giddings. THE GERMANS IN TEXAS; A STUDY IN IMMIGRATION. 1909. Reprint. Austin: Jenkins, 1974. 161 p. Bibliog.

> A well-documented study focusing on the period from 1815-48. Topics highlighted are: cultivation of cotton, the slavery issue, relations with Indians, and cultural and social life. The appendix lists Germans who took part in the 1836 Texas revolution, instructions to new settlers, and the Adelsverein constitution. The work includes several maps and a 150-item bibliography.

384 Tiling, Moritz Philip Georg. HISTORY OF THE GERMAN ELEMENT IN TEXAS FROM 1820-1850, AND HISTORICAL SKETCHES OF THE GERMAN TEXAS SINGERS' LEAGUE AND HOUSTON TURNVEREIN FROM 1853-1913. Houston: the author, 1913. 225 p. Bibliog.

> An introductory text on a popular level to supplement the official history of Texas. The emphasis is on the German contribution to the formation of the state of Texas.

385 Biesele, Rudolph Leopold. THE HISTORY OF THE GERMAN SETTLEMENTS IN TEXAS, 1831-1864. Austin: Press of Von Boeckman-Jones, 1930. 259 p. Bibliog., index.

> Working with primary resources, Biesele reconstructs the history of German settlement in Texas focusing on the Adelsverein settlement company. A great deal of documentary material is appended to the main body of the work, including plat maps delineating grant and settlement areas, muster rolls and various other contemporary documents. This work is central for the study of German settlements in Texas.

386 Geue, Chester William, and Geue, Ethel Hander, eds. A NEW LAND BECKONED: GERMAN MIGRATION TO TEXAS, 1844-1847. New and enlarged edition. Waco: Texian Press, 1972. 178 p. Bibliog., index.

387 Geue, Ethel Hander. NEW HOMES IN A NEW LAND; GERMAN IMMIGRATION TO TEXAS, 1847-1861. Waco: Texian Press, 1970. 166 p. Bibliog., index.

> These two monographs (386, 387) are devoted to the German contribution to the early period of Texas history. The purpose was not to produce an analytical, but a narrative or descriptive history. While an attempt is made to trace the reasons and consequences of the failure of the Verein Zum Schutze

Deutscher Einwanderer Nach Texas (Adelsverein), the thrust of the work is genealogical. The two works provide personal information on more than ten thousand settlers in the state. The names were compiled from passenger lists and other documents.

388 Roemer, Ferdinand. TEXAS; WITH PARTICULAR REFERENCE TO GERMAN IMMIGRATION AND THE PHYSICAL APPEARANCE OF THE COUNTRY; DESCRIBED THROUGH PERSONAL OBSERVATION. Translated from German by Oswald Mueller. San Antonio: Standard Printing, 1935. Reprint. Waco: Texian Press, 1967. 301 p.

The time-frame of this work is the 1850s when Roemer, a trained geologist, set out to survey parts of Texas. The work contains a thirty-four page preliminary in which the history of the German colonies in Texas, and in particular those established by the Mainzer Verein is described. The bulk of the book is the travelog in which considerable space is devoted to the description of the settlements at New Braunfels and Fredericksburg, and the daily life and adventures of their people. The story is set against the politics and colonization of the area. As an eyewitness account, Roemer's book is an important document for the study of German immigration to Texas.

389 Olmsted, Frederic Law. A JOURNEY THROUGH TEXAS: OR A SADDLE-TRIP ON THE SOUTHWESTERN FRONTIER: WITH A STATISTICAL APPENDIX. 1857. Reprint. Baker Texas History Center Series, no. 2. Austin: University of Texas Press, 1978. 516 p. Bibliog., index.

In the course of his journey through Texas, Olmsted visited and described in his diary German settlements as well. Therein lies the value of this work for the history of Germans in Texas.

390 King, Irene Marschall. JOHN O. MEUSEBACH: GERMAN COLONIZER IN TEXAS. Austin: University of Texas Press, 1967. 192 p. Bibliog., index.

John O. ·Meusebach was commissioner-general of the Verein Zum Schutze Deutscher Einwanderer (Adelsverein), the settlement company which promoted German immigration to Texas in the 1840s. This biography gives insight into the reasons behind the company's formation and the consequences of its failure. The work is divided into three sections: (1) Meusebach in Germany from 1812–45, (2) colonization from 1845–47, and (3) Meusebach's return to private life, 1847–97. The biography was written from manuscripts, correspondences, and published and unpublished archival materials found in Texas area archives. There are twenty-four portraits, photographs and facsimiles, and a map of Texas frontier settlements in 1851.

391 Dresel, Gustav. HOUSTON JOURNAL; ADVENTURES IN NORTH AMERICA AND TEXAS, 1837-1841. Translated from a German manuscript and edited by Max Freund. Austin: University of Texas Press, 1954. 168 p. Bibliog. notes, index.

> Dresel kept a personal journal when he traveled from Germany to New York, Iowa, New Orleans, Texas, Mississippi, and Alabama. He was most enthusiastic about Texas and eventually became active in the Adelsverein settlement company, which promoted German colonization of Texas. The journal did not appear in print until 1922, when it was first published in the YEARBOOK OF THE GERMAN-AMERICAN HISTORICAL SOCIETY OF ILLINOIS 1920-21 under the title, "Texanisches Tagbuch."

392 Jordan, Terry G. GERMAN SEED IN TEXAS SOIL; IMMIGRANT FARMERS IN NINETEENTH-CENTURY TEXAS. Austin: University of Texas Press, 1966. 237 p. Bibliog., index.

> Based on his doctoral dissertation, Jordan investigates in this work the evolution of agricultural methods in Texas in considerable detail, in order to determine whether the German settlers adopted local methods of farming, or vice-versa. The question was elicited by an impressive array of research techniques and instruments. There are 52 statistical tables and a 400-item bibliography complements the work.

393 Biggers, Don Hampton. GERMAN PIONEERS IN TEXAS: A BRIEF HISTORY OF THEIR HARDSHIPS, STRUGGLES, AND ACHIEVEMENTS. Fredericksburg, Tex.: Fredericksburg Publishing, 1925. 230 p.

> This study focuses on the city of Fredericksburg and Gillespie County, Texas, from 1828 to 1924. The supportive material includes vital statistics, church history, and lists of officeholders of Gillespie County. Heavy reliance was made on personal interviews in the compilation of the material.

393a Schmidt, Curt E. OMA AND OPA: GERMAN-TEXAN PIONEERS. New Braunfels, Tex.: Folkways Publishing, 1975. 129 p.

> A popularly written book on the customs and folkways of early German settlers in Texas with a section on German folksongs.

394 Justman, Dorothy E. GERMAN COLONISTS AND THEIR DESCENDANTS IN HOUSTON INCLUDING USENER AND ALLIED FAMILIES. Quanah, Tex.: Nortex Offset, 1974. 352 p. Bibliog., index.

395 Von Herff, Ferdinand. THE REGULATED EMIGRATION OF THE GERMAN PROLETARIAT WITH SPECIAL REFERENCE TO TEXAS, A TRANSLATION. Translated from German by Arthur L. Finck. San Antonio: Trinity University Press, 1978.

> Item not available for examination.

GERMANS IN THE WEST

California

396   Gudde, Erwin Gustav. GERMAN PIONEERS IN EARLY CALIFORNIA.
Concord Society Historical Bulletin, no. 6. 1927. Reprint. San Francisco: R and E Research Associates, 1970. 29 p.

> Subjects briefly discussed include: Father Kino and the Ger-
> man Jesuits; early explorers; John Sutter; gold and conquest;
> Los Angeles and San Francisco; cities and industries; and agri-
> culture and colonization.

397   Hammond, George Peter. GERMAN INTEREST IN CALIFORNIA BEFORE
1850. 1921. Reprint. San Francisco: R and E Research Associates,
1971. 85 p. Bibliog.

> Originally presented in 1921, Hammond's master's thesis dis-
> cusses early German settlement before the Gold Rush. He
> contends that the Germans were the largest ethnic element in
> that period in California. Some of the reasons for German
> migration there are also explored. A bibliography of over
> one hundred items brings together the essential literature for
> the study of the subject.

398   Paule, Dorothea Jean. THE GERMAN SETTLEMENT AT ANAHEIM. Los
Angeles: University of Southern California, 1952. Reprint. San Francisco: R and E Research Associates, 1974. 69 p. Bibliog.

Colorado

399   MacArthur, Mildred S. HISTORY OF THE GERMAN ELEMENT IN THE
STATE OF COLORADO. 1917. Reprint. San Francisco: R and E Research Associates, 1972. 51 p. Bibliog. notes.

> An introductory work giving an overview of German Americans
> in Colorado. It stresses German contribution to the develop-
> ment of the economy of the state with a discussion of their
> role in religion, education, and politics. It is the author's
> view that although the German element in Colorado is pro-
> portionally smaller than in states like Pennsylvania, Maryland,
> and Wisconsin, their influence was pervasive. The work was
> based on local archival sources, supplemented by the author's
> personal observations, correspondences, surveys, and interviews.
> The work also includes information on local German institutions
> and organizations. A list enumerates German-American office-
> holders in local government from 1864-76.

400   Hentschel, W. Reynold. THE GERMAN ELEMENT IN THE DEVELOP-
MENT OF COLORADO. Denver: the author, 1930. 24 p.

This discussion is limited to pioneers of German-American settlement in Colorado and of prominent Germans who played an
important part in the life of the state from the 1840s to World
War I.

401   Heitman, Sidney, ed. GERMANS FROM RUSSIA IN COLORADO. A
WSSA Monograph Series Study. Fort Collins, Colo.: Western Social
Science Association, 1978. 188 p. Bibliog.

The essays in this volume focus on the history, settlement,
and assimilation of the Colorado Russian-German. Sponsored
by a study project of Colorado State University, it provides
the first contribution to-Russian-German scholarship by ex-
clusively academic researchers as contrasted to earlier works
by authors from the ranks of the Russian-German community
itself. An additional feature of this work is an alphabetical
guide to the important research collection on German Russians
in the Colorado State University libraries.

402   Colorado State University, Fort Collins. Department of History. Germans
from Russia in Colorado Study Project. (Sidney Heitman, Project Coordinator).

The project was established in 1975 to carry out research,
teaching, publication, historic preservation, and public service. A variety of publications resulting from the research
program are part of the plans.

Washington

403   Wirsing, Dale R. BUILDERS, BREWERS AND BURGHERS: GERMANS OF
WASHINGTON STATE. Washington State American Revolution Bicentennial Commission Ethnic History Series. Tacoma: Washington State Historical Society, 1977. 74 p. Bibliog.

VI. HISTORY OF SPECIAL GROUPS

NATIONALITIES

Russian Germans

404 Sallet, Richard. RUSSIAN-GERMAN SETTLEMENTS IN THE UNITED
STATES. Translated by LaVern Rippley, and Armand Bauer. Fargo:
North Dakota Institute for Regional Studies, 1974. 207 p. Bibliog.,
index.

> A basic work on a subject which relatively little has been
> written about until recent times. Its information content has
> been augmented and updated by the translators. The origin
> and the intricate settlement patterns of Germans in Russian
> territories throughout the ages is thoroughly explored in the
> opening chapters. In addition to their completed regional
> distribution, Russian Germans have also been diversified by
> their religious allegiances. The book deals with many aspects
> of Russian-German immigration to the United States and the
> establishment of their communities in twenty-two states. The
> last chapter discusses their Americanization process. Demo-
> graphic statistics and an annotated bibliography are appended
> to the original work. The present edition includes three
> articles of which William C. Sherman's "Prairie Architecture
> of the Russian-German Settlers" is particularly informative.
> The value of the work is greatly enhanced by sixty-seven il-
> lustrations and a large number of maps showing Russian-German
> settlements by state.

405 Giesinger, Adam. FROM CATHERINE TO KHRUSHCHEV: THE STORY
OF RUSSIA'S GERMANS. Winnipeg, Manitoba: A. Giesinger, 1974.
443 p. Bibliog., index.

> A highly praised basic treatise which contains many references
> and a full chapter devoted to the Volga and Black Sea Ger-
> mans in the United States. There is a map showing their set-
> tlements on the North American prairie lands.

406   Koch, Fred C. THE VOLGA GERMANS: IN RUSSIA AND THE AMERI-
CAS, FROM 1763 TO THE PRESENT. University Park: Pennsylvania
State University Press, 1977. 365 p. Bibliog., index.

Two chapters of this journalistic work are devoted to the mi-
gration and settlement of Volga Germans in the United States.
A large bibliography provides further sources for research.
This work is especially useful for background information.

407   Eisenach, George John. PIETISM AND THE RUSSIAN GERMANS IN THE
UNITED STATES. Berne, Ind.: Berne Publishers, 1948. 218 p.

Swiss Germans

408   Swiss–American Historical Society. THE SWISS IN THE UNITED STATES.
A compilation prepared for the Swiss-American Society as the second
volume of its publications, by John Paul von Grueningen, editor. Madison, Wis.: Swiss-American Historical Society, 1940. Reprint. San
Francisco: R and E Research Associates, 1970. 153 p. Index.

A basic source for the immigration history of the Swiss with
an abundance of statistical and genealogical data. The Swiss
element in the population is surveyed by state and there are
also lists of settlers and organizations for cities with sizeable
Swiss populations. The bulk of the work is devoted to the
German-Swiss. A short chapter deals with the Italian-Swiss
colony in California. New York and New Jersey are given
extensive treatment.

408a   Meier, Heinz K. THE SWISS AMERICAN HISTORICAL SOCIETY 1927–
1977. Preface by Raymond A. Probst. Norfolk, Va.: Donning Company
Publishers, 1977. 82 p. Bibliog. notes.

The story of the society is told here in five chapters, tracing
the most important events and highlighting the personalities
who kept the organization alive over the years. The work
yields a considerable amount of biographical information on
contemporary American scholars of Swiss origin who were active
in the society and in Swiss American social and cultural life.
It is full of interesting details regarding the genesis of the
publications which the society sponsored and disseminated.
The bibliographic notes identify periodicals which are little
known outside the Swiss-American community. Appendix A
contains the society's consitution and bylaws and appendix B
gives the roster of officers.

408b   NEW SWITZERLAND IN ILLINOIS, AS DESCRIBED BY TWO EARLY
SWISS SETTLERS, KASPAR KOEPFLI AND JOHANN JACOB EGGEN
IN SPIEGEL VON AMERIKA UND AUFZEICHNUNGEN AUS HIGHLANDS
GRUENDUNGSZEIT. Translated from the German by Jennie Latzer Kae-

ser and Manfred Hartwin Driesner. Edited and annotated by Raymond Juergen Spahn and Betty Alderton Spahn. Foreword by John Cushman Abbott. Edwardsville: Friends of Lovejoy Library, Southern Illinois University at Edwardsville, 1977. 210 p. Bibliog.

> The chronological scope of this item is the period 1783-1848. This is a basic work on the history of settlement of Illinois by Swiss Germans.

408c THE SWISS-GERMANS IN SOUTH DAKOTA: FROM VOLHYNIA TO DAKOTA TERRITORY, 1874-1974. Freeman, S.Dak.: Published in conjunction with the Swiss-German Centennial Celebration, Pine Hill Press, 1974. 220 p.

> Item not available for examination.

408d Institute of Texan Cultures. THE SWISS TEXANS. San Antonio: Institute of Texan Cultures of the University of Texas at San Antonio, 1977. 23 p. Bibliog.

> Item not available for examination.

408e Schelbert, Leo, ed. NEW GLARUS 1845-1970. THE MAKING OF A SWISS AMERICAN TOWN. Glarus: Komm. Tschudi, 1970. 239 p.

> Item not available for examination.

RELIGIOUS GROUPS

General Bibliography

409 Burr, Nelson R., ed. A CRITICAL BIBLIOGRAPHY OF RELIGION IN AMERICA. 2 vols. In collaboration with editors, James Ward Smith, and A. Leland Jamison. Vol. 4 of RELIGION IN AMERICAN LIFE. Princeton Studies in American Civilization, no. 5. Princeton, N.J.: Princeton University Press, 1961. Index.

> In the panoramic survey of the evolution of American religion, the German religious sects receive substantial treatment. Major relevant works published up to 1960 are discussed in sections devoted to German Pietism, Moravians, Baptists, Mennonites, Brethren, and others.

Religious Life—General Works

410 Bittinger, Lucy Forney. GERMAN RELIGIOUS LIFE IN COLONIAL TIMES. Philadelphia: J.B. Lippincott, 1906. 145 p. Bibliog., index.

> Encompasses main-line religions, as well as sects, whose religious practices are discussed against the backdrop of religious

conditions in Germany. Heavy use was made of secondary sources. A bibliographic essay is provided at the end of each chapter. A companion volume to the author's THE GERMANS IN COLONIAL TIMES (see 224).

411 Sachse, Julius Friedrich. THE GERMAN PIETISTS OF PROVINCIAL PENNSYLVANIA, 1694-1708. 1895. Reprint: New York: AMS Press, 1970. 504 p. Bibliog., index.

An attempt at a comprehensive treatment of the subject. The author contends that the Pietists were historically significant, for they broke ground in Pennsylvania for the later religious and utopian movements. The work was based on primary resources some of which are reproduced in the text. The table of contents reflects the range of the subject matter discussed: Part 1: Woman in the Wilderness; exodus; voyage; arrival in Pennsylvania; Pietists in Germany and the New World; Woman in the Wilderness and Koester's rival community of Brethren; the divining rod, horoscope, and superstitions; mystics; the decline. Part 2: (Hermits on the Wissahickon) Magister Johannes Kelpius, Heinrich Bernard Koester, Daniel Falckner, Johann Gottfried Seelig, Dominie Justus Falckner, Conrad Matthaei, Dr. Christopher Witt; the romance of Spook Hill. Appendix: Benjamin Furly, Magister Johann Jacob Zimmerman, Dominie Andreas Rudmann. The volume is enriched by 240 items of illustrations.

412 Stoeffler, E. Ernest. MYSTICISM IN THE GERMAN DEVOTIONAL LITERATURE OF COLONIAL PENNSYLVANIA. Pennsylvania German Folklore Society Yearbook, vol. 14, 1949. Allentown: Pennsylvania German Folklore Society, 1950. 173 p. Bibliog.

The author contends that this type of literature was read intensely by German settlers. The discussion centers on Christian mysticism in sixteenth and seventeenth century Europe, and the influence of mysticism on the religious thought and daily living of the Moravians and the German Baptist Brethren (Ephrata). Mysticism, in the works of Arndt and Tersteegen and among other groups, is highlighted. The work is supported by primary resources referred to in the footnotes. In addition to a 120-item bibliography of secondary works, there is a list of devotional books analyzed with location symbols. Many of them are followed by comments about the books and their readers.

Amish

BIBLIOGRAPHY

413 Yoder, Don. "What to Read on the Amish." PENNSYLVANIA FOLKLIFE 18 (Summer 1969): 14-19.

A bibliographic essay discussing the best books and articles on the Amish for the general reader. The titles are organized under such subjects as religion, politics, language patterns, community and family, folk music, the Amish in fiction and theatre, art, pow-wow and braucherai, and journalistic writings in mass circulation magazines.

414 Hostetler, John Andrew. ANNOTATED BIBLIOGRAPHY ON THE AMISH; AN ANNOTATED BIBLIOGRAPHY OF SOURCE MATERIALS PERTAINING TO THE OLD ORDER AMISH MENNONITES. Scottdale, Pa.: Mennonite Publishing House, 1951. 100 p. Index.

Comprising more than four hundred entries, the list concentrates on the Old Order Amish. The chronological span of the writings inventoried here ranges from 1693 to 1950. All types of materials are listed. The entries are described fully with short, evaluative annotations. A map is added to the work showing Old Order congregations by state. (Updated by 320).

GENERAL WORKS

415 Hostetler, John Andrew. AMISH SOCIETY. Rev. ed. Baltimore: Johns Hopkins Press, 1968. 369 p. Bibliog., index.

A thoroughgoing inquiry into all aspects of this closed community with special emphasis on the tensions, both on the group and individual plane, caused by the pressures of the changing environment. The work is based on meticulous research and personal familiarity with Amish society. The author's family was expelled from the community during his childhood. The massive documentary evidence prompts the author in the last chapter to speculate about the future of Amish society. The attached documentary material includes statistics, photographs, maps, and a bibliography which concentrates on works dealing with change in Amish life.

416 _____. AMISH LIFE. Scottdale, Pa.: Herald Press, 1952. 39 p. Bibliog.

An easy-to-read essay on the religious and social organization of the Old Order Amish with many illustrations. A map shows the locations of their congregations east of the Mississippi. A brief annotated bibliography of popular works on the subject is included.

417 Newswanger, Christian, and Newswanger, Kiehl. AMISHLAND. New York: Hastings House, 1954. 128 p.

Inspired by personal observation, the authors intended to bear witness to "outer evidences of their [the Amish] grim determination to preserve intact a culture which was already

time-tested when they transplanted it from Germany to America
more than 200 years ago" (p. 9). The focus is on the daily
existence. The work is illustrated with pencil sketches.

418   Zielinski, John. THE AMISH: PIONEER HERITAGE. Des Moines:
      Wallace-Homestead, 1975. 174 p.

419   MEDICAL GENETIC STUDIES OF THE AMISH: SELECTED PAPERS. As-
      sembled, with commentary by Victor A. McKusick. Baltimore: Johns
      Hopkins University Press, 1978. 525 p. Bibliog., index.

REGIONAL STUDIES

420   Christner, Levi D. OLD ORDER AMISH CHURCH DISTRICTS OF INDI-
      ANA. LaGrange, Ind.: Wadell Print, [1949]. 24 p.

      This collection of maps of eight Amish Mennonite settlements
      in Indiana shows county boundaries, church district lines,
      roads, and bus and train routes. While the quality of the
      maps leaves something to be desired, the list of ministers by
      church district is a useful feature.

421   Schwieder, Elmer, and Schwieder, Dorothy. A PECULIAR PEOPLE: IO-
      WA'S OLD ORDER AMISH. Ames: Iowa State University Press, 1975.
      188 p. Bibliog., index.

      Produced by means of contemporary sociological methodology,
      the authors' intention was to provide an objective contempor-
      ary view of one of Iowa's significant minorities. The empha-
      sis is on the response of the Old Order Amish in Iowa to mod-
      ern development. The Amish v. Iowa School Board controversy
      is highlighted. Eighty personal interviews were conducted in
      the communities studied. The writers made heavy use of pri-
      mary and secondary materials. Maps and photographs accom-
      pany the text. One of the appendices contains the 1967 state
      statute entitled, "An Act Relating to the Compulsory School
      Attendance and Educational Standards," which provides exemp-
      tion from compulsory school attendance in Iowa. The bibliog-
      raphy includes books, articles, newspapers, unpublished works,
      and legal documents.

422   Wick, Barthinius Larson. THE AMISH MENNONITES; A SKETCH OF
      THEIR ORIGIN, AND OF THEIR SETTLEMENT IN IOWA, WITH THEIR
      CREED IN AN APPENDIX. Iowa City: State Historical Society of Iowa,
      1894. 60 p. Bibliog. notes.

      A concise comparative study of the Iowa Amish and Amana
      societies treated in a broad historical framework. The work
      was based on primary resources.

423   Schreiber, William Ildephonse. OUR AMISH NEIGHBORS. Chicago: University of Chicago Press, 1962. 226 p. Bibliog., index.

> A well documented study of the Amish of east central Ohio. The daily life and folkways are described in detail, and religious practices, community affairs, and social interaction are presented as they are revealed in the community newspaper, the Sugarcreek BUDGET. Much of the documentation is in the German language. There is a 150-item bibliography in the book. Drawings by Sybil Gould.

424   Bachman, Calvin George. THE OLD ORDER AMISH OF LANCASTER COUNTY. Pennsylvania German Society Proceedings and Addresses, vol. 49. 1941. Norristown: Pennsylvania German Society, 1942. Reprint. Pennsylvania German Society Publications, vol. 60. Lancaster, Pa.: Franklin and Marshall College, 1961. 297 p. Bibliog. notes, index.

> An ethnographic study of the Old Order Amish of Lancaster, Pennsylvania, made by the author while pastor at the Reformed Church in a neighboring area. The observation focused on the effects of encroaching technology on Amish life. It has been praised for its accuracy and sympathetic approach. Illustrations by Charles S. Rice.

425   Aurand, Ammon Monroe. LITTLE KNOWN FACTS ABOUT THE AMISH AND THE MENNONITES: A STUDY OF THE SOCIAL CUSTOMS AND HABITS OF PENNSYLVANIA'S "PLAIN PEOPLE." Harrisburg, Pa.: Aurand Press, 1938. 32 p.

> Personal glimpses presented in a slightly patronizing tone on such aspects of Amish folkways as dress, hair, religion and meeting houses, farms, holidays, marriage customs, funerals, superstitions, bundling, dialect, and others.

426   Smith, Elmer Lewis. THE AMISH PEOPLE: SEVENTEENTH-CENTURY TRADITION IN MODERN AMERICA; A COMPLETE ILLUSTRATED STORY OF THE "OLD ORDER" SECT OF SOUTHEASTERN PENNSYLVANIA. New York: Exposition Press, 1958. 258 p. Bibliog. notes.

> A sociological approach to the study of the Amish in the southeastern part of Pennsylvania. Findings of previous sociological writings on the subject were integrated into this work. The treatment is diagnostic, ending with a speculation on the future of the Amish. The book includes many photographs by Melvin J. Horst.

PICTORIAL WORKS

427   Warner, James A., and Denlinger, Donald M. THE GENTLE PEOPLE; A PORTRAIT OF THE AMISH. Soudersburg, Pa.: Mill Bridge Museum in cooperation with Grossman, New York, 1969. 185 p.

A beautifully executed photographic essay, mostly in color, showing scenes from Amish life and customs.

428 Tortora, Vincent R. THE AMISH FOLK OF PENNSYLVANIA DUTCH COUNTRY. Lancaster, Pa.: Photo Arts Press, 1958. 30 p.

A collection of 150 candid photographs on a wide variety of subjects.

429 Rice, Charles Scott, and Steinmetz, Rollin C. THE AMISH YEAR. New Brunswick, N.J.: Rutgers University Press, 1956. 224 p.

A pictorial chronicle documenting by month the life and pursuits of the Amish in Lancaster, Pennsylvania, during a typical year. The photographs are candid, and the subjects covered include an auction, dress and clothes shopping, farming processes, a funeral, buggies and their makers, a barn raising, Sabbath day, tobacco farming, an Amish rodeo, a young people's barn dance, a wedding, schooling, and holidays.

430 Rice, Charles Scott, and Shenk, John B. MEET THE AMISH: A PICTORIAL STUDY OF THE AMISH PEOPLE. New Brunswick, N.J.: Rutgers University Press, 1947. 96 p.

An assemblage of about two hundred black and white photographs conveying the sense of dignity of every facet of Amish life. Each picture is captioned.

FICTION

431 Yoder, Joseph Warren. ROSANNA OF THE AMISH. Huntingdon, Pa.: Yoder Publishing, 1940. Reprint. Scottdale, Pa.: Herald Press, 1974. 394 p.

A close-up view of Amish life-style through fictionalized biography of the author's mother who was raised in an Amish household. The time is the late nineteenth and early twentieth century. Illustrated by George Daubenspeck. A sequel was also written by Yoder, entitled, ROSANNA'S BOYS (Huntingdon, Pa.: Yoder Publishing, 1948).

Catholics

432 Schrott, Lambert. PIONEER GERMAN CATHOLICS IN THE AMERICAN COLONIES 1734-1784. United States Catholic Historical Society. Monograph Series, VIII. New York: Catholic Historical Society, 1933. 139 p. Bibliog.

A basic work originally prepared as a master's thesis at Catholic University of America which explores the early contacts of

German Catholics in North America, the reason of their emigration in the colonies, and in Louisiana. It focuses on pioneer German priests, the education of colonial German Catholics, and the German Catholic laity up to 1784. A list of German priests and the time they served in America, several biographies, and a 200-item classified bibliography complement the work.

433 Rothan, Emmet Herman. THE GERMAN CATHOLIC IMMIGRANT IN THE UNITED STATES (1830-1860). Washington, D.C.: Catholic University of America, 1946. 172 p. Bibliog., index.

Originally a doctoral dissertation, this work continues the study of German-Catholic immigration and the role of the Catholic Church among the immigrants in the various regions of the United States. The thematic scope extends to: (1) German immigration 1830-60; (2) German-Catholic immigrants in the East; (3) German-Catholic immigrants in the Midwest; (4) settlers in the Northwest and the Southwest; (5) apostolic immigrants from Germany; (6) life in the land of adoption; (7) German-Catholic schools; and (8) German Catholics and rural communities. The work is meticulously documented and includes a 160-item classified bibliography.

434 Barry, Colman J. THE CATHOLIC CHURCH AND GERMAN-AMERICANS. Catholic University of America. Studies in American Church History, vol. 40. Milwaukee: Bruce Publishing, 1953. 348 p. Bibliog., index.

An important contribution to the history of the Catholic Church in America, with reference to German Americans. It focuses on the nineteenth century, which was the period of great adjustments in the life of the Church. The central theme of the work was the conflict between the tendency of the German Catholic Church to retain its distinct identity, and the forces which aimed at integrating it into the main body of American Catholicism. The major themes discussed are: (1) background and beginnings 1800-84, (2) the German triangle of the West (St. Louis, Cincinnati, Milwaukee), (3) union and disunion, (4) the Cahenslyism turmoil of 1891, (5) Liberals v. Conservatives, and (6) unity. The role of the St. Raphael Society is highlighted. The work has some important supportive material in the appendix. An essay on the archival and manuscript sources, some reports and letters, several portraits of contemporary Church leaders, and immigration statistics should be mentioned among the addenda.

435 Gleason, Philip. THE CONSERVATIVE REFORMERS: GERMAN-AMERICAN CATHOLICS AND THE SOCIAL ORDER. Notre Dame, Ind.: University of Notre Dame Press, 1968. 272 p. Bibliog., index.

The Americanization of the German-American Catholic Church

is at the core of this scholarly exploration. The author's contention is that this process was shaped by the German Catholic Church's distinctive heritage, and by various historical contingencies and particularly by the problem of how the interest in social reform was related to the process of Americanization. The complex subject matter is discussed under the following chapter headings: (1) "Nineteenth Century Backgrounds," (2) "Crises and Reorganization," (3) "Social Reform Questions," (4) "New Leadership and the Creation of the Central Bureau," (5) "Social Reform Program in Action," (6) "Problems with Non-German Catholics and Non-Catholic Germans and Other Loyalties in Crises, 1908-1917," (7) "Alienated Reformers of the 1920s," and (8) "German American Catholics and Americanization." The work is well documented and the bibliographic essay appraises the archival and published literary sources consulted.

436   Fecher, Vincent J. A STUDY OF THE MOVEMENT FOR GERMAN NATIONAL PARISHES IN PHILADELPHIA AND BALTIMORE, 1787-1802. Analecta Gregoriana, vol. 77. Series Facultatis Historiae Ecclesiasticae, Sectio B, no. 11. Romae: Apud Aedes Universitatis Gregorianae, 1955. 283 p. Bibliog., index.

This work inquires into the inherent ethnocentric tendencies of early German Catholics through a case study involving the parishes of two major eastern cities. The author presents the documentary evidence of both sides: the German, as well as that of the Bishop. Much of the material was drawn from official records.

437   Dolan, Jay P. THE IMMIGRANT CHURCH; NEW YORK'S IRISH AND GERMAN CATHOLICS, 1815-1865. Foreword by Martin E. Marty. Baltimore: John Hopkins University Press, 1975. 212 p. Bibliog. notes, index.

A well-documented study in comparative social history.

German Baptist Brethren

438   Brumbaugh, Martin Grove. A HISTORY OF THE GERMAN BAPTIST BRETHREN IN EUROPE AND AMERICA. 2d ed. Elgin, Ill.: Brethren Publishing House, 1899. 559 p. Bibliog. notes.

For annotation, see 439.

439   Brumbaugh, Martin Grovek. A HISTORY OF THE GERMAN BAPTIST BRETHREN IN EUROPE AND AMERICA: INDEX. Knightstown, Ind.: Bookmark, 1977. 28 p.

Despite the years that have elapsed since its publication, this work (438) is still considered a classic treatise. The chronological scope covers the period between 1700 and 1850, and the discussion extends to the European as well as the American phase of the life of this distinct religious group which has stood apart from the other separatist denominations. The topical scope encompasses: (1) influences dominating Germany at the opening of the eighteenth century; (2) the Pietistic pathfinders; (3) mother congregation in Germany; (4) branches; (5) list of the members who joined the church in Europe; (6) the leaders in Germany; (7) Germantown, Pennsylvania, congregation; (8) leaders in colonial America; (9) colonial congregations, listed and described; (10) the two Christopher Sowers; (11) Ephrata's relation to the German Baptist Brethren; (12) early history of the annual meeting; and (13) doctrine and growth of the church. Because of the careful reporting of the people involved in the movement, the work provides valuable genealogical information. Much primary documentation was used in preparing the manuscript, but the description lacks bibliographic detail. Seventy-seven illustrations grace the text. An index (439) to the work was issued in 1977.

440 Falkenstein, George N. "The German Baptist Brethren or Dunkers." In PENNSYLVANIA GERMAN SOCIETY PROCEEDINGS AND ADDRESSES 10 (1900): 1-48. Lancaster: Pennsylvania German Society, 1900.

Item not available for examination.

441 Gillin, John Lewis. THE DUNKERS; A SOCIOLOGICAL INTERPRETATION. 1906. Reprint. New York: AMS Press, 1974. 238 p. Bibliog.

Traces the history and evolution from fifteenth-century Europe and the destiny of the group in the United States until 1905. Initially, their settlements concentrated along the standard routes to the West. Special emphasis is laid on Beissel's influence on the church. A bibliography of about seventy items is included.

Hutterites

442 Gross, Paul S. THE HUTTERITE WAY; THE INSIDE STORY OF THE LIFE, CUSTOMS, RELIGION, AND TRADITIONS OF THE HUTTERITES. Saskatoon, Saskatchewan: Freeman Publishing, 1965. 219 p. Bibliog.

An insider's account of the history, destiny, life, and customs of the Hutterites. The author traces the Hutterites' story from their European beginning, their arrival to North America, to the present day. The work is profusely illustrated, and a forty-four item bibliography of basic readings is included. Jacob Hutter's last epistle to his followers in Moravia in 1535 is given in the appendix.

443   Hostetler, John Andrew. HUTTERITE SOCIETY. Baltimore: Johns Hop-
       kins University Press, 1974. 403 p. Bibliog., index.

         Originated as research project number 1683 and funded by
         the U.S. Office of Education, this work has emerged as the
         definitive study of the Hutterites to date. It offers a broad
         historical view of the cultural, social, and economic organi-
         zation of the Hutterite communities with the view to eliciting
         the mechanisms of their survival. Research in records and
         literary sources are coupled with observations of the commu-
         nities themselves in the preparation of this study. A battery
         of sixteen appendices is added to the main body of the work.
         The additional material deals with: (1) Hutterite historiography;
         (2) chronology of Hutterite history 1525-1974; (3) Hutterite
         place names in Eastern Europe by language and country; (4)
         Hutterite school discipline, 1568; (5) table rules; (6) rites of
         passage from childhood to adulthood; (7) baptismal vows; (8)
         engagement and marriage vows; (9) ordination vows; (10) agree-
         ment of a divisional school board and a colony, Alberta; (11)
         holidays; (12) liturgical calendar; (13) colony menu for one
         week; (14) last words of Michael Waldner, 1823-89; (15) list
         of Hutterite colonies in North America (with year of founding,
         locale, parent colony); and (16) branching of Hutterite colo-
         nies in North America, 1874-1974. The work also includes
         photographs of the people and their buildings, questionnaire
         information in tabular form, and a map of the Hutterite colo-
         nies in North America. The bibliography of about 350 items
         is comprised of books, articles, conferences, theses, and other
         printed sources.

444   Hostetler, John Andrew, and Huntington, Gertrude Enders. THE HUTTE-
       RITES IN NORTH AMERICA. Case Studies in Cultural Anthropology.
       New York: Holt, Rhinehart and Winston, 1967. 119 p. Bibliog.

         A sociocultural study based on on-site observation and numer-
         ous interviews in more than 110 North American Hutterite co-
         lonies. The focus of the inquiry was to identify and analyze
         the forces which contributed to the survival of Hutterites as
         distinct groups. The authors present the Hutterite view of the
         world, the characteristics of the colony such as spatial allot-
         ments, weekly schedules, male-female roles, the church, work
         habits, property, the economics of the colony, socialization
         patterns, the impact of the English-language school, and the
         coping with disruptive events such as war, failure of leader-
         ship, and desertion of members. A bibliography of forty-two
         items is included.

445   Deets, Lee Emerson. THE HUTTERITES; A STUDY IN SOCIAL COHESION:
       WITH A NEW EPILOG BY THE AUTHOR AND AN APPENDIX, THE ORI-
       GINS OF CONFLICT IN THE HUTTERISCHE COMMUNITIES. American
       Utopian Adventure, series two. Philadelphia: Porcupine Press, 1975.
       87 p. Bibliog. notes.

A case study, originally written in 1939 and updated in 1974, constitutes the bulk of this work, which is expanded by the author's article "Origins of Conflict in the Hutterische Communities," published in the PUBLICATIONS OF THE SOCIOLOGICAL SOCIETY OF AMERICA, 25 (May 1931). The site of the study was the Hutterite community in Old Bon Homme, South Dakota.

446 Peters, Victor. ALL THINGS COMMON: THE HUTTERIAN WAY OF LIFE. Minneapolis: University of Minnesota Press, 1965. 233 p. Bibliog. notes, index.

While the focus of this inquiry is the Hutterites' colonies in Manitoba, the author has devoted considerable attention to American Hutterites in the Dakotas, Montana, and Minnesota as well. Their evolution from the 1870s to the present is described and analyzed. Material from primary and secondary sources is complemented by participation, observation, and personal interviews. The appendices greatly expand the information yielding value of this work; they include the reminiscences of a Hutterite girl in one of the "Bruederhofe," a copy of the constitution of the Hutterite Church, a list of Hutterite colonies founded between 1864 and 1964, and a map of Hutterite colonies as of 1965.

Jews

447 Glanz, Rudolf. STUDIES IN JUDAICA AMERICANA. Foreword by Jacob R. Marcus. New York: KTAV Publishing House, 1970. 407 p. Bibliog. notes.

This is a major contribution, consisting of a collection of essays on a broad range of topics affirming the significant role German Jews played in America. The emphasis is not so much on the achievement of a few successful individuals, but rather on the contributions of the common man. The essays are well documented throughout, but have no bibliography.

The individual essays are: (1) "Source Material on the History of Jewish Immigration to the United States, 1800-1880," (2) "The Immigration of German Jews up to 1880," (3) "Notes on Early Jewish Peddling in America," (4) "German Jews in New York City in the 19th Century," (5) "The History of the Jewish Community in New York," (6) "The Rise of the Jewish Club in America," (7) "The 'Bayer' and the 'Pollack' in America," (8) "Jews in Relation to the Cultural Milieu of the Germans in America up to the Eighteen Eighties," (9) "Jews in Early German-American Literature," (10) "German-Jewish Names in America," (11) "Jewish Names in Early American Humor," (12) "Jews and Chinese in America," (13) "Jew and Yankee: A Historic Comparison," (14) "The Rothschild Legend in Ameri-

ca," and (15) "Jewish Social Conditions as seen by the Muck-
rackers."

448   Hirschler, Eric E., ed. JEWS FROM GERMANY IN THE UNITED
STATES. New York: Farrar, Straus, and Cudahy, 1955. 182 p. Bibliog.

This collection of essays includes: (1) S. Stern-Tauebler,
"Problems of American Jewish and German Jewish Historiog-
raphy," (2) E. Hirshler, "Jews from Germany in the United
States," (3) B. Winryb, "German Jewish Immigrants to America, a Critical Evaluation," (4) A. Kober, "Aspects of the Influence of Jews from Germany on American Jewish Spiritual
Life of the Nineteenth Century," and (5) A. Friedlander,
"Cultural Contributions of the German Jew in America." Bibliography is provided for some of the essays. The appendix
includes a tentative list of rabbis and scholars who came to
America in earlier days. There is no index.

449   Kisch, Guido. "German Jews in White Labor Servitude in America."
PUBLICATIONS OF THE AMERICAN JEWISH HISTORICAL SOCIETY 34
(1937): 11-49. New York: American Jewish Historical Society, 1937.
Bibliog.

This work intends to shed light on German Jews as indentured
servants based on the interpretation of evidence provided by
letters of German-Jewish travelers, as well as the victims
themselves. Eight such letters are reprinted. The work is
abundantly footnoted, and includes a bibliography.

450   JEWISH IMMIGRANTS OF THE NAZI PERIOD IN THE U.S.A. 6 vols.
Boston: K.G. Saur Publishing, 1978. Bibliog.

"This series presents an in-depth history of the Jewish refugee
community. The documents and analysis presented detail the
social, political, economic history of the individual immigrant
organizations and their leaders. The broad coverage of various topics and the unusual source base which includes primary
sources, materials and interviews with immigrants will open up
new vistas for study of a group that has made a significant
and discernible impact on 20th century American society.

The first volumes include archival resources including holdings
in private and public repositories throughout the USA and an
annotated bibliography listing 1,600 books, articles and unpublished papers dealing with the Jewish immigrant between
1933 and 1945. Listings are grouped by topics such as: national and international politics of immigration, the image of
the USA in newspapers and specialized literature, and demographic and political aspects of resettlement. Succeeding
volumes list documents of a general nature as well as specific
'case studies' and recollections of a number of leading per-

sonalities. The final volumes present the immigrant community in the larger context with emphasis being placed on its unique character as well as on the social, intellectual and religious qualities of the immigrant." (publisher's announcement).

Lutherans

451 Bodensieck, Julius, ed. THE ENCYCLOPEDIA OF THE LUTHERAN CHURCH. 3 vols. Edited for the Lutheran World Federation. Minneapolis: Augsburg Publishing, 1965. Bibliog.

This first-rate reference work is a gold mine of information on the historical, organizational, and doctrinal aspects of the German Lutheran Church in America.

452 Wentz, Abdel Ross. A BASIC HISTORY OF LUTHERANISM IN AMERICA. Rev. ed. Philadelphia: Fortress Press, 1964. 439 p. Bibliog., index.

This is an updated and expanded version of the author's 1923 book, THE LUTHERAN CHURCH IN AMERICAN HISTORY (Philadelphia: United Lutheran Publication House, 1923). It surveys and interprets the evolution of the Lutheran Church in the broader framework of American history relating events in the life of the Church to the main trends in American society. The organization of the material is reflected in the chapter headings: (1) "Colonial Times (1625-1740)," (2) "Birth of the Nation (1740-1790)," (3) "Youth of the Republic (1790-1830)," (4) "Internal Discord (1830-1870)," (5) "Big Business Days (1870-1910)," (6) "In an Age of Larger Units (1910-1950)," and (7) "In an Age of Pluralism and Ecumenism (1950-1964)." The whole narrative is permeated with references to German-American history, particularly in the sections dealing with the Church in Pennsylvania, Maryland, Georgia, and in the general discussion of the Westward movement. The role of H.M. Muhlenberg is highlighted. The bibliography is especially valuable as it offers many leads to materials of interest for German-American research.

453 Schneider, Carl Edward. THE GERMAN CHURCH ON THE AMERICAN FRONTIER; A STUDY OF THE RISE OF RELIGION AMONG THE GERMANS OF THE WEST, BASED ON THE HISTORY OF THE EVANGELISCHER KIRCHENVEREIN IN DES WESTENS (EVANGELICAL CHURCH SOCIETY OF THE WEST) 1840-1866. St. Louis: Eden Publishing House, 1939. 579 p. Bibliog., index.

A comprehensive treatment of the subject appraising the reciprocal influence of the frontier on German settlers on the one hand, and the impact of the Germans on the molding of the frontier on the other. A contention is made that the German church played an important role in this process. The time

span covered extends from 1800-60, and the frontier comprised Missouri, Iowa, Minnesota, Illinois, Indiana, Ohio,
and Wisconsin. The author integrated into the narrative a
vast amount of topics, organized in the following chapters:
(1) "The German and American background," (2) "Religious
Origins Among the Germans in the West," (3) "Founding of
the Kirchenverein in des Westens," (4) "Pioneer Pastors of
the First Decade (1840-1850)," (5) "Pioneer Churches of the
First Decade (1840-1850)," (6) "Pastoral Labors on the Frontier," (7) "Frontier Churches and Their Organization," (8)
"Public Worship and Preaching," (9) "Educational Projects,"
(10) "Social Challenges of the Frontier," (11) "Interchurch
Relations," (12) "Theological Consciousness," (13) "Growth
and Expansion of the Church," (14) "Americanization of the
German Church." The following significant documents are an-
nexed to the main body of the work: I. "Missionary Report
of Ezra Keller"; II. "Constitution of Cincinnati German
Church" (excerpt); III. "Roster of Kirchenverein Pastors"; IV.
"Missionary aid to German Churches"; V. "Rubrics of Kirken-
verein Agende of 1857"; VI. "Preface to the Kirchenverein
Hymnal of 1862"; VII. "Roster of Marthasville Students";
VIII. "Financial Contributions Acknowledged in the FRIEDENS-
BOTE, 1850-1866"; IX. "Address of Peter G. Wall at the
Home Mission Congress of the German Evangelical Church,
Bremen, 1852"; X. "Churches Served by Kirchenverein Pas-
tors, 1840-1866"; XI. "Churches Affiliated with the Kirchenverein." Further supportive materials include: a bibliography
of 400 items of both primary and secondary materials; illustrations of churches, pastors, and facsimiles of documents; maps
showing distributions of Germans according to the 1860 census;
and a foldout map of Kirchenverein churches in the United
States between 1840-66.

454   Bernheim, Gotthardt Dellmann. HISTORY OF THE GERMAN SETTLE-
MENTS AND OF THE LUTHERAN CHURCH IN NORTH AND SOUTH
CAROLINA, FROM THE EARLIEST PERIOD OF THE COLONIZATION OF
THE DUTCH, GERMAN, AND SWISS SETTLERS TO THE CLOSE OF THE
FIRST HALF OF THE PRESENT CENTURY. 1872. Reprint. Spartanburg,
S.C.: Reprint Co., 1972. 557 p. Bibliog. notes.

Covers an important segment in German-American history and
in the history of the Lutheran Church based primarily on German-language records. Its scope encompasses the following
topics: (1) early colonization and settlements; (2) revolutionary
war period; (3) 1783-1803: Synod of North Carolina organized;
(4) formation of the first General Synod, to 1820; (5) to 1833,
with organization of the Tennessee Synod and the Theological
Seminary at Lexington, South Carolina; and (6) to 1850. All
chapters include discussions of histories of local congregations
and their leaders. The work lacks footnotes and a bibliography,
but there are documentary references in the text.

454a Vehse, Eduard. THE STEPHANITE MIGRATION TO AMERICA; WITH
DOCUMENTATION. Translated by Rudolph Fiehler. Tucson: M.R.
Winkler, 1975. 136 p.

Written by a Luthern layman, the former curator of the Saxon
State Archives, after spending barely a year in America in
1839, this work is considered an important contribution to
the history of American Lutheranism. The author chronicles
the internal ecclesiastical events of the German Lutheran
Church in Missouri. The text is translated from DIE STEPHAN'-
SCHE AUSWANDERUNG NACH AMERIKA and is keyed to the
German original.

454b Meyer, Carl Stamm, ed. MOVING FRONTIERS; READINGS IN THE
HISTORY OF THE LUTHERAN CHURCH--MISSOURI SYNOD. St. Louis:
Concordia Publishing House, 1964. 500 p. Bibliog.

The author brings together here essays and articles by various
writers which have appeared elsewhere. Together, these articles provide a panorama of the ecclesiastical and theological
evolution of the Missouri Synod over the past hundred years.

454c "Lutheran Church in America." THE ENCYCLOPEDIA OF THE LUTHERAN
CHURCH. Vol. 2. Minneapolis: Augsburg Publishing House, 1965.

Under the above title a 48-page entry is devoted to the discussion of the subject. The entry consists of a cluster of
authoritative signed articles on the background and evolution
of the Lutheran Church in America, giving separate treatment
to each national group and each component synod. The Missouri Synod which was organized as Die Deutsche Evangelisch-
Lutherische Synode von Missouri, Ohio und anderen Staaten is
discussed in considerable length, followed by a bibliography
of the most relevant works.

Mennonites

BIBLIOGRAPHY

455 Springer, Nelson P., and Klassen, A.J., comps. MENNONITE BIBLIOG-
RAPHY, 1631-1961. 2 vols. Scottdale, Pa.: Herald Press, 1977.
531 p.; 634 p. Index.

A comprehensive work in two volumes: volume one covers
the world outside of North America, and volume two is devoted to North America. It also includes an elaborate subject
index extending to over one hundred pages. In all, over
28,000 items of every kind are inventoried here. The work involved fifteen years of intermittent labor and is intended as
a continuation to Hans J. Hillerbrand, A BIBLIOGRAPHY OF
ANABAPTISM, 1520-1630 (Elkhart, Ind.: Institute of Men-

nonite Studies, 1962) and A BIBLIOGRAPHY OF ANABAPTISM, A SEQUEL, 1962-1974 (St. Louis: Center for Reformation Research, 1975). The material is organized into four sections: (1) periodicals; (2) history and descriptive works; (3) doctrine; and (4) miscellanea. For many periodicals, location is indicated.

456   Bender, Harold Stauffer. TWO CENTURIES OF AMERICAN MENNONITE LITERATURE: A BIBLIOGRAPHY OF MENNONITICA AMERICANA 1727-1928. Studies in Anabaptist and Mennonite History, vol. 1. Goshen, Ind.: Mennonite Historical Society, 1929. 181 p. Index.

Includes both religious and secular publications in the form of books, pamphlets, and periodicals produced in North America. The list was intended to be complete up to 1800 and representative after 1800. The presentation of the material is alphabetical by chronological periods. Many entries have brief annotations. Library locations for out-of-print titles are given, and reprints are listed whenever relevant. The appendix provides bibliographic information on a variety of related contributions, for example, works by Mennonite missionaries in Cheyenne and Hopi languages.

ENCYCLOPEDIA

457   THE MENNONITE ENCYCLOPEDIA: A COMPREHENSIVE REFERENCE WORK ON THE ANABAPTIST--MENNONITE MOVEMENT. 4 vols. Hillsboro, Kan.: Mennonite Brethren Publishing House, 1955-59. Bibliog.

A compendium of signed articles comprehensively treating all aspects of the Anabaptist movement on an international scale from the beginning to the present. Its major focus is history, theology, doctrines, ethics, and customs, but biographical material is limited to martyrs and the most prominent figures of the movement. The articles are complemented by bibliographies of works consulted. Illustrations are gathered at the end of each volume. There is a separate index to the illustrations in each physical unit. Numerous maps are added to the text, showing Mennonite settlements in the United States and elsewhere. The ultimate authority on all matters relating to the Amish, Hutterites, and the various Anabaptist groups.

DIRECTORY

458   MENNONITE YEARBOOK AND DIRECTORY. Edited by James E. Horsch. Scottdale, Pa.: Mennonite Publishing House, 1900-- .

This work combines the features of a directory and a fact book providing information on the Mennonite Church and related organizations, church calendar, a survey of annual events, services, statistical data, and a biographical section on Mennonite church personalities. The coverage is worldwide, but the emphasis is on North America.

GENERAL WORKS

459 Smith, Charles Henry. THE STORY OF THE MENNONITES. 2d ed. Berne, Ind.: Mennonite Book Concern, 1945. 844 p. Index.

A comprehensive treatment issued in several editions covering the history of the movement since the sixteenth century, written from a nonsectarian viewpoint. The first edition was published in 1920 under the title THE MENNONITES. In addition to religious aspects, the social and economic advancement of the movement is also brought under purview. The author states that he has done "careful research on all available resource materials," but this is not evidenced through documentary references or bibliography. A fourth edition, revised and enlarged by Cornelius Krahn was published in 1957 (Newton, Kans.: Mennonite Publishing Office).

460 Dyck, Cornelius J., ed. AN INTRODUCTION TO MENNONITE HISTORY; A POPULAR HISTORY OF THE ANABAPTISTS AND THE MENNONITES. Prepared under the direction of the Institute of Mennonite Studies. Scottdale, Pa.: Herald Press, 1967. 324 p. Bibliog., index.

Intended to serve as a textbook for denominational high schools and junior colleges. The treatment is partisan. The work provides a highly readable overview of the movement beginning in 1517 to recent times. Among the special features are chapter reading lists and a chart showing the dispersion of the various Mennonite groups in North America.

461 Burkholder, John Richard, and Redekop, Calvin, eds. KINGDOM, CROSS, AND COMMUNITY: ESSAYS ON MENNONITE THEMES IN HONOR OF GUY F. HERSHBERGER. Scottdale, Pa.: Herald Press, 1976. 323 p. Bibliog., index.

The essays assess the contribution of Hershberger as a Protestant theologian to the formulation of a Christian position on war, peace, nonresistance, and the new social issues such as labor unions, employer-employee relations, and urban life. Includes a 15-page bibliography of Hershberger's writings.

462 Hostetler, John Andrew. MENNONITE LIFE. Rev. ed. Scottdale, Pa.: Herald Press, 1959. 39 p. Bibliog.

The purpose of this booklet is to inform the general reader "on the most misunderstood group" among the smaller religious denominations. It provides an easy-to-read overview of all facets of the Mennonite religion, life-style, and services.

In addition, the author presents a great deal of useful information on congregations in the United States and Canada together with some attractive illustrative material.

REGIONAL STUDIES

463 Wenger, John Christian. THE MENNONITES IN INDIANA AND MICHIGAN. Studies in Anabaptist and Mennonite History, no. 10. Scottdale, Pa.: Herald Press, 1961. 470 p. Bibliog., index.

A scholarly study which took sixteen years to complete. In character, it is a composite work providing many layers of information, both historical and current on Mennonite and Amish congregations. Each congregation is treated separately in considerable depth. The descriptive section is followed by a biographical directory of 475 ordained preachers, deacons, and bishops, living and deceased. The textual material is expanded by a set of appendexes which among other things list congregations in Indiana and Michigan in 1910 and 1960. There is a reprint of the "Declaration of Commitment in Respect to Christian Separation and Non-Conformity to the World" (1955), which codifies the denomination's doctrinal positions. The author did not use any footnotes, but provided a three hundred-item classified bibliography of primary and secondary materials. The work is profusely illustrated with portraits and religious meeting houses. The descriptive and biographical sections are indexed, but the appendixes are not.

464 Gingerich, Melvin. THE MENNONITES IN IOWA; MARKING THE ONE HUNDREDTH ANNIVERSARY OF THE COMING OF THE MENNONITES TO IOWA. Iowa City: State Historical Society of Iowa, 1939. 419 p. Bibliog. notes, index.

A substantial work originating from a master's thesis at the State University of Iowa. The history of the Mennonite congregations in the various Iowa counties are explored in detail based on primary resources, many of which were consulted in archives. In addition to the standard aspects of congregations, the author describes many interesting economic and cultural sidelines. Documentary references are footnoted, and the very detailed index helps pinpoint specific information in the body of the text.

465 Stoltzfus, Grant M. MENNONITES OF THE OHIO AND EASTERN CONFERENCE; FROM THE COLONIAL PERIOD IN PENNSYLVANIA TO 1968. Studies in Anabaptist and Mennonite History, no. 13. Scottdale, Pa.: Herald Press, 1969. 459 p. Bibliog., index.

Originally a doctoral dissertation at Eastern Mennonite College (1958), the author gives comprehensive treatment of the subject in four parts: (1) the historical backgrounds and settlements; (2) religious conferences; (3) the inter-war period; and (4) religious programs, organizations, modern missions, and services. The text is complemented by many extra features including a directory of congregations, a list of leaders with key biographical data, a chronology of events from 1525, and a separate directory treatment for the congregations in the Ohio Conference. The sources are discussed in a bibliographic essay. The documentary value of the work is enhanced by numerous pertinent illustrations.

466   Smith, Charles Henry. THE MENNONITE IMMIGRATION TO PENNSYL-
       VANIA IN THE EIGHTEENTH CENTURY. Pennsylvania German Society
       Proceedings, vol. 35. Norristown, Pa.: Norristown Press, 1929. 412 p.
       Bibliog. notes.

       The chronological scope is broader than the title suggests, as
       events prior to the eighteenth century are also surveyed. The
       narrative concentrates on European conditions inducing depar-
       ture, settlement at Germantown, Skippack, and Pequea, the
       Amish, Revolutionary War nonresistance, religious literature
       and hymnology, religious doctrine and practice, pioneer life
       and culture, dress, and education. Every section is replete
       with biographical references to participants and contemporaries
       making the work eminently suitable for genealogical research.
       Documentation was drawn from local histories, private papers,
       newspapers, land records, and genealogical materials. Illus-
       trations consist of portraits, scenes, costumes, and others.

467   Brunk, Harry Anthony. HISTORY OF MENNONITES IN VIRGINIA.
       2 vols. Vol. 1, 1727-1900. Vol. 2, 1900-1960. Staunton, Va.: Mc-
       Clure Printing, 1959-72. Bibliog., index.

       An exhaustive work paying equal attention to the history of
       the Mennonite settlements in Virginia, as well as to the life
       and accomplishments of prominent members and their families.
       The Mennonite communites were divided into the Northern,
       the Middle, and the Southern Districts. The book traces the
       story of the community by district. The second volume brings
       the story up to the 1960s. The documentary material is listed
       in the references.

CUSTOMS

468   Gingerich, Melvin. MENNONITE ATTIRE THROUGH FOUR CENTURIES.
       Pennsylvania German Society Publications, vol. 4. Breinigsville: Penn-
       sylvania German Society, 1970. 192 p. Bibliog. notes, index.

       A discussion of the evolution of garments worn by members of
       the group in the framework of social history beginning with
       the sixteenth century. The research was done in archives and
       family photograph albums to find appropriate illustration. The

text is interspersed with footnotes that provide good leads for
further study. The work has sixty-six illustrations, and a glossary of terms clarifying pertinent denominational nomenclature.
The appendices include some interesting documentation: European Mennonite government clothing regulations of the 1600s,
costumes of women and girls in the Palatinate, Hutterite garb,
and excerpts from the 1921 Mennonite General Conference on
the dress question.

Moravians

469   Hamilton, John Taylor. A HISTORY OF THE CHURCH KNOWN AS THE
       MORAVIAN CHURCH, OR THE UNITAS FRATRUM, OR THE UNITY OF
       THE BRETHREN, DURING THE EIGHTEENTH AND NINETEENTH CEN-
       TURIES. 1900. Reprint. New York: AMS Press, 1971. 631 p. Bib-
       liog., index.

         Considered to be the most reliable and authoritative standard
         history of the church. The scope covers the entire range of
         activities from the early life of Count Zinzendorf to the Gen-
         eral Synod of 1899. The bulk of the narrative centers around
         the church in America, but missionary efforts in other parts of
         the world are also discussed in considerable depth. Much of
         the narrative is based on authentic primary sources. Appendix
         A consists of a list of the Bishops of the Resuscitated Moravian
         Church. Appendix B discloses the doctrinal position of the
         Moravian Church.

470   Gollin, Gillian Lindt. MORAVIANS IN TWO WORLDS: A STUDY OF
       CHANGING COMMUNITIES. New York: Columbia University Press,
       1967. 302 p. Bibliog., index.

         A comparative study of two Moravian communities in the
         eighteenth and nineteenth centuries, one in Herrnhut, Saxony
         and the other in Bethlehem, Pennsylvania. The social organi-
         zation and communal and religious life of the two communities
         were reconstructed from archival records, personal papers,
         legal documents, and biographical materials for the purpose
         of eliciting an understanding of the process of change of two
         ideologically identical groups coping with two different en-
         vironments. A classified bibliography of about 180 items ac-
         companies the work.

471   Sessler, Jacob John. COMMUNAL PIETISM AMONG THE EARLY AMERI-
       CAN MORAVIANS. Studies in Religion and Culture. American Religion
       Series, no. 8. New York: Holt, 1933. Reprint. New York: AMS
       Press, 1971. 265 p. Bibliog., index.

         A doctoral dissertation at Columbia University focusing on the
         history of the Moravian Church in Bethlehem, Pennsylvania, in
         the seventeenth century. The European background, the acti-

vities of Count Zinzendorf, and the economic development of
the Moravian communities are discussed in some detail. An
inventory of relevant materials is given in the bibliography
consisting of 220 entries.

472 Reichel, Levin T. THE MORAVIANS IN NORTH CAROLINA, AN
AUTHENTIC HISTORY. 1857. Reprint. Baltimore: Genealogical Publishing, 1968. 206 p.

A detailed study of the church, focusing on the communities,
the institutions, and missionary activities. It has a list of
ministers. The appendix includes an alphabetical enumeration
of the first settlers with date and place of birth, the location
from where the person came, and death data. In addition,
there is information on churches in each settlement, as well
as on houses, indicating the present use of the building.

473 Fries, Adelaide Lisetta. THE ROAD TO SALEM. Chapel Hill: University of North Carolina Press, 1944. 316 p.

Based on the 1803 autobiography of Anna Catharina Ernst which
was found in manuscript in the Salem Moravian Archives, this
story yields a great deal of information on the internal life of
the Moravian Church and its leaders in the early period. Settlements in Bethabara and Bethania are highlighted in addition to
the Salem settlement.

474 James, Hunter. THE QUIET PEOPLE OF THE LAND: A STORY OF THE
NORTH CAROLINA MORAVIANS IN REVOLUTIONARY TIMES. Old
Salem Series. Chapel Hill: University of North Carolina Press, 1976.
156 p. Bibliog., index.

By order of the British Parliament, Moravians in America were
exempt from military service, and since their pacifism prevented
them from taking part in the war on the side of the patriots,
they were generally mistrusted. Their peculiar situation is
explored in this narrative. The documentation is based on
archival material found mainly in the Southern Moravian Archives and the eleven-volume documentary set entitled REC-
ORDS OF THE MORAVIANS IN NORTH CAROLINA (see 482).
An interesting addition to the book is the "Revolutionary Calendar," 16 May 1771 to 20 January 1783, which chronicles
events of the war. A useful bibliography of thirty-five items
is included.

475 Reid, Grace Stuart. THE BARONY OF THE ROSE; A HISTORICAL
MONOGRAPH. New York: Grafton Press, 1904. 58 p.

This is a partisan account of the two hundred-year history of
the Moravian settlement in Nazareth, Pennsylvania. It contains numerous illustrations of buildings and interiors.

476   Fries, Adelaide Lisetta. THE MORAVIANS IN GEORGIA, 1735-1740.
      1905. Reprint. Baltimore: Genealogical Publishing, 1967. 252 p.
      Index.

      The work deals with the settlement near Savannah, Georgia,
      which could not develop into a permanent community. The
      book includes a great variety of data of particular interest
      to the genealogist.

477   McHugh, Thomas F. "The Moravian Mission to the American Indian:
      Early American Peace Corps." PENNSYLVANIA HISTORY 33 (1966):
      412-31. Bibliog. notes.

      Discusses the goals and methods of the Unitas Fratrum Church
      which sponsored the Moravian missionary activities in the
      eighteenth and nineteenth centuries, comparing them to the
      present day American "Peace Corps" concept.

478   Schwarze, Edmund. HISTORY OF THE MORAVIAN MISSIONS AMONG
      SOUTHERN INDIAN TRIBES OF THE UNITED STATES. Transactions of
      the Moravian Historical Society. Special Series, vol. 1. Bethlehem,
      Pa.: Times Publishing, 1923. 331 p. Bibliog. notes, index.

      This study deals with the missionary activities of Moravian
      settlers among the Cherokee and the Creek in North Carolina
      and the surrounding region, covering the period between 1734
      and 1906. The story was reconstructed from diaries, reports,
      letters, reminiscences, and some published material. Among
      the illustrations there are fifteen portraits of missionaries and
      their Indian counterparts.

479   Hutton, Joseph Edmund. A HISTORY OF MORAVIAN MISSIONS. Lon-
      don: Moravian Publication Office, 1923. 550 p.

480   Thompson, Augustus Charles, ed. MORAVIAN MISSIONS: TWELVE
      LECTURES. New York: Charles Scribner's Sons, 1882. 516 p. Bib-
      liog., index.

      The work surveys the worldwide missionary activities of the
      German-speaking Moravians. Of the twelve "lectures," four
      are devoted to their accomplishments in America, especially
      among the Indians. Each section of the book is accompanied
      by a bibliography, which contains German and English mate-
      rials.

481   Historical Records Survey. North Carolina. GUIDE TO THE MANU-
      SCRIPTS IN THE ARCHIVES OF THE MORAVIAN CHURCH IN AMERICA,
      SOUTHERN PROVINCE. Prepared by the Historical Records Survey, Di-
      vision of Professional and Service Projects, Works Projects Administration.
      Raleigh: North Carolina Historical Records Survey, 1942. 136 p. Index.

A descriptive listing of manuscript holdings covering the period 1753 to 1936. The subject categories in which the material is grouped include church history in general, and in North Carolina in particular; archival materials relating to the northern and southern provinces; individual settlements and congregations with special attention to the Salem congregation (Herbst Collection); church music and missionary work. In addition to official church records, the collection also encompasses memoirs, personal correspondences and diaries of church leaders, travel accounts, wills and settlements, and maps. The entries are fairly complete and some carry brief annotations. Up to 1865 the language of the records was German. The work has a fine index.

482 Fries, Adelaide Lisetta, ed. RECORDS OF THE MORAVIANS IN NORTH CAROLINA. 11 vols. Vol. 9 edited by Minnie J. Smith; vols. 10 and 11 edited by Kenneth G. Hamilton. Publications of the North Carolina Historical Commission. Raleigh: Edwards Broughton Print, 1922-54; North Carolina State Department of Archives and History, 1968-70. 6,175 p. Index.

A monumental compilation covering the period 1752 to 1879. It includes congregational records, minutes of councils, reports, minister lists, diaries of congregations, and memorabilia. The language of the documents disclosed here is English, although the original records were in German through 1856. In all, the set contains over six thousand pages and each volume is separately indexed. The arrangement of the material is according to year.

REFORMED CHURCH

482a Good, James Isaac. "The Founding of the German Reformed Church in America by the Dutch." AMERICAN HISTORICAL ASSOCIATION. ANNUAL REPORT, 1897, pp. 373-84.

This is a seminal essay by a distinguished church historian shedding light on the origin and early history of the German Reformed Church in America. The relationship between the Reformed Church of Holland and the early congregations of German immigrants to Pennsylvania from the Palatinate is discussed in detail with special reference to the difficulties and tensions which led to separation in 1792. A roster of thirty-nine ministers who served in America from 1737 to 1787 but were kept on the roll of the Holland Synods and the German Reformed Church of Pennsylvania is given at the end of the essay.

482b _____. HISTORY OF THE REFORMED CHURCH IN THE UNITED STATES, 1725-1792. Reading, Pa.: D. Miller, 1899. 701 p.

The author devotes considerable attention to the German Reformed Church in two places of his work. In chapter 1, the struggles and the religious life of German Reformed immigrants from the Palatinate in the first half of the eighteenth century are discussed on eleven pages. A portion of chapter 5 deals with the Philadelphia German Reformed congregation between 1755 and 1775.

482c _____. HISTORY OF THE REFORMED CHURCH IN THE U.S. IN THE NINETEENTH CENTURY. New York: The Board of Publication of the Reformed Church in America, 1911. 662 p.

The chronological scope of this work ranges from 1793 through 1910, but the bulk concentrates on the nineteenth century and focuses on the theological issues. References to the German Reformed Church in America are scattered in many parts of the book. The most important places in the book where pertinent material can be found are the following: part 1, chapter 3 deals with the founding of the Theological Seminary in Carlisle, Pennsylvania; part 2, chapter 1 discusses extensively the Mercersburg theological controversy in the years 1844-78 involving the professors Philip Schaff and J.W. Nevin; chapter 6 narrates the uprising of the German students at the Mercersburg Theological School against Nevin and gives the background of the organization of Marshall and Franklin College. Further on the author tells the story of the withdrawal of the Reformed Church of Germantown from the Synod and the role Rev. Jacob Helffenstein played in it. Of German-American interest is also the section on the first liturgical controversy of 1854-63, the account of the attack on the Mercersburg theology by the Reformed Church of Germany, and the three page unit on the Stiely Synod of Pennsylvania.

482d Bomberger, John Henry Augustus. THE REVISED LITURGY; A HISTORY AND CRITICISM OF THE RITUALISTIC MOVEMENT IN THE GERMAN REFORMED CHURCH. Philadelphia: J.B. Rodgers, 1867. 120 p.

A lucid exposition in an ecclesiastical context of the rise of the Mercersburg Theology and a discussion of the contributions of Frederick A. Rauch, John W. Nevin, and Philip Schaff, the chief exponents of its doctrines.

482e Apple, T.G. "The Theology of the German Reformed Church." PROCEEDINGS OF THE SECOND GENERAL COUNCIL OF THE PRESBYTERIAN CHURCH HELD IN PHILADELPHIA, 1880. Pp. 484-97.

Item not available for examination.

482f Dubbs, Joseph Henry. "History of the Reformed Church, German, by Joseph Henry Dubbs." In THE AMERICAN CHURCH HISTORY SERIES 8 (1895): 213-423.

Item not available for examination.

482g Appel, Theodore. RECOLLECTIONS OF COLLEGE LIFE, AT MARSHALL COLLEGE, MERCERSBURG, PA., FROM 1839 TO 1845: A NARRATIVE WITH REFLECTIONS. Reading, Pa.: D. Miller, 1886. 348 p.

Item not available for examination.

Schwenkfelders

483 Kriebel, Howard Wiegner. THE SCHWENKFELDERS IN PENNSYLVANIA, A HISTORICAL SKETCH. Pennsylvania German Society Proceedings, vol. 13. 1904. Reprint. New York: AMS Press, 1971. 232 p. Bibliog., index.

> An inquiry into the history and religious doctrines of the group founded by Kaspar Schwenkfeld. The historical survey begins in the 1500s in Europe, but the thrust of the work is the story of the Schwenkfelders in Pennsylvania in the eighteenth century. The author touched upon all aspects of the life of the group and its church. An excellent bibliographic essay appraises the sources and literature on the subject, providing information on the origin of diaries, letters, accounts, hymns, and others. Fifty-six facsimiles of manuscripts and eighteen pieces of illustrations by Julius F. Sachse contribute to the authentication of the text. There is in the appendix a sample marriage contract and a copy of the letter regarding the anti-military position of the Schwenkfelders in the Revolutionary War.

484 Brecht, Samuel Kriebel, ed. THE GENEALOGICAL RECORD OF THE SCHWENKFELDER FAMILIES, SEEKERS OF RELIGIOUS LIBERTY, WHO FLED FROM SILESIA TO SAXONY AND THENCE TO PENNSYLVANIA IN THE YEARS 1731-1737. Chicago: Printed for the Board of Publications of the Schwenkfelder Church, Pennsburg, Pa.: Rand McNally, 1923. 1,752 p. Index.

> A massive historical and genealogical study of Pennsylvania Schwenkfelders and their descendants. The cutoff date of coverage is the 1920s. Gives a historical background of the group's genesis in Germany which is followed by a discussion of six migratory waves. Includes name lists, marriage, birth, naturalization, death records, and maps of homesteads. Information can be easily located through a gigantic index. The text is complemented by over 130 illustrations, portraits, and facsimiles of documents.

Swiss Reformed Church

484a Good, James Isaac. HISTORY OF THE SWISS REFORMED CHURCH

SINCE THE REFORMATION. Philadelphia: Publication and Sunday School Board of the Reformed Church in the United States, 1913. 504 p.

Item not available for examination.

VII. UTOPIAN COMMUNITIES

GENERAL WORKS

485 Holloway, Mark. HEAVENS ON EARTH; THE UTOPIAN COMMUNITIES IN AMERICA, 1680-1880. 2d ed., rev. New York: Dover Publications, 1966. 246 p. Bibliog., index.

> Considered a basic treatment of communal settlements from 1680 to 1880 in America. The German-American communes treated individually are: Anabaptists (Mennonites), Labadists, Woman in the Wilderness, Ephrata, the Rappites' Harmony Society, Zoar, Bethel, Aurora, Amana, and the Hutterites. Intended for the general reader. The second revised edition has a bibliography of best sources consulted for each chapter. A map of utopian communities and twenty-four illustrations are attached.

486 Bestor, Arthur Eugene. THE SECTARIAN ORIGINS AND THE OWENITE PHASE OF COMMUNITARIAN SOCIALISM IN AMERICA: 1663-1829. 2d ed., enl. Philadelphia: University of Pennsylvania Press, 1970. 288 p. Bibliog., index.

> Addressing himself to the general discussion of communitarian experiments in the United States in the seventeenth and eighteenth centuries, Bestor devotes considerable attention to the German-American settlements of Ephrata, Moravians, Rappites, Zoarites, and some others. The work was based on meticulous research attested by copious footnotes and two major bibliographic essays elaborating on the sources of the study. Particularly relevant is the bibliographic essay, "Works on the Principal Sectarian Communities Founded Before 1830," which discusses the literary sources dealing with these communities. The value of the work is enhanced by a checklist of communitarian experiments between 1663 and 1858, summary data by year, and a richly detailed index providing access not only to the text, but to the supportive material as well. This work was originally titled, BACKWOODS UTOPIAS: THE SECTARIAN AND OWENITE PHASES OF COMMUNITARIAN SOCIAL-

ISM IN AMERICA, 1663–1829 (Philadelphia: University of Pennsylvania Press, 1950).

487 Nordhoff, Charles. THE COMMUNISTIC SOCIETIES OF THE UNITED STATES: ACCOUNTS OF THE ECONOMISTS, ZOARITES, THE SHAKERS, AMANA, ONEIDA, BETHEL, AURORA, ICARION, AND OTHER EXIST-ING SOCIETIES: THEIR RELIGIOUS CREEDS, SOCIAL PRACTICES, NUMBERS, INDUSTRIES, AND PRESENT CONDITION. 1875. Reprint. New York: Schocken Books, 1965. 439 p. Bibliog., index.

A fairly detailed discussion of communal societies in the United States encompassing eighteenth- and nineteenth-century developments. While the treatment is scholarly, the style of presentation is popular. It is especially valuable for its bibliography comprising almost 140 items, including primary and secondary materials.

488 Webber, Everett. ESCAPE TO UTOPIA: THE COMMUNAL MOVEMENT IN AMERICA. American Procession Series. New York: Hastings House, 1959. 444 p. Bibliog., index.

The German communes discussed in this work in the context of a general history of the movement include Ephrata, Woman in the Wilderness, Harmony Society, and Amana. The author pays particular attention to the causes that gave rise to the communitarian experiments and also analyzes the reasons for their decline. The personalities of the founders are brought into sharp relief. Has many valuable bibliographic leads.

489 Hinds, William Alfred. AMERICAN COMMUNITIES: BRIEF SKETCHES OF ECONOMY, ZOAR, BETHEL, AURORA, AMANA, ICARIA, THE SHAKERS, ONEIDA, WALLINGFORD, AND THE BROTHERHOOD OF NEW LIFE. Rev. ed. Enlarged to include additional societies, new and old, communistic, semicommunistic and cooperative. Chicago: Charles H. Kerr, 1902. 433 p. Bibliog. notes.

For annotation, see below.

490 _____. AMERICAN COMMUNITIES AND CO-OPERATIVE COLONIES. 2d ed., rev. Chicago: Charles H. Kerr, 1908. 608 p. Bibliog. notes.

This edition includes a considerable amount of information on German communal settlements, encompassing Ephrata and the Harmony Society. The work is based on the author's personal observations. Includes footnotes and contemporary photographs.

491 Lawson, Donna. BROTHERS AND SISTERS ALL OVER THIS LAND: AMERICA'S FIRST COMMUNES. New York: Praeger, 1972. 142 p. Index.

Popular discussion of communal settlements emphasizing nine-

teenth-century experiments. Of German-American interest are
Rapp's Harmony Society and Amana.

AMANA

492 Shambaugh, Bertha Maud (Horack). AMANA THAT WAS AND AMANA
THAT IS. Iowa City: State Historical Society of Iowa, 1932. Reprint.
New York: Benjamin Blom, 1971. 502 p. Bibliog. notes, index.

This is one of the few major treatments of the history and
destiny of the Inspirationists' communitarian experiment in
Iowa consisting of two main parts. The first part is a reprint
of the author's 1908 book entitled, AMANA: THE COMMU-
NITY OF TRUE INSPIRATION, which traces its history from
the European beginnings to the end of the nineteenth century.
The philosophy, government, religious life, social and educational aspects are highlighted. The second part is an extension of the story to the early 1930s, reporting on the organizational and technological changes which have transformed
the community in the intervening years. The narrative is based
on primary resources, much of it in German. The footnotes
explicate documentary references. Added to the text are:
(1) constitution and bylaws of 1843, and (2) the Articles of
Incorporation of Amana of 1927. The index is helpful in
locating specific information in the text.

493 Perkins, William Rufus, and Wick, Barthinius L. HISTORY OF THE
AMANA SOCIETY OR COMMUNITY OF TRUE INSPIRATION. 1891.
Reprint. Radical Tradition in America. Westport, Conn.: Hyperion
Press, 1976. 94 p. Bibliog.

A short but important history of Amana with strong reference
to its roots in European mysticism and pietism. Gives historical background of the founders' search for a community in
North America. Although originally published by the State
University of Iowa Press, it was based on the society's documents and was sanctioned by it. An interesting addition to
the text is a listing of assessed evaluation of Amana Society
property in Iowa County in 1890. A bibliography of some
source materials such as creed books and German-language
records, as well as twenty-six secondary sources, are included.

494 Yambura, Barbara S., in collaboration with Bodine, Eunice W. A
CHANGE AND A PARTING: MY STORY OF AMANA. Ames: Iowa
State University Press, 1960. 361 p.

A popular account based on personal experience by a former
member of Amana who spent her childhood and young adult
years in the community. The historical and religious traditions, social customs, and daily activities are detailed for
the record before modernization transformed them. The people

described are stereotypes. Additional materials include the "Twenty-Four Rules of True Godliness," a brief glossary, and some illustrations.

BETHEL AND AURORA

495 Hendricks, Robert J. BETHEL AND AURORA, AN EXPERIMENT IN COMMUNISM AS PRACTICAL CHRISTIANITY, WITH SOME ACCOUNT OF PAST AND PRESENT VENTURES IN COLLECTIVE LIVING. New York: Press of the Pioneers, 1933. Reprint. New York: AMS Press, 1971. 324 p. Index.

This work narrates the story of the communitarian settlement at Bethel, Missouri, inspired by teachings of religious and utopian social thinkers and its move from Missouri to Aurora, Oregon. The experiment's successful features are highlighted. A great deal of biographical information regarding William Keil and other prominent figures of the community are woven into the narrative. Excerpts from the writings of the settlers' spiritual forefathers and some illustrative materials of the community complement the text.

EPHRATA

496 Doll, Eugene Edgar, and Funke, Anneliese Marchwald, comps. THE EPHRATA CLOISTERS; AN ANNOTATED BIBLIOGRAPHY. Bibliographies on German American History, no. 3. Philadelphia: Carl Schurz Memorial Foundation, 1944. 140 p. Index.

Consists of two sections: section 1 is the work of Doll of the Carl Schurz Memorial Library and it lists about 360 items written about Ephrata between 1730 and 1940. The material ranges from newspapers, periodical articles, books, parts of books, speeches, and pamphlets, but no manuscripts. The newspapers included preceed 1800. The arrangement is alphabetic by author. The entries are briefly annotated. Section 2 was composed by Funke and comprises about one hundred items which were published by the Ephrata press from 1745-94. Here the arrangement is by year of printing. The entries are well annotated and for most items location is indicated. The bibliography does not include books by Ephrata residents printed elsewhere. (See also 504.)

497 Ernst, James Emanuel. EPHRATA, A HISTORY. Posthumously edited with an introduction by John Joseph Stoudt. Pennsylvania German Society Yearbook, vol. 25, 1963. Allentown: Pennsylvania German Folklore Society, 1963. 354 p. Bibliog. notes.

A key work on the history of Ephrata. Although the chronological coverage extends from 1690 to 1865, the story centers around Johann Conrad Beissel during whose lifetime the community reached its peak. The treatment is from the perspective of the broader social and cultural history of Pennsylvania. Ernst's manuscript was based on primary sources, and Stoudt put the work together after Ernst's death.

498 Sachse, Julius Friedrich. THE GERMAN SECTARIANS OF PENNSYLVANIA; A CRITICAL AND LEGENDARY HISTORY OF THE EPHRATA CLOISTER AND THE DUNKERS. 2 vols. 1899. Reprint. New York: AMS Press, 1971. 506 p.; 535 p. Bibliog. notes, index.

Considered to be a sequel to the author's THE GERMAN PIETISTS OF PROVINCIAL PENNSYLVANIA, 1694-1708 (see 411), the work follows the development of sectarian settlements from 1708 to the beginning of the nineteenth century. The following groups are dealt with: Palatines, Labadists, Baptist Brethren, New Dunkers, Unitas Fratrum (Moravians), Johann Conrad Beissel and Ephrata, and other sects and mystic groups. Other subjects discussed include Christopher Sower and his German Bible, industry and music at the Cloister, the Ephrata press, Conrad Weiser, education at the Kelpius and Ephrata communities, the valleys of Virginia, and Snow Hill.

Like the previous work, this treatise is well documented and illustrated. Added features include the death register of Ephrata from 1728 to 1800, with names listed by year of death, the register of the Snow Hill Community, giving baptisms and burials and other vital statistics, and a bibliographic essay of the press issuances of Ephrata's Kloster Press. Each volume is indexed separately in great detail.

499 Doll, Eugene Edgar. THE EPHRATA CLOISTER: AN INTRODUCTION. Ephrata, Pa.: Ephrata Cloister Associates, 1958. 32 p. Bibliog.

A popular introductory work on Ephrata in the eighteenth century with numerous illustrations by Ralph D. Dunkelberger.

500 Hark, Joseph Maximilian, trans. CHRONICON EPHRATENSE, A HISTORY OF THE COMMUNITY OF SEVENTH DAY BAPTISTS AT EPHRATA LANCASTER COUNTY, PENN'A. BY "LAMECH AND AGRIPPA." 1889. Reprint. Burt Franklin Research and Source Works Series. Philosophy and Religious History Monographs. New York: Burt Franklin, 1972. 288 p.

This is a translation, with some explanatory notes, of the original German published in 1786. The authors, two residents of the community, report their personal experiences and observations. The chronicle covers the period from 1708-86 in the life of the Ephrata community and the neighboring counties. An attempt was made to render in English the quaintness of the original work. Allegedly, only twenty copies of it still exist.

501 Reichmann, Felix, and Doll, Eugene Edgar, eds. EPHRATA AS SEEN BY CONTEMPORARIES. Pennsylvania German Folklore Society Yearbook, vol. 17, 1952. Allentown: Pennsylvania German Folklore Society, 1953. 216 p. Index.

The purpose of this work was to reexamine the prevailing knowledge about the Ephrata Cloister by making recourse to original resources. Sixty accounts from various provenances originating in the eighteenth century are disclosed here without editorial comment. The arrangement is chronological. The writings are introduced by a short statement about the author and the background of the piece. The contributors were mostly outsiders. To round out the picture, the editors added an appendix containing observations by residents of Ephrata. There are numerous photographs of buildings and interiors, as well as a chronology covering 1690 through 1796.

502 Zerfass, Samuel G. SOUVENIR BOOK OF THE EPHRATA CLOISTER: COMPLETE HISTORY FROM ITS SETTLEMENT IN 1728 TO THE PRESENT TIME: INCLUDED IS THE ORGANIZATION OF EPHRATA BOROUGH AND OTHER INFORMATION OF EPHRATA CONNECTED WITH THE CLOISTER. 1921. Reprint. Communal Societies in America [Series]. New York: AMS Press, 1975. 84 p.

The reprint copy was examined. The entry in Pochmann reads: Zerfass, Samuel G., HISTORY OF THE EPHRATA CLOISTER, Lititz, Pennsylvania, 1922. The author of this booklet was pastor at the Cloister who argued for the preservation of Ephrata as a historic monument. In addition to giving informative details, this booklet is valuable in that it includes poems written by inspired witnesses, and discloses many pictorial documents.

503 Klein, Walter Conrad. JOHANN CONRAD BEISSEL, MYSTIC AND MARTINET, 1690-1768. Pennsylvania Lives. Philadelphia: University of Pennsylvania Press, 1942. Reprint. Philadelphia: Porcupine Press, 1972. 218 p. Bibliog., index.

Placed against the background of seventeenth-century German radical versus conservative Protestantism, this critical history depicts a realistic tableau of Ephrata. In the core of it stands the psychobiography of its founder. The narrative is authenticated by many illustrative quotes from original sources, which are discussed in a special bibliographic essay.

504 Hollyday, Guy T., and Schweitzer, Christoph E. "The Present Status of Conrad Beissel/Ephrata Research." MONATSHEFTE 68 (Summer 1976): 171-78.

"Much research remains to be done on the early German-American religious leader Conrad Beissel (1690-1768) and his creation, the Ephrata community in Pennsylvania. After a

sketch of Beissel's life and the significance of the Ephrata
Cloister, the authors characterize and evaluate the chief
sources of information on the Cloister prior to 1944 and all
significant work published since THE EPHRATA CLOISTERS;
AN ANNOTATED BIBLIOGRAPHY by Eugene E. Doll and
Anneliese M. Funke (1944) (see 496). Since 1944 there has
been research on the buildings, the furniture, and the watermarks used by the press; also, scholars have given attention
to Beissel's sermons and the theory of composition and to
Ephrata hymns and Fraktur writing. Literary aspects of the
works by Beissel and his associates have not been investigated
extensively, in part because the authorship of many Ephrata
hymns is still uncertain." (Authors' abstract.)

505 Aurand, Ammon Monroe. HISTORICAL ACCOUNT OF THE EPHRATA
CLOISTER AND THE SEVENTH DAY BAPTIST SOCIETY. Harrisburg:
Aurand Press, 1940. 24 p.

A useful ancillary work which touches upon relations to Judaism
and Rosicrucianism, and provides biographical bits on Johann
Beissel, Christopher Sauer, and Peter Miller. Of some interest
is the description of printing and musical activities. Appended
is the reprinting of "An Historical Sketch of Ephrata," by William M. Fahnestock, from Hazard's REGISTER OF PENNSYL-
VANIA 15 (March 1835): 161-67.

506 Jacoby, John E. TWO MYSTIC COMMUNITIES IN AMERICA. Paris:
Les Presses Universitaires de France, 1931. Reprint. The Radical Tradition in America [Series]. Westport, Conn.: Hyperion Press, 1975.
104 p.

An offshoot of LE MYSTICISME DANS LA PENSEE AMERI-
CAINE (Paris: Les Presses Universitaires de France, 1931).
The first fifty pages of this book are devoted to Ephrata,
serving as an example of religious mysticism in action on
the American scene.

507 Whitney, Norman. EXPERIMENTS IN COMMUNITY: EPHRATA, THE
AMISH, THE DOUKHOBORS, THE SHAKERS, THE BRUDERHOF AND
MONTEVERDE. Pendle Hill Pamphlet 149. Wallingford, Pa.: Pendle
Hill, 1966. 40 p. Bibliog.

A useful overview treating German-American "intentional communities" in the broader context of the subject matter.

508 Hertz, Daniel Rhine. HISTORY OF EPHRATA, GIVING A BRIEF SKETCH
OF THE SETTLEMENT OF THE STATE AND COUNTY, THE BATTLE OF
BRANDYWINE, THE CLOISTER AND MONUMENT TO BE ERECTED AT
MOUNT ZION AND THE BOROUGH OF EPHRATA. Philadelphia: H.
Ferkler, printer, 1894. 80 p.

Although the occasion of this booklet was tangential to this history of Ephrata, the author digresses to give some glimpses into the region and the cloister itself.

509   Biever, Dale E. "A Report of Archaeological Investigations at the Ephrata Cloister, 1963-1966." FOUR PENNSYLVANIA STUDIES. Pennsylvania German Society Publications, vol. 3. Breinigsville: Pennsylvania German Society, 1970. Bibliog.

An important contribution based on two archaeological excavations at Ephrata in 1963 and 1966. The work's intention was to provide archaeological evidence to the understanding of the life-style of the community. Many photographs of the actual artifacts found are included.

HARMONY SOCIETY

510   Arndt, Karl John Richard. GEORGE RAPP'S HARMONY SOCIETY, 1785-1847. Rev. ed. Rutherford, N.J.: Fairleigh Dickinson University Press, 1972. 713 p. Bibliog., index.

511   _____. GEORGE RAPP'S SUCCESSORS AND MATERIAL HEIRS, 1847-1916. Rutherford, N.J.: Fairleigh Dickinson University Press, 1971. 445 p. Bibliog., index.

These two items are the products of Arndt's monumental undertaking to write a definitive history of the Harmony Society from its European origins to its communal experimentations in the United States and its dissolution. The first book (510) traces in its initial part the beginnings of the society in Wuertemberg, Germany, from 1757 to 1804. The subsequent sections deal with: (1) arrival in North America and the founding of the town of Harmony on the Connoquenessing River in Pennsylvania, where the society spent the first phase of its existence between 1804 and 1815; (2) the migration to Indiana and the founding of the settlement of Harmony on the Wabash River, from 1814-25, constituting the second phase; and (3) the return to Pennsylvania and the establishment of the community of Economy on the Ohio River in 1824, closing with 1847, the year George Rapp, its leader, died. All aspects of the society's life are covered. The work is based on meticulous examination and analysis of all types of relevant documents. The most important documents are disclosed in the form of appendices the range of which indicates the breadth of Arndt's inquiry: (a) George Rapp family line 1629-1889; (b) chronology of the Harmony Society 1757-1847; (c) signers of the Jefferson Petition for a land grant; (d) list of names of persons·appearing in the PITTSBURGH GAZETTE, 10 February 1832, denoucing George and Frederick Rapp, with age, date of arrival, and other remarks; (e) books printed on the Harmony Society press; and (f) families in Economy, January 1847 (327) names grouped into seventy families).

The second book (511) concentrates on the history of the society under Rapp's successors. It is conveniently divided into three chronological periods designated by three distinct trusteeships: (1) Baker-Henrici trusteeship, 1847-68, (2) Henrici-Lenz-Woelfel-Duss trusteeship, 1868-92, and (3) Duss-Siber-Riethmuller-Duss trusteeship, 1892-1916. A great deal of supplementary material is provided in the appendices which would be of interest to the serious researcher. They include: (a) survey of Harmony Society Archives at Economy, Pennsylvania; (b) 1829 "list of German books" in the Harmony Society Library at that time. Equally valuable are the illustrated materials, among which the following are to be found: I. Settlements made with members of the Society from 1890 to legal dissolution; II. 1927 list of bonds of Liberty Land Company given in payment for legal services and entitled to preference; III. Comparison of "donations of gifts" granted departing members of the society and lawyers' fees paid for legal services at various periods of the society's history. The index is an effective access tool to an extremely rich historical material.

At this writing, the documentary material upon which this study is based was in process to be published separately in a multiple volume set beginning in 1975 (see 512).

512   Arndt, Karl John Richard, comp. and ed. A DOCUMENTARY HISTORY OF THE INDIANA DECADE OF THE HARMONY SOCIETY, 1814-1824. 2 vols. Vol. 1, 1814-1819. Vol. 2, 1820-1824. Indianapolis: Indiana Historical Society, 1975-- . Index.

This is the first issue of a collection of documents related to the Rappist settlements projected to consist of six volumes. It brings together the primary evidence used by Arndt in his treatises described above (see 510, 511). The materials disclosed here encompass the whole spectrum of documentary species and throw light on both internal and external affairs of the society. The records are housed in the Harmony Society Archives of the Pennsylvania Historical and Museum Commission at Old Economy Village in Ambridge, Pennsylvania. The Indiana Historical Society is also a repository of Harmony Society papers. The initial volumes will deal with the Indiana period, while the Pennsylvania phase will take up two or three subsequent volumes. The last volume of the set will consist of a biographical dictionary and is contemplated to include all people involved in Harmony Society during its existence.

513   Bole, John Archibald. THE HARMONY SOCIETY: A CHAPTER IN GERMAN-AMERICAN CULTURE HISTORY. Americana Germanica, no. 2. 1904. Reprint. New York: AMS Press, 1973. 176 p. Bibliog.

A basic historical treatment covering both the Pennsylvania

and Indiana phases of the society from 1804–68. The author
worked with primary resources including private correspondences
of members, and business papers in German and English. The
internal records were in German, whereas the transactions of
the group with the surrounding world were usually written in
English. The work was originated as a doctoral dissertation
at the University of Pennsylvania in conjunction with the
American Ethnographic Survey. Some photographs and a source
list complement the study, but there is no index.

514 Knoedler, Christiana F. THE HARMONY SOCIETY, A 19TH-CENTURY
AMERICAN UTOPIA. New York: Vantage Press, 1954. 160 p. Index.

A popular account of the settlement written in a nostalgic
vein by a lifelong member of the Old Economy community.
The work's documentary value is enhanced by seventy-one
photographs.

515 Duss, John. THE HARMONISTS: A PERSONAL HISTORY. Harrisburg,
Pa.: 1943. Reprint. American Utopian Adventure [Series]. Philadelphia: Porcupine Press, 1972. 425 p.

An interesting document from the later phase of the Harmony
Society, produced by one of its members who later became
its leader. Written in a popular tone, the work offers an
insight into the causes leading to the society's dissolution.
Twenty-five photographs, portraits, and buildings illustrate
the work. The appendix contains the 1,805 Articles of Incorporation, and the official description of the society's as-
sets prior to its dissolution.

516 Williams, Aaron. THE HARMONY SOCIETY AT ECONOMY, PENN'A.
FOUNDED BY GEORGE RAPP, A.D. 1805. 1866. Reprint. New York:
A.M. Kelly, 1971. 329 p.

A composite work centering around Williams's tract written in
defense of the society against criticism which appeared in the
ATLANTIC MONTHLY (17 [May 1866]: 529–38). The work
is a cogent exposition of the religious, social, and moral
beliefs of the sect with an account of its history, life, and
customs. The main thesis of the tract is supported by essays
on the society's roots in the European movements of mysticism,
with special reference to the Zoarites. The two subsequent
sections of the book include the facsimile reproduction of the
1824 edition of George Rapp's THOUGHTS ON THE DESTINY
OF MAN, and John Duss's chronicle of the society based on
his unpublished memoirs.

517 Kring, Hilda Adam. THE HARMONISTS: A FOLK CULTURAL APPROACH.
ATLA Monograph Series, no. 3. Metuchen, N.J.: Scarecrow, American
Theological Library Association, 1973. 240 p. Bibliog., index.

Originally a doctoral dissertation at the University of Pennsylvania, this study offers a broad canvas of the life and customs of all three Harmony settlements. Topics include: the Harmonists, religious beliefs, the society's organization, places of worship, the Sabbath, rites of passage, feasts and holidays, music and hymns, home patterns, activities, community relationships, and the end of the society. Especially valuable is the bibliography which contains about five hundred items ranging from published materials to private papers and interviews. The twenty-eight photographs provide a unique pictorial documentation.

ZOAR

518 Randall, Emilius Oviatt. HISTORY OF THE ZOAR SOCIETY, FROM ITS COMMENCEMENT TO ITS CONCLUSION: A SOCIOLOGICAL STUDY IN COMMUNISM. 3d ed. 1904. Reprint. New York: AMS Press, 1971. 105 p. Bibliog. notes.

The most substantial discussion of this utopian communitarian experiment founded in 1717 in Tuscarawas County, Ohio, concentrating on the mid-nineteenth century phase of its existence. Randall examined the papers of the society and had visited the settlement interviewing some of its leaders. He found the experiment sociologically significant. Documentary references are explicated in lengthy footnotes. The narrative is complemented by the texts of incorporation, as well as the document of disbandment in 1898. A pullout plat map shows land distribution and there are several photographs of buildings. Also appears in OHIO ARCHAEOLOGICAL AND HISTORICAL QUARTERLY 8 (July 1899): 1-105.

519 Ohio Historical Society. Department of Research and Publications. ZOAR, AN OHIO EXPERIMENT IN COMMUNALISM. Columbus: Ohio Historical Society, 1972. 75 p. Bibliog.

A popular treatment, first published in 1952, dealing with the founding, the economic system, daily life, and the dissolution of the community. The work is richly illustrated with photographs.

520 Dobbs, Catherine R. FREEDOM'S WILL: THE SOCIETY OF THE SEPARATISTS OF ZOAR: AN HISTORICAL ADVENTURE OF RELIGIOUS COMMUNISM IN EARLY OHIO. New York: William-Frederick Press, 1947. 104 p.

Item not available for examination.

VIII. SOCIAL AND POLITICAL ASPECTS

521 Zenger, John Peter. THE TRIAL OF JOHN PETER ZENGER. Edited and with an introduction and notes by Vincent Buranelli. Washington Square: New York University Press, 1957. Reprint. Westport, Conn.: Greenwood Press, 1975. 152 p. Bibliog., index.

Useful for locating documentation on the Zenger case.

522 _____. A BRIEF NARRATIVE OF THE CASE AND TRIAL OF JOHN PETER ZENGER, PRINTER OF THE NEW YORK WEEKLY JOURNAL. By James Alexander. Edited by Stanley Nider Katz. 2d ed. Cambridge, Mass.: Harvard University Press, 1972. 250 p. Bibliog. notes, index.

An edited account of the celebrated 1738 trial of John Peter Zenger, German-born New York publisher. The trial was a landmark event in American constitutional history. An appendix cites a selection of publications issued by Zenger's publishing firm.

523 Higham, John. STRANGERS IN THE LAND: PATTERNS OF AMERICAN NATIVISM 1860-1925. New Brunswick, N.J.: Rutgers University Press, 1955. Corrected and with a new preface. New York: Atheneum, 1963. 431 p. Bibliog., index.

Considered as a basic treatise on the subject, this work is significant for the literature of the German-American experience. Nativistic prejudices have affected Americans of German origin during the rapid industrialization of the country, as well as through the campaign for restrictive immigration, and in outbursts of hostility against them during World War I. Although the scope is general, this book will prove highly informative for the student of German-American history.

524 Luebke, Frederick C., ed. ETHNIC VOTERS AND THE ELECTION OF LINCOLN. Lincoln: University of Nebraska Press, 1971. 226 p. Bibliog.

A collection of eleven essays from historical journals exploring the impact of ethnic groups on American politics preceding the

Civil War. Since numerically the German element loomed large in the population, the bulk of the essays deal with German political behavior. The key role of German Americans is investigated in the following essays: (1) V. Smith, "Influence of the Foreign-Born of the Northwest in the Election of 1860"; (2) C.W. Emery, "Iowa Germans in the Election of 1860"; (3) J. Schafer, "Who Elected Lincoln"; (4) J. Monaghan, "Did Abraham Lincoln Receive the Illinois German Vote?"; (5) A. Dorpalen, "German Element and the Issues of the Civil War"; (6) H.B. Johnson, "Election of 1860 and the Germans in Minnesota"; (7) G.H. Daniels, "Immigrant Vote in the 1860 Election: The Case in Iowa"; (8) R.P. Swierenga, "Ethnic Voter and the First Lincoln Election"; (9) P.J. Kleppner, "Lincoln and the Immigrant Vote: A Case of Religious Polarization"; (10) R.P. Formisano, "Ethnicity and Party in Michigan, 1854–60"; and (11) J.M. Bergquist, "People and Politics in Transition: The Illinois Germans, 1850–60."

525   David, Henry. THE HISTORY OF THE HAYMARKET AFFAIR; A STUDY IN THE AMERICAN SOCIAL-REVOLUTIONARY AND LABOR MOVEMENTS. New York: Farrar and Rinehart, 1936. Reprint. New York: Collier Books, 1963. 464 p. Bibliog., index.

A detailed study based on contemporary documents which is considered by experts as the definitive history of the subject. In tracing the events, the author wishes to establish the attendant facts, the reason why they occurred, and who should bear the responsibility for them. The discussion proceeds in a chronological sequence. The bibliography contains 350 items. The 1963 edition omits footnotes to the documentary references.

526   Foner, Philip Sheldon, comp. THE AUTOBIOGRAPHIES OF THE HAY-MARKET MARTYRS. American Institute of Marxist Studies, no. 5. New York: Humanities Press, 1969. 198 p. Bibliog., index.

The editor brings together biographical statements of the eight defendants originally carried in serialized form in the labor newspaper, THE KNIGHTS OF LABOR. Six of the eight defendants accused of exploding a dynamite bomb which killed seven policemen were of German descent. Of the two introductory essays, one was written by Foner, and the other by the defendents' chief legal counsel.

527   THE ACCUSED-THE ACCUSERS; THE FAMOUS SPEECHES OF THE EIGHT CHICAGO ANARCHISTS IN COURT. 1886. Reprint. THE ACCUSED AND THE ACCUSERS; THE FAMOUS SPEECHES OF THE EIGHT CHICAGO ANARCHISTS IN COURT. New York: Arno Press, 1969. 188 p.

A facsimile reprint of the reported addresses of the defendants August Spies, Michel Schwab, Oscar Neebe, Adolf Fischer, Louis Lingg, George Engel, Samuel Fielden, and Albert R. Parsons.

528 Joll, James. THE ANARCHISTS. Boston: Little, Brown, and Co., 1964. 303 p. Bibliog., index.

> The scope of this work is international, but important American representatives of anarchist thought, such as Wilhelm Weitling, are covered. It also includes a section on the Haymarket Affair.

529 Bruncken, Ernest. "Political Activity of Wisconsin Germans 1854-1860." PROCEEDINGS OF THE STATE HISTORICAL SOCIETY OF WISCONSIN 49 (1902): 190-211.

> This paper explores the political attitudes of German Americans in Wisconsin in the years preceeding the Civil War. Bruncken shows how the various political parties tried to appeal to German Americans in the state in view of their ability to sway elections. The documentation is based predominately on contemporary newspapers, state legislative materials, and other references.

530 Nelson, Clifford L. GERMAN-AMERICAN POLITICAL BEHAVIOR IN NEBRASKA AND WISCONSIN, 1916-1920. Lincoln: University of Nebraska, 1972. 114 p. Bibliog.

> This analysis concentrates on the 1916, 1918, and 1920 elections and examines the impact of the war and particularly of the nativist excesses on German-American voting patterns. Although the focus is localized, the author's inferences are general. The treatment is scholarly, supported by elaborate documentation, numerous tabular presentations, and a lavish display of documentary sources.

531 Luebke, Frederick C. IMMIGRANTS AND POLITICS: THE GERMANS OF NEBRASKA 1880-1900. Lincoln: University of Nebraska Press, 1969. 220 p. Bibliog., index.

> An examination of the voting behavior for the purpose of testing in the Nebraska context the validity of the assumption that the ethnic vote has been largely determined by the influence of the editors of ethnic newspapers. The treatment is broadly guaged, set against a historical background from which a collective portrait of the German body politic in Nebraska emerges. The characteristics were drawn from the careful analysis of relevant documentation, including census data, election results, and campaign related literature. Graphs and tables on the distribution of German population in Nebraska and a fine bibliography of primary and secondary materials accompany the narrative.

532 Knauss, James Owen. SOCIAL CONDITIONS AMONG THE PENNSYL-VANIA GERMANS IN THE EIGHTEENTH CENTURY AS REVEALED IN

GERMAN NEWSPAPERS PUBLISHED IN AMERICA. Pennsylvania German Society Proceedings, vol. 29. Lancaster: Pennsylvania German Society, 1922. 217 p. Bibliog.

A two-tier study: (1) a descriptive analysis of Pennsylvania German newspapers, and (2) social analysis of their readers. On the first, the history and characteristics of the newspapers and their publishers are described. On the second, the religious aspects, charities and humanitarian organizations, education, the language, occupational distribution, and political ideas and aspirations are explored. An important feature of the work is a checklist of German-language newspapers of the eighteenth century, and the U.S. libraries holding them.

533 Iverson, Noel. GERMANIA, U.S.A.: SOCIAL CHANGE IN NEW ULM, MINNESOTA. Minneapolis: University of Minnesota Press, 1966. 188 p. Bibliog., index.

A study in assimilation. The subject group is the "Turners" who came to the United States between 1830–48 and founded in 1856 Germania, a rural community, to insure political and religious freedom as well as economic security. The focus of the inquiry was to find out how status evolves in a community free from the pressures and prejudices that ethnic immigrants face in big cities. The work is based on questionnaires reprinted in the appendix. The results are displayed in forty-two tables. An extensive bibliography of primary and secondary sources is provided.

IX. ECONOMIC LIFE

AGRICULTURE

534 Long, Amos. THE PENNSYLVANIA GERMAN FAMILY FARM; A REGION-
AL ARCHITECTURAL AND FOLK CULTURAL STUDY OF AN AMERICAN
AGRICULTURAL COMMUNITY. Pennsylvania German Society Publica-
tions, vol. 6. Breinigsville: Pennsylvania German Society, 1972. 518 p.
Bibliog. notes, index.

An excellent source of information on Pennsylvania German
farm life, spiked with anecdotes culled firsthand from interviews and correspondence. A monument of the vanishing
Pennsylvania German life style, this work attempts to preserve
it through many photographs and illustrations. Especially interesting is the detailed treatment of the typical farm buildings:
the family home, smokehouse, icehouse, outhouse, barn, tool-
shed, smithy, chicken coop, milkhouse, tobacco barn, and
others.

535 Kollmorgen, Walter Martin. THE GERMAN-SWISS IN FRANKLIN
COUNTY, TENNESSEE; A STUDY IN THE SIGNIFICANCE OF CULTURAL
CONSIDERATIONS IN FARMING ENTERPRISES. Washington, D.C.:
U.S. Department of Agriculture, Bureau of Agricultural Economics, 1940.
113 p. Bibliog.

Using a broad gauged sociocultural approach, the author, an
agricultural economist, examines in minute detail all elements
that contributed to the formation of "cultural islands" in various farming areas of the country. The first part of the study
is a historical introduction to the county and its economy up
to the arrival of the first German-Swiss settlers immediately
after the Civil War. The rest of the work is a close analysis
of the farming methodology, land use patterns, and output of
the German-Swiss settlers, and the comparison of their farming program with three control groups in the county. Every
variable that accounted for the success of this program is
analyzed. Much of the data were drawn from official sources.
A good bibliography is appended.

536 _____. THE GERMAN SETTLEMENT IN CULLMAN COUNTY, ALABA-
MA, AN AGRICULTURAL ISLAND IN THE COTTON BELT. Washington,
D.C.: U.S. Department of Agriculture, Bureau of Agricultural Econo-
mics, 1941. 66 p. Bibliog. notes.

> The farming methods of the German settlements about fifty
> miles north of Birmingham, Alabama, originating in the 1870s,
> are the focus of this study. These methods differed greatly
> from the prevailing type of agriculture in the area. The study
> demonstrates the significance of cultural and social traditions.

537 _____. CULTURE OF A CONTEMPORARY RURAL COMMUNITY: THE
OLD ORDER AMISH OF LANCASTER COUNTY, PENNSYLVANIA. Rural
Life Studies, vol. 4. Washington, D.C.: U.S. Department of Agricul-
ture, Bureau of Agricultural Economics, 1942. 105 p. Bibliog. notes.

> Combining the methods of sociological inquiry with quantitative
> analysis of economics, the author investigates the factors that
> explain the stability and material growth of the group under
> study. The inquiry was carried out through a four-month field
> study, and the data were gathered from various sources. A
> map shows Amish and Mennonite communities in Lancaster
> County, and a chart gives the value of farmland between
> 1860 and 1935.

INDUSTRY AND CRAFTS

538 Schuyler, Hamilton. THE ROEBLINGS; A CENTURY OF ENGINEERS,
BRIDGE-BUILDERS AND INDUSTRIALISTS; THE STORY OF THREE GEN-
ERATIONS OF AN ILLUSTRIOUS FAMILY, 1831-1931. Princeton, N.J.:
Princeton University Press, 1931. Reprint. New York: AMS Press,
1972. 425 p. Bibliog. notes, index.

> A well-documented and illustrated dynastic biography focusing
> on the founder John August (1806-69) and his successors,
> Washington Augustus, Ferdinand William, and Charles Gusta-
> vus. The appendix includes comparative data on the suspen-
> sion bridges built by the company.

539 Baron, Stanley Wade. BREWED IN AMERICA; A HISTORY OF BEER AND
ALE IN THE UNITED STATES. Boston: Little, Brown and Co., 1962.
424 p. Bibliog., index.

> A general history covering the entire period from 1650, with
> a retrospective glance on the industry's origin in Europe. The
> role of Germans in the establishment of the industry is high-
> lighted. The bibliography contains many references document-
> ing German contribution to the industry.

540 Cochran, Thomas Childs. THE PABST BREWING COMPANY: THE HIS-
TORY OF AN AMERICAN BUSINESS. New York University, Graduate

School of Business Administration. Business History Series. New York:
New York University Press. Reprint. Westport, Conn.: Greenwood
Press, 1975. 451 p. Bibliog.

> Covers the first hundred years of the company's history from
> 1840, reconstructed from internal records and family papers.
> The narrative is complemented by supplementary materials
> which include, among others, a chronology and a roster of
> managerial and other staff.

541 Miller, Hugo. "Deutsch Amerikanische Typographia." In George A.
Tracy, comp., HISTORY OF THE TYPOGRAPHICAL UNION; ITS BEGIN-
NINGS, PROGRESS AND DEVELOPMENT, ITS BENEFICIAL AND EDU-
CATIONAL FEATURES TOGETHER WITH A CHAPTER ON THE EARLY
ORGANIZATIONS OF PRINTERS, COMPILED BY THE AUTHORITY OF
THE EXECUTIVE COUNCIL OF THE INTERNATIONAL UNION, compiled
by George A. Tracy, pp. 1069-94. Indianapolis: International Typo-
graphical Union, 1913.

> An important source of information on the German–American
> Typographical Union which was a branch of the International
> Union.

542 Omwake, John. THE CONESTOGA SIX-HORSE BELL TEAMS OF EAST-
ERN PENNSYLVANIA. Cincinnati: Ebbert and Richardson, 1930. 163 p.
Bibliog. notes.

> An interesting contribution to early regional transportation
> history with many passing references to Pennsylvania Germans.
> The lore of wagoneering is ably presented through abundant
> quotes and illustrations.

543 Shumway, George; Durell, Edward; and Frey, Howard C. CONESTOGA
WAGON, 1750-1850; FREIGHT CARRIER FOR 100 YEARS OF AMERICA'S
WESTWARD EXPANSION. New York: Early American Industries Asso-
ciation and George Shumway, 1964. 206 p. Bibliog. notes, index.

> This means of transportation spread from the Alleghenies region,
> which was heavily populated by Germans. The documentation
> gives many sources to German references. For example, there
> is a list of 194 wagoners with place of residence, and another
> list of wagonmakers of York County, Pennsylvania, active be-
> tween 1800 and 1850. The work is filled with fascinating bits
> of relevant information on the technology of the Conestoga
> wagon, early freight transportation, and roads and turnpikes.

544 Dillin, John Grace Wolf. THE KENTUCKY RIFLE; A STUDY IN THE
ORIGIN AND DEVELOPMENT OF A PURELY AMERICAN TYPE OF FIRE-
ARM, TOGETHER WITH ACCURATE HISTORICAL DATA CONCERNING
EARLY COLONIAL GUNSMITHS, AND PROFUSELY ILLUSTRATED WITH
PHOTOGRAPHIC REPRODUCTION OF THEIR FINEST WORK. 5th ed.
York, Pa.: George Shumway, 1962. 202 p. Index.

545   Lindsay, Merrill. THE KENTUCKY RIFLE. New York: Arma Press and
      Historical Society of York County, 1972. 101 p.

      Photographs by Bruce Pendleton.

546   Kauffman, Henry J. THE PENNSYLVANIA-KENTUCKY RIFLE. Harris-
      burg, Pa.: Stackpole, 1960. 376 p.

      The Kentucky rifle played an important role on the American
      frontier. Its manufacture has been associated by experts with
      Pennsylvania Germans. Items 544, 545 and 546 constitute an
      adequate array of sources of information on the history of the
      weapon and the Pennsylvania gunsmiths who introduced it in
      America.

NOTE: For the history of the achievements of individuals in industry and business, see the Biography section.

X. CULTURAL LIFE

547 Wish, Harvey. SOCIETY AND THOUGHT IN AMERICA. 2d ed. Vol.
1, SOCIETY AND THOUGHT IN EARLY AMERICA; A SOCIAL AND
INTELLECTUAL HISTORY OF THE AMERICAN PEOPLE THROUGH 1865.
New York: David McKay, 1950. 612 p. Bibliog., index. Vol. 2,
SOCIETY AND THOUGHT IN MODERN AMERICA; A SOCIAL AND
INTELLECTUAL HISTORY FROM 1865. New York: Longmans, Green
and Co., 1952. 618 p. Bibliog., index.

>A comprehensive discussion in two volumes of philosophical,
>literary, and artistic currents in American history. The author
>contends that the cultural evolution of America was propelled
>by a process of borrowing in which the Germans played an
>important role. The discussion of German influence is dispersed
>throughout the work, but there are some specific concentrations.
>In volume one, chapter ten deals expansively with German in-
>fluence on education and literature, and the impact of the
>"Forty-Eighters." Volume two considers German-American role
>in politics, music, literature, and in broader cultural areas
>as well. Additional subjects highlighted include German Jews,
>the Turnverein, the labor movement, and others. Among the
>personalities, Horace Mann, Carl Schurz, and George Ticknor
>receive special attention. The documentary sources of this
>work are discussed in bibliographic essays. They include many
>German-American items.

548 Pochmann, Henry August. GERMAN CULTURE IN AMERICA; PHILOSO-
PHICAL AND LITERARY INFLUENCES, 1600-1900. With the assistance
of Arthur R. Schultz, et al. Madison: University of Wisconsin Press,
1957. Reprint. Westport, Conn.: Greenwood Press, 1978. 865 p.
Bibliog., index.

>A monumental undertaking, hailed by critics when it was pub-
>lished, that has now become a classic. It surveys the impact of
>German thought, literature, education, and religion upon
>America by tracing influences in the works of outstanding
>American philosophers and authors, and in the manifestations
>of cultural movements, trends, and institutions. The first part

deals with German thought in America, in which ideas that
Americans studying in Germany borrowed are explored, together
with homegrown ideas, concepts, and issues generated by German-Americans themselves. The second part focuses on German literary influences in which the popularity and cultivation
of major German writers and poets in America are discussed.
Borrowings from German writers and their influences are traced,
for example, in the writings of Hawthorne, Poe, Longfellow,
Thoreau, Melville, and Whitman, to name only a few. Equal
in dimension are the notes covering almost three hundred pages
referring to an immense array of sources. The index takes up
sixty-three pages.

549 Vogel, Stanley M. GERMAN LITERARY INFLUENCES ON THE AMERI-
CAN TRANSCENDENTALISTS. Yale Studies in English, vol. 127. New
Haven, Conn.: Yale University Press, 1955. 196 p. Bibliog., index.

Consists of a survey of New England criticism of German literary and philosophical works which were current in America
during the first half of the nineteenth century, and an examination of German thought elements in the works of Emerson,
Channing, and the other major representatives of the Trans-
cendentalist movement. The sources from which the material
was drawn are given in the footnotes, often with library location. The book is enriched with a variety of supplementary
documentation of interest to the intellectual historian. For
example, there is a survey of German books in original and
in translation available in Boston during the period covered.
The author was able to compose a list of German titles in
Emerson's private library and trace in library circulation records are Emerson's readings of German literature through his borrowings.

550 Metzner, Henry Christian Anton. A BRIEF HISTORY OF THE AMERICAN
TURNERBUND. Rev. ed. Pittsburgh: National Executive Committee of
the American Turnerbund, 1924. 56 p.

A revised edition of the 1911 work surveying the history of
the organization of German gymnasts founded in 1848. The
study explores the organization's influence on public schools,
and the role of Friedrich Ludwig Jahn and the other leaders.
Additional topics include the Turnerbund's general philosophy
and the story of its teacher-training institutions.

551 Flanagan, John T. "The German in American Fiction." IN THE TREK
OF THE IMMIGRANTS: ESSAYS PRESENTED TO CARL WITTKE, edited
by Oscar Fritiof Ander, pp. 95-113. Augustana College Publications,
no. 31. Rock Island, Ill.: Augustana College Library, 1964. Bibliog.
notes.

552 Roucek, Joseph Slabey; Hero, Alice; and Downey, Jean, comps. THE IMMIGRANT IN FICTION AND BIOGRAPHY. New York: Bureau for Intercultural Education, 1945. 32 p.

> A useful but outdated list of annotated entries covering twenty-eight ethnic groups. Books for juvenile readers are marked.

553 Peschke, Melitta Diez. THE GERMAN IMMIGRANT AND HIS READING. Chicago: American Library Association, 1929. 32 p.

> A work of historical interest listing four hundred key titles on a variety of subjects, including citizenship. It was intended for American public libraries serving German-American readers who preferred to read works written in their mother tongue.

554 Fleming, Donald Harnish, and Bailyn, Bernard, eds. THE INTELLECTUAL MIGRATION; EUROPE AND AMERICA, 1930-1960. Cambridge, Mass.: Belknap Press of Harvard University Press, 1969. 748 p. Bibliog. notes, index.

> A collection of essays and personal testimonies illustrating the background, extent and impact of German-speaking intellectuals and artists, most of whom were refugees from the Nazis. Following an overview of the cultural climate of the Weimar Republic, the material is presented in chapters, each of which is devoted to a particular profession or field. Within the chapters, prominent representatives of the profession formulate personal statements about themselves and their field. The narrative is supported by many footnote references to a great variety of sources. The intellectual migration dealt with in this work encompasses German-speaking emigres, not only from Germany, but from other central European countries as well. The book includes three hundred biographical sketches, a list of artists who fled from fascism, and a collection of twenty-seven photographs showing works of German emigre architects.

555 Kent, Donald Peterson. THE REFUGEE INTELLECTUAL, THE AMERICANIZATION OF THE IMMIGRANTS OF 1933-1941. New York: Columbia University Press, 1953. 317 p. Bibliog., index.

> An interesting sociological study, based on questionnaires, probing into the background, social, and demographic characteristics. Most of the refugees surveyed came from Germany and Austria. In addition to the social and demographic characteristics, the study deals with their acculturation, livelihood, occupational adjustment, and attitudes toward America. The work is profusely documented with statistical data, official sources, excerpts from newspapers, and quotes from respondents.

556 THE LEGACY OF THE GERMAN REFUGEE INTELLECTUALS. Edited by

Richard Boyers. New York: Schocken Books, 1972. 325 p. Bibliog. notes.

Originally a special issue of the quarterly SALMAGUNDI (nos. 10-11, Fall 1969-Winter 1970) dealing with German philosophers and social thinkers and their impact on American thought. They include Walter Benjamin, Max Werthei-mer, Hannah Arendt, T.W. Adorno, Erich Kahler, Marcuse, Bertolt Brecht, Karl Mannheim, Otto Kirchheimer, Felix Kaufman, and Ernst Bloch. The essays are scholarly with footnotes, but no bibliographies.

557 Fermi, Laura. ILLUSTRIOUS IMMIGRANTS: THE INTELLECTUAL MIGRA-TION FROM EUROPE: 1931-41. 2d ed. Chicago: University of Chicago Press, 1971. 440 p. Bibliog., index.

The majority of the immigrants concerned came from Germany and Central Europe, and were men and women who received their higher education abroad and had achieved some stature before coming to the United States. This immigration was unique in American history. The German intellectual refugees of 1848 left their mark mainly in the realm of politics. This influx of German intellectuals had great influence on American science and culture. The author assesses the achievement of the refugee intellectuals of the 1930s in their respective fields of pursuit after their arrival, and describes their process of Americanization. A roster with biographical data is given separately at the end.

558 Mann, Erika, and Mann, Klaus. ESCAPE TO LIFE. Boston: Houghton Mifflin, 1939. 384 p. Index.

A highly readable personal account of the life of German emigre intellectuals in America, and of their reaction to their new environment. It is particularly interesting for the many intimate biographical details of some of the great writers, scientists, and artists of the twentieth century.

559 Committee for the Study of Recent Immigration from Europe. REFUGEES IN AMERICA; REPORT OF THE COMMITTEE FOR THE STUDY OF RECENT IMMIGRATION FROM EUROPE. By Maurice R. Davie with the colla-boration of Sarah W. Cohn, et al. New York: Harper, 1947. Reprint. New York: Greenwood Press, 1974. 453 p. Index.

An in-depth exploration covering the period from 1930 to the middle of the 1940s based on questionnaires. Eighty-two per-cent of the refugees surveyed were of German origin and they included both Jews and non-Jews. The work establishes key characteristics of the refugees, and discusses their major social, economical, and psychological problems. American reactions to the refugees are also described. The appendices focus on prominent refugees, Nobel Prize winners, scientists, and others.

In addition to the questionnaire, a great deal of data were gathered from government documents and periodicals.

XI. EDUCATION

GERMAN INFLUENCES

560 Walz, John Albrecht. GERMAN INFLUENCE IN AMERICAN EDUCA-
TION AND CULTURE. Philadelphia: Carl Schurz Memorial Foundation,
1936. Reprint. Freeport, N.Y.: Books for Libraries, 1969. 79 p.
Bibliog.

A succinct assessment of borrowed German theories and philo-
sophies on all levels of education on the one hand, and the
impact of thoughts and educational practices of immigrant German educators on the other. Originally, it was prepared as
a lecture at a round table of "American-German Relations"
at the University of Virginia in 1935. The work is well documented.

561 Baylor, Ruth M. ELIZABETH PALMER PEABODY: KINDERGARTEN PIO-
NEER. Philadelphia: University of Pennsylvania Press, 1965. 228 p.
Bibliog., index.

The movement to introduce kindergartens in the United States
received its initial inspiration from Friedrich Froebel's efforts
in Germany. It was also encouraged by Margaretta Schurz,
Carl Schurz's spouse, with whom Elizabeth P. Peabody kept
close contact. Footnotes lead to many pertinent references.
The bibliography is exhaustive. A chronology traces the development of kindergartens in America from 1836-92.

562 Jenkins, Elizabeth. "How the Kindergarten Found Its Way to America."
WISCONSIN MAGAZINE OF HISTORY 14 (September 1930): 48-62.
Bibliog. notes.

An essay on the three pioneers of kindergarten in America,
Margaretta Schurz, Elizabeth P. Peabody, and Caroline L.
Frankenberg. The treatment is biographical with references
to sources.

563 Hofstadter, Richard, and Metzger, Walter. THE DEVELOPMENT OF ACADEMIC FREEDOM IN THE UNITED STATES. New York: Columbia University Press, 1955. 527 p. Bibliog. notes, index.

> A general treatment which devotes about forty-five pages to the discussion of German influences in shaping American higher education. The bibliography offers further leads to writings on the subject.

564 Diehl, Carl. AMERICAN AND GERMAN SCHOLARSHIP, 1770-1870. Yale Historical Publications. Miscellany, 115. New Haven, Conn.: Yale University Press, 1978. 194 p. Bibliog., index.

> The subject of this monograph is American students in German universities between 1815 and 1870. The author describes and analyzes the nature of German scholarship in two distinct time periods and explores American attitudes toward it.

565 Thwing, Charles Franklin. THE AMERICAN AND THE GERMAN UNIVERSITY, ONE HUNDRED YEARS OF HISTORY. New York: Macmillan, 1928. 238 p. Bibliog. notes, index.

> A basic treatise aiming at "discovering and measuring the worth of contribution made by the German university in the last hundred years to higher education in the United States." The study explores the reasons why American students in the nineteenth century sought professional education in German rather than in English universities. A special chapter is devoted to teachers from Germany in American universities. The documentation is excellent.

566 Hart, James Morgan. GERMAN UNIVERSITIES: A NARRATIVE OF PERSONAL EXPERIENCE, TOGETHER WITH STATISTICAL INFORMATION, PRACTICAL SUGGESTIONS, AND A COMPARISON OF GERMAN, ENGLISH, AND AMERICAN SYSTEMS OF HIGHER EDUCATION. New York: G.P. Putnam's Sons, 1874. 398 p.

> A historically significant item which may have been influential in its time. In addition to providing practical information to prospective American students, it was also the intention of the author to promote the adoption of methods and standards of German universities in the United States.

EDUCATION IN PENNSYLVANIA

567 Wickersham, James Pyle. A HISTORY OF EDUCATION IN PENNSYLVANIA, PRIVATE AND PUBLIC, ELEMENTARY AND HIGHER. FROM THE TIME THE SWEDES SETTLED ON THE DELAWARE TO THE PRESENT DAY. 1886. Reprint. American Education: Its Men, Ideas, and Institutions [Series]. New York: Arno Press, 1969. 683 p. Index.

A comprehensive treatment devoting considerable attention to every segment of Pennsylvania German settlers. The work was written in a popular tone. The contributions of H.M. Muhlenberg, Count Zinzendorf, Christopher Dock, George Rapp, and the two Christopher Sowers (father and son), are highlighted.

568 Mulhern, James. A HISTORY OF SECONDARY EDUCATION IN PENNSYLVANIA. Philadelphia: Science Press Printing, 1933. Reprint. American Education: Its Men, Ideas, and Institutions. New York: Arno Press, 1969. 714 p. Bibliog., index.

A superbly documented comprehensive history, originally prepared as a doctoral dissertation at the University of Pennsylvania. The achievements of the German population in the field of education are not discussed in separate chapters, but their stories are interwoven in the body of the narrative. A great amount of relevant information can, however, be extracted through a detailed index. The bibliography lists almost 1,500 items.

569 Weber, Samuel Edwin. THE CHARITY MOVEMENT IN COLONIAL PENNSYLVANIA, 1754-1763; A HISTORY OF THE EDUCATIONAL STRUGGLE BETWEEN THE COLONIAL AUTHORITIES AND THE GERMAN INHABITANTS OF PENNSYLVANIA. 1905. Reprint. New York: Arno Press, 1969. 74 p. Bibliog., index.

The term refers to such organizations as the English Society for the Propagation of Christian Knowledge. Their activities in Pennsylvania among the German population from 1683 to the end of the eighteenth century are discussed here, together with the role of the press and publishing in the educational process. The author attributes their ultimate failure to the fact that these schools neglected to cultivate the German tongue and culture. A 70-item bibliography provides access to materials on the subject.

570 Klinefelter, Walter. THE ABC BOOKS OF THE PENNSYLVANIA GERMANS. Pennsylvania German Society Publications, vol. 7. Breinigsville: Pennsylvania German Society, 1973. 104 p. Bibliog. notes.

An analytical treatment covering the period from 1690 to the nineteenth century. Books of both secular and religious nature are dealt with. The work comes alive through many facsimile reproductions of title pages and illustrations. The material discussed is bibliographically described in a checklist consisting of 196 items. For many, library location is indicated.

Education

RELIGIOUS GROUPS

571   Haller, Mabel. EARLY MORAVIAN EDUCATION IN PENNSYLVANIA.
Transactions of the Moravian Historical Society, vol. 15. Nazareth,
Pa.: Moravian Historical Society, 1953. 423 p. Bibliog., index.

A detailed exposition of the history, objectives, methods,
institutions, and concentrations of education among the Moravians, with particular emphasis on the period from 1740 to
1840. The author encompasses a broad range of topics. First,
the story of Moravian schools in European and American locations is told in considerable detail. This is followed by a
section dealing with education in Moravian Indian missions.
The philosophical foundations, instructional practices, the
organization, control, and support of Moravian schools is explained. The material was drawn from primary sources such
as records of Moravian congregations, diaries of pastors, and
periodicals. Thirty-two illustrations and a lavish bibliography
of 760 items complement the text.

572   Hartzler, John Ellsworth. EDUCATION AMONG THE MENNONITES
OF AMERICA. Introduction by Elmer E.S. Johnson. Danvers, Ill.:
Central Mennonite Publishing Board, 1925. 195 p. Bibliog.

A systematic exploration of the evolution of the philosophical
and ethical foundations of Mennonite education. The institutions, the practices, and functions of which are discussed in
detail, include Sunday schools, German preparatory schools,
and higher education. The contribution of the influential
schoolmaster Christopher Dock is given considerable attention.
The material is drawn from church documents and a variety of
primary resources.

573   Hostetler, John. EDUCATIONAL ACHIEVEMENT AND LIFE STYLES IN
A TRADITIONAL SOCIETY, THE OLD ORDER AMISH. Final Report.
Washington, D.C.: U.S. Office of Education, Bureau of Research,
1969. 523 p. Bibliog.

A technical report of a research project for the U.S. Office
of Education, summarizing and documenting a variety of tests
given to Amish children. The purpose of the study was to
find out how the culture of a traditional society affects performance and personality. A historical essay discusses education and socialization practices of the Amish, beginning with
the sixteenth century. The many attachments include a list
of Old Order Amish elementary textbooks in print, papers
generated during the execution of the project, and a comprehensive bibliography.

574   Hostetler, Andrew, and Huntington, Gertrude Enders. CHILDREN IN
AMISH SOCIETY; SOCIALIZATION AND COMMUNITY EDUCATION.
New York: Holt, Rinehart and Winston, 1971. 119 p. Bibliog.

A popular treatment of the subject, based on Hostetler's research project for the U.S. Office of Education (see 573). The study offers many insights into the psychology of the Amish children. Much of the material was gathered in fieldwork in Pennsylvania, Indiana, and Ohio. The educational system of the Amish is given in-depth treatment. A map, photographs, and bibliographic citations complement the work.

575 Keim, Albert N., ed. COMPULSORY EDUCATION AND THE AMISH: THE RIGHT NOT TO BE MODERN. Boston: Beacon Press, 1975. 211 p. Bibliog., index.

A collection of important legal essays on court cases involving the reluctance of the Amish to expose their children to public education. The issues are discussed in a historical framework. There is a chronology of court cases between 1927-72 with appropriate citations and summaries of decisions. The various essays discuss landmark cases and evaluate their legal significance. They include D.A. Erickson's writings entitled "Showdown at an Amish Schoolhouse" (Iowa), and "Persecution of Leroy Garber" (Kansas). Other important articles in the collection include: (1) W.B. Ball, "Building a Landmark Case: Wisconsin v. Yoder"; (2) J.A. Hostetler, "Cultural Context of the Wisconsin Case"; and (3) L. Pfeffer, "The Many Meanings of the Yoder Case." In addition, two essays shed light on the matter from the Amish point of view: J. Stoll, "Who Shall Educate Our Children?", and Stephen Arons, "Compulsory Education: The Plain Peoples Resist." The appendix contains the text of the Supreme Court decision in the Wisconsin v. Yoder case (May 1972). All of the articles are well documented and there is a classified bibliography on the subject listing over 250 pertinent items.

576 Rodgers, Harrell R. COMMUNITY CONFLICT, PUBLIC OPINION, AND THE LAW; THE AMISH DISPUTE IN IOWA. Columbus, Ohio: Charles E. Merrill Publishing, 1969. 161 p. Bibliog. notes, index.

Originally a doctoral dissertation at the University of Iowa, the work deals with the confrontation in the 1960s between the Oelwein school district and the six conservative Mennonite groups in the district. Members of these religious communities refused to send their children to public schools beyond the eighth grade, fearing that its "corruptive" influence would turn the children away from their religion. The suit brought against the Mennonite communities by the state of Iowa hit national headlines. The study explores legal aspects of the case and sampled public opinion.

XII. LANGUAGE AND LITERATURE

GERMAN LANGUAGE IN AMERICA

General Studies

577   Fishman, Joshua A. LANGUAGE LOYALTY IN THE UNITED STATES:
THE MAINTENANCE AND PERPETUATION OF NON-ENGLISH MOTHER
TONGUES BY AMERICAN ETHNIC AND RELIGIOUS GROUPS. With
the assistance of Mary E. Warshauer, and with an introduction by Einar
Haugen. Janua Linguarum. Series Maior, vol. 24. The Hague: Mou-
ton and Co., 1966. Reprint. Bilingual-Bicultural Education in the
United States [Series]. New York: Arno Press, 1978. 478 p.

> A major study which explores the role of the ethnic press,
> foreign-language broadcasting, the ethnic group school, church,
> and other agencies. A special chapter is devoted to German-
> American language maintenance efforts, consisting of about
> fifty pages. This chapter has a sixty-item bibliography of
> relevant literature. Several maps show the distribution of
> German-speaking populations in the United States.

578   Gilbert, Glenn Gordon, ed. GERMAN LANGUAGE IN AMERICA: A
SYMPOSIUM. Austin: University of Texas Press, 1971. 217 p. Bibliog., index.

> Contains the papers presented at the Tenth German Language
> Symposium discussing the subject matter from a variety of
> perspectives. The following topics were dealt with: (1) dia-
> lectology of American Colonial German; (2) word geography
> of Pennsylvania German: extent and causes; (3) German in
> Wisconsin; (4) German in Virginia and West Virginia; (5)
> Pennsylvania German folklore research: a historical analysis;
> (6) German as an immigrant, indigenous, foreign, and second
> language in the United States; (7) a unified proposal for the
> study of the German language in the United States: a discus-
> sion; (8) German folklore in America: a discussion; and (9)
> German pedagogy and the survival of German in America: a

discussion. A bibliography of 360 items and some maps are appended to the work.

579   Arndt, Karl John Richard. "German as the Official Language of the United States of America?" MONATSHEFTE 68 (Summer 1976): 129-50.

"A source study of the 'legend' that German but for one vote would have replaced English as the official American language shows that, upon the request of Germans in Virginia to print the laws of the United States in German, two committees of Congress recommended that the request be granted. After assignment of the petition to a third committee the request was bypassed. New evidence is presented to show that the 'legend' applied to the State of Pennsylvania, but not to the exclusion of English. In conclusion, the 'legend' is not pure 'legend'; but both nationally and for the State of Pennsylvania there is sound evidence for the strength of the German language in America. This is further documented by the expansion of the German language as shown in Arndt and Olson: THE GERMAN LANGUAGE PRESS OF THE AMERICAS." (Author's abstract).

Bibliographies

580   Haugen, Einar Ingvald. BILINGUALISM IN THE AMERICAS: A BIBLIOGRAPHY AND RESEARCH GUIDE. American Dialect Society Publications, no. 26. University: University of Alabama Press, 1956. 159 p. Bibliog.

A scholarly treatment of the field, its concerns, and its literature. The author brings in a wealth of information on the languages, their influence on one another, their impact on the speakers and their communities, especially as it affects acculturation and education. More than 650 works are encompassed here, ranging from periodical articles to federal and United Nations documents. There is an index to the languages discussed which shows numerous references to the German language.

581   Viereck, Wolfgang. "German Dialects Spoken in the United States and Canada and Problems of German-English Language Contact Especially in North America: A Bibliography." ORBIS 16 (1967): 549-68; Supplement 17 (1968): 532-35.

In all, about three hundred items are identified here, predominately in English, encompassing surveys, studies, dictionaries, doctoral dissertations, and periodical articles on both scholarly and popular levels.

582   Eichhoff, Juergen. "Bibliography of German Dialects Spoken in the Uni-

ted States and Canada and Problems of German-English Language Contact, Especially in North America, 1968-1976, with Pre-1968 Supplements." MONATSHEFTE 68 (Summer 1976): 196-208.

This bibliography continues that which was published by Viereck (see 581).

Dictionaries

583 Lambert, Marcus Bachman. A DICTIONARY OF THE NON-ENGLISH WORDS OF THE PENNSYLVANIA-GERMAN DIALECT, WITH AN APPENDIX. Pennsylvania German Society Proceedings and Addresses, vol. 30. Lancaster: Pennsylvania German Society, 1924. 193 p.

A respected Pennsylvania German-English etymological dictionary with sixteen thousand entries.

584 Rahn, C.R. A PENNSYLVANIA DUTCH DICTIONARY. PENNSYLVANIA DUTCH WORDS TRANSLATED INTO ENGLISH. 2d ed. Quakerstown, Pa.: Meredith, 1948. 104 p.

A Pennsylvania Dutch-English dictionary of approximately 5,500 words. A brief review of Pennsylvania Dutch history, culture, and language as well as an obituary which assesses the contribution of A.H. Horne, a Pennsylvania Dutch linguist, are appended.

585 Danner, Edwin Russell. PENNSYLVANIA DUTCH DICTIONARY AND HANDBOOK, WITH SPECIAL EMPHASIS ON THE DIALECT THAT WAS, AND IS, SPOKEN IN YORK COUNTY, PENNSYLVANIA. York, Pa.: William Penn Senior High and Atreus Wanner Vocational School, 1951. 178 p.

An English-Pennsylvania Dutch dictionary of words and phrases with eighteen thousand entries. No pronunciation aids or other features.

586 Snader, Howard Benjamin. GLOSSARY OF 6,167 ENGLISH WORDS AND EXPRESSIONS AND THEIR PENNSYLVANIA DUTCH EQUIVALENTS. Reading, Pa.: Reading Eagle Press, 1949. 64 p.

An English-Pennsylvania Dutch dictionary in which the Pennsylvania Dutch version is given phonetically. The word usage is from the Berks County area.

587 Aurand, Ammon Monroe. QUAINT IDIOMS AND EXPRESSIONS OF THE PENNSYLVANIA-GERMANS; A COLLECTION OF CURIOUS PHRASES AND TERMS EMPLOYED BY GROUPS OF AMERICANS NUMBERING INTO THE MILLIONS, THAT TRULY FLAVOR THEIR ENGLISH. Harrisburg, Pa.: Aurand Press, 1939. 32 p.

Two types of idiomatic usage are covered: first, Pennsylvania German idioms that speakers mix into their English, and the other, misspelled or misused English words adapted to the local German dialect. These idiomatic oddities are illustrated in typical sentences for context.

Grammars

588 Buffington, Albert F., and Barba, Preston A. A PENNSYLVANIA GERMAN GRAMMAR. Rev. ed. Pennsylvania German Folklore Society Yearbook, vol. 27. Allentown: Pennsylvania German Folklore Society, 1965. 167 p. Bibliog.

A systematic treatment of Pennsylvania German Grammar, serving as a textbook, as well as a reference work. The initial part deals with the nature of the language, spelling, and punctuation followed by twenty lessons on points of grammar. A selection of readings in Pennsylvania German prose and poetry is provided. The authors designed a system of transliteration of Pennsylvania German, essentially an oral language, based on the German rather than the English orthography.

589 Frey, John William. A SIMPLE GRAMMAR OF PENNSYLVANIA DUTCH. Clinton, S.C.: J.W. Frey, 1942. 140 p.

Designed for the self-learner, this is a standard book focusing on the York County usage. It has been criticized for some errors and omissions.

German Dialects

590 Whyte, John. AMERICAN WORDS AND WAYS, ESPECIALLY FOR GERMAN AMERICANS. New York: Viking Press, 1943. 184 p. Bibliog., index.

The significance of this work is that it shows how American Germans see the culture and mores of their adopted country. It provides interesting glimpses into the acculturation process.

591 Learned, Marion Dexter. "The Pennsylvania-German Dialect." AMERICAN JOURNAL OF PHILOLOGY 9 (1888): 64-83, 178-97, 326-39, 425-56; 10 (1889): 288-317.

A study extending to 114 pages which was originally published in installments over a period of two years. The work is analytical as well as interpretive, seeking causes and laws underlying the change of the language. The main topics include: (1) early colonization to 1800; (2) phonology of vowels and consonants; (3) consonants; (4) inflection, verb tenses, noun cases; and (5) mixture with English.

592 Buffington, Albert F. "Linguistic Variants in the Pennsylvania German Dialect." PENNSYLVANIA GERMAN FOLKLORE SOCIETY YEARBOOK 13 (1948): 217-52. Allentown: Pennsylvania German Folklore Society, 1949.

> A report of a professional linguist made in the field in the 1940s, dealing with occurrences of some phonological, morphological, syntactical, and lexicographical phenomena of a set of words in a number of Pennsylvania counties.

593 Reed, Carroll Edward, and Seifert, Lester W. A LINGUISTIC ATLAS OF PENNSYLVANIA GERMAN. Marburg, Lahn, Germany: W.J. Becker, 1954. 6 p. 100 maps.

> A highly technical, graphic illustration of the use of stock phrases and idiomatic expressions in Pennsylvania counties and in some parts of Germany. Data were collected from questionnaire and personal interviews in the field. The introduction provides references to earlier studies of the Pennsylvania German dialect.

594 Gilbert, Glenn Gordon. LINGUISTIC ATLAS OF TEXAS GERMAN. Austin: University of Texas Press, 1972. 148 leaves. Bibliog.

> A collection of 154 maps and a twenty-five page interpretive text. The impact area is the southeast-central region of Texas, bounded roughly by Houston, San Antonio, Victoria, and Austin. The maps show phonological, syntactical, and lexical variations of specific words and phrases in German on the one hand, and German equivalents of English fixed phrases, as well as semantic variants for standard German lexical terms on the other. A complex system of codes is used to indicate occurrences. The work also includes a review of previous studies on Texas German, with a bibliography of seventy-one atlases and linguistic works.

595 _____, ed. TEXAS STUDIES IN BILINGUALISM: SPANISH, FRENCH, GERMAN, CZECH, POLISH, SERBIAN, AND NORWEGIAN IN THE SOUTHWEST; WITH A CONCLUDING CHAPTER ON CODE-SWITCHING AND MODES OF SPEAKING AMERICAN SWEDISH. Berlin: Walter de Gruyter, 1970. 223 p. Bibliog. notes, index.

> This compendium of highly technical essays by specialists devotes three entire chapters to German subjects: (1) Glen G. Gilbert, "The Phonology, Morphology, and Lexicon of a German Text from Fredericksburg, Texas"; (2) William Pulte, Jr., "An Analysis of Selected German Dialects of North Texas and Oklahoma"; and (3) Joseph B. Wilson, "Unusual German Lexical Items from the Lee-Fayette County Area of Texas." Much of the material is the result of the authors' fieldwork.

GERMAN-AMERICAN LITERATURE

General Works

596   GERMAN-AMERICAN LITERATURE. Edited by Don Heinrich Tolzmann.
       Metuchen, N.J.: Scarecrow Press, 1977. 328 p. Bibliog. notes, in-
       dex.

       An assemblage of articles and essays collectively intended to
       provide an introductory history of German-American literature.
       They were written by recognized authorities and originally
       published in scholarly journals. The material is presented in
       seven parts. They include broad treatments of themes such as
       regional literature, the German-American press, the German-
       American theatre, and German-American literature today. A
       special section is devoted to detailed discussions of the literary
       achievements of twenty-four German-American writers and
       poets.

597   GERMANICA-AMERICANA, 1976: SYMPOSIUM ON GERMAN-AMERI-
       CAN LITERATURE AND CULTURE AT THE UNIVERSITY OF KANSAS,
       LAWRENCE, KANSAS, OCTOBER 8-9, 1976. Edited by Erich A. Al-
       brecht, and J. Anthony Burzle. Lawrence: Max Kade Document and
       Research Center, University of Kansas, 1977. 129 p. Bibliog. notes.

598   Hofacker, Erich P. GERMAN LITERATURE AS REFLECTED IN THE GER-
       MAN LANGUAGE PRESS OF ST. LOUIS PRIOR TO 1898. Washington
       University Studies. New Series. Language and Literature, no. 16.
       Saint Louis: Washington University Press, 1946. 125 p. Bibliog. notes,
       index.

       The diffusion of German literature among German residents in
       America, especially in Missouri and adjacent areas by means
       of the local German-language newspapers, is the focus of this
       inquiry. To keep their readers informed and entertained, these
       dailies regularly printed novels, short stories, poems, and book
       reviews by contemporary and earlier writers of the old coun-
       try. The daily press thus became the prime force of the move-
       ment of ideas from Germany to America.

599   Kamman, William Frederic. SOCIALISM IN GERMAN AMERICAN LITE-
       RATURE. Americana Germanica, no. 24. 1917. Reprint. Radical Tra-
       dition in America [Series]. Westport, Conn.: Hyperion Press, 1975.
       124 p. Bibliog.

       A published doctoral dissertation at the University of Pennsyl-
       vania. It deals with ideas, the literary vehicles through
       which they were disseminated, authors, and organizations,
       such as the Freie Gemeinden, and the liberal athletic organi-
       zations. The impact of socialistic ideas on German-American

literature is explored in-depth and is interpreted as a revolt of rationalistic thought against revealed religion. The material was drawn mainly from German-language works.

600 Uhlendorf, Bernhard Alexander. "German-American Poetry, a Contribution to Colonial Literature." JAHRBUCH DER DEUTSCH-AMERIKANIS-CHEN HISTORISCHEN GESELLSCHAFT VON ILLINOIS 22-23 (1922-23): 109-295.

Provides a good sampling of poetry in the German language generated during the colonial period, written by natives or immigrants. Biographical and critical notes accompany the text.

Authors

601 Ward, Robert Elmer. DICTIONARY OF GERMAN–AMERICAN CREATIVE WRITERS: FROM THE 17TH CENTURY TO THE PRESENT. Vol. 1, BIBLIOGRAPHICAL HANDBOOK. Cleveland: German-American, 1978-- .

Pennsylvania German Literature

602 Robacker, Earl Francis. PENNSYLVANIA GERMAN LITERATURE; CHANGING TRENDS FROM 1683 TO 1942. Philadelphia: University of Pennsylvania Press, 1943. 217 p. Bibliog., index.

A survey divided into the following time periods: (1) period of greatest religious significance, 1683-1800; (2) period of transition, 1800-61; (3) the language-conscious period, 1861-1902; (4) the local color period, 1902-28; (5) the folk-conscious period, 1928-42; and (6) the scene as a whole. Literature is given a broad interpretation, but excludes devotional works, political tracts, textbooks, and journalistic works. The term "Pennsylvania German literature" implies any work written by a member of the group, in English, High German, or Pennsylvania German. The text contains a considerable amount of bibliographical detail about authors, and cited works are critically appraised. The appendix contains examples from the various genres. A bibliography of two hundred items accompanies the text.

603 Reichard, Harry Hess. PENNSYLVANIA-GERMAN DIALECT WRITINGS AND THEIR WRITERS. Pennsylvania German Society Proceedings, vol. 26. Lancaster: Pennsylvania German Society, 1918. 400 p. Bibliog.

A valuable source book of information about the lives, literary activities, and publications of thirty-two authors from the nineteenth and early twentieth centuries who wrote in the Pennsylvania German dialect. Following an introductory overview, the authors are treated individually, and for each, a

bibliography of their works and biographical details are given,
together with a critical appraisal of their accomplishments.
Several entries are illustrated with portraits. The next section
lists the primary and secondary materials which served as
sources for the book. In the subsequent part of the work,
the author provides an index to collections and compendia
where poetic and prose pieces of the authors treated can be
found. Further useful components include a list of Pennsylvania German lexical works, and a list of newspapers which
have regularly featured Pennsylvania German literary works
with directory information.

604   Reichard, Harry Hess, ed. PENNSYLVANIA GERMAN VERSE: AN
      ANTHOLOGY OF REPRESENTATIVE SELECTIONS IN THE DIALECT POPU-
      LARLY KNOWN AS PENNSYLVANIA DUTCH. Pennsylvania German So-
      ciety Proceedings and Addresses, vol. 48. Norristown: Pennsylvania
      German Society, 1940. 299 p.

      An anthology of nineteenth and twentieth century poetry writ-
      ten in the Pennsylvania Dutch dialect. The arrangement is
      by author. The poems were collected from newspapers, maga-
      zines, and private sources.

605   Buffington, Albert F., comp. THE REICHARD COLLECTION OF EARLY
      PENNSYLVANIA GERMAN DIALOGUES AND PLAYS. Pennsylvania Ger-
      man Society Publications, vol. 61. Lancaster, Pa.: Fackenthal Library,
      Franklin and Marshall College, 1962. 439 p.

      An important reference work that brings together dramatic
      works originally written in, or translated into the Pennsylvan-
      ia German dialect. The actual text of plays are given here
      and for works lacking standard transliteration, the transcription
      is indicated in brackets. Most of the original plays repro-
      duced here were written in the nineteenth and early twentieth
      century. A history of production by indigenous drama groups,
      staging directives, and a tribute to Harry Hess Reichard and
      his wife, Ida Ruch Reichard, collectors of Pennsylvania German
      drama, complements the text.

XIII. THEATRE

606   Bauland, Peter. THE HOODED EAGLE: MODERN GERMAN DRAMA
ON THE NEW YORK STAGE. Syracuse, N.Y.: Syracuse University
Press, 1968. 299 p. Bibliog., index.

A critical study of the modern German drama on the New
York stage from 1894 to 1964. Translations, as well as adaptations, are brought under purview. The impact of German
naturalism, neo-romanticism, realism, and other literary movements on the American stage is explored. Contemporary reviews and monographic works served as source materials. A
list of German plays produced on the New York stage during
the period covered and attendant data are provided in chronological arrangement.

607   Leuchs, Frederick Adolph Herman. EARLY GERMAN THEATRE IN NEW
YORK, 1840-1872. 1928. Reprint. New York: AMS Press, 1966.
298 p. Bibliog., index.

A penetrating study in cultural history focusing on the medium
of the German theatre in New York City. Chapters are devoted to the seasons and productions of the city's main German-language stages, the plays, playwrights, actors, and
drama criticism in contemporary periodicals. Sources used are
discussed in the introduction. The research and reference
value of the work is greatly enhanced by a succession of appendices which list halls and theatres in New York City used
for German-language productions (1840-48), plays produced
in German (1840-48), amateur theaters, a roster of the staff
of the Altes and Neues Stadttheater, a nearly complete list
of plays produced between 1854-72, and a chronological listing of German-American periodicals which regularly carried
critical reviews.

608   Baker, Louis Charles. THE GERMAN DRAMA IN ENGLISH ON THE
NEW YORK STAGE TO 1830. Americana Germanica, no. 31. Philadelphia: University of Pennsylvania Press, 1917. 168 p. Bibliog. notes.

A doctoral dissertation at the University of Pennsylvania covering the period from 1732. The dramatic works themselves,
their production, the cast, the performance, and their recep-
tion by critics are in the center of the author's attention.
The lack of an index is a serious drawback.

609 Brede, Charles Frederic. THE GERMAN DRAMA IN ENGLISH ON THE
PHILADELPHIA STAGE FROM 1794 TO 1830. Americana Germanica,
no. 34. Philadelphia: Americana Germanica Press, 1918. 295 p. Bibliog. notes.

A season-by-season survey and analysis of the theatrical life
of this culturally active city of Philadelphia. It was prepared
as a doctoral dissertation for the University of Pennsylvania.
Each major production is discussed with cited contemporary
critical comments.

610 Nolle, Alfred Henry. THE GERMAN DRAMA ON THE ST. LOUIS
STAGE. Americana Germanica, no. 32. Philadelphia: University of
Pennsylvania Press, 1917. 83 p. Bibliog.

The chronological scope of this study, originally a doctoral
dissertation at the University of Pennsylvania, ranges from
1842 to 1914. The material is discussed in five distinctive
time periods. Lengthy quotations, mostly in German, illustrate the type of plays produced. Local newspapers in German and English constituted the primary resources.

611 Loomis, Charles Grant. THE GERMAN THEATER IN SAN FRANCISCO,
1861-1864. University of California Publications in Modern Philology,
vol. 36, no. 8. Berkeley and Los Angeles: University of California
Press, 1952. 49 p.

The focus of this study is the German-language theatre of the
Adolph Meaubert repertoire company. The company's repertoire is listed in chronological sequence indicating the title,
and type of play, number of acts, playwrights, and a roster
of performers. The San Francisco ABEND-POST served as the
source of information.

XIV. MUSIC

COMPOSED MUSIC

612 National Society of the Colonial Dames of America. Pennsylvania.
CHURCH MUSIC AND MUSICAL LIFE IN PENNSYLVANIA IN THE
EIGHTEENTH CENTURY. 3 vols. in 4. Prepared by the Committee
on Historical Research. Publications of the Pennsylvania Society of the
Colonial Dames of America, 4. Philadelphia: Printed for the Society,
1926–47. Reprint. New York: AMS Press, 1972. Bibliog., index.

> Much of this work deals with German-American contributions.
> The discussion centers around the role of the various German
> religious groups and on such outstanding musicians as Johannes
> Kelpius, whose hymnal is reprinted here in facsimile, with
> its English translation by Christopher Witt. Other musicians
> treated extensively include Justus Falckner and Francis Daniel
> Pastorius. The work is heavily footnoted leading to many use-
> ful primary resources. A bibliography accompanies each vol-
> ume. Samples of various types of musical works are scattered
> throughout the book in facsimile. Volume three, which was
> issued later, consists of essays devoted to the music and musi-
> cal life of national and church groups during the colonial
> period in Pennsylvania. Each volume is separately indexed.

613 Drummond, Robert Rutherford. EARLY GERMAN MUSIC IN PHILADELPHIA.
Americana Germanica, New Series, no. 9. 1910. Reprint. New York:
AMS Press, 1972. 88 p. Bibliog. notes.

> A narrative history based on contemporary sources, relying
> mainly on information found in newspapers. The emphasis is
> on secular music. The discussion is divided into three sections.
> The first chapter casts a retrospective glance at church music
> and secular music before 1750. Chapter two, entitled "The
> Period of Progress" (1750-83), discusses concert music, music
> education, music publishing, and distribution. The third chap-
> ter, "Period of Greatest Development," centers around Alex-
> ander Reinagle, Philip Roth, and Philip Phile. The appendix
> comprises programs of concerns in 1791, and a chronological

list of the compositions of Alexander Reinagle, whom the author describes as "one of the ablest musicians in America at
that time." (p. 57)

614   Sachse, Julius Friedrich. MUSIC OF THE EPHRATA CLOISTER; ALSO
CONRAD BEISSEL'S TREATISE ON MUSIC AS SET FORTH IN A PRE-
FACE TO THE "TURTEL TAUBE" OF 1747, AMPLIFIED WITH FACSIMILE
REPRODUCTIONS OF PARTS OF THE TEXT AND SOME ORIGINAL
EPHRATA MUSIC OF THE WEYRAUCHS HUEGEL, 1739; ROSEN UND
LILIEN, 1745; TURTEL TAUBE, 1747; CHORAL BUCH, 1754, ETC. Penn-
sylvania German Society Proceedings and Addresses, vol. 12, 1901. 1903.
Reprint. New York: AMS Press, 1971. 108 p. Index.

The following are the topics dealt with: (1) "Music of the
Cloister" (melodies and unique notation, hymnbooks, role of
music); (2) "Beissel's Apology For Sacred Song" (the reasons
for singing); (3) "Music of the Kloster" (Beissel's system of
harmony); (4) "Hymn-books of the Community" (facsimiles of
title pages of various imprints); (5) "Turtel Taube of 1747"
(the foreword in facsimile, in English and German); (6) "Father Friedsam's Dissertation" (prologue to the TURTEL TAUBE);
(7) "Beissel's Dissertation on Harmony" (translation, with some
facsimiles of the German original); (8) "Original and Modern
Notation" (selected music score selections); and (9) "A Page
of Ephrata Theosophy" (Sachse translates Ephrata schoolmaster
Ludwig Hoecker's earliest plea for kindness to animals, and
the protection and revering of women). Sketches and facsimiles of musical notes, title pages, and a variety of pictures
are scattered throughout the book.

615   Seipt, Allan Anders. SCHWENKFELDER HYMNOLOGY AND THE
SOURCES OF THE FIRST SCHWENKFELDER HYMNBOOK PRINTED IN
AMERICA. Americana Germanica, no. 7. 1909. Reprint. New York:
AMS Press, 1971. 112 p. Bibliog.

Traces the European sources in the sixteenth century and the
evolution of Schwenkfelder hymnology in America through the
late eighteenth century. Christopher Sower's celebrated 1762
hymnbook is discussed in detail, together with the contributions
of composers and writers, Caspar and George Weiss, Balthasar
and Christopher Hoffman, Hans Christian Huebner, and Christopher Schultz. A chapter is devoted to the chronological listing from 1545 to 1869 of printed Schwenkfelder hymn collections in German with descriptive annotation.

616   Wetzel, Richard D. "The Music Collection of Georg Rapp's Harmonie
Gesellschaft (1805-1906)." MONATSHEFTE 68 (Summer 1976): 167-70.

"The article describes the contents of the music archives at
Economy Village, Ambridge, Pennsylvania, the third and final
home of Georg Rapp's Harmony Society. Rapp, a Separatist

preacher from Iptingen, Wuerttemberg, with several hundred followers, migrated to America in 1804. They organized themselves into a communal society and built and inhabited three villages: Harmony, Pennsylvania (1804-1814); Harmony, Indiana (1814-1824); and Economy, Pennsylvania (1824-1906). Deeply interested in music, the Harmonists maintained small vocal and instrumental ensembles, an orchestra of Classic proportions, numerous bands and choruses, and composed music for these as well as keyboard music and hymns. The article emphasizes the research potential of the collection (more than eight hundred items), particularly in the area of hymnody, and cites numerous rare German and German-American hymnals extant at Economy." (Author's abstract)

617 Gombosi, Marilyn, comp. CATALOG OF THE JOHANNES HERBST COLLECTION. Chapel Hill: University of North Carolina Press, 1970. 255 p. Index.

This catalog represents the holdings of the private library of the noted Moravian churchman and musician (1735-1812). They are manuscript copies of eighteenth and early nineteenth century musical works, vocal music, anthems, arias, and others, performed in American Moravian communities. The period covered was the time of vigorous growth of Moravian congregational music. Background information and the cataloging procedures applied are given in the preface. The entries consist of the name of the composer, title, specifications, and the musical notes of the first line. Among the additional materials, there is a chronology of major musical dates of the Moravian church year.

618 Rau, Albert George, and David, Hans T., comps. A CATALOGUE OF MUSIC BY AMERICAN MORAVIANS, 1742-1842, FROM THE ARCHIVES OF THE MORAVIAN CHURCH AT BETHLEHEM, PA. Bethlehem, Pa.: Moravian Seminary and College for Women, 1938. Reprint. New York: AMS Press, 1970. 118 p.

An inventory of musical works from the period 1742 to 1842 held at the Bethlehem Moravian Archives. The material originated from congregations in Bethlehem, Lititz, Lancaster, and Nazareth, all of which were Moravian settlements in Pennsylvania. The items included here were complete works in terms of texts and orchestration. They are given full bibliographic treatment and a short commentary. The listing is by composer. Biographical information and professional achievements of the composers are indicated.

619 David, Hans Theodore. "Musical Life in the Pennsylvania Settlements of the Unitas Fratrum: A Paper Read at the Annual Meeting of the Moravian Historical Society at Nazareth, Pa., October 13, 1938." TRANSACTIONS OF THE MORAVIAN HISTORICAL SOCIETY 13 (1942): 19-58. Reprint.

Foreword by Donald M. McCorkle. Moravian Music Foundation Publications, no. 6. Winston-Salem, N.C.: Moravian Music Foundation, 1959. 44 p. Bibliog. notes.

> This sketch dealing with the eighteenth and nineteenth-century musical life of the Moravians in Bethlehem, Pennsylvania, surveys the settlement's musical traditions and the major events of its musical culture. The contributions of the following composers are dealt with in some detail: Jeremiah Dencke, Immanuel Nitschman, Simon and Johann Friedrich Peter, Johannes Herbst, David Moritz Michael, and others. Documentation was based on biographies, hymn collections, and records from the Bethlehem Moravian Archives. There are references in the footnotes to "recent literature" (pre-1942) on this subject.

620 Grider, Rufus A. HISTORICAL NOTES ON MUSIC IN BETHLEHEM, PENNSYLVANIA FROM 1741 TO 1871. 1873. Reprint. Foreword by Donald M. McCorkle. Moravian Music Foundation Publications, no. 4. Winston-Salem, N.C.: Moravian Music Foundation, 1957. 41 p.

> Essentially, the main concern of this work is the secular and religious musical life of the Moravian community. Originally published in 1873, the work was partially based on the author's personal experiences and the reminiscences of older members of the community. Church music, concerts, serenades, musicians, composers and their works, primarily in the golden era from 1780 to 1820, constitute the subject matter. In addition to the narrative and references to groups and events, there is a list of four hundred names with dates of birth of individuals who were active in the city's musical life. A cautionary note in the foreword calls attention to some factual errors.

FOLK MUSIC

621 Korson, George Gershon, ed. PENNSYLVANIA SONGS AND LEGENDS. Philadelphia: University of Pennsylvania Press, 1949. Reprint. Baltimore: Johns Hopkins Press, 1960. 474 p. Index.

> General coverage, with the following chapters concentrating on German-American themes: (1) T.R. Brendle, and W.S. Troxell, "Pennsylvania German Songs"; (2) J.W. Frey, "Amish Hymns as Folk Music"; and (3) H.C. Frey, "Conestoga Wagoners." The chronological scope goes back to colonial times. The songs and stories were collected from oral sources. For the songs, the music, the original Pennsylvania German lyrics, and the English translation are usually provided.

622 Buffington, Albert F. PENNSYLVANIA GERMAN SECULAR FOLKSONGS. Pennsylvania German Society Publications, vol. 8. Breinigsville: Pennsylvania German Society, 1974. 182 p. Index.

A collection of eighty-five songs in Pennsylvania German with alternate versions and musical notes gathered by the author between 1946-64. English translation and a discussion of the origin and uses of the songs are also given. A bibliographic essay provides information on sources, publications of previous collections of folksongs, methods of transliteration from the vernacular into English, and on singers.

623   Yoder, Don. PENNSYLVANIA SPIRITUALS. Lancaster: Pennsylvania Folklife Society, 1961. 528 p. Bibliog., index.

The center of this study is the religious groups to which the author refers as the "Bush-Meeting Dutch." Many of the spirituals discussed here were collected in eastern Pennsylvania in the early 1950s. They were sung by revivalistic churches. The work consists of an introductory section discussing the origin and nature of the spirituals. This is followed by the text, notes, translation, and editorial information of 150 spirituals. The author addresses himself also to the bibliographic aspects, adaptions, and diffusion of these songs. The treatment is scholarly with splendid documentation. The bibliography lists about 220 general works and about eighty hymnals. The appendix contains a roster of the Evangelical Association's appointees, and facsimiles of hymns, posters, and others. Of the two maps, one shows the occurrences of the spirituals, and the second indicates where the recordings were made. The index is particularly useful as it provides access to topics, persons, places, song and hymn titles, and tunes.

624   Buffington, Albert F. DUTCHIFIED GERMAN SPIRITUALS. Pennsylvania German Society Publications, vol. 62. Lancaster, Pa.: Fackenthal Library, Franklin and Marshall College, 1962. 239 p. Bibliog.

A study of religious folksongs in a peculiar, adapted vernacular sung at meetings of German revivalistic churches in Pennsylvania during the latter half of the nineteenth century and the first half of the twentieth century. It could be considered as companion to Yoders's PENNSYLVANIA SPIRITUALS (see 623). The text of the songs is transcribed here according to the "Buffington-Barba phonetic system" which the author claims is a more scientific and usable rendering than any other suggested. In addition to the spirituals themselves and their translations, musical notes, and editorial comments, the study includes a bibliographic essay on the sources used.

XV. FOLK ART

BIBLIOGRAPHY

625 Riccardi, Saro John. "Pennsylvania Dutch Folk Art and Architecture."
BULLETIN OF THE NEW YORK PUBLIC LIBRARY 46 (June 1942): 471-
83. Index.

> An annotated subject bibliography reflecting the holdings of
> the New York Public Library as of 1942. It contains 138
> entries of books and periodical articles on popular art, frak-
> tur, buildings, interior decorations, and some industries; for
> example: the glass industry. The arrangement is by author,
> and the annotations are informative.

PENNSYLVANIA FOLK ART STUDIES

626 Stoudt, John Joseph. PENNSYLVANIA FOLK-ART; AN INTERPRETA-
TION. Allentown, Pa.: Schlechter's, 1948. 402 p. Bibliog. notes.

627 _____. PENNSYLVANIA GERMAN FOLK ART; AN INTERPRETATION.
Rev. ed. Pennsylvania German Folklore Society Yearbook, vol. 28.
Allentown, Pa.: Schlechter's, 1966. 386 p. Bibliog. notes.

> A scholarly work attempting an in-depth analysis of art as
> psychological and cultural expression. The themes dealt with
> encompass: (1) style, character, and culture in folk art;
> (2) sources of Pennsylvania German iconography and sym-
> bolism; (3) symbolic mood of Pennsylvania pietism; (4) symbol,
> image, and literary expression (motifs); and (5) symbolism and
> folk art; a psychological approach. More than two-thirds con-
> sists of illustrations of a wide spectrum of objects including:
> art of Ephrata; fractura; portraits; decorated household objects
> (furniture, utensils); ceramics; textiles; architectural decora-
> tion; and tombstones. Much of the documentation is in Ger-
> man. The 1948 edition (item 626) includes a bibliography of
> more than a hundred items. Both the 1948 and 1966 editions

are a revision of the author's CONSIDER THE LILIES, HOW THEY GROW--AN INTERPRETATION OF THE SYMBOLISM OF PENNSYLVANIA GERMAN ART. Pennsylvania German Folklore Society Yearbook, vol. 2. (Allentown: Pennsylvania German Folklore Society, 1937).

628 Adams, Ruth. PENNSYLVANIA DUTCH ART. Cleveland: World Publishing, 1950. 64 p.

A popular treatment of the subject focusing on homes, furniture, pottery, glass, textiles, woodcarving, metalwork, illuminated writing, barns, barnsigns, and others. It contains ten color plates and twenty-seven black and white illustrations.

629 Weygandt, Cornelius. THE RED HILLS; A RECORD OF GOOD DAYS OUTDOORS AND IN, WITH THINGS PENNSYLVANIA DUTCH. 1929. Reprint. Keystone State Historical Publications Series, no. 7. Port Washington, N.Y.: Ira J. Friedman, 1969. 251 p. Index.

A general treatment of Pennsylvania Dutch folk art written in a lyrical tone, showing not only the accomplishments of the folk genius but also telling how and why. The discussion of pottery and fraktur art is especially good. Nine illustrations are used to exhibit leading decorative motifs. This is a popular overview of the subject for the general reader.

630 Weygandt, Cornelius. THE DUTCH COUNTRY; FOLKS AND TREASURES IN THE RED HILLS OF PENNSYLVANIA. New York: D. Appleton-Century, 1939. 352 p. Index.

Essentially a follow-up to the author's 1929 work, THE RED HILLS (see 629), based on personal observations while living among the Pennsylvania Dutch. It is more tilted toward folkways and customs. Includes twenty-five illustrations.

Pictorial Works

631 New York. Metropolitan Museum of Art. PENNSYLVANIA GERMAN ARTS AND CRAFTS, A PICTUREBOOK. Rev. ed. New York: Metropolitan Museum of Art, 1949. 32 p.

A useful pictorial work showing typical specimens of furniture, fraktur, pottery, glass, and tinware.

632 PENNSYLVANIA GERMAN DESIGNS, A PORTFOLIO OF SILK SCREEN PRINTS. Index of American Design, National Gallery of Art, research by Pennsylvania Works Projects Administration Project. New York: Metropolitan Museum of Art, 1943. 20 plates.

A collection of twenty 11 x 14 inch prints of decorative designs used by settlers from the Palatinate in Pennsylvania in the eighteenth and early nineteenth centuries. Information is given on the verso.

633 Kauffman, Henry J. PENNSYLVANIA DUTCH AMERICAN FOLK ART. 2d ed. Rev. and enl. New York: Dover Publications, 1964. 146 p. Bibliog., index.

A short illustrated history of Pennsylvania Dutch arts and crafts with 120 pages of black and white illustrations giving identification, date, and the museum holding the piece.

634 Lichten, Frances. FOLK ART MOTIFS OF PENNSYLVANIA. New York: Hastings House, 1954. Reprint. Dover Pictorial Archive Series. New York: Dover Publications, 1976. 96 p.

A collection of a variety of decorative designs copied by the author, from antiques, tombstones, and other objects. The source is usually indicated. They include the typical motifs of tulips, hearts, birds, urns, flowers, barn symbols, borders, lettering, and quilts. The size and clarity of the sketches make them suitable for adaptions, and there are suggestions for enlarging and painting the motifs pictured.

635 Lichten, Frances. FOLK ART OF RURAL PENNSYLVANIA. London and New York: C. Scribner's Sons, 1946. 276 p. Index.

An oversize book systematically surveying categories of objects handcrafted by Pennsylvania Germans between 1750 and 1850. Most of these objects have long become collectors' items. The organization of the discussion is by source material: clay, flax, wool, straw, wood, stone, iron, tin, and quilts. The text is accompanied by 280 illustrations.

636 Stoudt, John Joseph. EARLY PENNSYLVANIA ARTS AND CRAFTS. New York: A.S. Barnes, 1964. 364 p. Index.

An attractive pictorial work providing representations of a variety of products of the Pennsylvania German arts and crafts from the 1680s to the 1850s. The subjects covered are: architecture, furniture styles, fine arts, crafts (glass, pottery, carving, iron, textiles, metalwork), and fraktur illuminating art.

637 Mercer, Henry Chapman. THE BIBLE IN IRON: PICTURED STOVES AND STOVEPLATES OF THE PENNSYLVANIA GERMANS; NOTES ON COLONIAL FIREBACKS IN THE UNITED STATES, THE TEN-PLATE STOVE, FRANKLIN'S FIREPLACE, AND THE TILE STOVES OF THE MORAVIANS IN PENNSYLVANIA AND NORTH CAROLINA, TOGETHER WITH A LIST OF COLONIAL FURNACES IN THE UNITED STATES AND CANADA. 3d ed. Rev., corrected, and enl. by Horace M. Mann, with further amendments and additions by Joseph E. Sanford. Doylestown, Pa.: Bucks County Historical Association, 1961. 256 p. Bibliog., index.

Consists of 256 pages of interpretive text and 409 illustrations, many of them plates. The book grew out of the author's work initially published in pamphlet form in 1899. The first full book edition appeared in 1914, and was issued in a second edition in 1941. The first part discusses the origin and motifs of this form of artistry. Many documentary references are given in footnotes. Part two presents 409 black and white photographs of stoves, stoveplates, and accessories giving their background and meaning of their symbolism. A bibliography of 250 titles, with many primary sources, is given.

ANTIQUES

638   Robacker, Earl Francis. PENNSYLVANIA DUTCH STUFF: A GUIDE TO COUNTRY ANTIQUES. Philadelphia: University of Pennsylvania Press, 1944. 163 p. Bibliog., index.

Intended for the layman wishing to use genuine designs, patterns, furniture, toys, and others, to create an authentic Pennsylvania Dutch atmosphere in the home. The bibliography includes an assortment of books aimed at providing the "spiritual equipment" to match the decor. A list of museums which collect Pennsylvania Dutch art and antiques complements the work.

639   _____. OLD STUFF IN UP-COUNTRY PENNSYLVANIA. South Brunswick, N.J.: A.S. Barnes, 1973. 283 p. Bibliog., index.

A pictorial guide to antiques of the Upper Poconos region. The whole range of arts and crafts are discussed. A long list of works on local history and the arts and crafts of the region are provided. Many illustrations accompany the work, some are in color. Photography by Stephen A. Karas, and Bryden Taylor.

640   Smith, Elmer Lewis. ANTIQUES IN PENNSYLVANIA DUTCHLAND. Witmer, Pa.: Applied Arts, 1963. 42 p. Bibliog.

An attractively illustrated booklet providing a quick overview of all facets of Pennsylvania Dutch arts and crafts. Beyond the usual subjects covered in similar works, the reader will find information on public auctions, and repositories of Pennsylvania Dutch antiques. Photographs by Mel Horst.

COPPERSMITHING

641   Kauffman, Henry J. "Coppersmithing in Pennsylvania, Being a Treatise on the Art of the Eighteenth Century Coppersmith, Together with a De-

scription of His Products and His Establishments." PENNSYLVANIA GER-
MAN FOLKLORE SOCIETY YEARBOOK 11 (1946): 83-153. Allentown: Pennsylvania German Folklore Society, 1948. Bibliog.

> Contains many references to the craft practiced by German
> Americans. The author traces the history of coppersmithing
> and in discussing the state of the craft in eighteenth century
> Pennsylvania, he deals with the making of sheet copper, the
> equipment used, the terminology of the trade, the training
> of the coppersmith, and the technique of making copper ves-
> sels. There is also a list of eighteenth-century Pennsylvania
> coppersmiths, with location of their shops. The black and
> white illustrations by Zoe T. Kauffman show sketches of vari-
> ous specimens of copper products, tools and trademarks, and
> facsimiles of contemporary advertisements.

FRAKTUR

642 Shelley, Donald A. THE FRAKTUR-WRITINGS OR ILLUMINATED MANU-
SCRIPTS OF THE PENNSYLVANIA GERMANS. Pennsylvania German
Folklore Society Yearbook, vol. 23. Allentown: Pennsylvania German
Folklore Society, 1961. 375 p. Bibliog., index.

> A landmark study which took twenty years to prepare. It is
> a scholarly history with pictorial analysis of fraktur writings
> and illuminations in the eighteenth and nineteenth centuries
> focusing on the period 1750 to 1850. The work has three
> components: (1) history and analysis, (2) bibliography, and
> (3) illustrations. The first part discusses the emergence of
> fraktur as a form of folk art with its European background.
> This is followed by a discourse on the types, techniques,
> materials, design, and motifs, the application of fraktur to
> various written, printed, engraved, and lithograph species,
> and the practice of fraktur by the Mennonites, Schwenkfelders,
> and at the Ephrata Cloister. The illustrations include repre-
> sentative specimens of birth and baptismal certificates, manu-
> scripts, books, religious broadsides, watercolor portraits, many
> of which have never been published before. The material was
> drawn from many museums and sixty-five private collections
> of fraktur materials. The work is extremely well documented.

> The bibliography is impressive, enumerating over eight hundred
> items of which 150 deal with fraktur. The rest is a bibliog-
> raphy of Pennsylvania German history, arts, and crafts. The
> appendix contains a roster of fraktur illuminators with their
> dates and activities, a list of printing centers, and a list of
> fraktur printers by place.

643 Borneman, Henry Stauffer. PENNSYLVANIA GERMAN ILLUMINATED
MANUSCRIPTS; A CLASSIFICATION OF FRAKTUR-SCHRIFTEN AND AN
INQUIRY INTO THEIR HISTORY AND ART. Pennsylvania German So-

ciety, 1937. Reprint. Corrected edition. New York: Dover Publications, 1973. 59 p. Bibliog. notes.

A beautifully illustrated oversize book consisting of a fifty-eight page narrative and thirty-eight 10 x 14 inch color plates. It discusses various fraktur manuscripts: birth certificates, baptismal records, a variety of family mementos, house blessings, book plates, and bookmarks. There is also a treatment of fraktur design, implements, materials, colors, and symbolism. The illustrations are copies of actual fraktur illuminations with information and explicative notes for each given on the opposite page.

644 Weiser, Frederick S., and Heaney, Howell J., comps. PENNSYLVANIA GERMAN FRAKTUR OF THE FREE LIBRARY OF PHILADELPHIA, AN IL-LUMINATED CATALOGUE. 2 vols. Pennsylvania German Society Publications, vols. 10 and 11. Breinigsville: Pennsylvania German Society and The Free Library of Philadelphia, 1976-77. Index.

This is a two-volume pictorial catalog, the first, the more sumptuous one, exhibiting in color the images of the stellar pieces held by the library. The second volume is more modest in appearance showing the replicas in black and white of lesser pieces. Each item is identified, its text translated and frequently commented upon. In addition to a general index for personal and place names, there are separate indexes for artists and scriveners, printers, engravers, lithographers and publishers, and of watermarks. The two volumes inventory 1,021 items of which 277 are found in the first volume.

645 Borneman, Henry Stauffer. PENNSYLVANIA GERMAN BOOKPLATES; A STUDY. Pennsylvania German Society Publications, vol. 54. Philadelphia: Pennsylvania German Society, 1953. 167 p. Bibliog. notes.

The study concentrates on the period 1798 to 1840, but the discussion is broader. The subjects dealt with include the uses of bookplates, typical designs and designers, migratory patterns of settlers, dialect, arts and crafts, fraktur, and hymnals. One hundred bookplates are cataloged here by the type of book from which they were taken. In addition, twenty-four plates are reproduced in color with translation. Ownership information is indicated on the facing page.

FURNITURE

646 Schiffer, Margaret Berwind. FURNITURE AND ITS MAKERS OF CHESTER COUNTY, PENNSYLVANIA. Philadelphia: University of Pennsylvania Press, 1966. 329 p. Bibliog.

A valuable study for the furniture specialist, focusing on the region which lies southeast of the Pennsylvania German coun-

ties. The bulk of the work is a collection of black and
white plates representing specimens of furniture with specifications, the name of craftsman, date, and comments. By
combing through a multitude of newspapers, letters, wills,
diaries, tax records, and others, Schiffer was able to produce
a biographical directory of Chester County furniture–makers
from 1680 to 1850. The information includes whatever the
author was able to glean: dates, family, characteristics of
their craftsmanship, inventory of their shops, advertisements,
obituaries, and others. Much of the documentary material
is given in facsimile.

647 Fabian, Monroe H. THE PENNSYLVANIA-GERMAN DECORATED CHEST.
Foreword by Frederick S. Weiser. Pennsylvania German Society Publications, vol. 12. New York: Universe Books, 1978. 230 p. Bibliog.,
index.

An authoritative, well-documented monograph giving not only
description, but history as well. The researcher can extract
a great deal of information on seventeenth and eighteenth century cabinetmaking in Pennsylvania. There are 250 illustrations of which 50 are in color.

NEEDLEWORK

648 Schiffer, Margaret Berwind. HISTORICAL NEEDLEWORK OF PENNSYL-
VANIA. New York: Scribner's, 1968. 160 p. Bibliog. notes, index.

Includes many samples of eighteenth- and nineteenth-century
Moravian and German needlework.

649 Haders, Phyllis. SUNSHINE AND SHADOW: THE AMISH AND THEIR
QUILTS. Clinton, N.J.: Main Street-Universe Books, 1976. 71 p.

"For Amish-quilt enthusiasts this book is a handy little compilation, chock-full of folksy narrative and full-color photos.

The author explores the Amish world of 'sunshine and shadow'
-- the use of deep, vibrant colors and dark, gloomy blacks.
Phyllis Haders draws heavily on her impressions of the Amish
handicraft and relates much of the first-hand knowledge she
garnered from her friendships with members of this closely knit
sect.

This slim volume includes a brief explanation of the Amish
attitude of noninvolvement in world or 'outside' affairs and
dwells at length on the patterns, materials, and colors involved in making Amish quilts, a craft that dates back for
generations.

The highlight of 'Sunshine and Shadow,' however, is Mrs.

Haders' compilation of pictures of one dozen striking, color-
ful quilts. The description and illustration of each quilt is
introduced with an appropriate Biblical or Amish quotation and,
opposite the full-page color photo, Mrs. Haders has included
an informative critique on each work." (Sara Terry, CHRIS-
TIAN SCIENCE MONITOR, 26 April 1977, p. 27).

POTTERY

650 Barber, Edwin Atlee. TULIP WARE OF THE PENNSYLVANIA GERMAN
POTTERS: AN HISTORICAL SKETCH OF THE ART OF SLIP-DECORATION
IN THE UNITED STATES. Art Handbook of the Pennsylvania Museum and
School of Industrial Art. 1903. Reprint. New introduction by Henry
J. Kauffman. New York: Dover Publications, 1970. 233 p. Index.

One of the contentions of the author is that from the seventeenth century onward the Pennsylvania Dutch settlers have
developed a homegrown version of pottery, and no longer re-
lied on patterns brought from Europe. The work discusses the
background of eastern Pennsylvania German settlers and their
various cultural traditions which influenced their pottery. The
processes of slip-ware manufacture, their subject and design,
and prominent eighteenth- and nineteenth-century patterns are
in the center of the study. The work includes ninety-four
black and white photographs of the objects d'art with all pertinent information. The index provides access to the subjects
of decoration and the potters.

TOMBSTONES

651 Barba, Preston Albert. PENNSYLVANIA GERMAN TOMBSTONES; A
STUDY IN FOLK ART. Pennsylvania German Folklore Society Yearbook,
vol. 18. Allentown: Pennsylvania German Folklore Society, 1954.
232 p. Bibliog.

A unique work consisting of a twenty-eight pages of descriptive and analytical discussion, followed by two hundred sketches
by Eleanor Barba. The tombstones described originate from the
1750-1850 period and were selected from a hundred graveyards.
Dates, location, and the authors' comments are given on the
page opposite the sketch. A bibliography of twenty-five items
in German and English is provided.

WEAVING

652 Reinert, Guy F. "Coverlets of the Pennsylvania Germans." PENNSYL-
VANIA GERMAN FOLKLORE SOCIETY YEARBOOK 13 (1948): 1-215.
Allentown: Pennsylvania German Folklore Society, 1949.

Traces the history of weaving of coverlets, a favorite household item in Pennsylvania Dutch homes, until the end of the nineteenth century. They were produced by professional weavers whose activities are discussed here. The work includes a list of pattern books and books on color dyeing that were used by weavers. The pictorial section consists of about 120 black and white photographs.

XVI. ARCHITECTURE

BIBLIOGRAPHY

653 Roos, Frank John. WITINGS ON EARLY AMERICAN ARCHITECTURE;
AN ANNOTATED LIST OF BOOKS AND ARTICLES ON ARCHITECTURE
CONSTRUCTED BEFORE 1860 IN THE EASTERN HALF OF THE UNITED
STATES. Ohio State University. Graduate School Studies. Contribu-
tions in the Fine Arts, no. 2. Columbus: Ohio State University Press,
1943. 271 p. Index.

> The listing consists of books and articles written between 1900–
> 40 that dealt with architectural subjects in the chronological
> span of 1611 to 1860 presenting their subject matter in a his-
> torical perspective. The geographic scope is limited to the
> eastern half of the United States. The organization of the
> material is mainly by region, state, and localities. A sepa-
> rate section groups works written about architects in the desig-
> nated period. The annotations are spotty. The work includes
> a considerable amount of German Americana which can be ac-
> cessed only through the name of a place or the name of the
> architect.

GENERAL WORKS

654 Brumbaugh, G. Edwin. COLONIAL ARCHITECTURE OF THE PENNSYL-
VANIA GERMANS. Pennsylvania German Society Proceedings, vol. 41,
(1930). Norristown, Pa.: Norristown Herald, 1933. 171 p.

> Of the 171 pages of this work, sixty are devoted to an intro-
> duction and an analysis, the message of which is that the ap-
> preciation of a people's architecture is essential to the under-
> standing of its genius. There are 105 full-page plates showing
> a variety of buildings, homes, churches, schools, stores, farm
> buildings, and others, with considerable detail. The majority
> of the buildings presented were built before the American Re-
> volution.

655 Van Ravenswaay, Charles. THE ARTS AND ARCHITECTURE OF GERMAN
SETTLEMENTS IN MISSOURI. Columbia: University of Missouri Press,
1977. 533 p. Bibliog., index.

"This monumental survey graphically portrays evidence of the
rich German influence upon the arts and architecture of the
lower Missouri River valley. Featuring more than six hundred
photographs (twenty color plates), this work is a fascinating
documentation of the remarkable success German immigrants
achieved in adapting to the Missouri environment, recreating
much of their traditional homeland culture in the process. The
settlers were forced to make inevitable compromises with conditions in Missouri that resulted in a legacy of particular interest to anyone concerned with the history of American design,
architecture, crafts, or Missouriana. . . . "

Topics covered: the beginnings of German settlement; the
emigration societies; the immigration of individuals; objects
brought by the immigrants; log construction; frame construction; half timbered buildings; later types of frame buildings;
stone construction; brick construction; barns; designers and
builders; the craftsmen; furniture, furniture types, and the
makers; musical instruments; wood carving; baskets; firearms;
tin and copperware; stonecutting and carving; textiles; pottery;
drawings, prints, and painting; miscellaneous crafts; black-
smiths, bookbinders, boxmakers, braziers, broom makers, glass-
makers, locksmiths, painters, sabots and woodenware, silver-
smiths, watchmakers, and jewelers. The book is complemented
by a 200-item bibliography.

PICTORIAL WORKS

656 Raymond, Eleanor. EARLY DOMESTIC ARCHITECTURE OF PENNSYL-
VANIA: PHOTOGRAPHS AND MEASURED DRAWINGS. Introduction
by R. Brognard Okie. New York: W. Helburn; Exton, Pa.: Schiffer,
1977. 98 p.

Contains 150 plates showing a variety of eighteenth-century
structures in eastern Pennsylvania. Much of it is in German.
Date of construction is often given.

657 Siskind, Aaron, photographer. BUCKS COUNTY: PHOTOGRAPHS OF
EARLY ARCHITECTURE. Text by William Morgan. New York: Published
for the Bucks County Historical Society by Horizon Press, 1974. 112 p.

Shows photographs of many fine models of German-American
buildings mostly from the eighteenth and nineteenth centuries.
The intention of the author is to document how the local population of German descent adapted the prevailing English style
to its needs and life style.

658 Synder, Karl H. AN ARCHITECTURAL MONOGRAPH: MORAVIAN
ARCHITECTURE OF BETHLEHEM, PENNSYLVANIA. White Pine Series
of Architectural Monographs, vol. 13, no. 4. New York: R.F. White-
head, 1927. 24 p.

> A brief pictorial essay of the architecture of the area between
> 1740 and 1800. In addition to the pictures there are four
> pages of detailed specifications of the frame buildings pre-
> sented.

BARNS

659 Dornbusch, Charles H. PENNSYLVANIA GERMAN BARNS. Pennsylvania German Folklore Society Yearbook, vol. 21 (1956). Allentown:
Pennsylvania German Folklore Society, 1958. 312 p.

> Comprised of 150 photographs, an introduction, and descrip-
> tive text by John K. Heyl. The barns are divided into ele-
> ven categories by type. For each barn, location and date
> are given.

660 Shoemaker, Alfred Lewis, ed. THE PENNSYLVANIA BARN. Lancaster:
Pennsylvania Dutch Folklore Center, 1955. 96 p.

> A compendium of essays to substantiate the editor's claim that
> the Pennsylvania German barn was the greatest original con-
> tribution to regional American architecture in the eighteenth
> century. The essays deal with the various types of barns,
> decorations, hex signs, methods of barn raising, and barn con-
> struction terminology. The contributors include Don Yoder,
> Henry J. Kauffman, J. William Stair, and Victor C. Dieffen-
> bach. The supplementary material contains many illustrations,
> statistical and tax records, and contemporary accounts of
> travelers. Of the three maps appended, one shows Pennsyl-
> vania counties as of 1798, the second indicates where hex
> signs were utilized, and the third outlines a tour to inspect
> existing brick barns.

661 Mahr, August C. "Origin and Significance of Pennsylvania Dutch Barn
Symbols." OHIO STATE ARCHAEOLOGICAL AND HISTORICAL QUAR-
TERLY 54, no. 1 (1945): 1-32. Bibliog.

> Explains the origin and significance of the various symbols
> used to decorate Pennsylvania Dutch barns. Many of these
> can be traced to Europe. Eighteen photographs exhibiting
> symbols and ornaments illustrate the text.

BRIDGES

662 Horst, Melvin, and Smith, Elmer L. COVERED BRIDGES OF PENNSYL-

VANIA DUTCHLAND. Lebanon, Pa.: Applied Arts Associates, 1960. 42 p.

The varieties of covered bridges are amply displayed with numerous photographs and illustrations.

XVII. SOCIAL LIFE AND CUSTOMS

BIBLIOGRAPHY

663 Haywood, Charles. A BIBLIOGRAPHY OF NORTH AMERICAN FOLK-LORE AND FOLKSONG. 2 vols. 2d rev. ed. New York: Dover Publications, 1961. 748 p.; 552 p. Index.

> The first volume of this classic inventories material related to German-American folklore. The listing is organized into two sections: (1) "Germans Outside of Pennsylvania," and (2) "Pennsylvania Germans." The sources enumerated include bibliographies, periodicals, general works, legends, customs, beliefs, superstitions, witchcraft, folk medicine, riddles, speech, games and rhymes, dances, and record collections. Some of the entries are annotated.

GENERAL WORKS

664 Rush, Benjamin. AN ACCOUNT OF THE MANNERS OF THE GERMAN INHABITANTS OF PENNSYLVANIA. 1789. Reprint. Notes added by I. Daniel Rupp. Philadelphia: Samuel P. Town, 1875. 72 p. Reprint. New introduction by William T. Parsons. Pennsylvania Dutch Studies, vol. 1. Collegeville: Institute on Pennsylvania Dutch Studies, 1974. 25 p. Bibliog. notes.

> The author was a native of Bucks County, Pennsylvania, who was also one of the signers of the Declaration of Independence and served as surgeon-general of the Continental army. His first hand observations on social life, customs, religion, education, and farming were expanded by I. Daniel Rupp in the 1875 edition only. This work is a valuable primary source of factual and biographical information in the context of the period covered.

665 Aurand, Ammon Monroe. SOCIAL LIFE OF THE PENNSYLVANIA GERMANS. Harrisburg, Pa.: Aurand Press, 1947. 31 p.

Concentrates on the eighteenth century and deals with marriage, funerals, parties, games, taffy pulls with recipes, sleighing, and other amusements. Sketches illustrate these activities.

666 Stoudt, John Baer. THE FOLKLORE OF THE PENNSYLVANIA-GERMAN; A PAPER READ BEFORE THE PENNSYLVANIA-GERMAN SOCIETY AT THE ANNUAL MEETING, YORK, PENNSYLVANIA, OCTOBER 14, 1910. Pennsylvania German Society Proceedings and Addresses, vol. 23, part 2. Lancaster, Pa.: New Era Printing, 1915. 155 p.

The fruit of fifteen years of labor, this collection was intended to "delve into Pennsylvania German inner life in their own words and thought forms." They were drawn from children, students, clergymen, and men and women from all walks of life. There is a rich assortment here of sayings, rhymes, ballads, proverbs, prayers, lullabies, riddles, new year wishes, and many other types of formulations, all in the Pennsylvania Dutch dialect without translation. A brief discussion introduces each genre. The author traces the place of origin of these pieces of folk wisdom and imagination, sometimes as far back as the German homeland.

667 Mitchell, Edwin Valentine. IT'S AN OLD PENNSYLVANIA CUSTOM. New York: Vanguard Press, 1947. 261 p.

A popular, general treatment which contains a considerable amount of information on the customs and folkways of Pennsylvania Germans. The subjects covered include dialect, beliefs, barns, the Kentucky rifle, music, cooking, courtship and marriage, dress, and decorative arts.

668 Korson, George Gershon. BLACK ROCK; MINING FOLKLORE OF THE PENNSYLVANIA DUTCH. Pennsylvania German Society Publications, vol. 59. Baltimore: Johns Hopkins University Press, 1960. 453 p. Bibliog. notes, index.

The role of the Pennsylvania Dutch in the anthracite coal industry and the folklore that developed around it in Schuykill County and the surrounding area in the latter half of the nineteenth century are explored in this work. It focuses on the Dutch dialect, courtship and marriage, folk medicine, religious lore, legends, superstitions, folksongs, and ballads. The work is well documented and drawn from primary sources. The section devoted to folksongs includes lyrics and music for many of them.

DOMESTIC LIFE

669 Schantz, F.J.F. THE DOMESTIC LIFE AND CHARACTERISTICS OF THE PENNSYLVANIA GERMAN PIONEER. Pennsylvania German Society Pro-

ceedings, vol. 10. Lancaster: Pennsylvania German Society, 1900. 97 p.

A popular account of all facets of the life of a typical nineteenth-century Pennsylvania German family. The subjects covered include founding a home, domestic economy, methods of soil cultivation and husbandry, clothing, the care of children, the aged, the infirm, the treatment of servants, domestic piety, hospitality, and special occasions. The text is supported by many illustrations and facsimiles of pages from religious books. There is a reference list of German-language religious books which were standard items in every household. The appendix contains Christopher Dock's one hundred rules of conduct for children.

670 Aurand, Ammon Monroe. CHILD LIFE OF THE PENNSYLVANIA GERMANS. Harrisburg, Pa.: Aurand Press, 1947. 32 p.

Provides glimpses of Pennsylvania German children's activities in the eighteenth and nineteenth centuries. The emphasis is on jobs children could do, games, holiday activities, pranks, and norms of behavior.

671 _____. HOME LIFE OF THE PENNSYLVANIA GERMANS. Harrisburg, Pa.: Aurand Press, 1947. 31 p.

The topics dealt with include food curing and canning, cooking, furnishing, quilting, methods of lighting in the home, techniques of sewing, tailoring, and shoemaking.

BELIEFS AND SUPERSTITIONS

672 Fogel, Edwin Miller. BELIEFS AND SUPERSTITIONS OF THE PENNSYLVANIA GERMANS. Americana Germanica. New Series, no. 18. Philadelphia: Americana Germanica Press, 1915. 387 p. Bibliog.

A compilation of more than two thousand sayings reflecting the beliefs and superstitions of Pennsylvania Germans, collected from oral sources. The sayings are given in the vernacular with their English translation and also in their original German version. The grouping of the sayings is by topic and are applied to such events and subjects as marriage, dreams, childhood, omens, cooking, trees, the moon, the weather, and others. Pronunciation is indicated.

673 Brendle, Thomas Royce. PENNSYLVANIA GERMAN FOLK TALES, LEGENDS, ONCE-UPON-A-TIME STORIES, MAXIMS, AND SAYINGS SPOKEN IN THE DIALECT POPULARLY KNOWN AS PENNSYLVANIA DUTCH. Collected, edited, and translated by Rev. Thomas R. Brendle, and William S. Troxell. Pennsylvania German Society Proceedings and

Addresses, vol. 50. Norristown: Pennsylvania German Society, 1944. 238 p.

The stories are grouped by type, and the collection is complemented by Swabian jokes, proverbs, and place names. Usual idioms used in the translation are referred to in the original in footnotes. In many cases, the name of the narrator, the place of origin of the story, and some other details are also indicated.

674 Hark, Ann. HEX MARKS THE SPOT, IN THE PENNSYLVANIA DUTCH COUNTRY. New York: J.B. Lippincott, 1938. 316 p. Bibliog.

Presents a potpourri of information on folklife, culture, and curiosities. The following topics are highlighted: hexerei, Ephrata, pow-wow, Conestoga wagon, notable Pennsylvania Dutch men, the Love Feast, food and cooking, home remedies, Baptism, Christmas, Moravian Bach music, Henry W. Stiegel and his glassworks, the Amish, the Pennsylvania Dutch language, pastries, legends, and an evening with the Amish. As an extra feature, the author gives the recipes of the various foods mentioned in the text. Illustrations and initials by Eleanor Hart Levis.

675 Hark, Ann. BLUE HILLS AND SHOOFLY PIE IN PENNSYLVANIA DUTCHLAND. Philadelphia: J.B. Lippingcott, 1952. 284 p.

Deals with events in the life of Pennsylvania German people in a calendarlike fashion on a year-round basis. The landmarks of each month are highlighted by related customs, folklore, superstitions, and celebrations. The author was a resident of the area and most of the information was gained through observation. The Amish and other "Plain People" are given particular attention. Recipes for foods for the appropriate occasion are added to the text.

CHRISTMAS

676 PENNSYLVANIA GERMAN SOCIETY YEARBOOK 6 (1941): Entire issue. Allentown: Pennsylvania German Society, 1941.

The whole issue is devoted to the theme of Christmas. It contains the following articles: (1) George E. Nitzsche, "Christmas Putz of the Pennsylvania Germans"; (2) Charles H. Rominger, "Early Christmases in Bethlehem, Pennsylvania (1742-1756)"; (3) Richmond Elmore Myers, "The Moravian Christmas Putz"; (4) Harry Hess Reichard, "The Christmas Poetry of the 'Pennsylvania Dutch' "; and (5) Edwin Miller Fogel, "Twelvetide."

677   Shoemaker, Alfred Lewis. CHRISTMAS IN PENNSYLVANIA, A FOLK-
      CULTURAL STUDY. Introduction by Don Yoder. Kutztown: Pennsyl-
      vania Folklife Society, 1959. 116 p. Bibliog. notes, index.

      Encompasses all aspects of Christmas celebration and examines
      how these practices survived the acculturation process. The
      text is illustrated with sketches of Christmas activities and
      tree decorations.

678   Hutchison, Ruth Shepherd. CHRISTMAS IN BETHELEHEM. New York:
      Oxford University Press, 1958. 30 p.

      A beautifully illustrated booklet showing glimpses of Christmas
      scenes among Moravians, intended for bibliophiles.

679   Pauli, Hertha Ernestine. THE STORY OF THE CHRISTMAS TREE. Boston:
      Houghton Mifflin, 1944. 69 p.

      Intended for young readers, the author tells the story of how
      the tree became part of the Christmas celebration in America.
      The chapters are filled with interesting episodes relating to
      the acceptance of this European custom by American Christian
      congregations. Illustrated by William Wiesner.

EASTER

680   Shoemaker, Alfred Lewis. EASTERTIDE IN PENNSYLVANIA, A FOLK-
      CULTURAL STUDY. Kutztown: Pennsylvania Folklife Society, 1960.
      96 p. Bibliog. notes, index.

      Copiously illustrated description of the customs and ceremonies
      connected with the observance of Shrove Tuesday, Ash Wednes-
      day, Good Friday, and Easter Sunday. Among the illustrations,
      there are many samples of Easter egg trees and decorated eggs.

681   Abernethy, Francis Edward, ed. THE FOLKLORE OF TEXAN CULTURES.
      Music editor, Dan Beatty. Publications of the Texas Folklore Society,
      no. 38. Austin: Encino Press, 1974. 366 p. Bibliog.

      A panorama of the twenty-five most numerous ethnic groups
      that make up the population of Texas. In each group some
      of the surviving customs are described. Two articles are de-
      voted to German Texans: one focusing on Gillespie County,
      and the second dealing with the custom of Easter fires in
      Fredericksburg. A third article of German-American interest
      is devoted to the Wends, a Germanized Slavic group whose
      ancestors came to Texas from the homeland in Germany in
      1854.

WILLS

682   Gilbert, Russell Weider. "Pennsylvania German Wills." PENNSYLVANIA
      GERMAN SOCIETY YEARBOOK 15 (1950): 1-107. Bibliog. notes.

> The author's interest in the subject rests on the assumption
> that "no other documentary evidence reveals more clearly the
> breadth and depth of character of the Pennsylvania German
> people. . . . " The wills processed originate from the
> eighteenth and nineteenth century and were taken from the
> books of seventeen counties. The majority were written in
> English with an admixture of Pennsylvania Dutch giving them
> a quaint flavor. A separate section discusses death and burial
> customs.

XVIII. COOKING

683 Randle, Bill. PLAIN COOKING; LOW-COST, GOOD-TASTING AMISH
RECIPES. Recipes edited by Nancy Predina. New York: Quadrangle,
1974. 270 p. Bibliog., index.

> A collection of the four hundred best recipes chosen from
> about one thousand which were tested and rated by outsiders.
> They include soups, stews, casseroles, vegetables, salads,
> breads and dumplings, sweet things, and canned goods. Photo-
> graphs by Perry Cragg.

684 Groff, Betty, and Wilson, Jose. GOOD EARTH AND COUNTRY COOK-
ING. Harrisburg, Pa.: Stackpole Books, 1974. 253 p. Index.

> This cookbook has a seasonal approach and suggests complete
> menus. In addition to the recipes, the authors offer advice
> on freezing, canning, pickling, and winemaking. A list of
> suppliers of equipment for home winemaking is given in the
> book. Some color photographs on food decoration and serving
> with Pennsylvania Dutch motifs complement the work.

685 Lestz, Gerald S., comp. THE PENNSYLVANIA DUTCH COOKBOOK.
New York: Grosset and Dunlap, 1970. 88 p. Index.

> Ninety recipes handed down from generation to generation are
> presented here. They consist of foods of a less common nature
> and concentrate on sweets and desserts. Illustrated by Walter
> Ferro.

686 Staebler, Edna Louis Cress. FOOD THAT REALLY SCHMECKS; MEN-
NONITE COUNTRY COOKING, AS PREPARED BY MY MENNONITE
FRIEND, BEVVY MARTIN, MY MOTHER, AND OTHER FINE COOKS.
Toronto and New York: McGraw-Hill, Ryerson, 1968. 297 p. Index.

> This collection contains the recipes of the favorite dishes of
> the Mennonites of Waterloo County, Ontario. Most of them
> require simple ingredients and the directions are easy to follow.

687 Hutchison, Ruth Shepherd. THE PENNSYLVANIA DUTCH COOKBOOK. New York: Harper, 1948. 213 p. Index.

688 _____. THE NEW PENNSYLVANIA DUTCH COOKBOOK. New York: Harper, 1958. 240 p. Index.

Illustrated by Tim Palmer.

689 _____. COOKING "DUTCH" WITH CALORIC/THE NEW PENNSYL-VANIA DUTCH COOKBOOK. New York: Benjamin, 1975. 240 p. Index.

Illustrated by Tim Palmer.

690 _____. THE PENNSYLVANIA DUTCH COOKBOOK. Bethlehem, Pa.: Moravian Book Shop, 1977. 240 p. Index.

A standard cookbook in successive editions (items 687, 688, 689) offering a wide variety of interesting recipes with easily obtainable ingredients and simple instructions. Illustrated by Philip B. Woodroofe.

691 Hark, Ann, and Barba, Preston A. PENNSYLVANIA GERMAN COOK-ERY, A REGIONAL COOKBOOK. Allentown, Pa.: Schlecter's, 1950. 258 p.

692 Aurand, Ammon Monroe, ed. COOKING WITH THE PENNSYLVANIA "DUTCH": A COLLECTION OF CHOICE AND TRIED OLD-TIME HOME AND FARM RECIPES. Harrisburg, Pa.: Aurand Press, 1946. 32 p. Index.

The recipes disclosed here would delight the "purist," as they focus on the authentic rather than on adaptations. A glossary of culinary terms and a table of measurements are added to the text.

693 PENNSYLVANIA DUTCH COOKBOOK OF FINE OLD RECIPES COM-PILED FROM TRIED AND TESTED RECIPES MADE FAMOUS BY THE EARLY DUTCH SETTLERS IN PENNSYLVANIA. Reading, Pa.: Culinary Arts Press, 1936. 48 p.

A selection of about 250 popular recipes with easy-to-follow instructions. The emphasis is on those items for which the ingredients are commonly available. An extra feature is a collection of sayings and rhymes in the dialect with the English equivalent.

694 Frederick, Justus George. PENNSYLVANIA DUTCH COOKERY: THEIR HISTORY, ART, ACCOMPLISHMENTS, ALSO A BROAD COLLECTION OF THEIR FOOD RECIPES. New York: Business Bourse, 1935. Reprint. Louisville: Famous Recipes Press, 1966. 275 p. Bibliog., index.

A treatise on the culinary art with a brief history of the people, their arts and crafts, and their contribution to America. The bulk of the book consists of recipes covering the whole range of foods.

XIX. BIOGRAPHIES

COLLECTIVE BIOGRAPHIES

695 Cunz, Dieter. THEY CAME FROM GERMANY: THE STORIES OF FA-
MOUS GERMAN-AMERICANS. New York: Dodd, Mead, 1966. 178 p.
Bibliog., index.

> A collective biography with some portraits, intended for the
> general reader, dealing with some prominent figures of Ger-
> man extraction. Detailed treatment is given to John Peter
> Zenger, F.W. von Steuben, Carl Follen, John Jacob Astor,
> Carl Schurz, J.A. Roebling, Thomas Nast, Otto Merganthaler,
> and Werner von Braun.

696 Cronau, Rudolph. GERMAN ACHIEVEMENTS IN AMERICA, A TRIBUTE
TO THE MEMORY OF THE MEN AND WOMEN WHO WORKED, FOUGHT
AND DIED FOR THE WELFARE OF THIS COUNTRY; AND A RECOGNI-
TION OF THE LIVING WHO WITH EQUAL ENTERPRISE, GENIUS AND
PATRIOTISM HELPED IN MAKING OUR UNITED STATES. New York:
the author, 1916. 233 p.

> Concentrates on German accomplishments in America from the
> beginning of the colonial period to the first decades of the
> twentieth century. These accomplishments are highlighted by
> means of biographical narratives of individuals who played a
> role in the conquest of the wilderness, in various wars, and
> in the development of science, industry, technology, and cul-
> ture. The presentation is in distinct topical chapters.

> The information provided in the text is rather sketchy, and
> there are no bibliographies to guide the reader to pertinent
> sources for further reading. Two chapters may be pointed out
> as having particular interest. The first is the chapter devoted
> to the story of the National German-American Alliance; and
> the second is the apologetic discourse entitled, "The Future
> Mission of the German Element in the United States." The
> chapter on the poetry of Germans in America contains a num-
> ber of representative selections.

Biographies

697 Schlegel, Carl Wilhelm. SCHLEGEL'S GERMAN-AMERICAN FAMILIES IN THE UNITED STATES GENEALOGICAL AND BIOGRAPHICAL. New York: American Historical Society, 1917. 401 p. Index.

An album of biographies, portraits, and family lines of prominent German-Americans from all walks of life, but predominantly from the late nineteenth-century business world. The album's value for genealogical research is enhanced by a detailed personal name index of all people mentioned in the text.

698 Skal, Georg von. HISTORY OF GERMAN IMMIGRATION IN THE UNITED STATES AND SUCCESSFUL GERMAN-AMERICANS AND THEIR DESCENDANTS. New York: Frank T. Smiley, 1910. 328 p. Index.

The essential part of this work is a collection of over two-hundred biographies of prominent German Americans in industry, finance, the sciences, and the professions, whose careers spanned across the nineteenth century. Both native and foreign-born people are included. The length of articles range from four-hundred words to several pages concentrating on the achievements of prominent German Americans. Many of the biographies are accompanied by portraits. While most of the articles seem to be well researched, especially those of scientists and scholars, the lack of documentation in general makes this work of limited value for further research. The biographical section is introduced by a forty-three page narrative giving broad overview of German immigration to North America.

698a Swiss-American Historical Society. PROMINENT AMERICANS OF SWISS ORIGIN. 2d ed. New York: Swiss-American Historical Society, 1953.

Item not available for examination.

INDIVIDUAL BIOGRAPHIES

Jane Addams

699 Linn, James Weber. JANE ADDAMS, A BIOGRAPHY. New York: Appleton-Century, 1935. Reprint. Westport, Conn.: Greenwood Press, 1968. 457 p.

John Peter Altgeld

700 Altgeld, John Peter. THE MIND AND SPIRIT OF JOHN PETER ALTGELD: SELECTED WRITINGS AND ADDRESSES. Edited by Henry M. Christman. Urbana, Ill.: University of Illinois Press, 1960. 183 p.

701 Fast, Howard. THE AMERICAN: A MIDDLE WESTERN LEGEND. New York: Duell, Sloan, and Pearce, 1946. 337 p.

John Jacob Astor

702 Porter, Kenneth Wiggins. JOHN JACOB ASTOR, BUSINESS-MAN. 2 vols. Cambridge, Mass.: Harvard University Press, 1931. Reprint. New York: Russell and Russell, 1966.

The Astor Family

703 Kavaler, Lucy. THE ASTORS: AN AMERICAN LEGEND. New York: Dodd, Mead, 1968. 211 p.

704 _____. THE ASTORS: A FAMILY CHRONICLE OF POMP AND POWER. New York: Dodd, Mead, 1966. 354 p. Bibliog.

705 O'Connor, Harvey. THE ASTORS. New York: Knopf, 1941. 488 p. Bibliog.

Johann Jakob Baegert

706 Baegert, Johann Jakob. OBSERVATIONS IN LOWER CALIFORNIA. Translated from original German with introduction and notes by M.M. Brandenburg, and Carl L. Baumann. Berkeley and Los Angeles: University of California Press, 1951. 218 p.

George Bancroft

707 Howe, Mark Antony DeWolfe. THE LIFE AND LETTERS OF GEORGE BANCROFT. 2 vols. 1908. Reprint. Port Washington, N.Y.: Kennikat Press, 1971.

Carl Leopold von Baurmeister

708 Baurmeister, Carl Leopold von. REVOLUTION IN AMERICA: CONFIDENTIAL LETTERS AND JOURNALS 1776-1784 OF ADJUTANT GENERAL MAJOR BAURMEISTER OF THE HESSIAN FORCES. Edited and translated by Bernhard A. Uhlendorf. New Brunswick, N.J.: Rutgers University Press, 1957. Reprint. Westport, Conn.: Greenwood Press, 1973. 640 p. Bibliog.

See 237.

Biographies

Johann Conrad Beissel

709   Klein, Walter Conrad. JOHANN CONRAD BEISSEL, MYSTIC AND MARTI-
       NET, 1690–1768. Pennsylvania Lives. Philadelphia: University of Pennsyl-
       vania Press, 1942. Reprint. Philadelphia: Porcupine Press, 1972. 218 p.

       See 503.

August Belmont

710   Katz, Irving. AUGUST BELMONT: A POLITICAL BIOGRAPHY. New
       York: Columbia University Press, 1968. 296 p. Bibliog.

Karl Bitter

711   Dennis, James M. KARL BITTER, ARCHITECTURAL SCULPTOR 1867–1915.
       Madison: University of Wisconsin Press, 1967. 302 p. Bibliog. notes.

712   Schevill, Ferdinand. KARL BITTER: A BIOGRAPHY. Issued under the
       auspices of the National Sculpture Society. Chicago: University of
       Chicago Press, 1917. 68 p.

Franz Boas

713   Goldschmidt, Walter, ed. THE ANTHROPOLOGY OF FRANZ BOAS:
       ESSAYS ON THE CENTENNIAL OF HIS BIRTH. American Anthropologi-
       cal Association, Memoir no. 89. San Francisco: Howard Chandler,
       1959. Reprint. Millwood, N.Y.: Kraus Reprint, 1974. 165 p. Bib-
       liog., index.

John Philip Boehm

714   Hinke, William John, ed. LIFE AND LETTERS OF THE REVEREND JOHN
       PHILIP BOEHM, FOUNDER OF THE REFORMED CHURCH IN PENNSYL-
       VANIA, 1683–1749. Philadelphia: Publication and Sunday School Board
       of the Reformed Church in the United States, 1916. 501 p.

The Bowman Family

715   Wayland, John Walter. THE BOWMANS, A PIONEERING FAMILY IN
       VIRGINIA, KENTUCKY AND THE NORTHWEST TERRITORY. Staunton,
       Va.: McClure, 1943. 185 p.

General Roeliff Brinkerhoff

716 Brinkerhoff, Roeliff. RECOLLECTIONS OF A LIFETIME. 2d ed. Cincinnati: Robert Clarke, 1904. 448 p.

John Carroll

717 Guilday, Peter Keenan. THE LIFE AND TIMES OF JOHN CARROLL, ARCHBISHOP OF BALTIMORE, 1735-1815. 1922. Reprint. Westminster, Md.: Newman Press, 1954. 864 p. Bibliog. notes.

Baron Ludwig von Closen

718 Closen, Ludwig von. THE REVOLUTIONARY JOURNAL OF BARON LUDWIG VON CLOSEN, 1780-1783. Translated and edited with an introduction by Evelyn M. Acomb. Chapel Hill: Published for the Institute of Early American History and Culture by the University of North Carolina Press, 1958. 392 p. Bibliog. notes.

Eugene V. Debs

719 Coleman, McAlister. EUGENE V. DEBS, A MAN UNAFRAID. New York: Greenburg, 1931. Reprint. Westport, Conn.: Hyperion Press, 1975. 345 p. Bibliog., index.

720 Currie, Harold W. EUGENE V. DEBS. Boston: Twayne Publishers, 1976. 157 p. Bibliog., index.

721 Ginger, Ray. THE BENDING CROSS: A BIOGRAPHY OF EUGENE V. DEBS. New Brunswick, N.J.: Rutgers University Press, 1949. Reprint. New York: Russell and Russell, 1969. 516 p. Bibliog.

Johann De Kalb

722 Zucker, Adolf Eduard. GENERAL DE KALB: LAFAYETTE'S MENTOR. Chapel Hill: University of North Carolina Press, 1966. 251 p. Bibliog.

Moses Dissinger

723 Brendle, Thomas R. "Moses Dissinger, Evangelist and Patriot." PENNSYLVANIA GERMAN SOCIETY PROCEEDINGS, vol. 58 (1959). Scottdale: Pennsylvania German Society, 1959. Bibliog. notes.

Biographies

Christopher Dock

724 Dock, Christopher. THE LIFE AND WORKS OF CHRISTOPHER DOCK: AMERICA'S PIONEER WRITER ON EDUCATION. Translated by Martin Grove Brumbaugh. 1908. Reprint. American Education: Its Men, Ideas, and Institutions [Series]. New York: Arno Press, 1969. 272 p.

725 Studer, Gerald C. THE BIOGRAPHY AND WRITINGS OF CHRISTOPHER DOCK: COLONIAL SCHOOLMASTER. Scottdale, Pa.: Herald Press, 1967. 445 p. Bibliog.

Gustav Dresel

726 Dresel, Gustav. HOUSTON JOURNAL; ADVENTURES IN NORTH AMERICA AND TEXAS, 1837-1841. Translated from a German manuscript and edited by Max Freund. Austin: University of Texas Press, 1954. 168 p. Bibliog. notes, index.

See 391.

Wyatt Earp

727 Lake, Stuart N. WYATT EARP, FRONTIER MARSHALL. Boston: Houghton Mifflin, 1931. Reprint. New York: Bantam Books, 1952. 372 p.

Hermann Ehrenberg

728 Ehrenberg, Hermann. WITH MILAM AND FANNIN: ADVENTURES OF A GERMAN BOY IN TEXAS' REVOLUTION. Translated by Charlotte Churchill; edited by Henry Smith; illustrated by Jerry Bywaters. Dallas: Tardy Publishing Co., 1935. Reprint. Austin: Pemberton Press, 1968. 224 p.

Max Ehrmann

729 Ehrmann, Bertha Pratt (King). MAX EHRMANN, A POET'S LIFE. Boston: Bruce Humphries, 1951. 118 p.

Jacob Eichholtz

730 Beal, Rebecca J. JACOB EICHHOLTZ, 1776-1842: PORTRAIT PAINTER OF PENNSYLVANIA. Philadelphia: Historical Society of Pennsylvania, 1969. 401 p. Bibliog.

731 Hensel, William Uhler. JACOB EICHHOLTZ, PAINTER; SOME "LOOSE LEAVES" FROM THE LEDGER OF AN EARLY LANCASTER ARTIST. Lancaster, Pa.: Brecht Printing Co., 1912. 39 p.

Dwight D. Eisenhower

732 Davis, Kenneth S. SOLDIER OF DEMOCRACY, A BIOGRAPHY OF DWIGHT EISENHOWER. Garden City, N.Y.: Doubleday, Doran, 1945. Rev. ed. New York: Bantam Books, 1952. 566 p.

733 Friedrichs, Heinz F., ed. PRESIDENT DWIGHT D. EISENHOWER'S ANCESTORS AND RELATIONS. Neustadt, Aisch, Germany: Deneger, 1955. 210 p.

734 Gunther, John. EISENHOWER, THE MAN AND THE SYMBOL. New York: Harper, 1952. 180 p.

735 Miller, Francis Trevelyan. EISENHOWER, MAN AND SOLDIER. Philadelphia: Winston, 1944. 278 p.

Peter Engelmann

735a Voight, Frieda Meyer, et al. THE ENGELMANN HERITAGE. Milwaukee: Milwaukee Alumni Association of the National Teachers' Seminary, 1951.

Justus Falckner

736 Clark, Delber Wallace. THE WORLD OF JUSTUS FALCKNER. Philadelphia: Muhlenberg Press, 1946. 189 p. Bibliog., notes.

737 Sachse, Julius Friedrich. JUSTUS FALCKNER, MYSTIC AND SCHOLAR, DEVOUT PIETIST IN GERMANY, HERMIT ON THE WISSAHICKON, MISSIONARY ON THE HUDSON: A BI-CENTENNIAL MEMORIAL OF THE FIRST REGULAR ORDINATION OF AN ORTHODOX PASTOR IN AMERICA, DONE NOVEMBER 24, 1903, AT GLORIA DEI, THE SWEDISH LUTHERAN CHURCH AT WICACO, PHILADELPHIA. Philadelphia: the author, 1903. 141 p.

Joseph Francl

738 Francl, Joseph. THE OVERLAND JOURNEY OF JOSEPH FRANCL: THE FIRST BOHEMIAN TO CROSS THE PLAINS TO THE CALIFORNIA GOLD FIELDS. Introduction by Richard Brautigan. San Francisco: Wreden, 1968. 55 p.

Biographies

Felix Frankfurter

739   Frankfurter, Felix. FELIX FRANKFURTER REMINISCES: RECORDED IN
       TALKS WITH DR. HARLAN B. PHILLIPS. New York: Reynal, 1960.
       Reprint. Westport, Conn.: Greenwood Press, 1978. 310 p.

Julius B. Friedlander

740   Freund, Elisabeth D. CRUSADER FOR LIGHT: JULIUS B. FRIEDLANDER,
       FOUNDER OF THE OVERBROOK SCHOOL FOR THE BLIND, 1832. Phil-
       adelphia: Dorrance, 1959. 153 p. Bibliog.

Ludwig Ernest Fuerbringer

741   Fuerbringer, Ludwig E. EIGHTY EVENTFUL YEARS: REMINISCENCES
       OF LUDWIG ERNEST FUERBRINGER. St. Louis: Concordia, 1944.

Eugene D. Funk

742   Cavanagh, Helen M. SEED SOIL AND SCIENCE: THE STORY OF
       EUGENE D. FUNK. Chicago: Lakeside, 1959. 544 p. Bibliog.

Otto Geist

743   Keim, Charles J. AGHVOOK, WHITE ESKIMO: OTTO GEIST AND
       ALASKA'S ARCHAEOLOGY. College: University of Alaska Press, 1969.
       313 p.

James Cardinal Gibbons

744   Ellis, John Tracy. THE LIFE OF JAMES CARDINAL GIBBONS, ARCH-
       BISHOP OF BALTIMORE, 1834-1921. 2 vols. Milwaukee: Bruce,
       1952. Bibliog. notes.

Colonel A.W. Gilbert

745   Smith, William Ernest, and Smith, Ophia D., eds. COLONEL A.W.
       GILBERT, CITIZEN-SOLDIER OF CINCINNATI. Cincinnati: Historical
       and Philosophical Society of Ohio, 1934. 122 p.

Samuel Gompers

746   Gompers, Samuel. SEVENTY YEARS OF LIFE AND LABOR: AN AUTO-
       BIOGRAPHY. 1925. Reprint. Revised and edited by Philip Taft, and

John A. Sessions. Foreword by George Meany. New York: Dutton, 1943. 334 p.

George Grosz

747 Grosz, George. A LITTLE YES AND A BIG NO; THE AUTOBIOGRAPHY OF GEORGE GROSZ. Translated by Lola Sachs Dorin. New York: Dial Press, 1946. 343 p.

The Guggenheim Family

748 Hoyt, Edwin P. THE GUGGENHEIMS AND THE AMERICAN DREAM. New York: Funk and Wagnalls, 1967. 382 p. Bibliog. notes.

Frederick Julius Gustorf

749 Gustorf, Frederick Julius. THE UNCORRUPTED HEART: JOURNAL AND LETTERS OF FREDERICK JULIUS GUSTORF, 1800-1845. Edited with introduction and notes by Fred Gustorf. Translated from German by Fred Gustorf, and Gisela Gustorf. Columbia: University of Missouri Press, 1969. 182 p. Bibliog. notes.

Herman Hagendorn

750 Hagedorn, Herman. THE HYPHENATED FAMILY; AN AMERICAN SAGA. New York: Macmillan, 1960. 264 p.

William Torrey Harris

751 Leidecker, Kurt Friedrich. YANKEE TEACHER: THE LIFE OF WILLIAM TORREY HARRIS. New York: Philosophical Library, 1946. 648 p.

Isaac Thomas Hecker

752 Burton, Katherine (Kurz). CELESTIAL HOMESPUN: THE LIFE OF ISAAC THOMAS HECKER. New York: Longmans, Green, 1943. 393 p.

753 Holden, Vincent F. THE YANKEE PAUL: ISAAC THOMAS HECKER. Milwaukee: Bruce, 1958. 508 p. Bibliog.

John Heckewelder

754 Heckewelder, John Gottlieb Ernestus. THIRTY THOUSAND MILES WITH JOHN HECKEWELDER. Edited by Paul A.W. Wallace. Pittsburgh: University of Pittsburgh Press, 1958. 474 p.

Biographies

Karl Heinzen

755 Wittke, Carl. AGAINST THE CURRENT, THE LIFE OF KARL HEINZEN (1809-1880). Chicago: University of Chicago Press, 1945. 342 p. Bibliog. notes.

Michael Heiss

756 Ludwig, Sister M. Mileta. RIGHT-HAND GLOVE UPLIFTED: A BIOG-RAPHY OF ARCHBISHOP MICHAEL HEISS. New York: Pageant, 1968. 567 p. Bibliog. notes.

John Martin Henni

757 Johnson, Peter Leo. CROSIER ON THE FRONTIER: A LIFE OF JOHN MARTIN HENNI, ARCHBISHOP OF MILWAUKEE. Madison: State Historical Society of Wisconsin, 1959. 240 p. Bibliog.

John Christian Frederick Heyer

758 Bachmann, Ernest Theodore. THEY CALLED HIM FATHER: THE LIFE STORY OF JOHN CHRISTIAN FREDERICK HEYER. Philadelphia: Muhlenberg, 1942. 342 p.

E.W. Hilgard

759 Jenny, Hans. E.W. HILGARD AND THE BIRTH OF MODERN SOIL SCIENCE. Pisa, Italy: Instituto de Chimica Agraria dell'Universita, 1961. 144 p. Bibliog. notes.

Michael Hillegas

760 Minich, Michael R. MEMOIR OF THE FIRST TREASURER OF THE UNITED STATES: WITH CHRONOLOGICAL DATA. Philadelphia: American Book and Job Printing, 1905. 208 p. Bibliog. notes.

Daniel Webster Hoan

761 Kerstein, Edward S. MILWAUKEE'S ALL-AMERICAN MAYOR: A PORTRAIT OF DANIEL WEBSTER HOAN. Englewood Cliffs, N.J.: Prentice-Hall, 1966. 237 p. Bibliog.

William Hoffman

762 Seitz, May Albright. THE HISTORY OF THE HOFFMAN PAPER MILLS IN MARYLAND. Towson, Md.: Seitz, 1946. 63 p. Bibliog.

Hans Hofmann

763 Wight, Frederick, Stallnecht. HANS HOFMANN. Berkeley: University of California Press, 1957. 66 p.

Caesar Hohn

764 Hohn, Caesar. DUTCHMAN OF THE BRAZOS: REMINISCENCES. Foreword by Agnes Meyer. Drawings by E.M. Schiwetz. Austin: University of Texas Press, 1963. 194 p.

Jacob Horner

765 Burdick, Usher L., and Hart, Eugene D. JACOB HORNER AND THE INDIAN CAMPAIGNS OF 1876 AND 1877. Cheltenham, Md.: Burdick, 1942. 30 p.

Dieter K. Huzel

766 Huzel, Dieter K. PENEMUENDE TO CANAVERAL. Introduction by Werner von Braun. Englewood Cliffs, N.J.: Prentice-Hall, 1962. 274 p.

William Travers Jerome

767 O'Connor, Richard. COURTROOM WARRIOR: THE COMBATIVE CAREER OF WILLIAM TRAVERS JEROME. Boston: Little, Brown and Co., 1963. 342 p.

Sylvester Judd

768 Brockway, Philip Judd. SYLVESTER JUDD (1813-1853): NOVELIST OF TRANSCENDENTALISM. Orono: University of Maine, 1941. 121 p. Bibliog.

Major-General John Kalb

769 Kapp, Friedrich. THE LIFE OF JOHN KALB, MAJOR-GENERAL IN THE REVOLUTIONARY ARMY. New York: H. Holt, 1884. 337 p.

Biographies

H.V. Kaltenborn

770   Kaltenborn, H.V. FIFTY FABULOUS YEARS, 1900-1950: A PERSONAL VIEW. New York: Putnam, 1950. 312 p.

Charles F. Kettering

771   Boyd, T.A. PROFESSIONAL AMATEUR, THE BIOGRAPHY OF CHARLES FRANKLIN KETTERING. New York: Dutton, 1957. Reprint. New York: Arno Press, 1972. 242 p.

Hermann Kiefer

772   Florer, Warren Washburn, ed. LIBERTY WRITINGS OF DR. HERMANN KIEFER. New York: Stechert, 1917. 511 p.

John Kline

773   Sappington, Roger E. COURAGEOUS PROPHET: CHAPTERS FROM THE LIFE OF JOHN KLINE. Elgin, Ill.: Brethren, n.d.

Karl Knaths

774   Mocsanyi, Paul. KARL KNATHS. Introduction by Duncan Phillips. Washington, D.C.: Phillips Gallery, 1957. 101 p.

Gustav Philipp Koerner

775   Koerner, Gustav Philipp. MEMOIRS OF GUSTAV KOERNER, 1809-1896, LIFE SKETCHES WRITTEN AT THE SUGGESTION OF HIS CHILDREN. 2 vols. Cedar Rapids, Iowa: Torch Press, 1909.

Henry Miller (née Heinrich Alfred Kreiser)

776   Treadwell, Edward Francis. THE CATTLE KING: A DRAMATIZED BIOGRAPHY. Boston: Christopher, 1950. Reprint. Fresno, Calif.: Valley Publishers, 1966. 375 p.

Max Amadeus Paulus Krueger

777   Krueger, Max Amadeus Paulus. SECOND FATHERLAND: THE LIFE AND FORTUNES OF A GERMAN IMMIGRANT. Edited with introduction by Marilyn McAdams Sibley. Rev. ed. Centennial Series of the Association of Former Students, Texas A & M University, no. 4. College Station: Texas A & M University Press, 1976. 161 p. Index.

Martin Kundig

778 Johnson, Peter Leo. STUFFED SADDLEBAGS: THE LIFE OF MARTIN
KUNDIG, PRIEST, 1805-1879. Milwaukee: Bruce, 1942. 279 p.
Bibliog.

John Lederer

779 Rights, Douglas L., and Cumming, William P. THE DISCOVERIES OF
JOHN LEDERER, WITH UNPUBLISHED LETTERS BY AND ABOUT LEDERER
TO GOVERNOR JOHN WINTHROP, JR., AND AN ESSAY ON THE
INDIANS OF LEDERER'S DISCOVERIES. Charlottesville: University Press
of Virginia, 1958. 148 p. Bibliog. notes.

Jacob Leisler

780 Reich, Jerome R. JACOB LEISLER'S REBELLION: A STUDY OF DEMO-
CRACY IN NEW YORK, 1664-1720. Chicago: University of Chicago
Press, 1953. 194 p. Bibliog.

Frederick Leypoldt

781 Beswick, Jay W. THE WORK OF FREDERICK LEYPOLDT, BIBLIOGRAPHER
AND PUBLISHER. New York: Bowker, 1942. 102 p. Bibliog.

Francis Lieber

782 Friedel, Frank. FRANCIS LIEBER, NINETEENTH CENTURY LIBERAL.
Baton Rouge: Louisiana State University Press, 1947. Reprint. Gloucester, Mass.: P. Smith, 1968. 445 p. Bibliog. notes.

Heinrich Lienhard

783 Lienhard, Heinrich. FROM ST. LOUIS TO SUTTER'S FORT 1846. Translated and edited by Erwin G. Gudde, and Elisabeth K. Gudde. Norman: University of Oklahoma Press, 1961. 204 p.

784 Lienhard, Heinrich. A PIONEER AT SUTTER'S FORT, 1846-1850: THE
ADVENTURES OF HEINRICH LIENHARD. Translated, edited, and an-
notated by Marguerite Eyer Wilbur from the original German manuscript.
Los Angeles: Calafia Society, 1941. 241 p. Bibliog.

Biographies

Walter Lippmann

785   Adams, Larry L. WALTER LIPPMANN. Boston: Twayne Publishers, 1977. 229 p. Bibliog., index.

786   Lushkin, John. LIPPMANN, LIBERTY, AND THE PRESS. University: University of Alaska, 1972. 273 p. Bibliog. notes.

787   Schapsmeier, Edward L. and Schapsmeier, Frederick H. WALTER LIPP-MANN: PHILOSOPHER-JOURNALIST. Washington, D.C.: Public Affairs Press, 1969. 188 p. Bibliog. notes.

788   Wellborn, Charles. TWENTIETH CENTURY PILGRIMAGE: WALTER LIPP-MAN AND THE PUBLIC PHILOSOPHY. Baton Rouge: Louisiana State University, 1969. 200 p. Bibliog.

Wilhelm Loehe

789   Greenholt, Homer Reginald. A STUDY OF WILHELM LOEHE, HIS COLONIES AND THE LUTHERAN INDIAN MISSION IN THE SAGINAW VALLEY OF MICHIGAN. Chicago, 1937.

Theodore Kepner Long

790   Long, Theodore Kepner. EMIGRE SAGA, A TALE OF EARLY AMERICA. New Bloomfield, Pa.: Carson Long Institute, 1943.

Henry C. Luckey

791   Luckey, Henry C. 85 AMERICAN YEARS: MEMOIRS OF A NEBRASKA CONGRESSMAN. New York: Exposition Press, 1955. 230 p.

Christopher Ludwick

792   Rush, Benjamin. AN ACCOUNT OF THE LIFE AND CHARACTER OF CHRISTOPHER LUDWICK. 1831. Reprint. Revised and republished by direction of the Philadelphia Society for the Establishment and Support of Charity Schools. New York: Garrett Press, 1969. 61 p.

Frank Luke

793   Hall, Norman S. THE BALLOON BUSTER: FRANK LUKE OF ARIZONA. Garden City, N.Y.: Doubleday, Doran and Co., 1928. 191 p.

Theodore Marburg

794 Atkinson, Henry A. THEODORE MARBURG, THE MAN AND HIS WORK. New York: Littmann, 1952. 221 p. Bibliog.

Andrew Mellick, Jr.

795 Mellick, Andrew D., Jr. THE OLD FARM. New Brunswick, N.J.: Rutgers University Press, 1948. 210 p.

H.L. Mencken

796 Anghoff, Charles. H.L. MENCKEN, A PORTRAIT FROM MEMORY. New York: T. Yoseloff, 1956. 240 p.

797 Bode, Carl. MENCKEN. Carbondale: Southern Illinois University Press, 1969. 452 p. Bibliog.

798 Enoch Pratt Free Library. Baltimore. H.L.M.; THE MENCKEN BIBLIOG-RAPHY. Compiled by Betty Adler with the assistance of Jane Wilhelm. Baltimore: Johns Hopkins University Press, 1961. 367 p.

799 Fecher, Charles A. MENCKEN: A STUDY OF HIS THOUGHT. New York: Random House, 1978. 391 p. Bibliog., index.

800 Mencken, Henry Louis. HAPPY DAYS, 1880-1892. New York: Knopf, 1940. 313 p.

801 _____. HEATHEN DAYS, 1890-1936. New York: Knopf, 1943. 299 p.

802 Nolte, William Henry. H.L. MENCKEN, LITERARY CRITIC. Middle-town, Conn.: Wesleyan University Press, 1966. 282 p. Bibliog. notes.

803 Stenerson, Douglas C. H.L. MENCKEN: ICONOCLAST FROM BALTI-MORE. Chicago: University of Chicago Press, 1971. 287 p. Bibliog.

Ottmar Mergenthaler

804 Mengel, Willi. OTTMAR MERGENTHALER AND THE PRINTING REVOLU-TION. Introduction by Lin Yutang. Brooklyn: Mergenthaler Linotype, 1954. 63 p.

805 Mergenthaler, Ottmar. BIOGRAPHY OF OTTMAR MERGENTHALER, AND HISTORY OF THE LINOTYPE, ITS INVENTION AND DEVELOPMENT. Baltimore, 1898. 71 p.

Biographies

John O. Meusebach

806 King, Irene M[arshall]. JOHN O. MEUSEBACH: GERMAN COLONIZER IN TEXAS. Austin: University of Texas Press, 1967. 192 p.

See 390.

Ernest Louis Meyer

807 Meyer, Ernest Louis. BUCKET BOY: A MILWAUKEE LEGEND. New York: Hastings House, 1947. 236 p.

Henry Meyer

808 Buffington, Albert F. "Henry Meyer: An Early Pennsylvania German Poet." PENNSYLVANIA GERMAN FOLKLORE SOCIETY YEARBOOK 19 (1954): 1-32.

HENRY MILLER. See Heinrich Alfred Kreiser

John Henry Miller

809 Dapp, Charles Frederick. "The Evolution of an American Patriot: John Henry Miller, German Printer, Publisher, and Editor of the American Revolution." PENNSYLVANIA GERMAN SOCIETY PROCEEDINGS AND ADDRESSES 32 (1924): 1-68. Lancaster: Pennsylvania German Society, 1924.

Lewis Miller

810 Turner, Robert P., ed. LEWIS MILLER, 1796-1882: SKETCHES AND CHRONICLES, THE REFLECTIONS OF A NINETEENTH CENTURY PENN-SYLVANIA GERMAN FOLK ARTIST. New York: Historical Society of York County, 1966.

Gottlieb Mittelberger

811 Mittelberger, Gottlieb. JOURNEY TO PENNSYLVANIA. Edited and translated by Oscar Handlin, and John Clive. 1898. Reprint. Cambridge, Mass.: Belknap Press of Harvard University Press, 1960. 102 p.

See 330, 331.

Aloisius Muench

812 Barry, Colman J. AMERICAN NUNCIO: CARDINAL ALOISIUS MEUNCH. Collegeville, Minn.: St. Johns University Press, 1969. 379 p. Bibliog.

Henry Melchior Muhlenberg

813 Frick, W.K. HENRY MELCHIOR MUHLENBERG, PATRIARCH OF THE
LUTHERAN CHURCH IN AMERICA. Philadelphia: Lutheran Publishing,
1902. 200 p.

814 Muhlenberg, Henry Melchior. JOURNALS. 3 vols. Vol. 1, 2 Jan.
1742-31 Dec. 1763; Vol. 2, 1764-76; Vol. 3, 1777-29 Sept. 1787.
Translated by Theodore G. Tappert, and John W. Doberstein. Philadelphia: Evangelical Lutheran Ministerium of Pennsylvania and Adjacent
States, and Muhlenberg Press, 1942-58.

815 _____. NOTEBOOK OF A COLONIAL CLERGYMAN. Edited and
translated by Theodore G. Tappert and John W. Doberstein. Philadelphia:
Muhlenberg Press, 1959. 250 p.

816 Seebach, Margaret R. AN EAGLE OF THE WILDERNESS: THE STORY
OF HENRY MELCHIOR MUHLENBERG. Philadelphia: United Lutheran,
1924. 139 p.

John Peter Gabriel Muhlenberg

817 Hocker, Edward W. THE FIGHTING PARSON OF THE AMERICAN RE-
VOLUTION, A BIOGRAPHY OF GENERAL PETER MUHLENBERG, LUTH-
ERAN CLERGYMAN, MILITARY CHIEFTAIN, AND POLITICAL LEADERS.
Philadelphia: Hocker, 1936. 191 p. Bibliog.

The Muhlenberg Family

818 Wallace, Paul A.W. THE MUHLENBERGS OF PENNSYLVANIA. Philadelphia: University of Pennsylvania Press, 1950. Reprint. Freeport,
N.Y.: Books For Libraries, 1970. 358 p. Bibliog.

William Nast

819 Wittke, Carl. WILLIAM NAST, PATRIARCH OF GERMAN METHODISM.
Detroit: Wayne State University Press, 1959. 248 p. Bibliog.

John Neumann

820 Curley, Michael J. VENERABLE JOHN NEUMANN, C. SS. R.,
FOURTH BISHOP OF PHILADELPHIA. Washington, D.C.: Catholic University Press, 1952. 547 p. Bibliog.

Biographies

Elisabet Ney

821 Fortune, Jan (Isabelle), and Burton, Jean. ELISABET NEY. New York: Knopf, 1943. 300 p. Bibliog.

822 Loggins, Vernon. TWO ROMANTICS AND THEIR IDEAL LIFE. New York: Odyssey, 1946. 385 p. Bibliog. notes.

823 Taylor, Bride Neil. ELISABET NEY, SCULPTOR. 1916. New ed., rev. Austin: n.p., 1938. 129 p.

Marta Nordlander

824 Pine, Hester. THE WALTZ IS OVER. New York: Farrar and Rinehart, 1943. 371 p.

Adolph S. Ochs

825 Johnson, Gerald W. AN HONORABLE TITAN, A BIOGRAPHICAL STUDY OF ADOLPH S. OCHS. New York: Harper, 1946. Reprint. Westport, Conn.: Greenwood Press, 1970. 313 p. Biliog. notes.

Philip William Otterbein

826 Drury, Augustus Waldo. THE LIFE OF PHILIP WILLIAM OTTERBEIN, FOUNDER OF THE CHURCH OF THE UNITED BRETHREN IN CHRIST. Dayton: United Brethren Publishing House, 1884. 384 p.

827 Milhouse, Paul W. PHILIP WILLIAM OTTERBEIN: PIONEER PASTOR TO GERMANS IN AMERICA. Nashville: Upper Room, 1968. 71 p. Bibliog. notes.

828 Zeigler, W.H. PHILIP WILLIAM OTTERBEIN, AN INTERPRETATION. Huntington, Ind.: United Brethren Publishing House, 1938. 96 p.

Reinhold Pabel

829 Pabel, Reinhold. ENEMIES ARE HUMAN. Philadelphia: Winston, 1955. 248 p.

Franz Daniel Pastorius

830 Learned, Marion Dexter. THE LIFE OF FRANZ DANIEL PASTORIUS, THE FOUNDER OF GERMANTOWN. Philadelphia: Campbell, 1908. 324 p.

Elizabeth Palmer Peabody

831   Baylor, Ruth M. ELIZABETH PALMER PEABODY: KINDERGARTEN PIO-
       NEER. Philadelphia: University of Pennsylvania Press, 1965. 228 p.
       Bibliog., index.

       See 561.

Samuel Whitaker Pennypacker

832   Pennypacker, Samuel Whitaker. THE AUTOBIOGRAPHY OF A PENN-
       SYLVANIAN. Philadelphia: J.C. Winston, 1918. 564 p. Bibliog.

John J. Pershing

833   O'Connor, Richard. BLACK JACK PERSHING. Garden City, N.Y.:
       Doubleday, 1961. 431 p.

The Pershing Family

834   Pershing, Edgar Jamison. THE PERSHING FAMILY IN AMERICA: A
       COLLECTION OF HISTORICAL AND GENEALOGICAL DATA, FAMILY
       PORTRAITS, TRADITIONS, LEGENDS AND MILITARY RECORDS. Phila-
       delphia: Ferguson, 1924. 434 p.

Friedrich Richard Petri

835   Newcomb, William Wilmon, Jr. GERMAN ARTIST ON THE FRONTIER:
       FRIEDRICH RICHARD PETRI. Austin: Published in collaboration with
       Texas Memorial Museum by the University of Texas Press, 1978. Bibliog.
       index.

Francis Xavier Pierz

836   Furlan, William P. IN CHARITY UNFEIGNED: THE LIFE OF FATHER
       FRANCIS XAVIER PIERZ. Patterson, N.J.: St. Anthony Guild, 1952.
       270 p.

Charles Preuss

837   Preuss, Charles. EXPLORING WITH FREMONT: THE PRIVATE DIARIES
       OF CHARLES PREUSS, CARTOGRAPHER FOR JOHN FREMONT ON HIS
       FIRST, SECOND, AND FOURTH EXPEDITION TO THE FAR WEST. Trans-
       lated and edited by Erwin G. Gudde, and Elisabeth K. Gudde. Norman:
       University of Oklahoma Press, 1958. 162 p.

Biographies

Heinrich Armin Rattermann

838 Spanheimer, Sister Mary Edmund. HEINRICH ARMIN RATTERMANN, GERMAN-AMERICAN AUTHOR, POET, AND HISTORIAN, 1832-1923. Washington, D.C.: Catholic University of America Press, 1937. Reprint. New York: AMS Press, 1970. 148 p.

839 Willen, Henry. HENRY ARMIN RATTERMANN'S LIFE AND POETICAL WORK. Philadelphia: University of Pennsylvania Press, 1939. 94 p. Bibliog.

Frederick Augustus Rauch

840 Ziegler, Howard J.B. FREDERICK AUGUSTUS RAUCH, AMERICAN HEGELIAN. Lancaster, Pa.: Franklin and Marshall College, 1953. 324 p. Bibliog.

Walter Rauschenbusch

841 Sharpe, Dores Robinson. WALTER RAUSCHENBUSCH. New York: Macmillan, 1942. 463 p.

Herman Francis Reinhart

842 Reinhart, Herman Francis. THE GOLDEN FRONTIER: THE RECOLLECTIONS OF HERMAN FRANCIS REINHART, 1854-1869. Austin: University of Texas Press, 1962. 353 p.

Robert Reitzel

843 Zucker, Adolph E. ROBERT REITZEL. Americana Germanica, new series, no. 25. Philadelphia: Americana Germanica, 1917. 74 p.

Walter Reuther

844 Dayton, Eldorous L. WALTER REUTHER, AUTOCRAT OF THE BARGAINING TABLE. New York: Devin-Adair, 1958. 280 p.

Conrad Richter

845 Barnes, Robert J. CONRAD RICHTER. Austin: Steck-Vaughn, 1968. 44 p. Bibliog.

846 Gaston, Edwin W., Jr. CONRAD RICHTER. New York: Twayne Publishers, 1965. 176 p. Bibliog.

Friederika von Riedesel

847 Riedesel, Friederika Charlotte Luise (von Massow) Friefrau von. LETTERS
AND JOURNALS RELATING TO THE WAR OF THE AMERICAN REVOLU-
TION, AND THE CAPTURE OF GERMAN TROOPS AT SARATOGA.
1867. Reprint. New York: New York Times, 1968. 235 p. Index.

See 238.

848 Tharp, Louise Hall. THE BARONESS AND THE GENERAL. Boston:
Little, Brown, 1962. 458 p. Bibliog.

David Rittenhouse

849 Ford, Edward. DAVID RITTENHOUSE, ASTRONOMER-PATRIOT, 1732-
1796. Philadelphia: University of Pennsylvania Press, 1946. 226 p.
Bibliog. notes.

William Rittenhouse

850 Rubincam, Milton. "William Rittenhouse, America's Pioneer Paper Manufacturer and Mennonite Minister." PENNSYLVANIA GERMAN SOCIETY
PROCEEDINGS 58 (1959). Scottdale: Pennsylvania German Society,
1959.

John Augustus Roebling

851 Trachtenberg, Alan. BROOKLYN BRIDGE: FACT AND SYMBOL. New
York: Oxford University Press, 1965. 182 p. Bibliog. notes.

The Roebling Family

852 Schuyler, Hamilton. THE ROEBLINGS, A CENTURY OF ENGINEERS,
BRIDGE-BUILDERS AND INDUSTRIALISTS: THE STORY OF THREE GEN-
ERATIONS OF AN ILLUSTRIOUS FAMILY, 1831-1931. Princeton, N.J.:
Princeton University Press, 1931. Reprint. New York: AMS Press,
1972. 424 p. Bibliog. notes, index.

See 538.

The Rothschilds Family

853 Morton, Frederic. THE ROTHSCHILDS, A FAMILY PORTRAIT. New
York: Atheneum, 1962. 305 p. Bibliog.

Biographies

Charles E. Ruthenberg

854 Johnson, Oakley C. THE DAY IS COMING: THE LIFE AND WORK OF CHARLES E. RUTHENBERG. New York: International Publishers, 1957. 192 p. Bibliog. notes.

Michael Sattler

855 Augsburger, Myron. PILGRIM AFLAME. Scottdale, Pa.: Herald Press, 1967. 288 p.

Jacob H. Schiff

856 Adler, Cyrus. JACOB H. SCHIFF: HIS LIFE AND LETTERS. 2 vols. 1928. Reprint. Freeport, N.Y.: Books for Libraries Press, 1972.

Theodore Emanuel Schmauk

857 Sandt, George W. THEODORE EMANUEL SCHMAUK, D.D., LL.D. A BIOGRAPHICAL SKETCH, WITH LIBERAL QUOTATIONS FROM HIS LETTERS AND HIS OTHER WRITINGS. Philadelphia: United Lutheran Publishing House, 1921. 291 p.

Ernst Ferdinand Felix Schmidt

858 Schmidt, Ernst Ferdinand Felix. HE CHOSE: THE OTHER WAS A TREADMILL THING. Edited and translated by Frederick Rehm Schmidt. Santa Fe: 1968. 187 p. Bibliog.

Samuel Simon Schmucker

859 Wentz, Abdel Ross. PIONEER IN CHRISTIAN UNITY: SAMUEL SIMON SCHMUCKER. Philadelphia: Fortress Press, 1967. 372 p. Bibliog. notes.

Charles Schreiner

860 Haley, J. Evetts. CHARLES SCHREINER, GENERAL MERCHANDISE: THE STORY OF A COUNTRY STORE. Austin: Texas State Historical Association, 1945. Reprint. Kerrville, Texas: C. Schreiner, 1969. 73 p. Index.

Charles Schreyvogel

861 Horan, James D. THE LIFE AND ART OF CHARLES SCHREYVOGEL, PAINTER-HISTORIAN OF THE INDIAN-FIGHTING ARMY OF THE AMERICAN WEST. New York: Crown Publishers, 1968. 62 p. Bibliog. notes.

Paul Schuman

862 Freeman, Joseph. NEVER CALL RETREAT. New York: Farrar and Rinehart, 1943. 756 p.

Carl Schurz

863 Easum, Chester Verne. THE AMERICANIZATION OF CARL SCHURZ. Chicago: University of Chicago Press, 1929. 374 p. Bibliog.

864 Fuess, Claude Moore. CARL SCHURZ, REFORMER: 1829-1906. New York: Dodd, Mead, 1932. Reprint. Port Washington, N.Y.: Kennikat Press, 1963. 421 p. Bibliog.

865 Schafer, Joseph. CARL SCHURZ, MILITANT LIBERAL. Evansville, Wis.: Antes, 1930. 270 p. Bibliog., index.

866 Schurz, Carl. INTIMATE LETTERS OF CARL SCHURZ, 1841-1869. Translated and edited by Joseph Schafer. Collections of the State Historical Society of Wisconsin, vol. 30. Madison: State Historical Society of Wisconsin, 1928. 491 p. Index.

867 _____. THE REMINISCENCES OF CARL SCHURZ. 3 vols. Illustrated with portraits and original drawings. New York: Doubleday, Page and Co., 1908. 405 p.; 443 p.; 486 p.

868 _____. SPEECHES, CORRESPONDENCE, AND POLITICAL PAPERS OF CARL SCHURZ. 6 vols. Selected and edited by Frederic Bancroft on behalf of the Carl Schurz Memorial Committee. 1913. Reprint. N.Y.: Negro Universities Press, 1969.

869 U.S. Library of Congress. Manuscript Division. CARL SCHURZ: A REGISTER OF HIS PAPERS IN THE LIBRARY OF CONGRESS. Washington, D.C.: Library of Congress, 1966. 17 p.

J. Otto Schweizer

870 Jockers, Ernst. J. OTTO SCHWEIZER, THE MAN AND HIS WORK. Philadelphia: Press of International Printing, 1953. 164 p.

Biographies

Charles Sealsfield

871 Jordan, Emil Leopold. AMERICA, GLORIOUS AND CHAOTIC LAND:
CHARLES SEALSFIELD DISCOVERS THE YOUNG UNITED STATES. Translated and adapted from the German original with introductions, notes,
and an account of Sealsfield's life by Emil L. Jordan. Englewood Cliffs,
N.J.: Prentice-Hall, 1969. 307 p. Bibliog. notes.

872 Faust, Albert Bernhardt. CHARLES SEALSFIELD (KARL POSTL): MATE-
RIALS FOR A BIOGRAPHY: A STUDY OF HIS STYLE: HIS INFLUENCE
UPON AMERICAN LITERATURE. Baltimore: Press of the Friedenwald
Co., 1892. 53 p. Bibliog.

Johann Gottfried Seume

873 Mueller-Borbach, Heinrich. DER LANDSTRASSE VERSCHWOREN; JOHANN
GOTTFRIED SEUME. East Berlin, Germany: Ruetten & Loening, 1957.

David Shultze

874 Shultze, David. THE JOURNALS AND PAPERS OF DAVID SHULTZE.
2 vols. Translated and edited by Andrew S. Berky. Pennsburg, Pa.:
Schwenkfelder Library, 1952-53.

Al Sieber

875 Thrapp, Dan L. AL SIEBER: CHIEF OF SCOUTS. Norman: University
of Oklahoma Press, 1964. 432 p. Bibliog.

William Sihler

876 Spitz, Lewis William. LIFE IN TWO WORLDS: BIOGRAPHY OF WIL-
LIAM SIHLER. St. Louis: Concordia, 1968. 198 p. Bibliog. notes.

The Spiegelberg Family

877 Fierman, Floyd S. THE SPIEGELBERGS OF NEW MEXICO, MERCHANTS
AND BANKERS 1844-1893. El Paso: Texas Western College Press, 1964.
48 p.

Claus Spreckels

878 Adler, Jacob. CLAUS SPRECKELS: THE SUGAR KING IN HAWAII.
Honolulu: University of Hawaii Press, 1966. 339 p. Bibliog. notes.

Joseph Lincoln Steffens

879 Steffens, Joseph Lincoln. THE AUTOBIOGRAPHY OF JOSEPH LINCOLN STEFFENS. New York: Harcourt, Brace, 1931. Reprint. New York: Harcourt, Brace, 1958. 884 p.

Charles Steinmetz

880 Thomas, Henry. CHARLES STEINMETZ. Illustrated by Charles Beck. New York: Putnam, 1959. 126 p.

George Wilhelm Steller

881 Ford, Corey. WHERE THE SEA BREAKS ITS BACK: THE EPIC STORY OF A PIONEER NATURALIST AND THE DISCOVERY OF ALASKA. Boston: Little, Brown and Co., 1966. 206 p. Bibliog.

Drawings by Lois Darling.

Friedrich William von Steuben

882 Kapp, Friedrich. LIFE OF FRIEDRICH WILLIAM VON STEUBEN, MAJOR GENERAL IN THE REVOLUTIONARY ARMY. New York: Mason, 1859. 735 p.

882a Palmer, John McAuley. GENERAL VON STEUBEN. New Haven, Conn.: Yale University Press, 1937. Reprint. Port Washington, N.Y.: Kennikat Press, 1966. 434 p. Bibliog.

Henry William Stiegel

883 Heiges, George L. HENRY WILLIAM STIEGEL AND HIS ASSOCIATES: A STORY OF EARLY AMERICAN INDUSTRY. Manheim, Pa.: Heiges, 1948. 2d ed. Mannheim, Pa.: Arbee Foundation, 1976. 227 p.

884 _____. HENRY WILLIAM STIEGEL: THE LIFE STORY OF A FAMOUS AMERICAN GLASS-MAKER. Manheim, Pa.: Heiges, 1937. 80 p.

Friedrich Armand Strubberg

885 Barba, Preston A. THE LIFE AND WORKS OF FRIEDRICH ARMAND STRUBBERG. Americana Germanica, no. 16. Philadelphia: Americana Germanica Press, 1913. 149 p. Bibliog.

Biographies

Elizabeth Kemp Stutzman

886 Stoll, Joseph. THE LORD IS MY SHEPHERD: THE LIFE OF ELIZABETH KEMP STUTZMAN. Aylmer, Ontario: Pathway, 1965.

Billy Sunday

887 McLoughlin, William Gerald. BILLY SUNDAY WAS HIS REAL NAME. Chicago: University of Chicago Press, 1955. 324 p. Bibliog.

Adolph Sutro

888 Stewart, Robert E., Jr., and Stewart, Mary Frances. ADOLPH SUTRO-- A BIOGRAPHY. Berkeley, Calif.: Howell-North, 1962. 243 p. Bibliog.

John A. Sutter, Jr.

889 Dana, Julian. SUTTER OF CALIFORNIA. New York: Pioneers, 1934. Reprint. New York: Greenwood Press, 1974. 423 p. Bibliog.

890 Dillon, Richard H. FOOL'S GOLD: THE DECLINE AND FALL OF CAPTAIN JOHN SUTTER OF CALIFORNIA. New York: Coward-McCann, 1967. 380 p. Bibliog.

891 Sutter, John Augustus. A STATEMENT REGARDING EARLY CALIFORNIA EXPERIENCE. Edited with a biography, by Allan R. Ottley. Sacramento, Calif.: Sacramento Book Collector's Club, 1943. 160 p.

892 _____. SUTTER'S OWN STORY: THE LIFE OF GENERAL JOHN AUGUSTUS SUTTER AND THE HISTORY OF NEW HELVETIA IN THE SACRAMENTO VALLEY. Edited by Erwin G. Gudde. New York: G.P. Putnam's Sons, 1936. 244 p.

893 Zollinger, James Peter. SUTTER, THE MAN AND HIS EMPIRE. New York: Oxford University Press, 1939. 374 p.

Gerard Swope

894 Loth, David. SWOPE OF G.E., THE STORY OF GERARD SWOPE AND GENERAL ELECTRIC IN AMERICAN BUSINESS. New York: Simon and Schuster, 1958. 309 p. Index.

Henrietta Szold

895 Zeitlin, Rose. HENRIETTA SZOLD, RECORD OF A LIFE. New York: Dial Press, 1952. 263 p.

David Tannenberg

896 Armstrong, William H. ORGANS FOR AMERICA: THE LIFE AND WORK OF DAVID TANNENBERG. Philadelphia: University of Pennsylvania Press, 1967. 154 p. Bibliog.

Bayard Taylor

897 Krumpelmann, John T. BAYARD TAYLOR AND GERMAN LETTERS. Hamburg, Germany: Cram, Gruyter, 1959. 235 p. Bibliog.

Rudolf Bolling Teusler

898 Robbins, Howard Chandler, and MacNaught, George K. DR. RUDOLF BOLLING TEUSLER: AN ADVENTURE IN CHRISTIANITY. New York: Scribner's, 1942. 221 p.

Theodore Thomas

899 Thomas, Theodore. A MUSICAL AUTOBIOGRAPHY. Edited by George P. Upton. New introduction by Leon Stein. New York: DaCapo Press, 1964. 378 p.

George Ticknor

900 Hillard, George S. LIFE AND LETTERS AND JOURNALS OF GEORGE TICKNOR. 2 vols. Boston: Houghton Mifflin, 1876.

Samuel G. Trexler

901 Devol, Edmund. SWORD OF THE SPIRIT: A BIOGRAPHY OF SAMUEL TREXLER. New York: Dodd, Mead, 1954. 298 p.

Henry Villard

902 Villard, Henry. MEMOIRS OF HENRY VILLARD, JOURNALIST AND FINANCIER, 1835-1900. 2 vols. 1904. Reprint. New York: DaCapo Press, 1969.

Biographies

Werner Von Braun

903 Bergaust, Erik. REACHING FOR THE STARS. Introduction by Frederick C. Durant III. New York: Doubleday, 1960. 407 p.

Abraham Wagner

904 Berky, Andrew S. PRACTITIONER IN PHYSICK: A BIOGRAPHY OF ABRAHAM WAGNER, 1717-1763. In PENNSYLVANIA GERMAN SOCIETY PUBLICATIONS 55 (1954): 1-175. Pennsburg, Pa.: Schwenkfelder Library, 1954. 175 p.

Philipp Waldeck

905 Learned, Marion Dexter. PHILIPP WALDECK'S DIARY OF THE AMERICAN REVOLUTION. Americana Germanica, new series, no. 6. Philadelphia: Americana Germanica Press, 1907. 146 p.

Jacob Walzer

906 Barnard, Barney, and Higham, Charles Frederick. TRUE STORY OF JACOB WALZER, A FASCINATING AND ROMANTIC TALE OF AN OLD GERMAN PROSPECTOR KNOWN TO FAME AS THE OLD DUTCHMAN AND WHOSE FAMOUS GOLD MINE IS STILL A MYSTERY OF SUPERSTITION MOUNTAIN. Apache, Arizona: Rancho Del Superstition, 1953. 66 p.

John Wanamaker

907 Appel, Joseph H. THE BUSINESS BIOGRAPHY OF JOHN WANAMAKER, FOUNDER AND BUILDER: AMERICA'S MERCHANT PIONEER FROM 1861 TO 1922: WITH GLIMPSES OF RODMAN WANAMAKER AND THOMAS B. WANAMAKER. New York: Macmillan, 1930. Reprint. New York: AMS Press, 1970. 471 p.

908 Gibbons, Herbert A. JOHN WANAMAKER. 2 vols. 1926. Reprint. Port Washington, N.Y.: Kennikat Press, 1971. Bibliog.

John Concord Weiser

909 Graeff, Arthur D. CONRAD WEISER, MAN OF AFFAIRS. Manheim, Pa.: John Conrad Weiser Family Association, 1964. 16 p.

910 Graeff, Arthur D. CONRAD WEISER, PENNSYLVANIA PEACEMAKER. Pennsylvania German Folklore Society Yearbook, vol. 8 (1943). Allen-

town: Pennsylvania German Folklore Society, 1945. 406 p. Bibliog. notes.

911 Wallace, Paul A.W. CONRAD WEISER, 1696–1760. FRIEND OF COLONIST AND MOHAWK. Philadelphia: University of Pennsylvania Press, 1945. Reprint. New York: Russell and Russell, 1971. 645 p. Bibliog. notes, index.

912 Walton, Joseph S. CONRAD WEISER AND THE INDIAN POLICY OF COLONIAL PENNSYLVANIA. 1900. Reprint. First American Frontier. New York: Arno Press, 1971. 420 p. Bibliog. notes.

913 Washington, Ida H. "Conrad Weiser in Fact and Fiction." MONATSHEFTE 68 (Summer 1976): 162–66.

914 Weiser, Clement Zwingli. THE LIFE OF JOHN CONRAD WEISER, THE GERMAN PIONEER, PATRIOT, AND PATRON OF TWO RACES. Reading, Pa.: D. Miller, 1899. 449 p.

The Weiser Family

915 Weiser, Frederick S. THE WEISER FAMILY, A GENEALOGY OF THE FAMILY OF JOHN CONRAD WEISER. Mechanicsburg, Pa.: John Conrad Weiser Family Association, 1960. 882 p.

916 _____, comp. A WEISER FAMILY ALBUM. Manheim, Pa.: John Conrad Weiser Family Association, 1971. 30 p.

Designed by Louise Z. Stahl.

Wilhelm Weitling

917 Wittke, Carl Frederick. THE UTOPIAN COMMUNIST, A BIOGRAPHY OF WILHELM WEITLING. Baton Rouge: Louisiana State University Press, 1950. 327 p.

Lewis Wetzel

918 Allman, Clarence Brent. LEWIS WETZEL, INDIAN FIGHTER: THE LIFE AND TIMES OF A FRONTIER HERO. New York: Devin-Adair Co., 1961. 237 p.

919 Meyers, L.C.V. LIFE AND ADVENTURES OF LEWIS WETZEL. Chicago: W.H. Harrison, 1883.

Biographies

Joseph Weydemeyer

920 Obermann, Karl. JOSEPH WEYDEMEYER, PIONEER OF AMERICAN
SOCIALISM. New York: International Publishers, 1947. 160 p.

Carl Wittke

921 Ander, Oscar Fritiof, comp. IN THE TREK OF THE IMMIGRANTS: ESSAYS
PRESENTED TO CARL WITTKE. Augustana College Publications, no. 31.
Rock Island, Ill.: Augustana College Library, 1964. 325 p. Bibliog.

> In addition to Harvey Wish's essay "Carl Wittke, Historian,"
> and C.H. Cramer's "Bibliography of Works by Carl Wittke,"
> the Festschrift also includes the study of John T. Flanagan's
> "The German in American Fiction."

Anna Zenger

922 Cooper, Kent. ANNA ZENGER, MOTHER OF FREEDOM. New York:
Farrar, Strauss, 1946. 325 p.

John Peter Zenger

923 Rutherford, Livingston. JOHN PETER ZENGER: HIS PRESS, HIS TRIAL,
AND A BIBLIOGRAPHY OF ZENGER IMPRINTS. 1904. Reprint. Westport, Conn.: Greenwood Press, 1975. 152 p.

924 Zenger, John Peter. A BRIEF NARRATIVE OF THE CASE AND TRIAL
OF JOHN PETER ZENGER, PRINTER OF THE NEW YORK WEEKLY JOUR-
NAL. 2d ed. By James Alexander. Edited by Stanley Nider Katz.
Cambridge, Mass.: Belknap Press of Harvard University Press, 1972. 250 p.

> See 522.

925 Zenger, John Peter. THE TRIAL OF PETER ZENGER. Edited, with introduction and notes by Vincent Buranelli. Westport, Conn.: Greenwood
Press, 1975. 152 p.

> See 521.

Nicholas Ludwig Graef Von Zinzendorf

926 Lewis, Arthur James. ZINZENDORF, THE ECUMENICAL PIONEER: A
STUDY IN THE MORAVIAN CONTRIBUTION TO CHRISTIAN MISSION
AND UNITY. Philadelphia: Westminster Press, 1962. 208 p. Bibliog.
index.

927 Mezezers, Valids. THE HERRNHUTERIAN PIETISM IN THE BALTIC, AND ITS OUTREACH INTO AMERICA AND ELSEWHERE IN THE WORLD. North Quincy, Mass.: Christopher Publishing House, 1975. 151 p. Bibliog.

928 Spangenberg, August Gottlieb. THE LIFE OF NICHOLAS LEWIS COUNT ZINZENDORF. Translated from German by Samuel Jackson. London: S. Holdsworth, 1838. 511 p.

929 Weinlick, John R. COUNT ZINZENDORF. Nashville: Abingdon Press, 1956. 240 p.

Illustrations by Fred Bees.

XX. SCHOLARLY SERIES

LIST OF VOLUMES PUBLISHED BY THE PENNSYLVANIA GERMAN SOCIETY AND THE PENNSYLVANIA GERMAN FOLKLORE SOCIETY

In 1890 the Pennsylvania German Society came into existence. Its aim was to record and preserve the history and lore of the Pennsylvania Germans. Between 1890 and 1966 it published 63 volumes of its PROCEEDINGS. In 1935 the Pennsylvania German Folklore Society was organized with similar aims. Until 1966 it published 28 volumes of its YEARBOOK. The two societies combined in November 1966 to form The Pennsylvania German Society. In that year, a new series of publications began, and a periodical, DER REGGEBOGE [The Rainbow], was launched.

For membership information, write to The Pennsylvania German Society, RD 1, Box 469, Breinigsville, Pa. 18031.

PENNSYLVANIA GERMAN SOCIETY PROCEEDINGS AND ADDRESSES, 1891-1966. Many of the volumes published in this series bear the heading: "Pennsylvania: The German Influence in Its Settlement and Development. A Narrative and Critical History."

Vol. 1 (1891)

930 PENNSYLVANIA GERMAN SOCIETY, SKETCH OF ITS ORIGIN, WITH THE PROCEEDINGS AND ADDRESSES AT ITS ORGANIZATION.

Vol. 2 (1892)

931 Sachse, Julius F. TRUE HEROES OF PROVINCIAL PENNSYLVANIA.

932 Egle, William H. THE PENNSYLVANIA GERMAN: HIS PLACE IN THE HISTORY OF THE COMMONWEALTH.

Vol. 3 (1893)

933 PENNSYLVANIA GERMAN DAY AT THE PENNSYLVANIA CHAUTAUQUA, MT. GRETNA, PENNSYLVANIA, MONDAY, JULY 17, 1893. LIST OF

MEMBERS OF THE PENNSYLVANIA GERMAN SOCIETY. BIRTH AND BAPTISMAL REGISTER OF TRINITY LUTHERAN CHURCH, LANCASTER, PENNSYLVANIA.

Vol. 4 (1894)

934   De Schweinitz, Paul. THE GERMAN MORAVIAN SETTLEMENTS IN PENNSYLVANIA, 1730-1800.

935   Levan, F.K. MAXATAWNY PRIOR TO 1800.

936   PENNSYLVANIA GERMAN DAY AT THE PENNSYLVANIA CHAUTAUQUA, MT. GRETNA, PENNSYLVANIA, THURSDAY, JULY 19, 1894.

937   Beehrle, R.K. THE EDUCATIONAL POSITION OF THE PENNSYLVANIA GERMANS.

Vol. 5 (1895)

938   Stahr, S. THE PENNSYLVANIA GERMANS AT HOME.

939   Hoffman, W.J. POPULAR SUPERSTITIONS.

940   Kuhns, L. Oscar. PENNSYLVANIA GERMAN SURNAMES.

941   Porter, Thomas Conrad. THE BUCHER ALBUM.

942   BIRTHS AND BAPTISMAL REGISTER OF TRINITY LUTHERAN CHURCH, LANCASTER PENNSYLVANIA. (Continued from vol. 3)

Vol. 6 (1896)

943   Sachse, Julius Friedrich, translator, collator, arranger. KIRCHEN-MATRI-CUL: DER EVANGELISCH LUTHERISCHEN GEMEINDE IN NEU PROVI-DENZ, PENNSYLVANIA, (Augustus Evangelical Lutheran Congregation, Trappe, Pa.)

944   BIRTHS AND BAPTISMAL REGISTER OF TRINITY LUTHERAN CHURCH, LANCASTER, PENNSYLVANIA. (Continued from vol. 5)

Vol. 7 (1897)

945   Sachse, Julius Friedrich. THE FATHERLAND: (1450-1750). (See 223).

946   Diffenderffer, Frank Ried. THE GERMAN EXODUS TO ENGLAND IN 1709. (Massenauswanderung der Pfaelzer.) (See 302).

947   Augustus Evangelical Lutheran Church, Trappe, Pennsylvania. RECORD OF MARRIAGES, CONFIRMATIONS AND BURIALS WITH A LIST OF THE CONTRIBUTORS TO PASTOR'S SALARY. NOV. 27, 1760.

948   THE RECORDS OF ST. MICHAELIS AND ZION CONGREGATION OF PHILADELPHIA.

Vol. 8 (1898)

949   Jacobs, Henry Eyster. THE GERMAN EMIGRATION TO AMERICA, 1709-1740. (See 303).

950 CHURCH REGISTER OF THE UNITED REFORMED AND LUTHERAN CHURCH, CALLED BLIMYERS, IN HOPEWELL TOWNSHIP, YORK COUNTY, PENN-SYLVANIA. Commenced March 19, 1767 by Rev. George Bager (Lutheran), and William Otterbein (Reformed).

951 THE RECORDS OF ST. MICHAELIS AND ZION CONGREGATION OF PHILADELPHIA. (Continued from vol. 7).

952 Richards, Henry Melchior Muhlenberg. AN ARGUMENT DEMONSTRATING THAT THE FIRST DISCOVERERS WERE GERMAN, NOT LATIN.

Vol. 9 (1899)

953 Pennypacker, Samuel Whitaker. THE SETTLEMENT OF GERMANTOWN, PENNSYLVANIA, AND THE BEGINNING OF GERMAN IMMIGRATION TO NORTH AMERICA. (See 343).

954 Richards, Matthias Henry. THE GERMAN EMIGRATION FROM NEW YORK PROVINCE INTO PENNSYLVANIA. (See 304).

955 THE RECORDS OF ST. MICHAELIS AND ZION CONGREGATION OF PHILADELPHIA. (Continued from vol. 8).

Vol. 10 (1900)

956 Sachse, Julius Friedrich. THE FIRST GERMAN NEWSPAPER PUBLISHED IN AMERICA.

957 Schantz, F.J.F. THE DOMESTIC LIFE AND CHARACTERISTICS OF THE PENNSYLVANIA GERMAN PIONEER. (See 669).

958 Diffenderffer, Frank Ried. THE GERMAN BAPTIST BRETHREN OR DUNKERS.

959 Hark, J. Max. PENNSYLVANIA GERMAN LITERATURE. AN HOND-FULL FARSH: EXPERIMENTS IN PENNSYLVANIA GERMAN VERSE, WITH AN INTRODUCTION ON THE CAPABILITY OF THE PENNSYLVANIA GERMAN FOR POETIC EXPRESSION.

960 Richards, Henry Melchior Muhlenberg. PENNSYLVANIA GERMAN GENEALOGIES: DESCENDANTS OF HENRY MELCHIOR MUHLENBERG.

Vol. 11 (1902)

961 Schmauk, Theodore Emanuel. THE LUTHERAN CHURCH IN PENNSYLVANIA (1638-1800). Vol. 1.

962 Dubbs, Joseph Henry. THE REFORMED CHURCH IN PENNSYLVANIA.

Vol. 12 (1903)

963 Sachse, Julius Friedrich. MUSIC OF THE EPHRATA CLOISTER. (See 614).

964 Schmauk, Theodore Emanuel. A HISTORY OF THE LUTHERAN CHURCH IN PENNSYLVANIA (1638-1820). (Continued from vol. 11).

965 Grumbine, Dee L. THE PENNSYLVANIA GERMAN DIALECT: A STUDY OF ITS STATUS AS A SPOKEN DIALECT AND FORM OF LITERARY EXPRESSION, WITH REFERENCE TO ITS CAPABILITIES AND LIMITATIONS, AND LINES ILLUSTRATING SAME.

966 Zimmerman, Thomas C. METRICAL TRANSLATIONS FROM THE GERMAN AND ENGLISH CLASSICS AND FROM THE IRISH AND SCOTCH DIALECTS INTO THE PENNSYLVANIA GERMAN.

Vol. 13 (1904)

967 Kriebel, Howard Wiegner. THE SCHWENKFELDERS IN PENNSYLVANIA, A HISTORICAL SKETCH. (See 483).

968 Rosengarten, J.G. AMERICAN HISTORY FROM GERMAN ARCHIVES WITH REFERENCE TO THE GERMAN SOLDIERS IN THE REVOLUTION AND FRANKLIN'S VISIT TO GERMANY.

969 Richardson, William H. THE PICTURESQUE QUALITY OF THE PENNSYLVANIA GERMAN.

Vol. 14 (1905)

970 Sachse, Julius Friedrich, translator and annotator. DANIEL FALCKNER'S CURIEUSE NACHRICHT FROM PENNSYLVANIA. THE BOOK THAT STIMULATED THE GREAT GERMAN IMMIGRATION TO PENNSYLVANIA IN THE EARLY YEARS OF THE XVIII CENTURY. RECORD OF THE MARRIAGES IN THE EVANGELICAL LUTHERAN CONGREGATION IN PHILADELPHIA: COMMENCED ANNO. 1745. (Continued from vol. 9).

Vol. 15 (1906)

971 Richards, Henry Melchior Muhlenberg. THE PENNSYLVANIA-GERMAN IN THE FRENCH AND INDIAN WAR. (See 329).

972 Rosengarten, J.G. FREDERICK THE GREAT AND THE UNITED STATES.

973 Keyser, Naaman Henry. OLD HISTORIC GERMANTOWN.

Vol. 16 (1907)

974 Sachse, Julius Friedrich. THE WRECK OF THE SHIP NEW ERA UPON THE NEW JERSEY COAST, NOVEMBER 13, 1854.

975 Richards, Henry Melchior Muhlenberg. GOVERNOR JOSEPH HIESTER: A HISTORICAL SKETCH.

976 _____. PENNSYLVANIA GERMAN GENEALOGIES: THE HIESTER FAMILY.

977 RECORD OF INDENTURES OF INDIVIDUALS BOUND OUT AS APPRENTICES, SERVANTS, ETC., AND OF GERMAN AND OTHER REDEMPTIONERS IN THE OFFICE OF THE MAYOR OF THE CITY OF PHILADELPHIA, OCTOBER 3, 1771 TO OCTOBER 5, 1773. (See 176).

Vol. 17 (1908)

978 Richards, Henry Melchior Muhlenberg. THE PENNSYLVANIA GERMAN IN THE REVOLUTIONARY WAR, 1775-1783.

979 Heller, William Jacob. THE GUN MAKERS OF OLD NORTHAMPTON.

Vol. 18 (1909)

980 Sachse, Julius Friedrich. DIARY OF A VOYAGE FROM ROTTERDAM TO PHILADELPHIA IN 1728.

981 Arfwedson, Carolus David. A BRIEF HISTORY OF THE COLONY OF NEW SWEDEN, 1825.

982 Sachse, Julius Friedrich. A CONTRIBUTION TO PENNSYLVANIA HISTORY: MISSIVES TO REV. AUGUST HERMAN FRANKE FROM DANIEL FALCKNER, GERMANTOWN, APRIL 16, 1702, AND JUSTUS FALCKNER, NEW YORK, 1704. SUPPLEMENTED WITH A GENEALOGICAL CHART OF DANIEL FALCKNER.

983 Koons, Ulysses Sidney. PENNSYLVANIA GERMAN LITERATURE, HAR-BAUGH'S HARFE (HARBAUGH'S HARP).

984 CHURCH RECORDS OF THE WILLIAMS TOWNSHIP CONGREGATION.

Vol. 19 (1910)

985 Rush, Benjamin. AN ACCOUNT OF THE MANNERS OF THE GERMAN INHABITANTS OF PENNSYLVANIA. Introduction and annotations by Theodore E. Schmauk. Notes by I. Daniel Rupp, revised. (See 664).

986 Miller, Daniel. EARLY GERMAN AMERICAN NEWSPAPERS. (See 142).

Vol. 20 (1911)

987 THE LUTHERAN CHURCH IN NEW HANOVER (FALCKNER SWAMP), MONTGOMERY COUNTY, PENNA.

Vol. 21 (1912)

988 Sachse, Julius Friedrich. A UNIQUE MANUSCRIPT BY REV. PETER MILLER (BROTHER JABEZ), PRIOR OF THE EPHRATA COMMUNITY, IN LANCASTER COUNTY, PENNSYLVANIA, WRITTEN FOR BENJAMIN FRANKLIN TOGETHER WITH A FACSIMILE AND TRANSLATION OF BEISSEL'S 99 MYSTICAL PROVERBS ORIGINALLY PRINTED BY BENJA-MIN FRANKLIN IN 1730.

989 Sachse, Julius Friedrich. THE WAYSIDE INNS ON THE LANCASTER ROADSIDE BETWEEN PHILADELPHIA AND LANCASTER.

990 Schutz, Augustus. GUIDE TO THE OLD MORAVIAN CEMETERY OF BETHLEHEM, PA. 1742-1910.

Vol. 22 (1913)

991 Sachse, Julius Friedrich. THE WAYSIDE INNS ON THE LANCASTER ROADSIDE BETWEEN PHILADELPHIA AND LANCASTER. (Continued from vol. 21).

992 Nead, Daniel Wunderlich. THE PENNSYLVANIA-GERMAN IN THE SETTLEMENT OF MARYLAND. (See 372).

Vol. 23 (1915)

993 Sachse, Julius Friedrich. QUAINT OLD GERMANTOWN IN PENNSYL-VANIA. (See 345).

994 Supplement: Stoudt, John Baer. THE FOLKLORE OF THE PENNSYL-VANIA-GERMAN. (See 666).

Vol. 24 (1916)

995 Wentz, Abdel Ross. THE BEGINNINGS OF THE GERMAN ELEMENT IN YORK COUNTY, PENNSYLVANIA.

Vol. 25 (1917)

996 Sachse, Julius Friedrich. THE BRADDOCK EXPEDITION: CONDITIONS OF PENNSYLVANIA DURING THE YEAR 1755. (Translation of a French pamphlet found in the Ducal Library at Gotha, Germany.)

997 THE PENNSYLVANIA GERMAN SOCIETY: CONSTITUTION AND BY-LAWS, FOUNDERS, ANNUAL MEETINGS, OFFICERS AND MEMBERS DURING THE FIRST TWENTY-FIVE YEARS OF ITS EXISTENCE, HISTORY AND CHURCH RECORDS PUBLISHED IN THE FIRST TWENTY-FIVE VOL-UMES OF ITS PROCEEDINGS.

Vol. 26 (1918)

998 Nead, Benjamin Matthias. THE PENNSYLVANIA GERMAN IN CIVIL LIFE.

999 Richards, Henry Melchior Muhlenberg. VALLEY FORGE AND THE PENNSYLVANIA GERMANS.

1000 Reichard, Harry Hess. PENNSYLVANIA-GERMAN DIALECT WRITINGS AND THEIR WRITERS. (See 603).

Vol. 27 (1920)

1001 Hinke, William John. A HISTORY OF THE GOSHENHOPPEN REFORMED CHARGE.

1002 Knipe, Irvin P. THE PENNSYLVANIA GERMAN IN THE CIVIL WAR.

1003 THE PENNSYLVANIA GERMAN SOCIETY: CONSTITUTION AND BY-LAWS, FOUNDERS, ANNUAL MEETINGS, OFFICERS AND MEMBERS

SINCE ITS ORGANIZATION, HISTORY AND CHURCH RECORDS PUB-
LISHED IN THE FIRST TWENTY-SEVEN VOLUMES OF ITS PROCEEDINGS.

Vol. 28 (1922)

1004 Hinke, William John. CHURCH RECORDS OF THE GOSHENHOPPEN RE-
FORMED CHARGE, 1731-1833.

Vol. 29 (1923)

1005 Knauss, James Owen, Jr. SOCIAL CONDITIONS AMONG THE PENN-
SYLVANIA GERMANS IN THE EIGHTEENTH CENTURY. (See 532).

Vol. 30 (1924)

1006 Lambert, Marcus Bachman. A DICTIONARY OF THE NON-ENGLISH
WORDS OF THE PENNSYLVANIA-GERMAN DIALECT, WITH AN APPEN-
DIX. (See 583).

Vol. 31 (1925)

1007 Hinke, William John. A HISTORY OF THE TOHICKON UNION
CHURCH, BEDMINSTER TOWNSHIP, BUCKS COUNTY, PENNSYLVANIA,
WITH COPY OF THE CHURCH RECORDS, REFORMED CONGREGATION,
1745-1869; LUTHERAN CONGREGATION, 1749-1840.

Vol. 32 (1924)

1008 Richards, Henry Melchior Muhlenberg. THE PENNSYLVANIA GERMANS
IN THE BRITISH MILITARY PRISONS OF THE REVOLUTIONARY WAR.

1009 Dapp, Charles Frederick. THE EVOLUTION OF AN AMERICAN PATRI-
OT, AN INTIMATE STUDY OF THE PATRIOTIC ACTIVITIES OF JOHN
HENRY MILLER.

1010 Richards, Henry Melchior Muhlenberg. THE WEISER FAMILY.

Vol. 33 (1923)

1011 Illick, Joseph S. REBUILDING OUR FOREST HERITAGE.

1012 Schmucker, Samuel C. THE RACIAL COMPOSITION OF THE PENNSYL-
VANIA GERMANS.

1013 Zundel, William A. FORT ALLEN, IN WESTMORELAND COUNTY, PA.

1014 Lick, David E., and Brendle, Thomas R. PLANT NAMES AND PLANT
LORE AMONG THE PENNSYLVANIA GERMANS.

Vol. 34 (1929)

1015 Smith, Edgar Fahs. EMINENT PENNSYLVANIA GERMANS.

1016 Meyers, Elizabeth Lehman. THE MORAVIAN REVOLUTIONARY CHURCH
AT BETHLEHEM.

1017 Hinke, William John. DIARIES OF MISSIONARY TRAVELS AMONG THE GERMAN SETTLERS IN THE AMERICAN COLONIES, 1743-1748.

1018 Illick, Joseph S. JOSEPH TRIMBLE ROTHROCK.

1019 Fackenthal, B.F., Jr. JOHN FRITZ.

Vol. 35 (1929)

1020 Smith, C. Henry. THE MENNONITE IMMIGRATION TO PENNSYLVANIA IN THE EIGHTEENTH CENTURY. (See 466).

Vol. 36 (1929)

1021 Landis, Charles I. CHARLES DANIEL EBELING.

1022 Cavell, Jean Moore. RELIGIOUS EDUCATION AMONG THE PEOPLE OF GERMANIC ORIGIN IN COLONIAL PENNSYLVANIA.

1023 Fogel, Edwin Miller. PROVERBS OF THE PENNSYLVANIA GERMANS.

Vol. 37 (1936)

1024 Stoudt, John Baer. THE LIBERTY BELLS OF PENNSYLVANIA.

Vol. 38 (1930)

1025 Johnson, Elmer E.S. THE TEST ACT OF JUNE 13, 1777.

1026 Livingood, Frederick George. EIGHTEENTH CENTURY REFORMED CHURCH SCHOOLS.

Vol. 39 (1931)

1027 Brumbaugh, Martin G. AN OUTLINE FOR HISTORICAL ROMANCE.

1028 Steele, Henry J. LIFE AND PUBLIC SERVICES OF GOV. GEORGE WOLF.

1029 Miller, Benjamin L. THE CONTRIBUTION OF DAVID O. SAYLOR TO EARLY HISTORY OF THE PORTLAND CEMENT INDUSTRY IN AMERICA.

1030 Kotz, A.L. SAMUEL DAVID GROSS, M.D., D.C.L., LLD.

1031 Roberts, Charles R. GERMANIC IMMIGRANTS NAMED IN EARLY PENNSYLVANIA SHIP LISTS.

1032 Gegley, H. Winslow. AMONG SOME OF THE OLDER MILLS OF EASTERN PENNSYLVANIA.

Vol. 40 (1932)

1033 Hinke, William John. THE LISTS OF IMMIGRANTS ENTERING PENNSYLVANIA FROM 1727 TO 1808.

1034 Maurer, Charles L. EARLY LUTHERAN EDUCATION IN PENNSYLVANIA.

Vol. 41 (1933)

1035 CHARTER AND BY-LAWS OF THE SOCIETY

1036 Rosenberry, M. Claude. THE PENNSYLVANIA GERMAN IN MUSIC.

1037 Brumbaugh, G. Edwin. COLONIAL ARCHITECTURE OF THE PENNSYL-
VANIA GERMANS. (See 654).

Vol. 42, 43, 44 (1934)

1038 Strassburger, Ralph Beaver, and Hinke, William John, eds. PENNSYL-
VANIA GERMAN PIONEERS. (See 174).

Vol. 45 (1935)

1039 Brendle, Thomas R., and Unger, Claude W. FOLK MEDICINE OF THE
PENNSYLVANIA GERMANS.

Vol. 46 (1937)

1040 Borneman, Henry S. PENNSYLVANIA GERMAN ILLUMINATED MANU-
SCRIPTS. (See 643).

Vol. 47 (1939)

1041 Landis, Henry Kinzer. EARLY KITCHENS OF THE PENNSYLVANIA
GERMANS.

1042 Graeff, Arthur D. THE RELATIONS BETWEEN THE PENNSYLVANIA
GERMANS AND THE BRITISH AUTHORITIES.

Vol. 48 (1940)

1043 Reichard, Harry Hess. PENNSYLVANIA GERMAN VERSE: AN
ANTHOLOGY. (See 604).

Vol. 49 (1941)

1044 Bachman, Calvin George. THE OLD ORDER AMISH OF LANCASTER
COUNTY. (See 424).

Vol. 50 (1944)

1045 Brendle, Thomas R., and Troxell, William S., eds. PENNSYLVANIA
GERMAN FOLK TALES, LEGENDS, ONCE-UPON-A-TIME STORIES,
MAXIMS, AND SAYINGS. Also includes fiftieth anniversary address
by Henry S. Borneman, president. (See 673).

Vol. 51 (1945)

1046 Kieffer, Elizabeth Clarke. HENRY HARBAUGH: PENNSYLVANIA
DUTCHMAN: 1817-1867.

Scholarly Series

Vol. 52 (1946)

1047 Rupp, William J. BIRD NAMES AND BIRD LORE AMONG THE PENN-
SYLVANIA GERMANS, CONTAINING A CHAPTER ON BELIEFS, SUPER-
STITIONS, AND SAYINGS.

Vol. 53 (1948)

1048 Hocker, Edward W. THE SOWER PRINTING HOUSE OF COLONIAL
TIMES. (See 130).

1049 Winters, R.L. JOHN CASPAR STOEVER, COLONIAL PASTOR AND
FOUNDER OF CHURCHES.

Vol. 54 (1953)

1050 Borneman, Henry S. PENNSYLVANIA GERMAN BOOKPLATES. (See
645).

Vol. 55 (1954)

1051 Berky, Andrew S. PRACTITIONER IN PHYSICK: A BIOGRAPHY OF
ABRAHAM WAGNER, 1717-1763.

Vol. 56 (1955)

1052 _____. THE SCHOOLHOUSE NEAR THE OLD SPRING: A HISTORY
OF THE UNION SCHOOL AND CHURCH ASSOCIATION. DILLINGERS-
VILLE, PA., 1735-1955.

Vol. 57 (1957)

1053 Reaman, G. Elmore. THE TRAIL OF THE BLACK WALNUT: PENNSYL-
VANIA GERMAN MIGRANTS TO PROVINCE OF ONTARIO, CANADA.

Vol. 58 (1959)

1054 Rubincam, Milton. WILLIAM RITTENHOUSE, AMERICA'S PIONEER
PAPER MANUFACTURER AND MENNONITE MINISTER.

1055 Brendle, Thomas R. MOSES DISSINGER, EVANGELIST AND PATRIOT.

Vol. 59 (1960)

1056 Korson, George. BLACK ROCK: MINING FOLKLORE OF THE PENN-
SYLVANIA DUTCH. (See 668).

Vol. 60 (1961)

1057 Bachman, Calvin George. THE OLD ORDER AMISH OF LANCASTER
COUNTY. (Reprint with new illustrations of vol. 49, 1941). (See 424).

Vol. 61 (1962)

1058 THE REICHARD COLLECTION OF EARLY PENNSYLVANIA GERMAN DIALOGUES AND PLAYS. Edited and retranscribed by Albert F. Buffington. (See 605).

Vol. 62 (1963)

1059 Buffington, Albert F. DUTCHIFIED GERMAN SPIRITUALS. (See 624).

Vol. 63 (1966)

1060 Rosenberger, Homer T. THE PENNSYLVANIA GERMANS, 1891-1965. (See 320).

1061 _____, ed. Special Publications: INTIMATE GLIMPSES OF THE PENN-SYLVANIA GERMANS. 1966. (See 332).

Series continued as PUBLICATIONS OF THE PENNSYLVANIA GERMAN SOCIETY, new series.

YEARBOOKS OF THE PENNSYLVANIA GERMAN FOLKLORE SOCIETY, 1936-1966.

Vol. 1 (1936)

1062 Ziegler, C.C. DRAUSS UN DEHEEM (dialect poems).

1063 Downs, Joseph. HOUSE OF THE MILLER, THE ARCHITECTURE, ARTS AND CRAFTS OF THE PENNSYLVANIA GERMANS.

1064 _____. THE PENNSYLVANIA GERMAN GALLERIES (IN THE METROPOLITAN MUSEUM OF ART).

1065 Hinke, William John, and Stoudt, John Baer. A LIST OF GERMAN IMMIGRANTS TO THE AMERICAN COLONIES FROM ZWEIBRUECKEN IN THE PALATINATE, 1728--49. (See 170).

1066 CATALOGUE OF THE PENNSYLVANIA FOLK ART EXHIBITION.

Vol. 2 (1937)

1067 Stoudt, John Joseph. CONSIDER THE LILIES, HOW THEY GROW. AN INTERPRETATION OF THE SYMBOLISM OF PENNSYLVANIA GERMAN ART. (See 626, 627).

Vol. 3 (1938)

1068 Birmelin, John. GEZWITSCHER (dialect verse).

1069 Beckel, C.E. EARLY MORAVIAN MARRIAGE CUSTOMS IN BETHLEHEM, PENNSYLVANIA.

1070 Landis, H.K. CONESTOGA WAGONS AND THEIR ORNAMENTAL IRONING.

1071 Eyster, Anita L. NOTICES BY GERMAN SETTLERS IN GERMAN NEWS-PAPERS.

Vol. 4 (1939)

1072 Iobst, C.F. EN QUART MILLICH UN EN HALB BEINT RAAHMN (a dialect comedy).

1073 LETTERS TO GOVERNOR MORRIS IN 1754 BY GERMAN PROTESTANT FREEHOLDERS, AND AN ANTI-FRANKLIN BROADSIDE.

1074 Barba, Preston, and Barba, Eleanor. LEWIS MILLER, PENNSYLVANIA GERMAN FOLK ARTIST.

Vol. 5 (1940)

1075 HECKWELDER'S INDIAN NAMES OF STREAMS, RIVERS, PLACES, ETC.

1076 Ziegler, S.H. THE EPHRATA PRINTING PRESS.

1077 Fogel, E.M. OF MONTHS AND DAYS.

1078 Connor, W.L. FOLK CULTURE OF THE PENNSYLVANIA GERMANS: ITS VALUE IN MODERN EDUCATION.

Vol. 6 (1941) (See 676)

1079 Nitzsche, G.E. CHRISTMAS PUTZ OF THE PENNSYLVANIA GERMANS.

1080 Rominger, C.H. EARLY CHRISTMASES IN BETHLEHEM, PENNSYLVANIA.

1081 Myers, R.E. THE MORAVIAN CHRISTMAS PUTZ.

1082 Reichard, Harry Hess. CHRISTMAS POETRY OF THE PENNSYLVANIA DUTCH.

1083 Fogel, E.M. TWELVE-TIDE.

Vol. 7 (1942)

1084 THE BUCKS COUNTY HISTORICAL SOCIETY, THE SCHWENKFELDER HISTORICAL LIBRARY, THE PENNSYLVANIA STATE MUSEUM, THE BERKS COUNTY HISTORICAL SOCIETY, THE HERSHEY MUSEUM, THE LANDIS VALLEY MUSEUM. (See 156).

1085 Landis, H.K., and Landis, G.D. LANCASTER RIFLES.

Vol. 8 (1943)

1086 Graeff, Arthur D. CONRAD WEISER, PENNSYLVANIA PEACEMAKER--A BIOGRAPHY. (See 910).

Vol. 9 (1944)

1087 Lichtenthaeler, F.E. STORM BLOWN SEED OF SCHOHARIE.

1088 Landis, H.K., and Landis, G.D. LANCASTER RIFLES ACCESSORIES.

1089 Kemp, A.F. PENNSYLVANIA GERMAN VERSAMMLINGE.

Vol. 10 (1945)

1090 Ludwig, G.M. INFLUENCE OF THE PENNSYLVANIA DUTCH IN THE MIDDLE WEST. (See 352).

1091 Yoder, Don H. EMIGRANTS FROM WUERTTEMBERG: THE ADOLF GERBER LISTS. (See 178).

Vol. 11 (1946)

1092 Graeff, Arthur D. THE PENNSYLVANIA GERMANS IN ONTARIO, CANADA.

1093 Kauffman, H.J. COPPERSMITHING IN PENNSYLVANIA. (See 641).

1094 Seifer, L.S.J. LEXICAL DIFFERENCES BETWEEN FOUR PENNSYLVANIA GERMAN REGIONS.

Vol. 12 (1947)

1095 Moll, L.A. AM SCHWARZE BAER (dialect).

1096 Yoder, Don H. LANGGUTH'S PENNSYLVANIA GERMAN PIONEERS FROM THE COUNTY OF WERTHEIM. (See 177).

Vol. 13 (1948)

1097 Reinert, Guy F. COVERLETS OF THE PENNSYLVANIA GERMANS.

1098 Kuder, Solomon. THE PRACTICAL FAMILY DYER (1858). Translated by Edwin M. Fogel.

1099 Buffington, Albert F. LINGUISTIC VARIANTS IN THE PENNSYLVANIA GERMAN DIALECT. (See 592).

Vol. 14 (1949)

1100 Stoeffler, E. Ernest. MYSTICISM IN THE GERMAN DEVOTIONAL LITERATURE OF COLONIAL PENNSYLVANIA. (See 412).

Vol. 15 (1950)

1101 Gilbert, Russell Weider. PENNSYLVANIA GERMAN WILLS: HUMOROUS PENNSYLVANIA GERMAN TALES. (See 682).

Vol. 16 (1951)

1102 THE LATER POEMS OF JOHN BIRMELIN (in dialect).

1103 Stoudt, John Joseph. PENNSYLVANIA GERMAN FOLKLORE--AN INTERPRETATION.

1104 Krebs, Friedrich. LIST OF GERMAN IMMIGRANTS TO THE AMERICAN COLONIES FROM ZWEIBRUECKEN (1750-1771).

1105 Steinemann, Ernest. LIST OF EIGHTEENTH CENTURY EMIGRANTS FROM THE CANTON OF SCHAFFHAUSEN.

Vol. 17 (1952)

1106 Reichmann, Felix, and Doll, Eugene E., eds. EPHRATA AS SEEN BY CONTEMPORARIES, (1734-1752). (See 501).

Vol. 18 (1953)

1107 Barba, Preston A. PENNSYLVANIA GERMAN TOMBSTONES--A STUDY IN FOLK ART. Drawings by Eleanor Barba. (See 651).

Vol. 19 (1954)

1108 Dundore, M. Walter. THE SAGA OF THE PENNSYLVANIA GERMANS IN WISCONSIN. (See 359).

1109 Buffington, Albert F. HENRY MEYER--AN EARLY PENNSYLVANIA GERMAN POET.

Vol. 20 (1955)

1110 Stoudt, John Joseph. PENNSYLVANIA HIGH GERMAN POETRY--1685-1830, AN ANTHOLOGY.

Vol. 21 (1956)

1111 Dornbusch, Charles H., and Heyl, John K. PENNSYLVANIA GERMAN BARNS--THEIR TYPES AND ARCHITECTURE. (See 659).

Vol. 22 (1957)

1112 Nitzsche, Elsa Koenig. MARRIAGE BY LOT--A NOVEL BASED ON MORAVIAN HISTORY.

Vol. 23 (1958 and 1959)

1113 Shelley, Donald A. THE FRAKTUR-WRITINGS OR ILLUMINATED MANU-SCRIPTS OF THE PENNSYLVANIA GERMANS. (See 642).

Vol. 24 (1960)

1114 Smith, Elmer Lewis. THE AMISH TODAY: SOCIOLOGICAL STUDIES OF THEIR PRESENT BELIEFS AND WAYS OF LIFE.

Vol. 25 (1961)

1115 Ernst, James E. EPHRATA, A HISTORY. (See 497).

Vol. 26 (1962)

1116 Smith, Elmer Lewis; Stewart, John; and Kyger, M. Ellsworth. THE PENNSYLVANIA GERMANS OF THE SHENANDOAH VALLEY. (See 374).

Vol. 27 (1964)

1117 Buffington, Albert F., and Barba, Preston A. A PENNSYLVANIA GER-MAN GRAMMAR. Rev. ed. (See 588).

Vol. 28 (1966)

1118 Stoudt, John Joseph. PENNSYLVANIA GERMAN FOLK ART. 1966. (See 627).

Series continued as the PUBLICATIONS OF THE PENNSYLVANIA GERMAN SOCIETY beginning in 1968.

PUBLICATIONS OF THE PENNSYLVANIA GERMAN SOCIETY; or PENNSYL-VANIA GERMAN SOCIETY PUBLICATIONS; or SERIES OF THE PENNSYLVANIA GERMAN SOCIETY. This new series of publications began in 1968 with the merger of the Pennsylvania German Society and the Pennsylvania German Folklore Society.

Vol. 1 (1968)

1119 Wood, Ralph Charles. THE FOUR GOSPELS TRANSLATED INTO THE PENNSYLVANIA GERMAN DIALECT.

1120 Weiser, Frederick S. DANIEL SCHUMACHER'S BAPTISMAL REGISTER.

Vol. 2 (1969)

1121 Treher, Charles M. SNOW HILL CLOISTER.

1122 Barba, Preston A. DIALECT POEMS OF RALPH FUNK.

Vol. 3 (1970)

FOUR PENNSYLVANIA GERMAN STUDIES:

1123 Biever, Dale E. ARCHAEOLOGICAL INVESTIGATIONS AT THE EPHRA-TA CLOISTER. (See 509).

1124 Barba, Preston A. RACHEL BAHN, PENNSYLVANIA GERMAN POETESS.

1125 Buffington, Albert F. SIMILARITIES AND DISSIMILARITIES BETWEEN PENNSYLVANIA GERMAN AND THE RHENISH PALATINATE DIALECTS.

1126 PAROCHIAL REGISTERS OF THE INDIAN CREEK REFORMED CHURCH 1753-1851.

Vol. 4 (1970)

1127 Gingerich, Melvin. MENNONITE ATTIRE THROUGH FOUR CENTURIES. (See 468).

Vol. 5 (1971)

1128 SELECTIONS FROM ARTHUR D. GRAEFF'S "SCHOLLA."

Vol. 6 (1972)

1129 Long, Amos. PENNSYLVANIA GERMAN FAMILY FARM. (See 534).

Vol. 7 (1973)

1130 Klinefelter, Walter. THE ABC BOOKS OF THE PENNSYLVANIA GER-MANS. (See 570).

1131 Heckman, Marlin L. ABRAHAM HARLEY CASSEL, NINETEENTH CEN-TURY PENNSYLVANIA GERMAN AMERICAN BOOK COLLECTOR. (See 133).

1132 Braun, Fritz, and Weiser, Frederick S., eds. MARRIAGES PERFORMED AT THE EVANGELICAL LUTHERAN CHURCH OF THE HOLY TRINITY IN LANCASTER, PENNSYLVANIA, 1748-1767. (See 179).

Vol. 8 (1974)

1133 Buffington, Albert F. PENNSYLVANIA GERMAN SECULAR FOLK-SONGS. (See 622).

Vol. 9 (1975)

1134 BILDER UN GEDANKE, THE POEMS OF RUSSELL W. GILBERT.

Vol. 10 and 11 (1976 and 1977)

1135 Weiser, Frederick S., and Heaney, Howell J. THE PENNSYLVANIA GERMAN FRAKTUR OF THE FREE LIBRARY OF PHILADELPHIA. (See 644).

Vol. 12 (1978)

1136 Fabian, Monroe. PENNSYLVANIA-GERMAN DECORATED CHESTS. (See 647).

AMERICANA GERMANICA

New series. Monographs devoted to the comparative study of the literary, lin-guistic, and other cultured relations of Germany and America.

This series was initiated in 1901 by the German-American Histori-cal Society affiliated with the University of Pennsylvania. It was intended to provide a systematic publishing outlet for doctoral dissertations and other scholarly works separate from the journal, GERMAN AMERICAN ANNALS, of the same provenance. The series ceased publication in 1919 with number 35.

1137 Davis, Edward Ziegler. TRANSLATIONS OF GERMAN POETRY IN AMERICAN MAGAZINES, 1741-1810. (No. 1).

1138 Bole, John Archibald. THE HARMONY SOCIETY: A CHAPTER IN GERMAN AMERICAN CULTURE HISTORY. (No. 2). (See 513).

1139 Parry, Ellwood Comly. FRIEDRICH SCHILLER IN AMERICA, A CONTRIBUTION TO THE LITERATURE OF THE POET'S CENTENARY, 1905. (No. 3).

1140 Reed, Bertha. THE INFLUENCE OF SALOMON GESSNER UPON ENGLISH LITERATURE. (No. 4).

1141 Bek, William G. THE GERMAN SETTLEMENT SOCIETY OF PHILADELPHIA AND ITS COLONY, HERMANN, MISSOURI. (No. 5). (See 355).

1142 Learned, Marion Dexter. PHILIPP WALDECK'S DIARY OF THE AMERICAN REVOLUTION. With introduction and photographic reproductions. (No. 6).

1143 Seipt, Allen Anders. SCHWENKFELDER HYMNOLOGY AND THE SOURCES OF THE FIRST SCHWENKFELDER HYMNBOOK PRINTED IN AMERICA. With photographic reproductions. (No. 7). (See 615).

1144 Deiler, J. Hanno. THE SETTLEMENT OF THE GERMAN COAST OF LOUISIANA AND THE CREOLES OF GERMAN DESCENT. With illustrations. (No. 8). (See 369).

1145 Drummond, R.R. EARLY GERMAN MUSIC IN PHILADELPHIA. (No. 9). (See 613).

1146 MacLean, Grace Edith. "UNCLE TOM'S CABIN" IN GERMANY. (No. 10).

1147 Benjamin, Gilbert Giddings. THE GERMANS IN TEXAS; A STUDY IN IMMIGRATION. (No. 11). (See 383).

1148 Learned, Marion Dexter. THE AMERICAN ETHNOGRAPHIC SURVEY: CONESTOGA EXPEDITION. (No. 12).

1149 Johnson, Amandus. SWEDISH SETTLEMENTS ON THE DELAWARE, 1638-1664. 6 maps and 150 illustrations and photographic reproductions. (No. 13).

1150 Perring, Roy H. NATIONAL UNITY IN THE GERMAN NOVEL BEFORE 1870. (No. 14).

1151 Epping, Charlotte S.J., translator. JOURNAL OF DU ROI THE ELDER, LIEUTENANT AND ADJUTANT IN THE SERVICE OF THE DUKE OF BRUNSWICK, 1776-1778. (No. 15).

1152 Barba, Preston A. THE LIFE AND WORKS OF FRIEDRICH ARMAND STRUBBERG. (No. 16).

1153 _____. BALDWIN MOELLHAUSEN, THE GERMAN COOPER. (No. 17).

1154 Fogel, Edwin M. BELIEFS AND SUPERSTITIONS OF THE PENNSYLVANIA GERMANS. (No. 18). (See 672).

1155 Geissendoerfer, J. Theodore. DICKENS' EINFLUSS AUF UNGERN-STERNBERG, HESSLEIN, STOLLE, RAABE UND EBNER-ESCHENBACH. (No. 19).

1156 Eastburn, Iola Kay. WHITTIER'S RELATION TO GERMAN LIFE AND THOUGHT. (No. 20).

1157 Victory, Beatrice Marguerite. BENJAMIN FRANKLIN AND GERMANY. (No. 21).

1158 Betz, Gottlieb. DIE DEUTSCHAMERKANISCHE PATRIOTISCHE LYRIK DER ACHTUNDVIERZIGER UND IHRE HISTORISCHE GRUNDLAGE. (No. 22).

1159 Sachs, H.B. HEINE IN AMERICA. (No. 23).

1160 Kamman, William Frederic. SOCIALISM IN GERMAN AMERICAN LITERATURE. (No. 24). (See 599).

1161 Zucker, Adolf E. ROBERT REITZEL. (No. 25).

1162 Schappelle, Benjamin Franklin. THE GERMAN ELEMENT IN BRAZIL, COLONIES AND DIALECT. (No. 26).

1163 Haussmann, C.F. KUNZE'S SEMINARIUM AND THE SOCIETY FOR THE

PROPAGATION OF CHRISTIANITY AND USEFUL KNOWLEDGE AMONG THE GERMANS IN AMERICA. (No. 27).

1164 Steinke, Max. YOUNG'S CONJECTURES ON ORIGINAL COMPOSITION IN ENGLAND AND AMERICA. (No. 28).

1165 Learned, Henry Dexter. THE SYNTAX OF BRANT'S NARRENSCHIFF. (No. 29).

1166 Sladen, Charles Fischer. THE APPROACH OF ACADEMIC SPOKEN STYLE IN GERMAN: A STUDY IN POPULAR SCIENTIFIC PROSE FROM 1850 TO 1914. (No. 30).

1167 Baker, Louis Charles. THE GERMAN DRAMA IN ENGLISH ON THE NEW YORK STAGE TO 1830. (No. 31). (See 608).

1168 Nolle, Alfred Henry. THE GERMAN DRAMA ON THE ST. LOUIS STAGE. (No. 32). (See 610).

1169 Scholz, W.H. THE ART OF TRANSLATION, WITH SPECIAL REFERENCE TO ENGLISH RENDITIONS OF PROSE DRAMAS OF GERHART HAUPT-MANN AND HERMANN SUDERMANN. (No. 33).

1170 Brede, Charles F. THE GERMAN DRAMA IN ENGLISH ON THE PHILA-DELPHIA STAGE. (No. 34). (See 609).

1171 Vollmer, Clement. THE AMERICAN NOVEL IN GERMANY, 1871-1913. (No. 35).

XXI. JOURNALS AND PERIODICALS

1172 AMERICAN-GERMAN REVIEW. Philadelphia: Carl Schurz Memorial
Foundation, vols. 1-36. 1934-70. Monthly.

    Continued as RUNDSCHAU.

1172a AMERIKANISCHE SCHWEIZER ZEITUNG. New York: Swiss Publishing
Co., 1868-- . Weekly.

1173 AMERIKASTUDIEN/AMERICAN STUDIES. Stuttgart: Deutsche Gesellschaft fuer Amerikastudien (German Association for American Studies),
1959-- . Semiannual.

    English, or German with summaries in English.

1174 ANGLO-GERMAN AND AMERICAN-GERMAN CROSS CURRENTS.
Chapel Hill: University of North Carolina Press, 1957-- .

    Subseries of University of North Carolina Studies in Compara-
tive Literature.

1175 BROWN COUNTY'S HERITAGE. New Ulm, Minn.: Brown County Historical Society, 1958-- .

1176 DER DEUTSCH AMERIKANER. Chicago: German-American National
Congress, 1886-91. Monthly.

    English and German language.

1177 DEUTSCH-AMERIKANISCHE GESCHICHTSBLAETTER. Chicago: Deutsche-
amerikanische Historische Gesellschaft von Illinois. (German-American
Historical Society of Illinois), vols. 1-33. 1901-37 (suspended 1933-36).
Annual.

1178 DEUTSCHE PIONIER: ERINNERUNGEN AUS DEM PIONEER-LEBEN DER
DEUTSCHEN IN AMERIKA. Cincinnati: Deutscher Pionierverein von

Cincinnati, vols. 1-18. 1869-87. Monthly. From 1869-76 title read: DER DEUTSCHE PIONIER; EINE MONATSCHRIFT FUER ERINNERUNGEN AUS DEM DEUTSCHEN PIONIER-LEBEN IN DEM VEREINIGTEN STAATEN. Continued as DEUTSCHER PIONIERVEREIN VON CINCINNATI VOR-STANDSBERICHT.

1179 DEUTSCHER PIONIERVEREIN VON CINCINNATI. VORSTANDSBERICHT. Cincinnati: Deutscher Pionierverein von Cincinnati, vol. 20--. 1887/88-1931?.

Formerly DEUTSCHE PIONIER. 1887/88-1888/89 as its JAH-RESBERICHT.

1180 DUTCHMAN. See PENNSYLVANIA FOLKLIFE.

1181 ECK. See 'S PENNSYLFAWNISCH DEITSCH ECK.

1182 THE GERMAN-AMERICAN GENEALOGIST. Cleveland: Institute for German-American Studies, March 1975-- . Quarterly.

"A journal of ancestral research."

1183 GERMAN-AMERICAN STUDIES. Youngstown, Ohio: Society for German-American Studies, 1969-- . Quarterly.

Described as "a journal of history, literature, biography and genealogy," was continued with vol. 11 in Spring 1976 as JOURNAL OF GERMAN-AMERICAN STUDIES.

1184 GERMANIC GENEALOGICAL HELPER. Harbor City, Calif.: Augustan Society, 1975-- . Quarterly.

Continued with vol. 7 in April 1976 as GERMANIC GENEA-LOGIST.

1185 GERMANIC GENEALOGIST. Harbor City, Calif.: Hartwell no. 7-- , April 1976-- . Quarterly.

1186 THE GERMANNA RECORD. Harrisonburg, Va.: Memorial Foundation of the Germanna Colonies. July 1961-- . Irregular.

1187 GERMAN QUARTERLY. Philadelphia: American Association of Teachers of German, 1928-- . Quarterly.

Since 1961, the membership directory of the association is published in September as a special unnumbered issued. A major book reviewing medium.

1188 HARMONIE HERALD. Ambridge: Pennsylvania Historical and Museum Commission, Old Economy Village, 1966-- . Occasional.

1189 HISTORIC SCHAEFFERSTOWN RECORD. Schaefferstown, Pa.: Historic Schaefferstown, 1967-- . Quarterly.

1190 JAHRBUCH DER DEUTSCH-AMERIKANISCHEN HISTORISCHEN GESELLSCHAFT VON ILLINOIS. See DEUTSCH-AMERIKANISCHE GESCHICHTSBLAETTER.

1191 JOURNAL OF GERMAN-AMERICAN STUDIES. Cleveland: Published in collaboration with the Society for German-American Studies. Vol. 11-- , Spring 1976-- . Quarterly.

> Formerly GERMAN-AMERICAN STUDIES.

1192 LEO BAECK INSTITUTE OF JEWS FROM GERMANY. Yearbook. London: East and West Library, 1956-- .

1193 MENNONITE HISTORICAL BULLETIN. Scottdale, Pa.: Historical Committee of the Mennonite Church, April 1940-- . Quarterly. Semiannual 1940-41.

> Published by the Historical and Research Committee [called Historical Committee 1940-59] of the Mennonite General Conference.

1194 MENNONITE LIFE. North Newton, Kans.: Bethel College, 1946-- . Quarterly.

1195 MENNONITE QUARTERLY REVIEW. Goshen, Ind.: Mennonite Historical Society, 1927-- .

1196 MENNONITE RESEARCH JOURNAL. Lancaster, Pa.: Lancaster Mennonite Conference Historical Society, April 1960-- . Quarterly.

1197 MONATSHEFTE: A JOURNAL DEVOTED TO THE STUDY OF GERMAN LANGUAGE AND LITERATURE. Madison: University of Wisconsin Press Press, Dec. 1899-- . Quarterly.

> Organ of Nationaler deutsch-amerikanischer Lehrerbund from 1899-1926. Title varies: PAEDAGOGISCHE MONATSHEFTE 1899-1905; MONATSHEFTE FUER DEUTSCHE SPRACHE UND PAEDAGOGIK 1906-27; MONATSHEFTE FUER DEUTSCHEN UNTERRICHT 1928-45. Suspended 1919-27 when JARHBUCH was issued.

1198 MORAVIAN HISTORICAL SOCIETY. Transactions. Nazareth, Pa.: Moravian Historical Society, 1857-- . Annual.

1199 MORAVIAN MUSIC FOUNDATION. NEWS BULLETIN. Winston-Salem: Moravian Music Foundation, 1957-- . Semiannual.

1200 _____. PUBLICATIONS. Winston-Salem: Moravian Music Foundation, September 1956-- .

1201 PENN GERMANIA . . . A POPULAR JOURNAL OF GERMAN HISTORY AND IDEALS IN THE UNITED STATES. Cleona, Pa.: H.W. Kriebel. Vols. 1-15, no. 3, 1900-November, December 1914. Monthly. Formerly THE PENNSYLVANIA GERMAN. Vols. 1-12, 1900-1911.

1202 PENNSYLVANIA DUTCHMAN. See PENNSYLVANIA FOLKLIFE.

1202a PENNSYLVANIA DUTCH NEWS AND VIEWS. Lenhartsville, Pa.: Pennsylvania Dutch Folk Culture Society. 1965-- . Biennial.

1203 PENNSYLVANIA DUTCH STUDIES. Collegeville: Institute of Pennsylvania Dutch Studies, 1974-- .

1204 PENNSYLVANIA FOLKLIFE. Lancaster: Pennsylvania Folklife Society, May 1949-- . 5 issues per year.

> Title varies: PENNSYLVANIA DUTCHMAN, Vols. 1-5, 8; DUTCHMAN, vols. 6-7.

1205 THE PENNSYLVANIA-GERMAN: A POPULAR MAGAZINE OF BIOGRAPHY. HISTORY, GENEALOGY, FOLKLORE, LITERATURE, ETC. Lebanon, Pa.: P.C. Croll. Vol. 1-12, 1900-11. Quarterly; 1906-14, monthly.

> Continued as PENN GERMANIA. Vols. 13-15, 1913-14.

1206 PENNSYLVANIA GERMAN FOLKLORE SOCIETY. Yearbook. Allentown: Pennsylvania German Folklore Society, vols. 1-28. 1936-66.

> Continued as PENNSYLVANIA GERMAN SOCIETY. PUBLICATIONS.

1207 PENNSYLVANIA GERMAN SOCIETY. PROCEEDINGS AND ADDRESSES. Philadelphia: Pennsylvania German Society, vols. 1-63. 1891-1966. Annual.

> Title varies: PENNSYLVANIA GERMAN SOCIETY. PROCEEDINGS. Continued as PENNSYLVANIA GERMAN SOCIETY. PUBLICATIONS.

1208 _____. PUBLICATIONS. Breinigsville: Pennsylvania German Society, 1968-- . Annual. Formerly PENNSYLVANIA GERMAN SOCIETY.

PROCEEDINGS AND ADDRESSES. Absorbed PENNSYLVANIA GERMAN FOLKLORE SOCIETY. Yearbook.

1209 PENNSYLVANIA MENNONITE HERITAGE. See MENNONITE RESEARCH JOURNAL.

1210 PENNSYLVANIA MAGAZINE OF HISTORY AND BIOGRAPHY. Philadelphia: Historical Society of Pennsylvania, 1877-- . Quarterly.

   Issues for 1877-1935 also designated as nos. 1-233.

1210a THE PENNSYLVANIA TRAVELER-POST; RECORDS, FAMILY HISTORY AND DATA RELATING TO PENNSYLVANIA AND SURROUNDING STATES. Danboro, Pa.: Richard T. and Mildred C. Williams, publishers and owners, P.O. Box 307, 1964-- . Quarterly.

1211 DER REGGEBOGE (The Rainbow). Breinigsville: Pennsylvania German Society, 1966-- . Quarterly.

1212 RUNDSCHAU. Philadelphia: National Carl Schurz Association, April 1971-- . 9 issues per year.

   "An American-German review." At head of title: N.F.S.G. [National Federation of Students of Germany].

1212a DER SCHWEIZER. Cleveland: North American Swiss Alliance, vols. 1-59, 1865-November 1941. Monthly.

   Continued as THE SWISS AMERICAN.

1212b SCHWEIZER JOURNAL. San Francisco: Swiss Journal Co., 1918-- . Weekly.

   Also known as SWISS JOURNAL.

1213 'S PENNSYLFAWNISCH DEITSCH ECK. Weekly Saturday feature of the newspaper. THE MORNING CALL. Allentown, Pa., 1935-- . Weekly.

   Reprints of the column have been gathered in the seven volume set: 'S PENNSYLFAWNISCH DEITSCH ECK: DEVOTED TO THE LITERATURE, LORE, AND HISTORY OF THE PENNSYL-VANIA GERMANS. Edited by Preston A. Barba. Allentown, Pa.: The Morning Call, 1935-69.

1214 SOCIETY FOR THE HISTORY OF THE GERMANS IN MARYLAND. ANNUAL REPORT. Baltimore: Society for the History of the Germans in Maryland, 1887-- . Triennial.

   Suspended 1908-28, 1930-38, except for 150th anniversary report issued 1933.

1215 THE STEUBEN NEWS. New York: The Steuben Society, n.d. Monthly.

1216 STUDIES IN ANABAPTIST AND MENNONITE HISTORY. Scottdale, Pa.: Published in cooperation with the Mennonite Historical Society, Goshen, Ind., 1929-- .

1216a THE SWISS AMERICAN. Cleveland: North American Swiss Alliance, vol. 60-- , December 1941-- . Monthly.

Formerly DER SCHWEIZER.

1216b SWISS-AMERICAN HISTORICAL SOCIETY. NEWSLETTER. Norfolk, Va.: Old Dominion University, 1927-- . 3 times per year.

1216c SWISS-AMERICAN REVIEW. New York: Swiss Publishing Co., 1868-- . Weekly.

1216d SWISS JOURNAL: See SCHWEIZER JOURNAL.

1216e THE SWISS RECORD: YEARBOOK OF THE SWISS AMERICAN HISTORI-CAL SOCIETY. Madison, Wis.: Swiss American Historical Society, 1949-- .

1217 VIRGINIA MAGAZINE OF HISTORY AND BIOGRAPHY. Richmond: Virginia Historical Society, July 1893-- . Quarterly.

XXII. DIRECTORY OF SPECIALIZED GERMAN-AMERICAN ARCHIVAL AND LITERARY RESOURCES

CALIFORNIA

1218 The Huntington Library, 1151 Oxford Road, San Marino, Calif. 91108. Tel. (213) 792-6141, ext. 57.

> Open to serious researchers only; must apply for reading privileges. Mon. - Sat. 8:30 a.m. - 5:00 p.m. Photocopying on demand.

> Subject area: The researcher of German Americana will note that the library has extensive holdings of printed, manuscript and archival materials related to the entire range of American history, literature, and the American West. Materials of German and American interest are not treated as a distinct collection.

1219 Hoover Institution on War, Revolution and Peace--Stanford University (founded 1919), Stanford, Calif. 94305. Tel. (415) 497-2058.

> Open to public, Mon. - Fri. 8:00 a.m. - 5:00 p.m., Sat. 8:30 a.m. - 1:00 p.m. Photocopying facilities available; microfilm and Xerox copies may be ordered through the reference department, photoduplication service. Limited interlibrary loan service. Periodicals and archival materials are not lent but photocopies of selected sections may be ordered.

> Subject area: This is a specialized library dealing with history, politics, and government of the twentieth century throughout the world. Materials dealing with German-American relations form part of the collections and are not specially emphasized.

> Holdings: Among the institution's abundant holdings the following may be of interest to researchers of German Americana: Christopher T. Emmet collection (American Council on Germany 1940-70); George Sylvester Viereck collection (journalist -papers, memoirs, scrapbooks 1903-42); and Franz Schoenberner collection (editor and writer-papers 1899-1970).

> Major periodicals files: AMERIKA'S DEUTSCHE POST, New

York, 1933-34; see also DEUTSCHER BEOBACHTER, 1934-35; NATIONAL AMERICAN, 1935; AUFBAU, New York, 1941-64; CALIFORNIA STAATSZEITUNG, Los Angeles, 1944-48; DEUTSCH-AMERIKA, New York, 1915-27; FREE AMERICAN AND DEUTSCHER WECKRUF UND BEOBACHTER, New York, 1935-41; GERMAN AMERICAN, New York, independent publication, 1943-49; DER HERMANN-SOHN, San Francisco, 1942-48; NATIONAL AMERICAN, New York, 1938-39; NEW YORK STAATS ZEITUNG, New York, 1915-19; NEW YORKER STAATSZEITUNG UND HEROLD, New York, 1940-54; DER RUF, New York, Zeitung der deutschen Kriegsgefangener in USA, 1945-46; SONNTAGSBLATT, STAATSZEITUNG UND HEROLD, New York, 1940-54; STEUBEN NEWS, New York, 1939-48.

COLORADO

1220 American Historical Society of Germans From Russia Archives and Historical Society Library, Greeley Public Library (founded 1968), City Complex Building, Greeley, Colo. 80631. Tel. (303) 353-6123.

Open to public, Mon. - Thurs. 9:00 a.m. - 9:00 p.m. Fri. - Sat. 9:00 a.m. - 6:00 p.m. Interlibrary loan; copying available. Must be society member to check out materials.

Subject area: Emigration; settlements; family histories.

Holdings: 745 books, 4 periodical, and 7 newspaper titles, some archival materials, maps, microfilm, tapes, phonograph records.

Notable items: DAKOTA FREIE PRESS, 1909-16; DAKOTA FREE PRESS, 1903-31; NEUES LEBEN, 1970-73; NORD DAKOTA HERALD, 1907-60; ODDESAIR ZEITUNG, 1890, 1897-1900, 1902-14; VOLKS ZEITUNG, 1912-14; DIE WELT POST, 1916-72. (All dates are approximate.) In addition: MENNONITE LIFE, 1946-date; ZEITSCHRIFT FUER KULTURAUSTAUSCH, 1967-date; DER KIRCHENBOTE, 1954-64; RELIGION IN COMMUNIST LANDS, 1973-date.

Publication: BIBLIOGRAPHY OF THE AHSGR ARCHIVES AND HISTORICAL LIBRARY, available from headquarters: AHSGR, 631 D Street, Lincoln, Nebr. 68502. $2.00 per copy.

CONNECTICUT

1221 Yale University Library, New Haven, Conn. 06520.

The library has most standard printed materials for the study of the history of German communities in America, especially in the West, but has no unusually strong holdings in the more ephemeral primary source material.

ILLINOIS

1222 Archives of Lutheran Church in America (founded 1962 but the origin of the collections dates back to 1870). Lutheran School of Theology at Chicago, 1100 East 55th Street, Chicago, Ill. 60615. Tel. (312) 667-3500.

> Open to serious researchers only, credentials required; Mon. - Fri. 8:30 a.m. - 4:30 p.m.; interlibrary loan requests are honored; copying available.
>
> Subject area: National and some regional and local records of the Lutheran General Synod (1820-1918); Lutheran General Council (1867-1918); Lutheran United Synod in the South (1863-1918); United Lutheran (1918-62) and Lutheran Church in America (1962 to present); religious and ecclesiastical materials; biographical records; church music.
>
> Holdings: 400 books, 20 periodical and 8 newspaper titles, 3,000 shelf feet of archival materials, photographs, sound recordings. Note: The bulk of the material in this archive dealing with German Americans and their descendants comes from the period after full Americanization. Materials from earlier periods can be found in the Archives of Gettysburg Seminary, Gettysburg, Pennsylvania, the Lutheran Seminary in Philadelphia, as well as the regional archives of the New York, North Carolina, Ohio, and the various Pennsylvania Synods of the Church.
>
> Publications: A guide to the holdings is available on request.

1223 The Newberry Library (founded 1887). 60 West Walton Street, Chicago, Ill. 60610. Tel. (312) 943-9090.

> Open to serious researchers only, with credentials. Tues. - Thurs. 9:00 a.m. - 10:00 p.m., Fri. - Sat. 9:00 a.m. - 5:00 p.m.; no interlibrary loan; copying available.
>
> Subject area: German Americans is only one area of the library's very substantial holdings in American history up to about 1925. Strong on local and family history, music.
>
> Holdings: Books, periodicals, local newspapers, archival materials. Among the holdings is the former library of the Germania Club.
>
> Notable holdings: Several Chicago German newspapers; papers of Hermann Raster and Wilhelm Rapp.
>
> Publications: NEWBERRY NEWSLETTER, 1973-- , free.

1224 The University of Chicago, The Joseph Regenstein Library, 1100 East 57th Street, Chicago, Ill. 60637.

> The library does not have a special collection relating to the

general subject of German Americana, but has considerable amount of material diffused within its general collection.

1225 The Library of Bethany and Northern Baptist Theological Seminaries (founded by merger, 1975), Bethany Theological Seminary, Butterfield and Meyers Roads, Oak Brook, Ill. 60521. Tel. (312) 620-2214.

Open to public: (1) General collection--Mon. - Thurs. 8:00 a.m. - 10:30 p.m., Fri. 9:00 a.m. - 5:00 p.m., Sat. 2:30 p.m. - 5:00 p.m., Sun. 6:30 p.m. - 10:00 p.m.; interlibrary loan, copying available. (2) Special collections-- open to researchers with credential. Mon. - Fri. 9:00 a.m. - 1:00 p.m.; no interlibrary loan; copying available.

Subject area: Church of the Brethren; Mennonites; Baptists; Schwenkfelder Churches; German-American Christian communities, especially Ephrata. Special collections contain 12,000 items from the Abraham Cassel Collection.

Holdings: 2,500 books, 50 periodical titles.

1226 Illinois Historical Survey Library, University of Illinois Library (founded 1909), Urbana, Ill. 61801. Tel. (217) 333-1777.

Open to public, Mon. - Fri. 9:00 a.m. - 12:00 p.m.; 1:00 p.m. - 5:00 p.m., Tues. and Wed. 7:00 a.m. - 9:30 p.m., Sat. 9:00 a.m. - 12:00 p.m., interlibrary loan for recent books; copying available.

Subject area: History of nineteenth-century German immigration to the Midwest.

Holdings: 130 books, one retrospective periodical, 32 cubic feet archival materials.

Notable items: Papers of Heinrich A. Rattermann (poet, musician, author, and editor of the Cincinnati DER DEUTSCHE PIONIER), journal of the Belleville, Illinois, German Library Corporation, 1836-61.

Publications: Maynard J. Brichford, Robert M. Sutton, and Dennis F. Walle, MANUSCRIPTS GUIDE TO COLLECTIONS AT UNIVERSITY OF ILLINOIS AT URBANA-CHAMPAIGN (Urbana: University of Illinois Press, 1976). A GUIDE TO THE HEINRICH RATTERMANN COLLECTION by Dennis F. Walle is in preparation.

INDIANA

1227 Lilly Library, Indiana University, dedicated 1960, Bloomington, Ind. 47401. Tel. (812) 337-2452.

Open to public, Mon. - Thurs. 9:00 a.m. - 5:00 p.m. and

6:00 p.m. - 10:00 p.m., Fri. 9:00 a.m. - 5:00 p.m., Sat.
9:00 a.m. - 12:00 p.m., no interlibrary loan; copying on a
selective basis; microfilming generally available.

Subject area and holdings: 12 printed contemporary Rappite
materials; 400 issues of German-language almanacs printed in
the United States during the nineteenth century; 17 books
printed by the Christopher Sower family of Germantown, Pa.,
18 other pre-1821 U.S. imprints in German; approximately
200 pieces of American nineteenth century sheet music, German language or melodies.

1228 Associated Mennonite Biblical Seminaries Library (founded 1958: Mennonite Biblical Seminary 1945; Goshen Biblical Seminary 1958), 3003
Benham, Elkhart, Ind. 46514. Tel. (219) 295-3726, ext. 34, 37.

Open to public, during the academic year, Mon. - Thurs.
8:00 a.m. - 11:00 p.m., Fri. 8:00 a.m. - 5:30 p.m., Sat.
8:00 a.m. - 12:00 p.m., 1:00 p.m. - 5:00 p.m.; vacation
periods, Mon. - Fri. 8:30 a.m. - 12:00 p.m., 1:00 p.m. -
5:00 p.m., interlibrary loan; copying available.

Subject area: Mennonitica.

Holdings: 100 books, 200 periodical titles.

1229 Mennonite Historical Library (founded 1907), Goshen College and Associated Mennonite Biblical Seminaries, Goshen, Ind. 46526. Tel. (219)
533-3161, ext. 337.

Open to public, but appointment is advisable if assistance is
required, Mon. - Sat. 8:00 a.m. - 12:00 p.m., 1:00 p.m. -
5:00 p.m.; library closed on Saturdays in the second half of
April, August, and December; interlibrary loan requests honored
on a case-by-case basis; copying available.

Subject area: Mennonites; Church of the Brethren; Moravians;
Schwenkfelders; regional materials representing areas with concentrations of Mennonite populations. In addition, the library
has holdings in missions, conscription, colonization and migration, biography, genealogy, belles-lettres, art, cookery, and
works by Mennonite authors.

Holdings: The total collection amounts to over 21,000 books,
9,000 bound periodicals, 400 maps, vertical file materials,
yearbooks, reports, and official publications of various Mennonite bodies and institutions. There is a large file of unpublished papers, many of them student research papers from
Goshen College and the Associated Mennonite Biblical Seminaries.

Special service: The library maintains an obituary index to
the HERALD OF TRUTH (1864-1908) and its successor, the
GOSPEL HERALD. There is a computerized index to more than
one hundred Amish genealogies.

1230 Manchester College Library (founded 1889), North Manchester, Ind. 46962. Tel. (219) 982-2141, ext. 231.

Open to public, but under supervision, credentials required. Mon. - Fri. 8:00 a.m. - 10:30 p.m., Sat. 9:00 a.m. - 5:00 p.m., Sun. 1:30 p.m. - 10:30 p.m. during school year; interlibrary loan limited to photocopies of old materials, or to duplicates; copying available.

Subject area: Family and church histories of the Church of the Brethren, and books by Brethren authors; local church histories; district church histories by states or parts of states.

Holdings: 1,500 books, 10 periodical titles, 3,000 pieces of archival materials.

Notable runs of periodicals: THE INGLENOOK, 1900-13; THE GOSPEL VISITOR, 1851-73.

KANSAS

1231 Mennonite Brethren Historical Library, Tabor College (founded 1936), 400 S. Jefferson, Hillsboro, Kans. 67063. Tel. (316) 947-3121, ext. 254.

Open to public, but credentials are required. Mon. - Fri. 8:30 a.m. - 4:30 p.m.; interlibrary loan permitted on certain materials; copying available.

Subject area: Mennonite Brethren Church; Mennonite life and history; family and local histories pertaining to Mennonite Brethren settlements and church life, church archives.

Holdings: 1,200 books, 100 periodicals, and one newspaper title, 500 square feet of archival materials, films, tapes, photographs.

Notable items: CHRISTIAN LEADER, 1937-- ; VORWAERTS, 1919-40; WAHRHEITSFREUND, 1915-47; ZIONSBOTE, 1890-1960.

Museum: Hillsboro Adobe House in the vicinity.

1232 Max Kade Document and Research Center, the University of Kansas, 2080 Wescoe Hall (356-7 Watson Library), Lawrence, Kans. 66045. Tel. (913) 864-4657 and 864-3028.

Open to public: access to the collections by appointment; interlibrary loan; copying available.

Subject area: German-American literature until 1920.

Holdings: The nature of the collection was originally determined by a substantial gift of books received from the Milwaukee Historical Society and from the former Milwaukee Turnverein. The collection contains several thousand German and German-American books reflecting the reading interests of German immigrants.

Publications: A listing of the center's holdings was published in the Catalogue dated October 1976. Supplements are contemplated at irregular intervals.

1233 Miller Library, McPherson College (founded 1906), 1600 East Euclid, McPherson, Kans. 67460. Tel. (316) 241-0731, ext. 67.

Open to public, Mon. - Thurs. 8:00 a.m. - 10:00 p.m., Fri. 8:00 a.m. - 5:00 p.m., Sat. 1:00 p.m. - 5:00 p.m., hours reduced during summer; interlibrary loan; copying available.

Subject area: Church of the Brethren; biographical materials on members.

Holdings: 616 books, 12 periodical titles, more than 6 drawers of archival papers.

Notable items: (periodicals) BRETHREN AT WORK, 1877, 1880-82; CHRISTIAN FAMILY COMPANION, 1865, 1871-73; CHRISTIAN FAMILY COMPANION AND GOSPEL VISITOR, 1874-75; GOSPEL PREACHER, 1881; GOSPEL VISITOR, 1851-56, 1858, 1860, 1862-73; MISSIONARY VISITOR, 1908-30; PILGRIM, 1876; PRIMITIVE CHRISTIAN, 1876, 1880-83; PRIMITIVE CHRISTIAN AND PILGRIM, 1877-79; SCHWARZENAU, 1939-40; GOSPEL MESSENGER, 1884-1913; MESSENGER, 1914-date.

Museums: McPherson Museum has some relevant material as the city and the county have a high percentage of German Americans in the population.

MASSACHUSETTS

1234 Harvard College Library, Harvard University (founded 1636), Cambridge, Mass. 02138. Tel. (617) 495-2411.

Open to serious researchers with credentials, appointment required. Mon. - Sat. 9:00 a.m. - 5:00 p.m.; interlibrary loan, a fee of $8 per volume.

Subject area: Materials of German-American interest are part of the general collections.

Holdings: Books, periodicals, newspapers, rich retrospective runs of serials.

Museum: Busch-Reisinger Museum.

1235 American Antiquarian Society Library (founded 1812), 185 Salisbury Street, Worcester, Mass. 01609. Tel. (617) 755-5221.

Open for graduate research use; readers must apply for access to collection.

Subject area: American history, culture, and life through 1876.

Holdings: The library concentrates, among other things, on early American imprints. It holds 56 percent of book titles listed in Oswald Seidensticker's THE FIRST CENTURY OF GERMAN PRINTING IN AMERICA 1728-1830, and 5 percent of the periodical titles. (By a rough estimate this holding may consist of 1,500 items.) In addition, the library also has the Rowell Collection of 1876.

MICHIGAN

1236 University of Michigan Library, Department of Rare Books and Special Collections; Labadie Collection (established 1911). 711 Hatcher Library, Ann Arbor, Mich. 48109. Tel. (313) 764-9377.

Open to qualified researchers, but it is advisable to write a letter before planning a trip. Hours are Mon. - Fri. 10:00 a.m. - 12:00 p.m. and 1:00 p.m. - 5:00 p.m., Sat. 10:00 a.m. - 12:00 p.m. during regular semesters; during intersessions, Mon. - Fri. 1:00 p.m. - 5:00 p.m. may be closed between Christmas and New Year's day; copying available; interlibrary loan considered individually.

Subject area: Social protest materials; especially strong in the fields of anarchism, socialism, communism, civil liberties, early labor history, Spanish Civil War 1936-39, radical right, and forms of contemporary social and political liberation.

Holdings: 5,000 cataloged books; 15,000 uncataloged pamphlets; 8,000 serials; 95 vertical file drawers of clippings, leaflets, organizational records, manuscripts, photographs, and memorabilia.

Special services: 94 drawers of local indexing cards provide access by person, group, and subject to materials in the collection.

Note: Although there is no approach to materials by way of national background, a check reveals many names suggesting German-American ancestry or association. Such prominent radical journalists as Karl Heinzen (1809-80), Johan Most (1846-1906), and Robert Reitzel (1849-98) are represented, with noteworthy runs of their papers, JANUS and DER ARME TEUFEL being complete and FREIDENKER and FREIHEIT very nearly so. There are in the collection approximately thirty German-language serials published in the United States as well as many English-language publications to which German Americans contributed. In the manuscript correspondence, the four hundred letters from and to Karl Heinzen and his family are outstanding, covering his friendship with the poet, Ferdinand Freiligrath, the 1848 Revolution, and his manifold activities during his American years. The extensive correspondence and other manuscript writings of the Slavonian anarchist, Stephanus Fabrijanovic, are almost entirely in German.

1237 Detroit Public Library, Burton Historical Collection (founded 1914). 5201 Woodward Avenue, Detroit, Mich. 48202. Tel. (313) 833-1000.

Open to public, no credentials necessary but identification is requested. Hours: Mon., Tues., Thurs., Fri., Sat. 9:30 a.m. - 5:30 p.m.; Wed. 9:00 a.m. - 9:00 p.m., Sun. (school year) 1:00 p.m. - 5:00 p.m. Orders are taken for copying, camera copy 50 cents per page, xerox 15 cents per page.

Subject area: Detroit, Great Lakes area, history, genealogy, heraldry.

Holdings: In 1971 the resources of the Burton Historical Collection consisted of over 200,000 volumes; 12,000 cataloged pamphlets and many as yet uncataloged; 5,000 bound newspaper volumes; 6,800 scrap books; 4,000 maps; 3,300 reels of microfilm; 1,000 color transparencies; 1,000 lantern slides; 5,000 glass negatives; and millions of manuscripts. The book stock dealing with Germans comprises hundreds of volumes covering not only Michigan but the entire country. The archival collection is particularly strong in its coverage of Germans in Detroit and the Bay area. The library houses the papers of German societies and families going back to the early period.

Notable holdings: DETROITER ABEND POST, complete run 1916-1956.

Publications: None, but the library has several analytical catalogs and indexes providing multiple accesses to the material.

MINNESOTA

1238 Brown County Historical Society (founded 1930), 27 North Broadway, New Ulm, Minn. 56073. Tel. (507) 354-2016.

Open to public, Mon. - Sat. 1:00 p.m. - 5:00 p.m.; no interlibrary loan; copying available.

Subject area: German settlement of the New Ulm, Minnesota; files on about 1,800 German-American families who have settled in Brown County.

Holdings: 100 books, 20 periodical and 9 newspaper titles, many items of archival materials.

Publications: BROWN COUNTY'S HERITAGE (annual), circulation 325, distributed to society members.

Special services: Lectures and slide programs.

Museum at the same address; tours provided.

1239 Volkfest Association of Minnesota (founded 1958), 301 Summit Avenue, St. Paul, Minn. 55102. Tel. (612) 222-7027.

Open to public: Mon., Wed., Fri. 12:00 p.m. - 5:00 p.m., and during all Volkfest functions; no interlibrary loan; no copying available.

Subject area: Local and regional German culture.

Holdings: Undetermined quantity of books, periodicals, newspapers, archival materials.

Publications: VOLKFEST NEWSLETTER (monthly), 1957-- , circulation 2,700.

Special services: Conversational German courses for beginners and intermediates; annual "German Day."

Museum: History room is maintained at the same location.

1240 Carver County Historical Society (founded 1940), 119 Cherry Street, Waconia, Minn. 55387. Tel. (612) 442-4234.

Open to public: Sun., Tues., Fri. 1:00 p.m. - 4:30 p.m.; no interlibrary loan; copying available.

Subject area: Local history; genealogy; religious works; music; cookbooks (German and English).

Holdings: Over 10,000 books, county newspapers, hundreds of archival records.

Notable items: The Deutscher Leserverein collection dating back to 1856; some German-language magazines; early collections from St. Anscara Academy in East Union, Carver County, now Gustavus Adolphus, St. Peter, Minn.

Publications: NEWSLETTER (six times per year).

MISSOURI

1241 Concordia Historical Institute, Lutheran Church--Missouri Synod (founded 1927), 801 DeMun, St. Louis, Mo. 63105. Tel. (314) 721-5934, ext. 320, 321.

Open to public: Credentials required. Mon. - Fri. 8:00 a.m. - 5:00 p.m.; interlibrary loan; service charge $3 per volume; copying available.

Subject Area: History of Lutheranism in North America; Archives of the Lutheran Church--Missouri Synod and related bodies; personal papers of individuals; local and family history; special collections of Bibles, hymnals, and devotional literature.

Holdings: 57,500 books, periodicals, pamphlets, tracts; archival materials, audio-visual materials, museum artifacts.

Notable items: Periodicals dealing with early German Lutherans; museum artifacts on nineteenth-century pioneer way of life.

Publications: CONCORDIA INSTITUTE HISTORICAL QUARTERLY, 1928-- , circulation 1,600, subscription $10 per year.

Museum on premises.

1242 Missouri Historical Society (founded 1866), Jefferson Memorial Building, St. Louis, Mo. 63112. Tel. (314) 361-1424.

Open to serious researchers only, fee $3 per day for non-members of the society. Library and archives, Tues. - Sat. 9:30 a.m. - 4:45 p.m.; museum, daily 9:30 a.m. - 4:45 p.m.; interlibrary loan for microfilm, with postage and insurance; copying of non-fragile materials is permitted.

Subject area: St. Louis Germans (materials about and by them).

Holdings: Books, periodicals, newspapers, archival materials.

Notable runs: AMERIKA, 1872-1923 (bound); WESTLICHE POST, 1857-1938 (microfilm).

Publications: THE BULLETIN, (quarterly) 1944-- , $7.50 per year.

Museum: Exhibits on industrial St. Louis, which includes material on German Americans.

1243 Washington University Libraries (founded 1853), Lindell and Skinker Boulevards, St. Louis, Mo. 63130. Tel. (314) 889-5400.

Open to public, Mon. - Thurs. 8:00 a.m. - 12:00 a.m., Fri. 8:00 a.m. - 10:00 p.m., Sat. 9:00 a.m. - 10:00 p.m., Sun. 1:00 p.m. - 12:00 a.m.; interlibrary loan requests honored; copying available.

Subject area: German-American history and literature.

Holdings: About 1,000 books, 20 periodical titles.

NEBRASKA

1244 American Historical Society of Germans From Russia (founded 1968), 631

D Street, Lincoln, Nebr. 58502. Tel. (402) 477-4524.

Open to members only, but the general public is invited to visit the international headquarters on site and use some of the materials. Hours: 8:00 a.m. - 12:00 p.m., 1:00 p.m. - 4:30 p.m.

Subject area: History and culture of Germans from Russia; history of Russian-German settlements; family histories; religious studies; music.

Holdings: Over 40 books, three periodical and two newspaper titles, over 600 archival materials, three films, 25 maps.

Special services: Assistance in genealogical research; publishing programs by specific groups; informative presentations by volunteers to interested groups.

Publications: AHSGR NEWSLETTER (3 issues per year), 1969-- , circulation 3,000; WORK PAPER (the society's historical journal with informative articles on Germans from Russia) (3 issues per year) 1969-- ; CLUES (devoted to genealogical research and surname exchange) (annual) 1969-- .

Museum: 615 D Street, Lincoln, Nebr. 68502. The society's archives are located at the Greeley, Colorado, Public Library; materials are available to AHSGR only through interlibrary loan.

NEW YORK

1245 Leo Baeck Institute, Inc. (founded 1955), 129 East 73rd Street, New York, N.Y. 10021. Tel. (212) 744-6400.

Open: Mon. - Thurs. 9:00 a.m. - 5:00 p.m., Fri. 9:00 a.m. - 3:00 p.m.; limited interlibrary loan; copying available.

Subject area: German Jewish immigrants to the United States; family histories; papers; memoirs.

Holdings: Extensive, especially in the institute's primary interest area (history, literature, and thought of German-speaking Jewry in Central Europe from the second half of the eighteenth century to the beginning of the Hitler era). The institute has a full run of the weekly AUFBAU.

Publications: LBI NEWS (semiannual); LBI LIBRARY AND ARCHIVES NEWS (semiannual) 1975-- ; BULLETIN DES LEO BAECK INSTITUTE (in German) (quarterly) 1957-- ; LEO BAECK INSTITUTE YEARBOOK (annual) 1956-- , price $15.

Exhibits: Current and alternating exhibits of archival material, art work, and new library accessions on the premises.

1246 New York Public Library--The Research Libraries (founded 1895), 5th Avenue and 42nd Street, New York, N.Y. 10018. Tel. (202) 790-6253.

> Open to public (over age 18): hours vary, generally open Mon., Tue., Wed., Fri., Sat. 10:00 a.m. - 6:00 p.m.; no interlibrary loan; copying available.

> Subject area: Materials of German-American interest are included in the general collection; strong in history, religion, Bibles, poetry, description and travel, pre-1801 imprints.

> Holdings: Books, periodicals, newspapers, archival materials (no separate tally of German-American materials is made).

> Notable Holdings: Many rare items; runs of periodicals; the file of DEUTSCH-AMERIKANISCHE DICHTUNG, 1889-90.

1247 Frederick W. Crumb Library, State University of New York at Potsdam (founded 1880), Pierrepont Avenue, Potsdam, N.Y. 13676. Tel. (315) 268-4991.

> Open to public during regular hours; interlibrary loan; photocopying.

> Subject area: Northern New York State history.

> Notable holdings: Snell Collection of public and private papers.

NORTH CAROLINA

1248 Moravian Archives, Southern Province, Drawer M Salem Station, Winston-Salem, N.C. 27108. Tel. (919) 722-1742.

> Open to serious researchers, with credentials and appointment (hourly service fee). Mon. - Fri. 9:00 a.m. - 12:00 p.m., 1:00 p.m. - 4:30 p.m.; no interlibrary loan; limited copying available.

> Subject area: Records of the Moravian Church in America, Southern Province, since 1754.

1249 Moravian Music Foundation, P.O. Box Drawer Z, Salem Station, Winston-Salem, N.C. 27108. Tel. (919) 725-0651.

> Open to public, Mon. - Fri. 8:30 a.m. - 12:00 p.m., 1:00 - 4:00 p.m.; no interlibrary loan but will supply photocopies when possible; copying available for private use.

> Subject area: Moravian music and hymnology in the German language; hymnological material in German from the Lutheran, Reformed, and Mennonite churches.

> Holdings: Collection of over 10,000 pieces of manuscripts of

eighteenth and nineteenth century American Moravian music, principally in the German language, 3,000 German-texted church services (love feasts), 1,000 books, 2 periodicals.

Publications: THE MORAVIAN MUSIC FOUNDATION BULLE-TIN (semiannual), 1956-- , free, circulation 4,000; address: P.O. Box Drawer Z, Salem Station, Winston-Salem, N.C. 27108.

Special service: Inquiries are invited about Moravian music or hymnology from all users.

NORTH DAKOTA

1250 North Dakota Historical Society of Germans From Russia (founded 1971), 219 - Seventh Street North, P.O. Box 1641, Bismarck, N. Dak. 58501. Tel. (701) 223-6167.

Open to serious researchers, Mon., Wed., Fri., 10:00 a.m. - 4:00 p.m.; no interlibrary loan; no copying.

Subject area: History and family genealogies of persons who emigrated from Germany from 1763 through 1850 to the Volga River, Black Sea, and Crimean areas of Russia, and subsequently immigrated to the United States, Canada, and South America from 1860 through 1930.

Holdings: 25 books, 40 periodical titles, numerous genealogical records.

Notable items: Songbooks and a cookbook of items submitted by the society members and members of the group.

Special services: Genealogy assistance to members of the society.

Publications: HERITAGE REVIEW (3 times a year) 1971-- , subscription $10 per year, circulation 1,200; address: P.O. Box 1671, Bismarck, N. Dak. 58501.

OHIO

1251 Mennonite Historical Library, Bluffton College (founded 1935), Bluffton, Ohio 45817. Tel. (419) 358-8015, ext. 114.

Open to public, but credentials and appointment are required. Mon. - Fri. 9:00 a.m. - 3:00 p.m.; interlibrary loan, except for rare or out-of-print books, return postage requested; copying available.

Subject area: Mennonites, Anabaptists, Amish, Hutterian Brethren.

Holdings: 3,000 books, 150 periodicals, 20 newspaper titles,

10 feet of archival materials, 100 reels of microfilm, miscellaneous audio-visual materials.

Museum: Swiss Community Historical Museum in the vicinity.

1252 Public Library of Cincinnati and Hamilton County (founded 1854), 800 Vine Street, Cincinnati, Ohio 45202. Tel. (513) 369-6000.

Open to public, Mon. - Fri. 9:00 a.m. - 9:00 p.m., Sat. 9:00 a.m. - 6:00 p.m.; rare book room open Mon. - Sat. 9:00 a.m. - 5:00 p.m.; interlibrary loan permitted, charge $5 per volume outside Ohio; photocopy $.15 per page; copying available.

Subject area: German-language materials published in Cincinnati; German immigration to the United States; genealogy; local history; fiction in the German language.

Holdings: Undetermined number of books, 22 periodicals, 15 newspaper titles.

Notable periodicals: CINCINNATI TAEGLICHE ABEND POST, 1877-1880; CINCINNATI ABEND POST, 1877-1880; CINCINNATI SONNTAGS CHRONIK, 1877-1880; CINCINNATI ANZEIGER, 1880-1901; TAEGLICHER CINCINNATI COURIER, 1871-1874; CINCINNATIER FREIE PRESSE, 1874-1963; SONNTAGSBLATT DER CINCINNATIER FREIE PRESS, 1874-1941; CINCINNATI KURIER, 1964-- ; CINCINNATI TAGEBLATT, 1895-1896; TAGLICHES CINCINNATIER VOLKSBLATT, 1836-1919; WESTLICHE BLAETTER, 1865-1919; CINCINNATI VOLKSFREUND, 1850-1908; SONNTAGSMORGEN, 1867-1908; CINCINNATIER ZEITUNG, 1886-1901; CINCINNATIER ZEITUNG SONNTAGS AUSGABE, 1887-1901; DER DEUTSCHE PIONIER, Vol. 1-70, 1869-1938.

1253 University of Cincinnati Libraries, Special Collections Department (founded 1973), 610 Main Library, University of Cincinnati, Cincinnati, Ohio 45221. Tel. (513) 475-6459.

Open to serious researchers only, Mon. - Fri. 8:00 a.m. - 5:00 p.m.; credentials are required for manuscript consultation, no interlibrary loan, copying available.

Subject area: The Fick Collection of German-American prose and poetry, covering the years 1850-1935.

Holdings: 1,000 books, Cincinnati German publications, unpublished autobiographies, literary manuscripts, and rare materials such as the first anthology of German-American poetry, DEUTSCH-AMERIKANISCHER DICHTERWALD, published in Detroit in 1856, materials relating to the German literary societies of Cincinnati.

1254 North American Swiss Alliance (founded 1865), 33 Public Square, Suite 404, Cleveland, Ohio 44113. Tel. (216) 771-2414.

Open to public, credentials and appointment required. Mon.
- Fri. 9:00 a.m. - 4:30 p.m.; no interlibrary loan; no copying facilities.

Publications: THE SWISS AMERICAN (monthly), subscription
$5 per year, circulation 3,400.

PENNSYLVANIA

1255 Muhlenberg College Library (founded 1848), Allentown, Pa. 18104.
Tel. (215) 433-3191.

Open to serious researchers with credentials, appointment advisable. Mon. - Fri. 8:00 a.m. - 11:30 p.m., Sat. 9:00
a.m. - 5:00 p.m., Sun. 1:00 p.m. - 11:30 p.m.; interlibrary
loan; copying available.

Subject area: Church histories of individual churches and of
the Evangelical Lutheran Church in North America--Pennsyl-
vania Synod; Pennsylvania German literature; Muhlenberg
family; local history.

Holdings: 1,150 books, 42 periodicals, (7 current, 35 retrospective), 9 newspaper titles, 12 tapes, 9 land deeds, undetermined amount of archival materials.

Notable items: BRUEDER BOTSCHAFTER, 1871-1906; FRIE-
DENS BOTE, 1834-56; LEHIGH COUNTY PATRIOT, 1829-
72; PENNSYLVANIA-GERMAN, 1900-1914; WELT-BOTE,
1856-1907 (the runs are not complete); various publications
from the press of Christopher Sauer (Sower) from 1744-80, including Bibles of 1743, 1763 and 1776; Ralph S. Funk's index
to Pennsylvania German poetry; various quantities of manuscripts by Charles C. More, and Lloyd A. Moll.

1256 Old Economy Village (founded 1824), Pennsylvania Historical and Museum
Commission, Fourteenth and Church Streets, Ambridge, Pa. 15003. Tel.
(412) 266-4500.

Open to serious researchers with credentials and appointment.
Mon. - Sat. 8:30 a.m. - 5:00 p.m., Sun. 1:00 p.m. - 5:00
p.m.; interlibrary loan selectively, depending upon material,
copying available.

Subject area: History of the Harmony Society, 1805-1905;
preserved center German village (1825-1905) complete with
buildings, archives, and collections.

Holdings: 12,000 books, 100 periodicals, 100 newspaper titles,
600 cubic feet of archival materials.

Publications: HARMONIE HERALD, (irregular), 1966-- , subscription $10 a year, circulation 250-300.

1257 The Moravian Archives, 41 West Locust Street, Bethlehem, Pa. 18018. Tel. (215) 866-3255.

Open to public, but credentials are required. Mon. - Fri. 9:00 a.m. - 12:00 p.m., 1:00 p.m. - 5:00 p.m.; no interlibrary loan; copying available.

Subject area: Moravian Church history, theology, and archival records in North America and worldwide; the first hundred years of Bethlehem, Pennsylvania; art and music of the colonial era and later.

Holdings: Books, periodicals, newspapers, archival materials, audiovisual materials.

Special services: Tours available.

1258 Reeves Library, Moravian College (founded 1807), Bethlehem, Pa. 18018. Tel. (215) 865-0741.

Open to public, during academic year, Mon. - Thurs. 8:00 a.m. - 12:00 a.m., Fri. 8:00 - 9:00 p.m., Sat. 9:00 a.m. - 5:00 p.m., Sun. 10:00 a.m. - 12:00 a.m.; interlibrary loan; copying available.

Subject area: Moravian Church; Pennsylvania Germans.

Holdings: Several hundred books on the subject, 6 periodicals, 1 newspaper.

1259 Spruance Library, Bucks County Historical Society (founded 1880), Pine Street, Doylestown, Pa. 18901. Tel. (215) 345-0210.

Open to public, Tue. 1:00 p.m. - 9:00 p.m., Wed. - Fri. 10:00 a.m. - 5:00 p.m.; no interlibrary loan; copying available.

Subject area: Pennsylvania German history and genealogy in Bucks County; folk art, crafts, industries and cultural life; collection of early American tools many of which originated from Pennsylvania Germans.

Holdings: Undetermined number of books, periodicals, newspapers, archival materials, audiovisual materials.

Notable items: DOYLESTAUN EXPRESS, 1827-28, 1838-39, 1845-46; DER MORGENSTERN, 1851-54; PATRIOT AND REFORMER (Milford Square and Quakertown), 1867-86.

Publications: BUCKS COUNTY HISTORICAL SOCIETY JOURNAL (semiannual), 1972-- , $15, includes membership in society.

Museum: The Mercer Museum of the Bucks County Historical Society, Pine Street, Doylestown, Pa. 18901.

1260 Pennsylvania State Archives, Pennsylvania Historical and Museum Commission (founded 1913), Box 1026, Harrisburg, Pa. 17120. Tel. (717) 787-3023.

> Open to public, Mon. – Fri. 8:30 a.m. – 5:00 p.m.; copying available.

> Subject area: State and local history.

> Holdings: Archival materials, newspapers.

> Notable holdings: Archival materials: Harmony Society Papers, 1742–1905, ca. 303 cubic feet; correspondence and papers of Frederick Rapp, George Rapp, R.L. Baker, and so forth, 1812–80, 13 volumes; George Krause and Company (Lebanon) Collection, 1848–1909. Newspapers: BANNER VON BERKS (Reading), 1867–88; DER PILGER, 1871–81; DER READINGER POSTBOTHE (Reading), 1816–22; PHILADELPHIA TAGEBLATTE, 1877–1929; READING ZEITUNG, 1789–1802; REPUBLIKANER VON BERKS (Reading), 1869–98.

> Publications: A printed detailed guide to the holdings is available upon request.

1261 State Library of Pennsylvania (founded 1745), Commonwealth and Walnut Streets, Box 1601, Harrisburg, Pa. 17126. Tel. (717) 787-4440.

> Open to public, but appointment is required for the use of rare books. Mon. – Fri. 8:30 a.m. – 5:00 p.m., open Saturdays also, except the period between Memorial Day and Labor Day; interlibrary loan; copying available.

> Subject area: History, language, and culture of the Pennsylvania Germans; state and local history; genealogy; Mennonites and other religious groups; pre-1850 Pennsylvania imprints.

> Holdings: 850 books, 31 periodicals, 49 newspapers, journals of the Pennsylvania Assembly.

> Notable items: Sizeable collection of newspapers of German-American interest, including Karl John Richard Arndt's MICRO-FILM GUIDE AND INDEX TO GERMAN PRISONERS OF WAR PAPERS PUBLISHED IN THE UNITED STATES OF NORTH AMERICA FROM 1943 TO 1946, 56 volumes on 15 reels; many items listed in Karl J.R. Arndt, GERMAN AMERICAN NEWS-PAPERS AND PERIODICALS 1932-1955.

> Special services: Library orientation to users.

> Publications: YEARS' WORK IN PENNSYLVANIA STUDIES (annual), 1965-- , circulation 1,200, free. Intended for librarians and historians.

1262 Juniata College Library (founded 1876), Eighteenth and Moore Streets, Huntingdon, Pa. 16652. Tel. (814) 643-4310, ext. 57, 58.

Open to public, but appointment required. Mon. - Thurs.
8:00 a.m. - 11:00 p.m., Fri. 8:00 a.m. - 10:00 p.m., Sat.
9:00 a.m. - 5:00 p.m., Sun. 2:00 p.m. - 11:00 p.m.; interlibrary loan; copying available.

Subject area: Early Pennsylvania imprints, many in German,
including a large collection from Christopher Sauer's (Sower's)
press; Early Brethren, Schwenkfelder, Anabaptist tracts from
Pennsylvania and Europe.

Holdings: 5,000 books.

1263 Kutztown State College Library (founded 1866), Kutztown, Pa. 19530.
Tel. (215) 683-3511.

Open to public, Mon. - Thurs. 7:45 a.m. - 11:00 p.m.,
Fri. 7:45 a.m. - 5:00 p.m., Sat. 9:00 a.m. - 5:00 p.m.,
Sun. 2:00 p.m. - 11:00 p.m.; interlibrary loan; copying
available.

Subject area: Pennsylvania German history and folklore.

Holdings: Books, periodicals.

1264 Evangelical and Reformed Historical Society, 555 West James Street,
Lancaster, Pa. 17603. Tel. (717) 393-0654, ext. 46.

Open to public, Mon. - Fri. 8:30 a.m. - 12:30 p.m., 1:30
- 4:30 p.m., except holidays and vacation periods; no interlibrary loan; copying available.

Subject area: Colonial Church records of German Reformed
Congregations; family histories; religious materials.

Holdings: About 6,000 books, periodicals, about 6,000 pieces
of archival material, microfilms of church records.

Publications: NEWS FROM THE EVANGELICAL AND RE-
FORMED HISTORICAL SOCIETY, (3 times yearly), free to society members.

Special services: Microfilms of church records sent directly to
individuals for a rental fee of $2 per microfilm.

1265 Fackenthal Library, Franklin and Marshall College (founded 1937), College Avenue, Lancaster, Pa. 17604. Tel. (717) 291-4216.

Open to public, but credentials are required. Mon. - Sat.
8:00 a.m. - 12:00 a.m., Sun. 1:00 p.m. - 12:00 a.m.; interlibrary loan; copying available.

Subject area: Mennonite catechisms and creeds, hymns, church
discipline; Lutheran Church catechisms and creeds, hymns,
prayer books and devotions, liturgy and rituals; Church of the
Brethren collected works, doctrinal and controversial works;
Schwenkfelders prayer books and devotional literature; religious
education, and others.

Holdings: 3,380 books, 30 retrospective periodicals, five newspapers, 560 broadsides.

Notable items: "Penn Collection," a collection of books and periodicals containing the histories of all areas of Pennsylvania. The library possesses long runs of early local and statewide German-language periodicals: HAUS UND HERD; EIN FAMILIEN-MAGAZIN, 1–6, Cincinnati, 1873; PENNSYL-VANISCHER CALENDER, Ephrata, 1796–97; AMERICANISCHER CALENDER, Ephrata, 1799, 1802, 1809; DER HOCH-DEUTSCH AMERICANISCHE CALENDER, Germantown, 1749–1833; GEIST-LICHES MAGAZIEN, Germantown, series 1, nos. 4, 8–50; Pennsylvania Department of Public Instruction, BERICHT, Harrisburg, 1861, 1863, 1864–68; Pennsylvania State Geologist, JAHRLICH BERICHT DES STAATE GEOLOGEN...Harrisburg, 1838; Pennsylvania Constitutional Convention, VERHANDLUN-GEN UND DEBATTEN 1837–1838 DER CONVENTION DER REPUBLIK PENNSYLVANIEN, Harrisburg, Vol. 1–3, 5–14; DER AMERIKANISCHE BAUER, Harrisburg, Vol. 3; DER GANTZ NEUE VERBESSERTE NORD-AMERICANISCHE CALENDER, Lancaster, 1779, 1781–89; DER REPUBLIKANISCHE CALENDER, Lancaster, 1781; DER NEUE GEMEINNUTZIGE LANDWIRT-SCHAFTS, CALENDER, Lancaster, 1787–1832; DER NEUE AL-LGEMEIN NUTZLICHE VOLKS-CALENDER, Lancaster, 1801, 1803; DER VOLKS FREUND UND BEOBACHTER, Lancaster, scattered issues from 1816–96; DES LANDWIRTHS UND SEI-DENBAUERS CALENDER, Lancaster, 1840; NEUER GEMEIN-NUTZIGER PENNSYLVANISCHER CALENDER, Lancaster, 1833–1918; DER REFORMER; EIN RELIGIOSES WERK, Lancaster, Bd. 1, no. 1–2; DER PENNSYLVANISCHE ANTI-FREIMAURER CALENDER, Lancaster, 1832–33; DAS BRUDERBLATT, ENTHAL-TEND ALTES UND NEUES AUS DER BRUDER-KIRCHE, Lan-caster, 1854–61; NEUER HAUSWIRTHSCHAFTS CALENDER, Lebanon, 1807–12, 1814; JAHRES-BERICHT UBER DIE VOLKS SCHULEN, Lebanon, 1841; MEYER'S MONATS-HEFTE, DEUTSCH-AMERIKANISCHE ZEITSCHRIFT FUR LITERATUR, KUNST UND GESELLSCHAFT, New York, Vols. 2, 3, 4–5; WALHALLA; EINE MONATSCHRIFT ZUR BELIHRUNG UND ERHEITERING, Philadelphia, 2 vols. in 1; PHILADELPHIER MAGAZIN FUR FREUNDE DER DEUTSCHEN LITERATUR IN AMERIKA, Reading, 1824–25; DEUTSCHER HAUSSCHATZ IN WORT UND BILD, Regensburg, 1874.

Museums: Pennsylvania Farm Museum of Landis Valley, 2451 Kissel Hill Road, Lancaster, Pa. 17601; Ephrata Cloisters Mu-seum, 632 East Main Street, Ephrata, Pa. 17522; Historical Society of York County, 250 East Market Street, York, Pa. 17403.

1266 Lancaster County Library, 125 North Duke Street, Lancaster, Pa. 17602. Tel. (717) 394-2651.

Open to public, Mon. - Fri. 9:00 a.m. - 9:00 p.m., Sat.
9:00 a.m. - 5:30 p.m.; interlibrary loan, except rare books;
copying facility on the premises.

Subject area: Social life and customs, history, religion, no-
vels, literature, folk art, cookbooks, music, family and local
histories, especially about Lancaster and its residents.

Holdings: 300 books, 10 periodical titles, newspapers, various
audiovisual materials, the Lancaster collection, an assemblage
of materials by Lancastrians on and about Lancaster. Many
of these deal with Pennsylvania Germans.

Publications: The library publishes occasional bibliographies
on the Pennsylvania Germans.

Museum: Lancaster County Historical Society.

1267 Lancaster Mennonite Conference Historical Society (founded 1958), 2215
Millstream Road, Lancaster, Pa. 17602. Tel. (717) 393-9745.

Open to public, Mon. 8:30 a.m. - 9:00 p.m., Tue. - Sat.
8:30 a.m. - 5:00 p.m.; no interlibrary loan; copying available for specific items.

Subject area: Religious thought and expression, Pennsylvania
Dutch genealogy, culture of Mennonite-related groups originating Pennsylvania, including their European backgrounds, from
1525; Southeastern Pennsylvania secular and denominational
history, especially the historic Peace churches; quilting;
hymnology.

Holdings: 10,000 books, 100 periodical and 25 newspaper
titles, 10 cubic feet archival materials, some tapes and slides,
deeds.

Notable Runs: Complete file of the BUDGET, an Amish newspaper printed in Sugarcreek, Ohio.

Publications: PENNSYLVANIA MENNONITE HERITAGE (quarterly), January, 1978-- , circulation 1,200, distributed to
Society members, $10 per year; THE MIRROR (bimonthly news-
letter), 1969-- .

Special services: Tours for school children and cultural groups.

Museum: Hans Herr House, 1849 Hans Herr Drive, Willow
Street, Pa. 17584, oldest house in Lancaster County, built
1719. Open daily, except Sundays, Christmas and New Year's.
Admission fee.

1268 Pennsylvania Farm Museum of Landis Valley, 2451 Kissel Hill Road, Lancaster, Pa. 17601. Tel. (717) 569-0401.

Open to public. Appointment is required for the use of the
research collection. Mon. - Sat. 9:00 a.m. - 4:30 p.m.,
Sun. 12:00 p.m. - 4:30 p.m.; no interlibrary loan; no copying.

Subject area: Pennsylvania German folklore, agricultural history, cookbooks.

Holdings: 5,000 books, 1,000 periodical titles.

Museum: Same address with restored houses, farm buildings, and other buildings.

1269 Eastern Pennsylvania Mennonite Library, Mennonite Historians of Eastern Pennsylvania, Christopher Dock Mennonite High School, 1000 Forty Foot Road, Lansdale, Pa. 19446. Tel. (215) 362-2675.

Open to public, Mon.-Fri. 8:00 a.m. - 12:00 p.m., 1:30 p.m. - 3:30 p.m.; copying available; no interlibrary loans.

Subject area: Mennonites in eastern Pennsylvania; Anabaptists; Reformation; religious literature.

Holdings: Undetermined quantity of archival materials; 150 books; 5 periodicals.

Publications: NEWSLETTER OF THE MENNONITE HISTORIANS OF EASTERN PENNSYLVANIA (quarterly), 1974-- . Address: Historical Library, Christopher Dock Mennonite High School, 1000 Forty Foot Road, Lansdale, Pa. 19446.

1270 Moravian Historical Society, 214 East Center Street, Nazareth, Pa. 18064. Tel. (215) 759-0292.

Open to public: Tues., Fri., Sat. 2:00 p.m. - 5:00 p.m. No interlibrary loan; no copying.

Subject area: Moravian Church and social history, theology, Bibles, hymnbooks; seventeenth and eighteenth century German imprints in America; archival records, artifacts; museum pieces.

Holdings: The library of Bishop Spangenberg, containing seventeenth and eighteenth century German imprints; imprints of the Ephrata Cloisters and the Christopher Saur (Sower) Press of Germantown, Pennsylvania; productions from the press of Benjamin Franklin; a large collection of rare Bibles, dating from 1636; a great number of antique hymn books, and many other volumes of historical interest.

Publications: TRANSACTIONS OF THE MORAVIAN HISTORICAL SOCIETY (biannual), 1867-- , price varies, circulation, 500.

Museum: The Whitefield House, 208 East Center Street (Route 191), Nazareth, Pa. 18064. Has large collection of musical instruments, pottery, clothing, and textiles, and a variety of artifacts documenting the life and religious activities of Moravian settlers.

1271 Schwenkfelder Library (founded 1884), Pennsburg, Pa. 18073. Tel. (215) 679-7175.

Open to public: Mon.-Fri. 9:00 a.m. - 5:00 p.m.; inter-library loan; copying available.

Subject area: The Schwenkfelders in America; Pennsylvania-German materials; Montgomery County family histories and lists.

Holdings: 30,000 books, 100 newspaper titles, 500 bound volumes of manuscripts, 2,500 pieces of archival material.

Notable runs: THE SCHWENKFELDIAN.

Publications: Occasional monographs on Schwenkfelder theology and history.

1272 Free Library of Philadelphia--Rare Books Department (founded 1891), Logan Square, Philadelphia, Pa. 19103. Tel. (215) MU 6-5416.

Open to serious researchers only: The general public admitted to the exhibits; appointment is not required, but advisable. No interlibrary loan; very limited copying allowed due to the fragility of materials.

Subject area: Pennsylvania German Fraktur; Pennsylvania German imprints, books, and broadsides to 1850.

Holdings: 2,400 books, 1,100 Fraktur, and folk art items.

Special services: Materials for purposes of exhibitions are available on loan.

1273 German Society of Pennsylvania, Horner Memorial Library (founded 1764), 611 Spring Garden Street, Philadelphia, Pa. 19123. Tel. (215) MA 7-4365.

Open to serious researchers with credentials: Borrowing privileges for members only. Wed. 10:00 a.m. - 5:00 p.m., Thurs. 10:00 a.m. - 6:00 p.m., Sat. 10:00 a.m. - 4:00 p.m. Interlibrary loan requests honored, charge for postage; copying available, $.15 per page when ordered.

Subject area: Local Pennsylvania and Philadelphia history; German clubs and associations history; family genealogies; publishes history and records of the society; archival collections in Americana Germanica; German literature; the arts, history, reference, and so forth. Numerous broken runs of nineteenth century periodicals.

Holdings: 80,000 books, 20 periodicals, and 5 ongoing newspapers, 6,000 pieces of archival materials, microfilms, pictures, memorabilia, various audiovisual materials.

Publications: Membership NEWSLETTER (monthly), free to members.

Special services: Hosts literary and cultural performances; visits of school groups can be arranged. Custom-search in the genealogical records severely limited.

1274 Germantown Historical Society Library (founded 1907), 5214 Germantown Avenue, Philadelphia, Pa. 19144. Tel. (215) 844-0514.

> Open to public: Tue., Thurs., Sat. 1:00 p.m. - 5:00 p.m., and by special appointment. Interlibrary loan; no copying facilities.

> Subject area: Local history; genealogy; religious materials, music, cookbooks; local press.

> Holdings: 2,000 volumes, periodicals from 1830, 8 cubic feet of archival materials.

> Notable items: Complete German imprints of Christopher Sower and Michael Billmeyer, 185 columns; runs of GERMANTOWN TELEGRAPH; GERMANTOWN CHRONICLE (weekly), 1830-72 with index (also on microfilm).

> Publications: GERMANTOWN CRIER (quarterly), 1924-- , $4 per year, circulation 850. Address: the Baynton House, 5208 Germantown Avenue, Philadelphia, Pa. 19144.

> Special service: Study groups in German-American culture.

> Museum: 5214 Germantown Avenue, Philadelphia, Pa.

1275 University of Pennsylvania, The Charles Patterson Van Pelt Library, Philadelphia, Pa. 19104.

> Holdings: In addition to the standard materials one would expect to find in a large academic library, the rare book collection includes the originals of "Daniel Sower's Day Book" (Accounts, 1786-92); lists of deaths in Reading, Pa. 1795-1850; Francis Daniel Pastorius, "The Beehive" (a commonplace book, written in Germantown, Pa., 1696-1719); 891 folios.

1276 Reading Public Library, 5th and Franklin Streets, Reading, Pa. 19602.

> Open to public, Mon.-Thurs. 9:00 a.m. - 9:00 p.m., Fri. 9:00 a.m. - 5:30 p.m., Sat. 9:00 a.m. - 5:00 p.m. Interlibrary loan; copying available.

> Subject area: Germans in Pennsylvania; books in Pennsylvania German dialect; Berks County history; Amish and Mennonite history in Lancaster County.

> Holdings: 5,000 books, 2,000 periodicals, 10 newspaper titles, several records and films.

> Special services: Small collection of German-language materials in both adult and children's departments.

1277 Zion Mennonite Church Library (founded 1945), 149 Cherry Lane, Souderton, Pa. 18964. Tel. (215) 723-3592.

> Open to public: daily 9:00 a.m. - 4:00 p.m. Interlibrary loan; no copying available.

Subject area: Mennonite history.

Holdings: 75 books, two periodicals, and one newspaper title.

Notable holdings: Runs of MENNONITE LIFE; MENNONITE QUARTERLY REVIEW; MENNONITE WEEKLY REVIEW.

Museum: Mennonite Historical Museum, Souderton, Pa.

1278 The Allison-Shelley Collection (founded 1975), Pennsylvania State University, W342 Pattee Library, University Park, Pa. 16802. Tel. (814) 865-1793.

Open to public: Mon.-Fri. 8:00 a.m. - 5:00 p.m. Occasional interlibrary loan; copying available.

Subject area: Germans in Pennsylvania; Pennsylvania German imprints; German literature in English translation; German children's literature in translation; Anglo-German cultural relations; Anglo-German literature; the Christmas tree in art and literature; Pennsylvania German folklore and dialects.

Holdings: 10,000 books, 25 periodicals, 4 newspaper titles, 10 linear feet of archival materials.

Publications: ANGLO-GERMAN AND AMERICAN-GERMAN CROSS CURRENTS (irregular), 1957-- , Pennsylvania State University Press, University Park, Pa. 16802.

1279 D. Leonard Corgan Library--King's College (founded 1946), West Jackson Street, Wilkes-Barre, Pa. 18711. Tel. (717) 824-9931.

Open to public, appointment advisable. Special collection: Tues. 9:00 a.m. - 12:00 p.m., 1:00 p.m. - 5:00 p.m.; Thurs. 2:00 p.m. - 5:00 p.m. No interlibrary loan; limited copying.

Subject area: Taped interviews with Pennsylvania Germans on folklore, folklife, customs, and so forth.

Holdings: Audio tapes.

SOUTH DAKOTA

1280 South Dakota Historical Resource Center (founded 1901), Memorial Building, Pierre, S. Dak. 57501. Tel. (605) 224-3615.

Open to public: Mon.-Fri. 8:00 a.m. - 12:00 p.m., 1:00 p.m. - 5:00 p.m. Some interlibrary loan; copying available.

Subject area: Early Dakota history; pioneer homesteaders; immigrant groups to the Dakotas, including Russian-Germans.

Holdings: Approximately 2,000 catalogued and 5,000 uncatalogued or uninventoried items; retrospective periodicals; 5 newspaper titles.

Special services: Subject search and lending of all types of materials to libraries upon request, in accordance with the interlibrary loan policies.

TEXAS

1281 Catholic Archives of Texas, Catholic Church of Texas (founded 1923), P.O. Box 13327, Capitol Station, Austin, Tex. 78711. Tel. (512) 476-4888.

Open to public: Mon.-Fri. 9:00 a.m. - 4:30 p.m. Limited library loan; copying available.

Subject area: Religious materials pertaining to the Catholic Church of Texas.

Holdings: Records of parishes with large German populations (Frelsburg, Castroville, New Braunfels). Scattered accounts of German missionaries, sisters in various congregations; books on the history of German settlements in Texas.

Notable items: Diocesan newspapers: ALAMO REGISTER (San Antonio), 1944-- ; LONE STAR CATHOLIC (Austin), 1959-- ; TEXAS CATHOLIC (Dallas), 1952-- ; TEXAS CATHOLIC HERALD (Galveston-Houston), 1964-- .

Publications: TEXAS CATHOLIC HISTORICAL SOCIETY NEWSLETTER (twice a year), 1976-- , circulation 300.

Museum: Nimitz Museum, Fredericksburg, Tex.

1282 De Golyer Foundation Library, Southern Methodist University (founded 1956), Box 396, SMU Station, Dallas, Tex. 75275. Tel. (214) 692-2253.

Open to public: Mon.-Fri. 8:30 a.m. - 4:30 p.m. No interlibrary loan; copying available.

Subject area: Local history of the Trans-Mississippi West; family history.

Holdings: Library has an indeterminate number of relevant books on German-Americana.

VIRGINIA

1283 Bridgewater College Library (founded 1880), Bridgewater, Va. 22812. Tel. (703) 828-2501.

Open to serious researchers with appointment; Mon.-Fri. 8:00 a.m. - 10:00 p.m. Weekend hours vary; interlibrary loan permitted for circulation materials; copying available.

Subject area: History of the Shenandoah Valley area, including family histories; church records; hymnals; Henkel Press materials.

Holdings: Books, archival materials.

1284 Menno Simons Historical Library (founded mid-1950's), Eastern Mennonite College, Harrisonburg, Va. 22801. Tel. (703) 433-2771, ext. 153.

Open to public: Appointment advisable during vacation periods. Mon.-Fri. 8:30 a.m. - 12:00 p.m., 1:00 p.m. - 5:00 p.m.; Sat. 9:00 a.m. - 12:00 p.m.; as a rule. No interlibrary loan; copying available.

Subject area: Mennonite-related local history, specific family histories, religious materials, music, cookbooks.

Holdings: 6,000 books, 40 periodical and 5 newspaper titles, 84 linear feet of archival materials.

Notable runs: Fairly complete set of THE MUSICAL MILLION and some WATCHFUL PILGRIM.

Publications: Special historical library issues of the EASTERN MENNONITE COLLEGE BULLETIN.

Special service: Limited assistance in genealogical research.

WISCONSIN

1285 State Historical Society of Wisconsin, Archives Division (founded 1846), 816 State Street, Madison, Wis. 53706. Tel. Archives Reading Room (608) 262-3338.

Open to public: Must show credentials at request. Hours: Mon.-Fri. 8:00 a.m. - 5:00 p.m.; Sat. hours vary; closed Sunday and major holidays. Copying available for material in good condition; fees are charged; interlibrary loan only for microfilms.

Subject area: German immigrants and German Americans in Wisconsin. A great deal of the material is national in scope, i.e., labor history, socialism, and so forth.

Holdings: Undetermined volume of archival records and papers; audiovisual materials.

Publications: Guides to the various collections.

Special services: Tours can be tailored arranged to special interest groups.

1286 State Historical Society of Wisconsin Library, 816 State Street, Madison, Wis. 53706. Tel. (608) 262-3421.

Open to public: Mon.-Thurs. 8:00 a.m. - 10:00 p.m.,
Fri.-Sat. 8:00 a.m. - 5:00 p.m. Interlibrary loan; copying
available.

Subject area: History broadly interpreted; especially strong
in local history; genealogy; labor and religious history.

Holdings: Undetermined quantity of books and periodicals;
substantial runs of German-American periodicals.

Publications: WISCONSIN MAGAZINE OF HISTORY (quarterly), 1917-- , subscription $10 per year, circulation 6,500.

Museum: Old World Wisconsin (the society's outdoor ethnic
museum), Route 1, Box 12-A, Eagle, Wis. 53119.

1287 Milwaukee County Historical Society (founded 1935), 910 North Third
Street, Milwaukee, Wis. 53203. Tel. (414) 273-8288.

Open to public: Credentials required. Mon.-Fri. 9:00 a.m.
- 12:00 p.m., 1:00 p.m. - 5:00 p.m. Interlibrary loan;
copying available.

Subject area: German history in Milwaukee; Milwaukee German-language imprints; family histories.

Holdings: 86 books, periodicals in 12 subjects, 13 newspaper
titles, 78 individual archival collections, individual and institutional photos and scrapbooks of numerous German organizations, i.e., Turnverein, German theater, Musikverein; the
Frank-Kerler family papers; large collection of German works
published in Milwaukee.

Notable items: DER PIONIER (Boston), 1844-73, incomplete
run.

Publications: HISTORICAL MESSENGER (quarterly), 1940-- ,
cost $1 plus tax, circulation 1,000.

ADDENDUM

1288 Campen, Richard N. GERMAN VILLAGE PORTRAIT. Including a section on Restoration Practices by Robert E. Harry. Chagrin Falls, Ohio: West Summit Press, 1978. 102 p. Bibliog.

1289 Gibson, John, ed. HISTORY OF YORK COUNTY, PENNSYLVANIA FROM THE EARLIEST PERIOD TO THE PRESENT TIME, DIVIDED INTO GENERAL, SPECIAL, TOWNSHIP AND BOROUGH HISTORIES, WITH A BIOGRAPHICAL DEPARTMENT APPENDED. 1886. Part 2 reprinted as A BIOGRAPHICAL HISTORY OF YORK COUNTY, PENNSYLVANIA. Baltimore: Genealogical Publishing Co., 1975. 772, 207 p.

1290 Heinicke, Milton H. HISTORY OF EPHRATA. Compiled by Ralph M. Hartranft. Ephrata, Pa.: The Historical Society of the Cocalico Valley, 197?-74. 12 vols. in 1.

1291 Murtagh, William J. MORAVIAN ARCHITECTURE AND TOWN PLANNING, BETHLEHEM, PENNSYLVANIA, AND OTHER EIGHTEENTH-CENTURY AMERICAN SETTLEMENTS. Chapel Hill, N.C.: University of North Carolina Press, 1967. 224 p. Bibliog.

1292 Wust, Klaus German. THE SAINT-ADVENTURERS OF THE VIRGINIA FRONTIER; SOUTHERN OUTPOST OF EPHRATA. Edinburg, Va.: Shenandoah History Publishers, 1977. 125 p. Bibliog., index.

1293 Yoder, Don. AMERICAN FOLKLIFE. Austin, Texas: University of Texas Press, 1976. 304 p. Bibliog., index.

1294 Yoder, Don. "Hohman and Romanus: Origins and Diffusion of the Pennsylvania German Powwow Manual." In UCLA Conference on American Folk Medicine, AMERICAN FOLK MEDICINE: A SYMPOSIUM. Ed. by Wayland D. Hand. Publication of the UCLA Center for the Study of Comparative Folklore and Mythology; 4. Berkeley: University of California Press, 1976, pp. 235-48. 347 p. Bibliog. notes, index.

AUTHOR INDEX

In addition to authors, this index includes all translators, illustrators, photographers, editors, and compilers cited in the text. References are to entry numbers and alphabetization is letter by letter.

Author Index

Author Index

Author Index

Author Index

Author Index

TITLE INDEX

This index includes titles of books and journal articles which are cited in the text. The book titles are listed in their shortened form and journal articles appear within quotation marks. Alphabetization is letter by letter and numbers refer to entry numbers.

Title Index

Title Index

Title Index

Title Index

Frederick Augustus Rauch, American
Hegelian 840
Frederick the Great and the United
States 972
Frederick the Great's Influence on the
American Revolution 234
Free American and Deutscher Weckruf
und Beobachter 1219
Freedom's Will: The Society of the
Separatists of Zoar 520
Free German and Free Austrian Press
and Booktrade in the United States,
The 137
Freidenker 1236
Freiheit 1236
Friedensbote 1255
Friedrich Schiller in America 1139
From Catherine to Khrushchev: The
Story of Russia's Germans 405
From St. Louis to Sutter's Fort
1846 783
Furniture and Its Makers of Chester
County, Pennsylvania 646

G

Der Gantz Neue Verbesserte Nord-
Americanische Calender 1265
Geistliches Magazien 1265
Genealogical Record of the Schwenk-
felder Families, The 484
Genealogies in the Library of Congress
162
Genealogy of the Kemper Family 382
General DeKalb: Lafayette's Mentor
722
General von Steuben 882a
Gentle People, The 427
"Geographical Origins of German
Immigration to Wisconsin" 361
George Rapp's Harmony Society,
1785-1847 510
George Rapp's Successors and Material
Heirs, 1847-1916 511
German Achievements in America 696
German Allied Troops in the North
American War of Independence,
1776-1783, The 236
German American 1219
German American, The 230

German-Americana: A Bibliography
124
German American Annals 51,
1137-71
German-American Catholics and the
Social Order 435
German-American Families in the
United States Genealogical and
Biographical 697
German-American Genealogical
Research Monograph(s): nos. 1-5
243-47
German-American Genealogist, The
1182
German-American Historical Society
of Illinois 600, 1177, 1190
German-American Literature 596
"German-American Migration and the
Bancroft Naturalization Treaties,
1868-1910" 206
German-American Newspapers and
Periodicals, 1732-1955 139
German-American Pioneers in
Wisconsin and Michigan 365
"German-American Poetry, a Con-
tribution to Colonial Literature"
600
German-American Political Behavior
in Nebraska and Wisconsin, 1916-
1920 530
German American Press Research from
the Time of the Revolution to the
Bicentennial 140
German-Americans, an Informal
History, The 216
German-Americans, The 212
German-Americans and the World
War 257
German-Americans and World War 1
256
German-Americans in Politics, 1914-
1917, The 255
German-American Studies 1183,
1191
German and German-Swiss Element
in South Carolina, 1732-1752,
The 375
German and Swiss Settlements of
Colonial Pennsylvania, The 317
German Artist on the Frontier:
Friedrich Richard Petri 835

Title Index

Title Index

M

Title Index

T

Title Index

SUBJECT INDEX

This index is alphabetized letter by letter; numbers refer to entry numbers.

Subject Index

American Nazi Party 69. See also
 Nazi Movement in the
 United States
American Philosophical Society 849
American Revolution
 army rolls 163, 245
 battles 235, 238
 diaries 237, 238, 847, 848,
  905
 Germans in 210, 231-36, 968
 German sources 235
 Maryland 372
 Mercenaries in. See Hessians
 officers 231, 817
 Pennsylvania Germans in 327, 999
 prisoners of war 245, 1008
Amerikadeutsche (der) 69
Amerika-Deutscher Volksbund. See
 German-American Bund
Amish 2, 313, 334, 418, 457,
 507, 674
 bibliography 413, 414
 biography 463
 education 421
 fictional works 431
 genealogy 1229
 history 209, 316, 463
 in Indiana 420, 463
 medical studies 419
 in Michigan 463
 in Ohio 423
 in the Ozarks 357
 pacifism 279
 in Pennsylvania 425
 pictorial works 300, 426-30
 popular works 413, 416, 417,
  425
 quilts 649
 Revolutionary War 466
 sociological studies 415, 426,
  1114
 statistics 415
 See also Amish Mennonites; Old
  Order Amish
Amish Mennonites 422, 457
Amman, Jakob 4
Amusements 665, 670
Anabaptism, bibliography 455
Anabaptists 5, 77, 316, 457, 485,
 1262, 1269

periodicals 1216
popular works 460
See also Amish; Mennonites;
 Swiss-Germans
Anaheim (Calif.) 398
Anarchism 525-28
Ansbach (Germany), emigrants 244
Anti-Clericalism 114
Anti-Defamation League of B'nai
 B'rith 266
Antiques
 Missouri 655
 Pennsylvania 312, 634, 635,
  638-40
Anti-Semitism 272
Architecture 308, 323, 335, 396,
 636, 654, 655, 1063
 bibliography 625, 653
 farms 534, 654
 Moravian 658, 1291
 pictorial works 654-57
 See also Barns
Archival materials, bibliography
 123, 124, 146, 147, 151-
 55, 157
Archives (Europe)
 Austria 152
 France 152
 Germany 151, 152, 159
 Italy 152
 Switzerland 152
Archives (United States) 123, 124,
 146, 147, 153, 155
 North Carolina 481, 482
 Pennsylvania 320
Archives of Gettysburg Seminary
 1222
Archives of the Lutheran Church in
 America 1222
Arendt, Hanna 556
Arizona 793, 906
Arndt, Karl J.R.
 bibliography 228
 Festschrift 228
Art 210, 308, 314, 322, 1064
 bibliography 127, 625
 Pennsylvania 625-29, 631,
  633-36, 639, 642, 1063
 pictorial works 631-37, 639,
  642
 See also Folk art; Painters

Asheville (N.C.) 103a
Assimilation 213, 226, 256, 553, 555, 557, 558, 580, 590
Associated Mennonite Biblical Seminaries Library (Elkhart, Ind.) 1228
Association for the Protection of German Immigrants in Texas. See Adelsverein
Associations, bibliography 123
Astor family 703-5
Astor, John Jacob 695, 702-5
ATLANTIC MONTHLY 516
Atlantic states, bibliography 148
Auctions 429
Augusta County (Va.) 378
Augustus Evangelical Lutheran Congregation (Trappe, Pa.) 944, 947
Aurora (Oreg.) 6, 485, 487, 489, 490, 495
Auslandsdeutsche 31
Austrian National Library 144

B

Baden (Germany) 106
Baden-Wuerttemberg, emigration from 161
Baegert, Johann Jakob 706
Bager, George 950
Bahn, Rachel 1124
Baker, R.L. 1260
Baker-Henrici Trusteeship (Harmony Society) 511
Ballads 666, 668
Baltimore (Md.) 744
Bancroft, George 707
Bancroft Naturalization Treaties 206
Banking 856, 879
Baptism 674
Baptismal certificates 642, 643
Baptists. See Church of the Brethren
Barba, Preston A. 13
Barn dance 429
Barns 7, 301, 313, 429, 534, 628, 654, 655, 659, 660, 667
    hex signs 313, 628, 634, 660, 661

Bartholdt, Richard 255
Basket weaving 655
Baurmeister, Karl Leopold [von] 708
Bayreuth (Germany), emigrants 244
Beachy Amish 8, 77. See also Amish
Beachy, Moses M. 8
Bedminster Township (Bucks County, Pa.) 1007
Beer 539, 540
Beissel, Johann Conrad 347, 497, 498, 503, 504, 614, 709, 988. See also Ephrata
Beliefs 672, 1047. See also Folklore
Belleville, Illinois, German Library Corporation 1226
Belmont, August 710
Benjamin, Walter 556
Berks County (Pa.) 102, 313, 323, 909-16
    dialect 586
    local history 157, 1276
    pictorial works 301
Berks County Historical Society 156
Berne (Switzerland) 108
Bernville (Pa.) 335a
Bessarabia (Russia) 100
Bethabara (N.C.) 120, 473, 1291
Bethania (N.C.) 120, 473, 1291
Bethany and Northern Baptist Theological Seminaries Library, Oak Brook, Illinois 1225
Bethel (Mo.) 6, 9, 485, 487, 489, 490, 495
Bethlehem (Pa.) 334, 336-38
    architecture 658, 1291
    Christmas 676, 678
    chronology 337, 338
    Moravians 470, 471, 618, 620, 1016, 1291
    musical life 620
    pictorial works 337, 338, 678
    poems 309
    travel 311
Bibles, rare 1270

Subject Index

Subject Index

Subject Index

Subject Index

Subject Index

Subject Index

Subject Index

Mississippi Valley, Germans in 210
Missouri
    architecture 655
    Catholic Church 434
    Evangelical Church Society of the
        West 453
    Germans in 210, 226, 228,
        355-57
    handicrafts 655
    territory 58
Missouri Historical Society 1242
Mittelberger, Gottlieb 330, 811
Moellhausen, Baldwin 1153
Mohawk Indians 909-14
Mohawk Valley (N.Y.) 290, 291,
    909-16
Moll, Lloyd A. 1255
Monteverde 507
Montgomery County (Pa.) 102, 323,
    987, 1271
Montgomery County (Va.) 378a
Moral influence 210
Moravian Archives, Northern
        Province 481, 619, 1257
Moravian Archives, Southern
        Province 474, 481, 482,
        1248
Moravian Church 10, 20, 146,
        470-72, 1229
    archives 481, 482, 1248
    bibliography 409
    doctrines 469
    General Synod (1899) 469
    history 469, 473, 926-29
    missionaries 379, 469, 477-81,
        1229
    music 481, 616, 618-20
Moravian College (Bethlehem, Pa.)
    1258
Moravian Historical Society 1270
Moravian Music Foundation 1249
Moravian Revolutionary Church at
        Bethlehem (Pa.) 1016
Moravians 470, 471, 486, 926-29
    American Revolution 336, 474
    architecture 658, 1291
    artifacts 1270
    Christmas 676, 678
    Civil War 336
    education 571

    genealogy 336
    in Georgia 476
    handicrafts 637
    industry 336
    music 617-20, 674
    mysticism 412
    in North Carolina 472-74, 478
    pacifism 279, 474
    in Pennsylvania 313, 319, 334,
        336, 470, 471, 475, 498,
        934
    periodicals 1198-1200
    relations with Indians 336, 477,
        478, 480, 571
More, Charles C. 1255
Mormon Church Archives. See
        Church of Jesus Christ of
        Latter-day Saints, Genea-
        logical Society
MORNING CALL (newspaper),
        Allentown, Pa. 1213
Morris County (N.J.) 288
Most, Johan 1236
Mount Airy (Pa.) 341, 342
Mount Morris College (Ill.) 133
Mt. Olive Churches (N.J.) 288
Muckrakers 447
Muench, Alosius 812
Muhlenburg College Library 1255
Muhlenberg family 818, 960,
    1255
Muhlenberg, Henry Melchior 76,
    304, 452, 567, 813-16
Muhlenberg, John Peter Gabriel
    817
Museums 638
    directories 150, 156a, 188
    Pennsylvania 156, 311, 312
Music 209, 210, 214, 313, 547,
    896, 899, 1227
    church music 612
    Harmony Society 616
    Moravians 617, 618, 619, 620,
        674
    Pennsylvania 612, 613, 614,
        621, 622, 623, 624,
        1036
    revivalistic 623, 624
    See also Folk music; Hymns;
        Sprituals

Subject Index

Subject Index

Subject Index

Subject Index

WITHDRAWN from AMBS LIBRARY

WITHDRAWN from AMBS LIBRARY